'WHAT I REALLY WANT TO DO IS PRODUCE . . .'

Of related interest from Faber and Faber

MY FIRST MOVIE
By Stephen Lowenstein

SCREENWRITER'S MASTERCLASS
Screenwriters Talk About Their Greatest Movies
Edited by Kevin Conroy Scott

THE PITCH
Eileen Quinn & Judy Counihan

'What I Really Want To Do Is PRODUCE . . .'

Top Producers Talk Movies & Money

Helen de Winter

faber and faber

First published in 2006
by Faber and Faber Limited
3 Queen Square London WC1N 3AU

Photoset by RefineCatch Ltd, Bungay, Suffolk
Printed in England by Mackays of Chatham plc

A CIP record for this book
is available from the British Library

ISBN 978-0-571-21744-1
ISBN 0-571-21744-3

2 4 6 8 10 9 7 5 3

Contents

Plates

1. A band apart: Lawrence Bender (right) with Quentin Tarantino circa *Pulp Fiction*.
2. Cubby Broccoli (left), probably the most famous independent movie producer of all time, here sharing in a sodality with Sean Connery among others.
3. Bond co-producers Barbara Broccoli and Michael G. Wilson, here relishing the red-carpet part of their demanding job.
4. Stephen Woolley, expressing himself on set for his directorial debut, *Stoned*.
5. Working Title co-producer Tim Bevan and director Sydney Pollack on location for *The Interpreter* at the United Nations, New York, 2004.
6. Eric Fellner with Working Title colleague Liza Chasin on location at Lake Tahoe during the shoot of *Smokin' Aces* in November 2005. Photograph by Jaimie Trueblood.
7. Alison Owen on the set of *Sylvia*, overseeing the work of director Christine Jeffs and cinematographer John Toon.
8. Stephen Evans in conversation with Helena Bonham Carter and financier David Wickens in the penthouse of the Danielli, Venice, during work on *The Wings of the Dove*.
9. JoAnne Sellar with Paul Thomas Anderson on the set of *Magnolia*.
10. Paul Brooks on the set of *Hellion*.
11. During the filming of *Fade to Black*, from left to right, Oliver Parker (director), Barnaby Thompson, Diego Luna.
12. Mike Medavoy.
13. Jennifer Todd (standing) and Suzanne Todd (seated) with John Cusack on the set of *Must Love Dogs*.
14. Robert Shaye in relaxed pose.
15. The Professor: James Schamus.

Overture

'So, you're a producer? What do you actually do . . .?'

ALAN GREENSPAN (*Donnie Brasco, High Fidelity*):
I ask myself the same question . . .

BARBARA BROCCOLI (*GoldenEye, Die Another Day*):

Most people have absolutely no concept of what producers do, even people in the film business . . .

STEPHEN WOOLLEY (*The Crying Game, Interview with the Vampire*):

It's complex. And that may be one of the reasons there are so few books about producers.

SYDNEY POLLACK (*The Quiet American, Cold Mountain*):

You know, you have a tough job here — because I don't think any two people you talk to are going to agree on what a producer does. Every producer is different — it's been so different on every movie that I've worked on. For me, there *is* no definition.

ERIC FELLNER (*Four Weddings and a Funeral, Bridget Jones's Diary*):

Ultimately a producer is the instigator . . . the cheerleader.

JENNIFER TODD (*Austin Powers, Memento*):

I always say I'm the head firefighter.

SYDNEY POLLACK:

Sometimes the best thing you can do as a producer is be a traffic cop.

SIMON CHANNING-WILLIAMS (*Vera Drake, The Constant Gardener*):

I tend to think of producers as 'caring administrators'. I have always rather laughingly said that we look after the three Ts — teas, transport and toilets — which sort of breaks things down to the lowest common denominator . . .

BARNABY THOMPSON (*Wayne's World, Spice World*):

I think of a producer in terms of old-style Hollywood producers — Selznick, Spiegel, Goldwyn — those are the people you aspire to be. I think if the job is done properly then you are literally doing *everything*.

STEPHEN EVANS (*The Madness of King George, Confessions of a Dangerous Mind*):

People ask me, 'Oh so do you *just* raise the money?' And, cynically, I say, 'Yeah, if someone asks me can they make a movie I just get out my chequebook.' I can't explain to them — nor do I want to — the whole process of finding a property, bringing in a writer and a director, looking for actors, working out deals, sorting out the money, talking to the studio or the sales agents, seeing a film into production, keeping the director and the actors happy on set, watching dailies, commenting on the edit . . . or sometimes doing fuck-all and smoking a cigar, which does happen sometimes but, overall, not enough.

ERIC FELLNER:

I think too many people forget that this is called 'the film business' — so there are people who make films without thinking about the business side, and others who make films thinking *only* about the business. You need to think about both. You need some creative insight to make the right choices, and you need business acumen to set the whole thing up properly.

ARNIE MESSER (*Basic, All the King's Men*):

Producers range from people who take credit and do nothing to people who are solely responsible for every decision that's made and everything in-between. Some are really hard-working creative producers who are very close to the director. Some are 'packagers', and once the movie is packaged you don't see them again.

JENNIFER TODD:

Often in Hollywood you meet producers who used to be studio executives or lawyers, and a lot of them have never had any hands-on
experience, so suddenly they get very daunted by the physical aspects
of budgeting and scheduling and everything else you have to do to get
a movie through production.

SYDNEY POLLACK:

There are producers I know who are extraordinarily gifted from a creative point of view, but not very sophisticated in terms of management
and finance issues. So I wouldn't want them going off and managing a
difficult movie in a foreign country where you might have weather
problems, or diplomatic issues with local governments . . .

SID SHEINBERG (former President, Universal Studios):

The Producer's Guild has come up with certain rules to define who is a
producer, because the producing credit was going to people who didn't
have that customary definition. When you take a look at all these
pictures that come out of Miramax and you see Harvey Weinstein's
name — I don't know exactly what he does on all these pictures.

ALAN GREENSPAN:

Credits *are* important. Producers' credits are their currency. This is
agent-speak but, as they say in Hollywood, 'It's cash or credit', and
credit is a commodity that you can trade for cash and vice versa.

JENNIFER TODD:

The best credit to have on a movie is just a plain old 'Produced by' —
because if the movie wins an award then you're the person who gets it.

SYDNEY POLLACK:

Here's what happens. Legally, according to the Academy, you can have
three people as the Producers of a movie . . .

STEPHEN WOOLLEY:

The Academy restricted the Best Picture Oscar to three producers
because after *Shakespeare in Love* they decided that they didn't want
more than three people on the stage . . .

SYDNEY POLLACK:

Then you have the executive producers, co-producers, associate producers and line producers. The only *real* producers are the producers ... other than the line producer who does the day to day grunt work. Everyone else is usually somebody who's getting paid off with a credit of some kind, or because they own the company ...

ARNIE MESSER:

Today some of the producer's credit goes to the star's manager, or if the director has a guy who works with him then sometimes he'll get it. The credit has clearly been debased. But I don't really think people in the audience care. Somebody sitting in the audience in Iowa ... what difference does it make to them?

STEPHEN EVANS:

Frankly the more you explain what you do, the more pathetic you sound: 'I did this and that and you don't realize what I've been through ...' You just sound like a fully paid-up member of the Sad Fuckers Club. That doesn't mean it's not a worthwhile trip.

JENNIFER TODD:

You have to do it on the grounds that *you* know what you did — you can't really do the job for outside validation. It's nice when it happens, but you can't really look to it for that. If you do, then you should be a writer or director, because then you earn your craft by yourself. But movies, just by the very nature of them, take a hundred people to make them, and so you only get to own a piece of it.

JAMES SCHAMUS (*Crouching Tiger, Hidden Dragon, Brokeback Mountain*):

At the end of the day, producing is simply having the will to get something done, and figuring out a way to make sure that thousands of people help you.

STEPHEN WOOLLEY:

It's like being in charge of a mob of unruly children — you know that there are some people you have to be gentle with to get the best out of them, and people you have to be quite rough with. But you try to make people feel that they have an important role to play on the film, even if they are just the runner, or bashing nails into a wall. You need the runner to be smiling when he's taking tea to Julianne Moore. You need to make people feel good when they are working under stressful, arduous conditions, doing things that are, let's face it, pretty strange — whether it's taking your clothes off, or diving headfirst through a window . . .

ERIC FELLNER:

You have to be cool of head and heart to ensure that you get to the finish line. And there are many times on projects when it's just too difficult. But you can't stop, because if *you* stop then everything stops . . .

PAUL BROOKS (*My Big Fat Greek Wedding*):

There are so many reasons why producing is something that a sane human being shouldn't do. But as a producer you just have to force the films to move ahead. You have to have the courage of your convictions. Don't listen to the doubters, because it's very easy to be waylaid. I simply refuse to listen, I just zip up my rhino-skin and get on with it.

JASON HOFFS (*The Terminal*):

A producer said something to me once that I have always remembered — and this is probably going to sound terrible — but he said that a movie project is like a very sick patient who is dying in the emergency room, and you are the ER doctor who needs to keep the patient alive — except that the patient *wants* to die. It's not like he's fighting for his life. And as a producer, even if your project is on the fast track, the amount of care, energy, ideas and passion you need to keep pumping into these things to get them made is *staggering*. Along the way there are going to be thousands of roadblocks thrown in front of you. But you have to keep going. So that's what a producer does. Everything possible . . .

Introduction

Once upon a time in the glorious history of film, names such as Samuel Goldwyn, Louis B. Mayer, David O. Selznick and Cubby Broccoli meant something to the general public. They were the titans and impresarios widely identified as 'The Producers', inhabitants of a fabled realm known as 'The Film World' wherein power, largesse and social prominence were synonymous with the movie stars they created. These producers had a habit of being photographed with beautiful actresses and leading men, in exotic locations or on set at the studio. They were rich, wildly successful, and their aura of power was as alluring as the trail of smoke from their fat cigars . . .

How times change. Today, outside of Hollywood and perhaps a few London postal districts, the reality is that most people haven't the faintest idea who movie producers are or what they do. The very term 'producer' seems nebulous and evasive, revealing nothing and concealing everything. As someone says elsewhere in these pages, it 'has no real definition', and is not even acknowledged as an occupation by US Immigration at Los Angeles airport (which must cause delays on a daily basis). Social gatherings can be galling things for producers, as it is not uncommon to hear 'I know what writers and directors do, but what *exactly* does a producer do?' Or 'So what's the difference between an *executive* producer and a *line* producer? And how's that different from an *associate* producer . . .?'

What is thought to be known about what a producer does borders on the cliché. To wit, they raise the money — or, most irritatingly for some, they *just* raise the money — and they have something to do with the production of a film. Period. The public might just note the presence of the producer's credit at the start of a movie or on its poster. And, come the awards season, the prestigious Best Picture Oscar, crowning award of the night, is handed out to the winning film's producer(s). But still, I suspect that most people will remember the name of the film and forget that of the flushed and euphoric producer flourishing the statuette. Today there are less than a handful of globally recognizable producer's names. More people than ever before are conversant with how much a film made at the box office last week, yet the producer who assembled the financing and whose career hinges on those receipts remains largely anonymous. Beyond the obvious media interest in actors-turned-producers, the most publicity a producer can hope for is to be namelessly assimilated into the marketing of a film. Thus 'the producer' who brought you last year's blockbuster is now the individual 'proud to present' this summer's tent-pole movie. Or a new film 'from the makers of . . .' reminds us that these people have a track record and are a busy lot.

As a devotee of behind-the-scenes film books, I had long been struck by the anomaly that there exist plenty of books about directors and screenwriters but hardly anything about producers. One or two excellent biographies are published most years, but there is virtually nothing on offer that gives a feel for the day-to-day dimensions of the profession, and the personalities at the heart of the business. I began to wonder whether the producer's involvement in the authorship and creation of a movie was in danger of being terminally overlooked. Certainly it is rare that a producer will be interviewed upon the release of a film, given the ascendancy of the director and the importance of stars. And if a producer is finally asked for an audience, it's as though all the imagination and interest the journalist had in the movie is subjugated to the usual tired questions about money and schedules. Why is it blankly assumed that the producer won't have just as many illuminating stories to share about the filmmaking process as anyone, particularly as very often he or she is the person who initiated the project and developed it for years?

I approached Faber and Faber and proposed a book of interviews with leading film producers in a similar vein to Faber's series of 'in conversation' books with directors. I felt that the accessibility of the format would be ideal for interviewees to simply tell it the way it is. My pitch had a personal dimension because I had been working in the business for a few years. I got started having participated in a writing seminar attended by five erudite and successful producers who — in-between pitching to the screenwriters of the group (I wasn't one of them) — talked about what they did. I was captivated by their accounts of finding ideas, developing scripts, and juggling film production with the business of selling and distributing films. Thus I made the decision that 'this was what I wanted to do'. Like many entering the business before me I grafted my way through the ranks of film production and post-production. I worked for producers and read and edited their scripts. Along the way I was commissioned by FilmFour and BBC Films to make a short film and went on to raise further funds to produce other shorts in my spare time. I also lost money developing a couple of features that didn't happen and those experiences were sobering, but in my mind this was all part of an integrated course of action that would make me a producer. Then, along the way, I began to realize that this wasn't necessarily the case. Through personal disappointment, a proximity to other working producers, and an almost forensic interest in what was going on in the business through trade papers and industry gossip, I came to see that producing was about something more elusive and challenging, more risky, than I had previously imagined. I suspected that luck — which might be described as having the right project at the right time, being friendly with the right people, or perhaps even being married to a billionaire (I am not) — might play a part in getting a film made. I also suspected that, on top of skill, a producer's sheer force of personality could be crucial, no matter how comparatively invisible these people were to the public.

In the course of my work there have been plenty of times when I have wondered to myself, 'Is this normal? Do other people go through this?' But because the film industry is such an elaborate hierarchy — even in the UK where it is very small — I have never been in a position to call anyone to find out. When you are on someone else's payroll you just have to manage the problems as they arise. Money disappearing and a film going into hiatus, a star walking off the set, an executive producer diverting production funds to a relative in Lebanon — these are just some of the 'mishaps' I have experienced on other people's movies. One of my formative experiences came when I was on a production recce with the director and key heads of department for some short films I was producing, this only a few days before we were due to start principal photography. Late in the afternoon I got a call from the investor who was ringing to say he was unable to cash-flow the films because he had a problem with the agreement. Worse, because he was busy he wasn't going to be able to address the issues until a few days after we were scheduled to start shooting. It was an interesting moment: should I tell everyone else the news, and give up on the day? Or not tell anyone, and hope that I could persuade him later on the phone to work through the contract and sign off so that much needed funds would start to flow? I decided on the latter course, withdrew a wad of cash from my bank account for the various heads of department, and carried on with the job. What was significant was that for a moment I felt completely and utterly alone. Film crews have an unerring instinct for when things go wrong and as I sat watching a group of people eyeing me with caution and pretending to talk among themselves, it was the first time I had a sense that filmmaking has its own rules and that much of how you determine success has something to do with how you navigate the possibility of failure.

Success in film creates its own mythology, and once a filmmaker has broken through we rarely discover much about how they made their way up. I began to wonder about the experiences of producers I admired — established producers, individuals I had dreamt of meeting. What had been their experience of becoming producers, and what were their reflections having made the ascent? What were the best or worst of times? How had they prepared for the job, and what had they learned along the way? How much of this wisdom could they pass on to novices and disciples?

Faber were immediately receptive and, unlike the development of most film projects, the book quickly secured a green light. I had several ambitions. I wanted to meet as diverse a group of people as possible in the UK and US — it wasn't going to be possible to fly round the world. I wanted to meet producers from the self-starting independent world — particularly in London and New York — and I wanted to talk to producers set up with deals and offices at the Hollywood studios. Some producers straddle both worlds, but I was interested in exploring the significant cultural and business differences (if any) between these camps. I wanted to gather a diverse set of interviewees who would illustrate, through their different backgrounds, the particular sets of skills and good practices necessary to get the job done. I am often amazed when friends who work in unrelated businesses express regret at not having the skills to produce movies. My experience is that what makes many producers interesting is their seemingly unrelated skills. For instance, entrepreneurs are rarely defined by a thorough knowledge of the business they are in, but rather by their canny ability to bring the right people together. I wondered how many such personalities operate in the film business today?

More than anything I wanted to talk to the interviewees about their life in film, in order to show the reader that producing is not just a job. There is nothing nine-to-five about this business: film is an international industry, and it is routine for people to start their day in one time zone and carry on into another, making for a fifteen-to-eighteen hour day and six-to-seven-day-a-week commitment. And finally I hoped that the people I encountered would be freely open to discussing their backgrounds, their experiences and their films in a way that defined not just what they do but who they are. In all, it was an ambitious brief, but I was hopeful that, through the accumulation of detail, the essence of what producing is would emerge.

I decided that I would try and interview the producers over a six-to-eight month period. I knew that there would be a long period of editing (or 'post-production') and that the nature of publishing is such that by the time the book appeared there would be an additional off-the-page story about the ultimate destiny of the films discussed, and an opportunity for postscripts about additional completed projects. I drafted an extended wish list and wrote and fired off my letters. What was immediately obvious was just how busy producers are. A few were out of town and would be on location for several months. A few weren't interested. There were some I never heard from. With one or two I had a suspicion that a whole book devoted to them, rather than an individual chapter, would have been of greater interest. Some people were naturally suspicious of my intentions; after all, I was a complete stranger proposing to ask intimate details about their career. How many executives in any industry agree to discuss the finer aspects of their business to a stranger? But I persisted, and gradually the process of development gave way to production.

When contacting US producers I decided it was insane to try and set up interviews long distance from a different continent and time zone. As soon as I could, I got on a plane and headed out to LA. Getting to know agents, their assistants and colleagues was a vital part of the process in securing a producer's involvement and I discovered that there are producers in Hollywood who have the same level of agent representation as directors, writers and talent. I also discovered that in LA I wasn't always pitching the idea of the book so much as the participation of whoever had already said yes. One assistant said, 'Well, if X is doing it, then Y will definitely do it because he loves his movies . . .'

A journalist friend asked me how long I expected to have with each interviewee and was surprised that I was looking for more than half an hour . . . Often I was lucky beyond belief. Chris Hanley had three hours to offer. Lawrence Bender generously made time for two meetings. Eric Fellner had forty-five minutes, after eight months of pursuit. When I arrived to meet Sydney Pollack he was enjoying a surprise birthday celebration sprung by his assistants and colleagues, but was gracious in sticking to the schedule. Most had an hour to spare but, amusingly, almost everyone had an unerring instinct for when the hour was up — the sign, no doubt, of a well-developed sense of time management. When I met Bob Shaye the interview strayed over the hour and I was hoping he hadn't noticed until he was discreetly prompted by his assistant. As he was midway through a point we had a robust negotiation about extra time, for which I was grateful. Many interviews were interrupted by the constant peeping of messages on cellphones; assistants would routinely interrupt to put through calls. I would respectfully offer to leave the room but one interviewee took so many calls from the director he was working with that, in the end, he suggested I stay put.

Interviews were mostly conducted in company offices. In London these were mainly small rooms in run-down Victorian buildings, in Manhattan they were similarly old buildings on the Lower East Side — both something of a contrast to the light-strewn glass edifices of LA. Collecting studio maps and passes at Paramount, Sony and Universal provided me with a fascinating geography, and I was amused to discover that a part of Paramount Pictures backs on to the celebrated Hollywood cemetery Hollywood Forever — an interesting corporate metaphor . . . After arriving at the Universal lot to interview Jennifer Todd — then based at DreamWorks with her sister Suzanne — I was walking towards their bungalow when the Universal tour bus swept by me, and a loud pre-recorded commentary was blaring out: 'So, finding a good script is a bit like winning the lottery, right Brian . . .?' Brian Grazer, of course, is the uber-producer whose partnership with director Ron Howard in Imagine Entertainment has brought Universal such smash hits as *A Beautiful Mind*. It was funny to think that Grazer's disembodied voice was now imparting wisdom to the hordes of tourists who visit the Universal buildings looking for some kind of back-stage insight into the making of movie magic. This book, too, is an attempt to shed some light on the process, at what I trust is a greater length and depth, and I hope you will find the voices of the twenty-one producers herein sufficiently informative, amusing and inspiring as to spare you the price of a trip on that bus . . .

Helen de Winter
June 2006

Part One

CASE STUDIES

I want to begin this book with two very disparate but equally inspiring examples of how the producer's job gets done at the highest level. The first is a producer who arrived at the profession by somewhat roundabout means, but who, once there, used every ounce of his drive and ingenuity to produce, independently, some of the seminal movies of his generation. The second is a pair of co-producers who, essentially, inherited the reins of one of the greatest franchises in movie history — a huge responsibility as well as a blessing, and one that involves production logistics of an order almost unparalleled elsewhere.

Take 1

LAWRENCE BENDER

People may follow many and varied paths into the job of producing movies, and indeed they may embark from unlikely starting points. A background in the arts is not essential but clearly can be helpful — and those arts need not be movies. Consider Lawrence Bender. His first ambitions lay in performing, but events and friendships conspired to mould him into a budding producer. Then at a party he met a guy called Quentin who had a movie script . . . and so he was set on a journey, the first landmark of which was *Reservoir Dogs* (1992), now widely considered one of the outstanding directorial debuts. As Bender here relates, that picture so nearly didn't happen, such are the rigours of securing low-budget finance. But Bender made the deal, and the rest is history: he became one of the key producers of his generation, and within a few years found himself in Malaysia, producing a big movie for Fox and being responsible for the welfare of horses and elephants. I met and talked with Lawrence in Los Angeles, in conditions of relative calm.

1. *'I want to produce . . .'*

HELEN DE WINTER: *Am I right in thinking you started out as a dancer?*

LAWRENCE BENDER: When I was in college I dated a girl who was a dancer, and one day she said they needed guys in the dance department. I was at the University of Maine, and a guy called Arthur Hall — a beautiful black man and African dancer — had a company called Ile Ife. Arthur's whole thing was outreach to men, to get young men to dance. I learned a lot of African dances, and that's really how I fell in love with dance. It kind of became my drug. Then Ralph Robinson, who had run the Maine State Ballet, formed his own company, and he saw me dance and invited me to join the company. I danced for about five or six years, and during that time I also studied civil engineering and got my degree, then from ballet I segued into modern dance. But because I started late I got injured relatively quickly.

At the same time as you were dancing were you also interested in movies?

I went to the movies all the time, but it wasn't like they were in my head — because I was a dancer, and that was my life. But with the injuries I picked up, it became obvious I wasn't going to make it as a dancer, so I joined an acting class and started transitioning from dance to acting. This was in the early 1980s when Lee Strasberg was still alive and I would go to the Actors Studio and watch Strasberg moderate. I was in acting class with Jessica Lange, Mickey Rourke, Marlo Thomas and Christopher Reeve. Sandra Seacat was our teacher, and one time I got up and did a scene for Eli Wallach. Then I started taking classes at the Strasberg Institute, and also began studying with Stella Adler — so I was around interesting groups of people, and it was a great time to be in the New York acting scene. Then in 1985 I moved out to Los Angeles to find work. There is nothing worse than being a male out-of-work actor in LA. Who wants to meet another unemployed actor? For a time it was very depressing, a real struggle. When I came out I had one friend, so I called her before I arrived and she said I could stay on her couch for a couple of nights. I had a few hundred bucks, so if it didn't work out at least I knew I could sleep in the car, because it's warm out here . . .

How did you survive?

It was really tough. I called everybody I knew, but I didn't really know *anyone*. I would walk around trying to get jobs, but I couldn't get hired because I didn't have any experience. It was impossible to get an agent. I got a walk-on in *General Hospital* or something like that, and took some classes. I tried to get a job in the mailroom at a talent agency but, again, I didn't know anyone, plus I couldn't type, and there are a million people going for those jobs. Eventually, I got a job as a waiter. Then I started working on film sets to try and make some money, but that was difficult too, because it's not like you suddenly start working on a movie. I ended up going over to the American Film Institute when they were doing their end-of-term student films and offered to work for free. I went into the office and they said, 'What do you want to do?' so I said, 'I want to produce', and they looked at me and rolled their eyes as if to say, 'Great, another out-of-work actor who wants to produce . . .' But they said they needed extra guys to lug stuff around and they put me in the grip department. The script supervisor let me stay on the couch in her apartment — I ended up staying there for six months — and I got fed on set. I worked on two projects for six weeks where I learned how to do grip work. I enjoyed it, and I was learning a skill. The guy who worked the dolly showed me how to use a pee-wee dolly, and I went over to one of the rental houses and got a book on grip equipment and memorized all the names. On one movie I worked as a dolly grip for the cinematographer Russell Carpenter — who later won an Academy Award for *Titanic* — because the dolly grip had just gotten fired. And I spent the next two and a half years working in production.

How, then, did you start producing?

As I was working on set as a crew member and looking around at what people did, I realized what I wanted to do was produce. A friend of mine, Boaz Yakin, suggested I talk to a friend of his, Scott Spiegel, who had co-written *Evil Dead 2* [1987, dir. Sam Raimi]. Scott is a great guy and very talented, so we ended up sitting down together and he wrote a great little horror story, 'Night Crew', which ultimately became my first movie, *Intruder*.

How did you put the film together?

We found a guy who offered us $100,000 to make the film. The whole thing took place in a grocery store, so I found a bankrupt store — the owner was out of town so I said to the manager, 'I will pay you $2,500 if we can use your store for two months, and we will be out before the owner gets back.' And for $1,000, Ralph's Grocery Store gave us two five-ton trucks of spoiled, dented boxes to stock the place. Then we lost the $100,000, because the guy decided he didn't want to make the movie since the last video he made didn't sell. So, suddenly, we had nothing and I was running around worried we were going to lose our location. Eventually we found another investor and made the film. Sam Raimi has a small part, and I had a *tiny* part playing a cop.

Did you feel comfortable in your first time producing? Did you know what you were doing?

It was a very intense low-budget movie and a genuine guerrilla experience, but we had a pretty good crew and most people were doing it for the first time. Everyone did everything and we had a lot of fun making the film, it was all new and exciting, I was like a sponge and I learned so much as I went along. Even though I was in charge of the production, I was the one who knew the least, and it was then I learned that if I didn't know something, I needed to make sure I had people around me who knew more. A friend showed me how to do a budget in Lotus, and I would take pieces of paper, write up a cash-flow, and put it on the walls. I didn't have an accountant, so someone showed me how to set up books and I entered the cheques and wrote stuff down in pencil. I think everyone got paid $150 a week. I remember Sheldon Lettich — a friend of Boaz and Scotty and mine, who's directed some movies — well, he came on set and said, 'Lawrence, this is a really great set, man, it's running smoothly and you did a really good job.'

Charlie Band[1] financed the film and he had a post-production set-up and someone to set it up for me, so we did post in his building. At the end we had a beautiful 35mm print, but instead of putting the film in theatres Charlie broke our hearts and sold it directly to Paramount Video for $500,000. Of course we didn't see a dime of that, he made all the money. As it was a gore-fest, Paramount couldn't get an acceptable rating, so they had to cut a lot of the great shots. There was a scene where Sam Raimi gets killed with a meat hook and another character gets killed by a trash compactor — all kinds of fun stuff. So, at the end of this long process, I was broke again . . .

Didn't you have a formal agreement with Charles Band with profit participation?

At that point in my life, I didn't know there was such a thing as a back-end. I didn't have a lawyer, and it was more that I just wanted to go and make the movie because someone had given us $100,000.

2. 'Let's go make this happen . . .'

Did it get any easier for you to raise money having produced Intruder?

Well, I tried, but I got into some odd situations. It would be 'This guy knows a Swiss financier . . .' or 'That guy knows somebody . . .' but, of course, nobody really delivered anything. At the same time people were sending me scripts and I was reading everything I could. Then one day Scott Spiegel, who directed *Intruder*, said, 'You've got to meet my friend Quentin, he has a bunch of really cool scripts that you guys

1. Head of the low-budget horror specialist Empire Pictures, later Full Moon Pictures, later still Shadow Entertainment.

should talk about.' Soon after, Scott had a party and it was there I met Quentin.

I'm so bad with names, and at the party I said, 'Quentin Tarantino? That name sounds familiar . . . I know! I read a script by a guy with a name that's similar to yours, called *True Romance*.' Quentin said, 'That's my script!' I said, 'Are you sure?' He said, 'Yes, yes, that's me!' I don't remember who sent me the script but the funny thing is that *True Romance* was sitting by my bed. So I ended up telling Quentin how much I liked it.

What was Tarantino doing at this time?

He was trying to raise money with a friend to make *Natural Born Killers*. And he was shooting a movie. What he would do was work for a few months and get a bit of money together for stock, then shoot something and edit it together a few months later. When we met he had a few scenes cut together and he showed me one sequence that I liked quite a bit.

For a while I tried to help him make *Natural Born Killers*, but it didn't work out. Then he said, 'I have this great idea, it's something I've had in my head for a long time — it's about a bunch of guys who pull a jewellery heist, but you never see the heist, and all the action takes place at one location, back at a warehouse.' And from the way Quentin told the story and described the action I got very excited, there was something about the enthusiasm in the room between us that really got to me. I had this amazing feeling that we *were* going to make the movie. Honestly — I had a feeling in my stomach and I thought 'Let's go make this happen.' But I had no idea how to do it because, again, it wasn't like I knew anything. I was still struggling, I was broke, I didn't know anyone and I had only made one low-budget horror movie.

But Quentin literally went off and wrote the heist script in three and a half weeks, and I read it and it was great. He wrote it on an old type-writer with bad spelling and it was improperly formatted — but it was fantastic. He said, 'I'm going to call this *Reservoir Dogs*.' Then we knew we could make it, because at that time Cinetel was going to make *True Romance* and Quentin was going to get paid $50,000 for the script. So we were thinking we would make *Reservoir Dogs* for $50,000 and shoot it on 16mm in black and white.

He was prepared to invest his entire True Romance *fee into* Reservoir Dogs?

Absolutely one hundred per cent. One of the reasons why he connected with me was because he had seen *Intruder* which I had made for $100,000, so he knew I could do it. But when I read the script I thought 'This is too good', and I said to Quentin, 'We've got to do this for more than $50,000.' But Quentin said, 'No, I've been trying to raise money for years now and it doesn't work. I'm a director who hasn't directed, therefore I don't exist. And I *need* to direct.' I said, 'Give me two months.' So on a piece of paper he wrote out an option for two months. Within that time I found somebody who agreed to give us $100,000. So when Quentin saw it ramping up, he allowed me to continue. Basically, I was giving the script to anybody I knew and asking them to give it to anyone *they* knew, and so on.

When we first talked about making the movie, acting was still a big part of my life, I was really an actor trying to produce, and the agreement I had with Quentin was I would play a part in *Reservoir Dogs*. I had two acting teachers in New York, Peter Flood and Lilly Parker, who was Peter's wife at the time. Lilly is a member of the Actors Studio so I asked her if she would give the script to Harvey Keitel. We didn't have a casting wish-list but Harvey was the dream guy. Then a couple of weeks later I got a phone call: 'Lawrence, this is Harvey Keitel. I just read the script by Quentin Tarantino. He's very talented and I would love to get involved in any way I can, so please call me.' It was an interesting moment for me, because I had two feelings. One was the producer-half of me saying, 'Wow, Harvey Keitel wants to do this movie, that's totally amazing.' The other part was the actor-half of me, and the producer-half said to the actor-half, 'This movie is going to become a bigger project than you, and you are not going to end up acting in it.' So I had to make a choice, and my acting career was going to go away and my producing career was going to start to happen. In the end I had a small part in the movie — I played a cop running down the street . . .

What else did you do to get Reservoir Dogs *off the ground?*

I gave the script to a friend who gave it to Monte Hellman, who gave it to Richard Gladstein at Live Entertainment, Richard gave it to his boss Ronna Wallace, and they decided they wanted to make the movie. So that was our team, and Richard Gladstein became our executive producer. Then Quentin, Richard and I went over to Harvey Keitel's house in Santa Monica and had some espresso with him. We talked all about the movie and Quentin and I were sitting there thinking 'This is amazing . . .' After that, Harvey signed up and got involved, and from time to time he would come to castings and it would be Quentin, Harvey and me, with fifty guys waiting. Each actor would take a minimum of half an hour to read because the scenes were really long. We all played different parts and it was really exciting. Then Harvey said, 'Quentin, Lawrence, you have amazing actors here in LA but you also have wonderful actors in New York. It's an extraordinary movie and you owe it to yourself to go to New York.' I said, 'Harvey, the financing hasn't come through yet, we're broke, we don't have any money, we *can't* go to New York.' He said, 'OK, I'm going to fly you out there.' So we got the red eye to New York on a Friday night, Harvey was in first class and Quentin and I were in coach. At about three in the morning we met in the midway section for a drink and we were talking, and Harvey says, 'Boys, I know I'm in first and you're in coach, but we're on my dime. But when this movie is over you're going to be in first class too . . .'

Harvey put us up in a hotel, the casting director Todd Thaler gave us his space for two days, and we cast solidly, morning, noon and night. It was pretty wild, I was always the one who ended up having to play the cop tied to the chair — so I was knocked over, strangled and beat up. One guy came in and pulled a real gun and we're like 'Sorry, no guns!' He shows us the barrel and says, 'Look, it's not loaded . . .' But quite a few guys brought in weapons, and it was a real sweatbox full of testosterone. Then Steve Buscemi came in, and it was funny, because Steve didn't necessarily give the best audition but we felt he was great and had to be in the movie. So he became Mr Pink. If Harvey hadn't taken us to New York, we would never have cast Steve. After the casting, Harvey took Quentin and I to the Russian Tea Room. I was born in the Bronx and spent a lot of time in New York but I had never had the money to go to the Russian Tea Room. After dinner, I said to Harvey, 'We're going to make you a co-producer.' And Harvey said, 'Lawrence, it's about time. What took you so long?' and we all laughed.

3. 'This is not going to happen . . .'

As *Reservoir Dogs* was a negative pick-up[2] there was no cash-flow until we had a signed deal, which meant getting a bond and having to close. At a certain point I think Live gave us a few thousand dollars

---

2. Prior to production a financier agrees with a producer to purchase the film's negative for a pre-negotiated fee. The actual deal requires a letter of intent from a distributor, supported by the same from a 'bonding' insurance company, which then form the collateral for a loan from the financier.

for offices, but in the beginning there wasn't much money up-front. Our attorney to this day is Carlos Goodman, whom I had met through my room-mate Chris Broncato. Carlos was new in the entertainment business and this was his first negative pick-up. It was tough because we were in pre-production without cash-flow, so everyone was working in good faith for free, including Ronnie Yeskel, our casting director. Ronnie was on the Fox lot, so we would cast out of her office. At the same time I was negotiating equipment deals, looking for locations, crewing up . . . and then — because I was broke — I was working once a week as a PA on commercials to make $100 to eat, making copies of the *Reservoir Dogs* script and sending them out. It was OK, they all knew what I was doing. But I think I was the only PA working in commercials who had produced a movie.

A couple of days before the closing, I was in the negotiation with Live Entertainment, and it was going on and on and on — and at the time I didn't know this was normal. There were certain things they wanted me to do, and I said, 'No way.' One I remember was that they wanted me to be responsible for paying all the actors their back-end. And I said, 'That's ridiculous. I'm an out-of-work broke guy who doesn't have an accounting firm, I can't be responsible for analysing and sorting out back-end payments for years to come. I can't do it and I'm not going to do it.' I was so angry I stood up to leave, I was literally going to throw the whole movie away. So they left the room for a while, and when they came back they said, 'OK.'

Before we secured the loan, Michael Mendelssohn, head of entertainment for Bank Paribas, asked me to come in because they wanted me to meet the bankers. I said, 'I've never met bankers before. What do I say? What am I supposed to wear? Should I be a working guy or wear a suit?' But they said, 'Come as you are, you'll be fine. They just want to meet the producer, the guy they are going to loan the money to.' It turned out I didn't need to know anything about banking because that was their job. My job was to produce the movie. And though I wasn't a big producer, I knew enough from producing a horror movie to make them feel confident. I said, 'I guess you needed to come down and check out the guy you're giving the money to.' And they said, 'Didn't they tell you? We're not *giving* you anything. We're loaning you the money and you've got to pay us back.' That was a little unsettling . . .

The day of the closing was like running a marathon. Carlos Goodman was there with Quentin and I at the banker's law firm of Loeb & Loeb. We sat round a huge round table with fifteen big law-firm chairs that I had only ever seen in movies. And every one of these chairs had a pile of folders in front of them, and all the documents had to be negotiated, and there were about fifty people who had to sign them. And there were about twenty-five points that hadn't been negotiated — mainly the intricacies of the inter-party agreement. So we spent all day sitting round the table negotiating, and then there would be side-meetings, after which we would come back and they would re-type and red-line the documents and I would sit there and read them. I remember saying, 'If we can't get this done today we can't make the movie . . .' I had five weeks left of pre-production before we shot, and there still wasn't a cash-flow. Finally, I'm reading the contract and everyone is waiting for me to finish, because I am not a fast reader. And one of the bankers comes up to me and whispers in my ear, 'Lawrence, it gives me a lot of confidence that you're reading these things.' Little did I know that the producer never reads these documents — they usually leave it to their lawyer. I just wanted to make sure that everything I needed was in there.

But there were times during the day when I thought 'This is not going to happen, we are not going to close.' At one stage the lawyer from the opposing party came over and said, 'Lawrence, you *never* get to this stage and it doesn't close. No matter how difficult you think it is, no matter how bad you are feeling at this moment . . .' So at the end of the day all these people had to sign the inter-party agreements but then it came down to this one document, the promissory loan note. And there was only one person who could sign, and that person was me. The document was for a $1.3-million loan and I was thinking 'Wow, I just signed a loan for 1.3 million bucks . . .'

It's funny, but I haven't read an inter-party agreement since that day. I don't read any of that stuff any more — I completely depend on Carlos's law firm. Today I will have a conversation with Carlos, he knows what I'm looking for, and then he comes back to me. And thank God, because there is just too much to do. But we got through that day, and at the end we were congratulating each other.

4. *I could pay my bills . . .*

So, once the finance was secure, were you confident about the actual production?

We had a friend who had just gotten fired off a movie, so we knew it *could* happen. If you talk to Richard Gladstein he'll say, 'That's crazy, we were never thinking of firing you . . .' But in our little world we had to make sure we were protected, so what I did was put the scenes with more coverage at the beginning of the schedule. I figured by the time we got to the areas where there was less coverage it wouldn't bother them, they would just find it interesting.

Before we shot, Quentin was invited to go to the Sundance Institute and shoot some scenes. It was perfect timing, and while he was there we made the final casting decisions on the phone. Our dream was that the finished film would go to Sundance, win — which we didn't do — get bought by Miramax, and go to Cannes . . . Then we scheduled two weeks of rehearsal, and Quentin shot-listed almost the entire movie, so by the time we started shooting he was really, really prepared. When you shoot it's inevitable that some things change, but for Quentin the concept was always solid. For instance there's a particular scene in the film where you are looking down a hallway and Steve Buscemi is off-camera and Harvey is on-camera, and Quentin had *always* visualized the scene that way.

How does a producer support a director during the shoot?

A director needs to have a producer who will be his sounding-board, backboard, safety net and buffer to the outside world. You need to support his vision, help create a great team of cast and crew, be the collaborator and push for the best. Every director is different, but it's like dating. You get to understand what each other's needs are and you just start giving to that person. And when you've been going out longer, you know more . . . I think pretty much every producer has some kind of major argument with every director they work with at some point during the movie, because you are pushing to create the best vision. Laura Ziskin once told me while we were shooting *Anna and the King* that you weren't doing your job if you didn't get to that point.

What were you thinking when you saw the dailies for Reservoir Dogs?

It was like the experience of being in the room when we first auditioned. One shot would cover the whole scene, so sometimes it was like watching theatre, it was beautiful. And Andrzej Sekula's lighting was spectacular to look at. We both knew we were doing something special. I don't think we knew *how* special but it certainly didn't seem like anything we had seen before.

There's a fun story about Andrzej — it was about two and a half weeks before we started shooting, and we still didn't have a director of photography. It was between Andrzej — who had never shot a feature film before, just some shorts — and someone else who had shot several movies. Everyone was saying, 'Go with the other guy who's shot some movies', and, of course, that made sense. The question was, do we go with a DP who has never shot a feature when *we* have never shot a feature? Isn't it better to go with someone who has a lot of experience and knows a lot more about shots, angles, lenses and so on? It was a risk because Andrzej didn't know the crews and the labs in the US. But there was something really special about Andrzej. We had seen a short film that he had shot and it was phenomenal. But we hadn't met him, and he was in Greece on vacation. He woke me up at 1 a.m. in the morning from Greece and said, 'Lawrence I need to meet you guys because I have got to make this movie.' I said, 'Andrzej, I don't know what to say, I can't have you fly all the way out here because I can't promise you the job and I will feel really bad if you come over and don't get it.' He said, 'I don't care, I'm flying out.' So he came to LA and we met with him and with the other DP on a Sunday two weeks before we started shooting. We were so glad we hired Andrzej because the look of *Reservoir Dogs* and *Pulp Fiction* became synonymous with Quentin's shooting style for those movies.

Were the songs used in Reservoir Dogs *written into the script?*

Quentin wrote all the songs into his script. At the auditions, Quentin would many times give actors the note to 'bring whatever song inspires you'. So the cop scene was a lot of fun to work on. 'Stuck in the Middle with You' was the most important song to Quentin and the one he said he absolutely had to have.

Having hoped that the film would get into Sundance, what was it like to present the film there?

Very exciting. Meeting all the other filmmakers was a great thrill. In the first screening the movie was a little bit out of focus and on the sides of the walls, so I was sweating the whole time and I thought 'Oh my God, the movie is a failure', but afterwards everyone was applauding and it was a great success.

   After Sundance I visited Quentin in Amsterdam where he was chilling out and writing *Pulp Fiction*, then I went to Cannes where the film was screening at midnight in the Official Selection, out of competition. I remember getting off the bus from Nice Airport in Cannes, and I was dragging my luggage up the Croisette and sweating when I ran into Jere Hausfater (then of Buena Vista). He said, 'Lawrence, didn't they tell you? Someone's supposed to be *carrying* your bags for you now!'

Were you surprised by the subsequent success of the film?

Miramax saw it at Sundance and when we got back from the festival we found out that they wanted to buy it, so we were excited about that. But when Live sold it to Miramax, it turned out that they had held back the video and foreign rights. This ended up being a problem because Miramax didn't have any other rights except theatrical to recoup their prints and advertising costs from. So Miramax didn't put much money into the P&A for the US theatrical release and we ended up with a small domestic release. In England, though, it was a box office smash, it was just huge — it wasn't just a cult thing. Quentin ended up travelling all over the world with the movie. When the film was released on video in the US, it became really huge, and by the time we did *Pulp Fiction* everyone had seen *Reservoir Dogs* on video. We believed that if we made *Pulp Fiction* for between $6 to 8 million it would make its money back because so many people had seen *Reservoir Dogs*. But all the studios passed on *Pulp Fiction,* so we went out to a bunch of foreign financiers, and there were several companies vying for it but ultimately Miramax swooped in and made the deal.

Did life change for you after Reservoir Dogs?

I worked hard before that movie and I was working hard after. The only thing that changed was that I could pay my bills. I was paid $40,000 on *Reservoir Dogs* so I was able to pay off my credit cards and survive for a year and a half. At the time I was living in a two-bedroom apartment and sharing with a room-mate, but I couldn't afford to move out — actually I produced *Pulp Fiction* out of that apartment . . .

While Quentin was writing Pulp Fiction *were you working on anything of your own?*

Quentin had a friend, Roger Avary, and while we were scouting locations for *Reservoir Dogs* one of the places we scouted was a bank, so I had called Roger and said I had found a closed-down bank and how it was a great location. I asked him if he had any ideas for a film that took place in a bank and Roger said, 'Yeah . . .' So that's how *Killing Zoe* got started. We shot the film in LA except for a day in Paris.

Then Boaz Yakin had left for Paris where he was hanging out writing a book and taking a break from the film business. I told him I was making a movie with Quentin, and I suggested he write something that he could direct, so Boaz said he would come up with an idea, which turned out to be *Fresh*. Later we were sitting around with a bunch of friends and one of them said to Boaz, 'Let me get this straight, the movie is about a young black kid in New York City, so the lead can't be a star, and the cast is all black, so you're not going to be able to raise any money from foreign.' His friend continued to try and dissuade him from writing the idea, but I said to Boaz that every movie is a challenge, he should write the script and if we failed, at least we tried. When I was in Cannes with *Reservoir Dogs* I had met a bunch of foreign financiers and distributors including a French company called Lumière and, ironically, it was Lumière who bought and financed *Fresh*. The film ended up being in Director's Fortnight at Cannes the same year that *Pulp Fiction* was in competition.

When did you and Quentin decide to set up a company together?

Quentin and I formed A Band Apart in-between *Reservoir Dogs* and *Pulp Fiction* because we decided we wanted a long-term partnership. Quentin is great with titles and he came up with the name, because he was a fan of Godard and we both felt like a band of outsiders.

I also started A Band Apart Music and Videos with Michael Bodnarchek, who I had met when I was working as a grip on some AFI movies and he was an electrician. Michael started line-producing big commercials while I continued to try to act and work on crews. When Michael approached me about starting a video and music division, I was producing *Four Rooms*. We signed up a bunch of directors and eventually McG came on board. He was shooting music videos and we helped transition him into commercials. He always had an enormous amount of energy; he used to come up to my office all the time and say, 'Lawrence, I want to make a movie', and I would say, 'Great, let's make one!' When the script for *Charlie's Angels* came in he said, 'I don't know what to do.' I looked at the script and said, 'The script is terrible but you should do the movie.' He said, 'How can you tell me to do a terrible script?' and I said, 'Because you know how to make this movie and I know you'll be able to pull the script together . . .'

5. *Harvey said, 'You're my A-list producer . . .'*

Pulp Fiction *made money and got nominated for Oscars. Is that the main objective for a producer?*

I think the main objective is to make great movies that people want to see and that have their own distinctive, artistic vision. Interestingly enough, it doesn't ever seem to get easier, you are always struggling to find good material and develop great screenplays. Today the variety of movies the studios are trying to make is diminishing; it's much harder to make dramas because there are fewer and fewer buyers. Many times it takes more than one producer to get a movie made. Often young producers will bring me material and I will partner up with them.

Is that how Good Will Hunting *came about?*

It came about when I was at the New York Film Critics Awards — we were at the Four Seasons Hotel, there was a big blizzard outside, we were drinking away and Harvey said, 'Lawrence, I've got next year's Academy Award-winning movie and I want to give it to you because you are my A-List Producer and I want you to get this movie made.' Harvey got me incredibly excited, so I read the script immediately and really liked it — I cried. I told Harvey I thought it was fantastic but I also thought it needed a little bit of work. So Harvey said, 'Great, meet with Matt and Ben and if they like you, go and make the movie.' So I met with them and we got on great and decided to make the movie together. Then I ended up bringing Gus Van Sant on board by convincing Harvey to hire him, and that was a big part of getting the movie to the place where it was. Everyone liked Gus a lot, but he wasn't an obvious choice. While he had made a lot of great movies, he had never made a commercial, mainstream movie. Harvey wanted to make a commercial movie and Gus had just directed *To Die For*, which, in a sense, was a cooler film emotionally. Also Gus had experienced a tough time on *To Die For*, he had got a bad rap coming off it, so Harvey was also worried about that. So you wouldn't have looked at Gus and thought *Good Will Hunting*, but after meeting with him, I felt very strongly about him. One of the things I took away was that he was at a time in his life when he wanted to make a commercial movie.

How do you define 'commercial'?

That's a difficult question. But to make a commercial movie, you have to juggle two things in your mind: you have to maintain the integrity of the creative vision you are going for but you also take into account the needs of the audience. *Good Will Hunting* had a lot of heart, Gus wanted to make a film that would appeal to a mass audience, and he believed the material could do that.

Am I right in thinking you had two other productions on the go at the time of Good Will Hunting?

We had a massively expedited period getting *Good Will Hunting* into production while at the same time I had *Jackie Brown* starting up with Quentin. When Robin Williams read *Good Will Hunting* and we got the call he was interested, he had a three-week window, six weeks from the time we got the call, so we had to hurry up and close the deal because Miramax wasn't going to cash-flow the movie until Robin's deal was done. In the meantime we did get a location scout, started scouting in Boston and sent someone up to Toronto. I was flying from LA to Toronto, then on to Boston, New York, and back to LA again, back and forth like that every week. But I wasn't alone because I brought producer John Penotti on to the third film I was making — *A Price Above Rubies*, with Boaz Yakin. John has Green Street Productions now, but back then he was starting out.

My agreement with Miramax was that I would be on *Good Will Hunting* for pre-production and the first month of production, and hopefully things would then be on track. There was an overlap of one week with *Jackie Brown* so it wasn't too bad, but I was taking a lot of red eyes because I couldn't miss a day of work. What helped on *Good Will Hunting* was that Gus already had most of his crew because he tended to work with the same people. But it was a massive amount of work to pull off in five weeks of pre-production in two cities and two countries.

How closely were you involved in the casting of the movie?

It was a big ensemble effort with Matt, Ben, Chris Moore and Gus. One of the last roles we ended up casting was Stellan Skarsgård's part, late in pre-production. We had so many good actors interested but we couldn't find the right guy until Stellan, who was shooting another movie at the time, drove into New York to audition. The second he came in, we knew we had the guy. The other role that was interesting to cast was Skylar. We had some good choices, but I knew about a relatively unknown actress at that time, Minnie Driver from *Circle of Friends*. Then I was talking to Minnie's agent — who at that time was Hilda Quilley at the William Morris Agency — and she told me that Minnie was in London but on her way to LA so she could stop by New York. So I arranged to have a read-through with Gus, Matt, Ben, Chris Moore and myself. It was five guys in a room with Minnie. She was reading with Matt and she just blew us all away, we all had tears in our eyes. When she left, we got on the phone with Harvey and said, 'We have found the girl.'

Good Will Hunting was a smooth shoot. Everyone did a great job, there were no problems on set, we were on schedule, and everyone was happy with the dailies. It was a good, well-oiled machine. We were lucky because once we started shooting the script was locked. We fought like cats and dogs *before* it was locked, but we were all excited when it was complete. Very often you go into a movie and if the script isn't locked it creates a lot of tension because you have to work on it during the shoot. It can be a nightmare if you have the studio, the director, the producer and the actors all suggesting different ways to finish it. So the script becomes a moving target. You do everything you can to avoid it but sometimes there is nothing you can do.

With so much going on, how did you manage to be in three places at once effectively? Doesn't a little part of you go insane?

Well, there's no such thing as having a life . . . With *Jackie Brown*, the thing about Quentin and I at that point was that we were good friends and had already worked together a lot, and in terms of my commitment Quentin always came first. I figured out a way to work everything so I was always there for Quentin and I was in LA for pretty much the entire movie. As usual, Quentin put together an incredible cast. His movie sets are always a place you want to be because the crew are all family, the actors are always really special, and Quentin is the visionary who brings everybody together.

Have you believed in every project or idea Quentin has written?

Everything. Even things we haven't made together, like *True Romance*. Let me put it this way — if the scripts for *Reservoir Dogs, True Romance, From Dusk Till Dawn, Pulp Fiction, Jackie Brown* and *Kill Bill* came across your desk, is there one script there that wouldn't blow your mind?

6. A hundred horses and twenty elephants

Your next picture was Anna and the King *for Fox 2000. Did that constitute a leap in scale?*

Anna and the King was one of the toughest movies I have ever made. We started the movie with a script that ultimately wasn't finished until three-quarters of the way through the shoot. Plus there were huge construction issues. We originally wanted to shoot in Thailand because that's where the movie took place and all the temples and buildings in the movie exist there. The authorities kept on saying,

'Yes, yes, we will give you permission.' I flew over there several times with the director, Andy Tennant, to meet various officials, including royalty. They had many problems, starting with the issue that they didn't like us calling it *Anna and the King* — they felt it should be 'The King and Anna', because in Thailand the king is regarded as a celestial being. It's not that we were trying to be disrespectful in any way, we just couldn't fit the drama we wanted to make with their requests. Gradually, we realized that they were never going to say yes, even though they never said no. This really screwed us up because we knew now that we would have to build all these sets . . . Fortunately, we had been scouting fairly extensively and we knew the area pretty well. The temples in Malaysia were all wrong for the story, but they have an infrastructure there — roads, telephones, and basic services that make it easier for a production company to come in and shoot. So we ended up shooting in Malaysia. Because we had so much construction, this caused us a lot of delays. At one time we had five hundred people building a palace. Then we were moving around the country to different locations. We went from Kuala Lumpur to Ipoh in the Cameron Highlands then on to Penang and Langkawi Island. Between every location we were carrying a hundred horses and twenty elephants. That means feeding and stabling, as well as employing people to look after them. Every time we changed location, it was like moving a city of two hundred and fifty people. It was a massive operation.

Would you do it again?

I would, even though at the time I said I wouldn't, because it felt like I was going into a world war. Another difficulty was that we were on the other side of the world from the studio, so the middle of the day for us was the middle of the night for them, and communication was difficult. In that situation the tension is higher, particularly when you have to have long conversations in the middle of the night.

7. 'Look, I'm a dancer . . .'

How would you describe your instinct for material? What drives your interests?

I think ultimately my instincts draw me to interesting characters. It doesn't matter if I'm trying to make a thriller or a genre movie, it's the characters that draw me in. The other thing that excites me are directors. Of course, Quentin is the ultimate example of both, he is an extraordinary director who creates incredible characters.

Would you describe yourself as an independent producer?

I consider myself a hybrid, and I don't just mean the car I drive . . . I enjoy making independent financed movies as well as studio pictures.

When did you feel that you had established yourself as a producer?

It's only in the last few years that I have realized I am a professional producer.

After you have been producing for fifteen years?

I think it's because I am always struggling, and it never seems to get easier . . . I'm not Jerry Bruckheimer.

Do you want to be Jerry Bruckheimer?

Honestly, I don't — and I wouldn't know how. He is, by far, one of the most successful producers in Hollywood. I guess what I am trying to say is there are certain producers like Bruckheimer and Imagine who have achieved a certain branding and that makes it easier for producers at that level. If you are not in that top tier, it's always hard and extremely competitive.

As your career progresses, do you feel under pressure to make more obviously commercial movies?

I *want* to be making more commercial movies. I haven't made a tent-pole movie yet, the summer blockbuster that keeps the studio afloat. It's become incredibly important, and I want to do that.

Do tent-pole movies have their own rules?

Tent-pole movies rely on stories that incorporate large action set-pieces, and the emotions between the characters seem to be less complicated. When you're dealing with drama you can explore the complexity between people, but a more commercial movie has to appeal to the lowest common denominator. There was a quote recently about a movie that said if it was ten per cent smarter it would have made fifty per cent less money.

Did you develop the Dirty Dancing *sequel* Havana Nights *because of your passion for dance?*

The independent company Artisan had been trying to do a *Dirty Dancing* sequel for years, but they were never able to put together a movie that they were happy with, so they approached Miramax. I guess the idea was that Miramax would be able to help creatively, put it together and distribute it. When I first heard about it, it was a salsa story about a Cuban girl, set in the present in South Beach, Miami. So I said to Harvey, 'Look, I'm a dancer, I love salsa and I love Cuba so I'm the perfect person to do this.' At the same time, I had a script in my discretionary fund that I had been developing; it was a story based on the life of a very good friend of mine, JoAnn Fregalette Jansen — about her life in Cuba during the period when Castro overthrew Batista. JoAnn, an American, was there with her family and she met Castro and Che Guevara when she was a teenager. So JoAnn and I developed a screenplay called *Cubra Libre* about a teenage girl coming of age during the Cuban Revolution.

JoAnn spoke to our friend Boaz Yakin and asked him to think about converting this teenage coming of age story in Cuba to a *Dirty Dancing* idea. We went in and pitched it to Miramax and they bought the screenplay, with the idea that Boaz would rewrite it to make it into the *Dirty Dancing* franchise.

Do you have any regrets about not having become a professional dancer?

Dance was the thing I loved more than anything, it was my life. And even to this day I feel in my heart that I'm a dancer. It's funny, I once looked back at my college files and found a recommendation letter from the Dean and what he said was, 'Lawrence has a great combination of the arts and sciences, and someday he's going to make a great manager . . .'

Since our interview Lawrence has completed and seen the release of Tarantino's *Kill Bill, Vols 1 & 2*, *The Great Raid*, *Innocent Voices*, *88 Minutes*, *The Chumscrubber*, *Goal!*, and a documentary made with Al Gore, *An Inconvenient Truth*, which screened at the Sundance and Cannes festivals in 2006.

Take 2

BARBARA BROCCOLI
AND MICHAEL G. WILSON

It can be contended that the late Albert R. 'Cubby' Broccoli remains the best-known movie producer who ever lived — this is the consequence of Broccoli's massive success in bringing Ian Fleming's celebrated James Bond novels to the screen, and also the passionate attention lavished by loyal Bond fans on every off-screen aspect of the movies' celebrated wizardry. Since Cubby Broccoli's passing, the mantle of the Bond franchise has been picked up and carried by his daughter Barbara and his stepson Michael G. Wilson, working as co-producers.

It was not long after Barbara's birth in 1960 that her father — an independent American producer based in England — resolved to get Bond on film. Together with Harry Saltzman, who then held the option on Fleming's books, Broccoli formed Eon Productions Ltd and a holding company, Danjaq, and, with the financing of United Artists, they produced *Dr No* (1962). On the heels of that triumph came *From Russia with Love* (1963), *Goldfinger* (1964), *Thunderball* (1965), *You Only Live Twice* (1967), *On Her Majesty's Secret Service* (1969), *Diamonds Are Forever* (1971), *Live and Let Die* (1973) and *The Man with the Golden Gun* (1974).

Saltzman then sold up to UA and Broccoli became sole Bond producer. He brought Michael G. Wilson on board the series, first as an assistant on *The Spy Who Loved Me* (1977), then as executive producer of *Moonraker* (1979), *For Your Eyes Only* (1981), and *Octopussy* (1983). Wilson would further co-write the screenplays of five films. With Cubby, Wilson then co-produced *A View to a Kill* (1985), *The Living Daylights* (1987), and *Licence to Kill* (1989).

Barbara Broccoli had grown up travelling the world with the Bond filming units, loaning a helping hand along the way. She was associate producer on *The Living Daylights* and *Licence to Kill*, the latter would be the last of her father's sixteen Bond productions, not to say the last Bond film prior to a six-year hiatus. Cubby's failing health saw him turn control of Eon over to Michael and Barbara. Meantime, from 1990 there were some legal matters between Danjaq and MGM. Once the litigation was settled, Bond returned in *GoldenEye* (1995, dir. Martin Campbell), produced by Michael and Barbara. Cubby Broccoli's health precluded his participation, and he passed away on June 27 1996.

Michael and Barbara have since produced *Tomorrow Never Dies* (1997, dir. Roger Spottiswoode), *The World is Not Enough* (1999, dir. Michael Apted), *Die Another Day* (2002, dir. Lee Tamahori) and they are currently producing *Casino Royale* (2006, dir. Martin Campbell). They have also produced the hit London stage show *Chitty Chitty Bang Bang* — based on the 1968 film produced by Cubby Broccoli, itself adapted from a children's novel by Ian Fleming, the rights for which Broccoli acquired at the same time as the 007 option.

1. *The family business*

HELEN DE WINTER: *Do you suppose it was inevitable that you would both come to be involved with the Bond films eventually?*

MICHAEL G WILSON: It wasn't inevitable for me, because first I studied law at Stanford University, then I went on to become a partner in a law firm in Washington. At a particular point, Cubby asked me to assist him in a legal capacity, helping to resolve disputes between him and Harry Saltzman from his point of view. So I took a leave of absence from my partnership. But film is such an exciting business, it just sort of grabs you — so I found myself getting more and more involved. Cubby became my mentor, and I never went back to law . . .

BARBARA BROCCOLI: For me, I think my involvement started because it was about my wanting to spend time with my dad. So my interest in the movies was an extension of what was going on at home. Growing up, Dad would be getting calls at home all the time, so I used to like to be his secretary. Then, after school on Fridays, my sister and I would go to the studio. I saw that my dad was very committed and passionate about what he did — he loved it. So in the beginning I think it was about being around him, *then* it was exciting being with the extended family that Cubby created. Because he made a lot of films with the same people, they became the people we socialized with. Ken Adam[3] was 'Uncle Ken' . . . in fact *everyone* was considered an uncle.

3. Celebrated production designer, b.1921, designer on seven Bond films, twice winner of the Academy Award — for *Barry Lyndon* (1975, dir. Stanley Kubrick) and *The Madness of King George* (1994, dir. Nicholas Hytner).

With Bond in the family, so to speak, what then does the experience of now producing the Bond films mean to you personally?

BB: I think we care a great deal about them and that's why we're very hands-on. We understand that audiences come in with expectations. The people who started this — Cubby, Harry, Ken Adam, Terence Young — set a template and kept a very high standard. So when you take that over you don't want to let the audience down, you don't want people to think you have ripped them off — they should have had a worthwhile experience. I think, at the moment, we have the audience's good will . . .

Normally people make a movie and the press people don't really know very much about it until it's released. In our case, we have a lot of interest during the making of the film, so we have a lot of set visits and press queries. I'm sure a franchise movie like *The Terminator* or the *Matrix* movies have that too, but Bond is not like the average movie. Everybody knows what it's about and the reaction is, 'Oh, it's a Bond movie, let's go and see it.' To create that excitement, journalists don't just want to interview James Bond, they want to be on the set and see the spectacle that's being made. It's the circus — they want to come to the circus, and I understand that, because *I* want to go to the circus every morning, that's the feeling I have. When we're shooting I can't wait to get to the set, and I *love* that moment — and we got this from our dad — that moment when you're standing there on location, and the sun is coming up, and the tea urn is next to you, and everyone starts to arrive. Then it all happens and unfolds in the next couple of hours. It's fantastic.

How do you divide the responsibilities of the producing job?

MW: Barbara does all the work and I take all the credit . . .

BB: Fortunately, we are very different and have different interests, but we tend to agree on most things. Michael has an engineering, legal and writing background, so he brings a lot to the table. And I like the organizational things . . .

MW: After she got out of school, Barbara worked her way up through the various departments and became an associate producer, before we made *GoldenEye* together. So she knows the nuts and bolts, and all about scheduling and budgeting.

BB: We do a lot of stuff together, and then we end up covering specific tasks separately.

MW: On *GoldenEye* Barbara went out and did all the scenes in Russia, and I stayed in the studio. Then I went up to Iceland a few times on *Die Another Day*.

BB: During production we tend to be in the same room most of the time. Then we call one another to check on what's happening. We know when we need to communicate, and so do our people. We delegate a lot of responsibility to particular people, we hand things over — just as we hand over responsibility to the director, and then he hands over certain things to the second unit director. You can control and control, but at a certain point you have to turn it over — because you can't be up in every helicopter, you can't be behind every camera. And these are productions that have model units, special effects units, aerial units, sky-diving units and underwater units to supervise. There's a *lot* going on.

Do you have one line producer or two?

MW: We have two.

BB: Then there are production managers and a whole system of crew.

MW: And once the material starts pouring in — and when it does, it just *floods* in — then there is a whole editorial department just trying to keep up with that.

When you're shooting, are you both there at call and wrap times?

BB: We're there all the time . . .

MW: And as we're shooting we're also in the edit looking at rushes as we go along.

BB: As well as being on phone calls to the States until all hours of the night. It's very, very hard, both physically and mentally. The thing is, you have to really know the script and everything in it, inside and out, because months later, when you're editing and you're talking to the studio and they're saying 'Can we change this?' or 'Can we do that?' or whatever, it has to be in your memory bank . . .

MW: You know whether you have the shot or you *don't* have the shot to make a change — because you've seen all the rushes.

You tend to work with the same creative team and regular crew. Would you say that makes it even more of a family business?

MW: If you look at *Dr No* — the cameraman, the writers, a lot of the actors, the designers, *everybody* had already worked for Cubby on other films. You work hard to put a team of people together who are reliable and who like the project.

BB: The first thing we do when we start working on the script and we're thinking about locations and whether we can do this or that is call up Peter Lamont. He's an Oscar-winning designer, a great guy, and he's worked on these films since *Goldfinger* when he was a draughts-man. He's the guy we call and say, 'What do you think?' With the ice hotel on *Die Another Day*, we said to Peter, 'How would we tackle that?' Within a week of that conversation Peter went to the ice hotel and spent the night there, because it was going to melt, and we were going to want to replicate that a year later. When he came back he had so much information about it — photographs, notes and observations. So when we met with the writers, Peter came in and told us all a lot of stuff, and it went into the script.

Sometimes in development we might have a question about an aerial shot, and the second-unit director's son will then come up with some fantastic aerial idea, and a couple of weeks later they will come back to us with a tape of what can be done there. So the people we work with get very involved — and often early on, when we're addressing the script.

You make the Bond films on a very tight schedule.

MW: We've had films that had a twelve-week post-production period . . .

A tight schedule doesn't allow for error. Do you ever do re-shoots?

MW: We've done tiny pick-ups but not a re-shoot. There isn't time for that. You've got to get it right, and you should have it right the first time.
BB: It goes back to what we were saying about working with the same crew. When you have people you know you can rely on and they say, 'I can have that ready by October first', you know that's a certainty. You're not thinking 'Gee, I haven't worked with this guy before, I hope when he says October first that he means it.' We know that when our people say they can deliver something, they are telling us the truth. It's the same with the writers. You can sit tight for six weeks and wait for someone to deliver you a draft and then read it and it's completely wrong. Or you can sit in a room every day with the writers and *know* that you are going to get the draft on a specific date, because you have been through the process with them.

With the benefit of Cubby's influence would you say you came to the Bond job with a thorough understanding of what was involved?

MW: I think our close involvement comes, firstly, from the tradition of Cubby having loved the movies, and the way he came to see the work, and then secondly from observing *how* it was actually done. We both enjoy very much the creative aspect of putting the story and script together, putting the right team of people in place, and casting the films correctly — all of those things being the work that we as producers do in the making of the films. Then there's the business and administrative side, which is a huge part of the process — because if you want to keep the business going, you have to make it feasible, and that means it has to be profitable.

BB: When we made *GoldenEye* we met a lot of writers and read a lot of material before we selected Michael France.4 Then we worked through the different drafts with him. It was a sort of evolution from *GoldenEye* on to *Tomorrow Never Dies*, where we brought on Bruce Feirstein. But I think we feel the development of the stories and scripts is an on-going process, even though we know the character and Bond's world very well. Just as Cubby and Harry set clear parameters for Bond from the novels, and in their work with Ken Adam and their collaborators, so for us when it came to *GoldenEye* we realized we had to adjust those parameters to be in tune with how the world has evolved and changed.

We also find that it takes a while to bring people into the process and get writers and directors and new people accustomed to what Bond is about — because there has to be *some* consistency. But, generally, we find we want people who will challenge our notions. Then, once we have people we believe in, it becomes a lot easier.

2. *The formula*

In terms of the parameters you mention — how do you keep Bond modern? How much of a formula is it?

MW: He changes with the times.

BB: There are a set of rules in the Bond movies, and you change some of them to a certain extent. But I don't think you'd want to see Bond escaping from the villain with a Big Mac in his hand . . . There are things that just wouldn't fit.

MW: Our basic philosophy is that we are making action-adventure films, and therefore the audience is going to expect certain elements. There's got to be a character going out on a quest, with villains along the way, challenges, reversals, and a romantic plot. In other words, all of the things that are typical of a film in a well-known genre, and of course we have to be inventive like everyone else. But the second

4. Previously the writer of *Cliffhanger* (1993), latterly credited on *The Hulk* (2003), *The Punisher* (2004), and *Fantastic Four* (2005).

element for us is that we are developing James Bond and his world. And, as Barbara says, there are some unique parameters that are Bond. Early on, we identified and documented the novel and film elements of the James Bond character that the audience expects him to be 'about'. Our challenge is to try to be inventive in *both* genres — the action/adventure and Bond's world.

BB: The character Fleming created is pretty fascinating and contradictory. He was complex, and in the early films they accentuated certain elements of his character according to each actor. He's *flawed* too, and I think that was one of the most appealing things about him when he first appeared. His contradictions showed that he wasn't just a plain old knight-in-shining-armour, and because of that, I think, he captured the imaginations of a lot of people. We have quite a lot to work with, and we like to exploit all the elements.

It's been a while since a Bond film was adapted from one of Fleming's novels or stories.

MW: Today, the character in the Bond films is a derivative of the character in the books, one that has its own levels of character, that's different.[5]

Do you continue to have a relationship with the Fleming estate?

BB: Oh yeah, absolutely. We still have a financial relationship with them. There are family members who keep in regular contact with us. They're always welcome to come to the set, and they're invited to premieres.

Do the Bond spoofs or imitators out there ever affect how you think about Bond?

BB: We pretty much ignore them . . . although occasionally when we're talking about something we'll say, 'That's a bit *too Austin Powers* . . .'[*laughs*].

Was it your decision to permit the usage of Bond in Austin Powers?

BB: It just kind of happened. I thought the first movie was very funny. And the spoofs are not our competitors.

MW: The parodies show you where you can go wrong. It's quite easy to fall into the ridiculous if you're not careful — Bond should never be

5. Ian Fleming's US copyrights are now held under the MGM/UA-Danjaq banner.

a parody of himself. But if you're talking about people who have attempted to duplicate Bond, such as the Matt Helm books[6], I think they really suffered from not understanding the importance of complexity in the character that Barbara mentioned. The Helm books went from one superficial aspect to the next, so one moment he's very charming, or suddenly he's very brutal. For us the Bond character is a combination of elements. Humour is very important, but it has to be a certain *kind* of humour — edgy, ironic, and slightly black.

3. *The talent*

Are you continuing to work with the writing team of Neal Purvis and Robert Wade, who scripted The World is Not Enough *and* Die Another Day?

BB: I think so . . .
MW: Cubby had Dick Maibaum, who wrote — or at least participated in — about twelve of them. There is something to be gained from having someone who understands the character. But occasionally you need to inject new life. That's why we have been bringing in different directors for each film, which, I think, energizes the series.

What do you look for in hiring a Bond director?

BB: Stamina!
MW: Confidence . . .
BB: It sounds banal, such a page-one thing, but you really want somebody who can tell a story — and it's *very* hard to find directors who can tell stories. We also want someone who will help with the development of the script and understand the characters, and work well with actors. Also we need someone with a great visual sense, because the films *have* to be visually entertaining and interesting. It has to be someone who will accept that these films are made on a very large scale with multiple units, so they have to be able to visualize the film they want to make, and then be able to communicate that vision to a lot of people, and help those people provide the resolve they need to get the job done. It's very challenging — which is why we try to have a pretty lengthy pre-production period.
MW: We like the director to participate in the script and work on it for a while. We bring it to a certain point and then the director comes in and refines it. That seems to be the most efficient way of working.

6. Series of novels by Donald Hamilton, filmed by Columbia Pictures with Dean Martin as the eponymous spy-hero.

BB: A director also has to be brought up to speed on the history of Bond because often you'll be sitting there and they will say, 'Wouldn't it be great if he wore a kilt . . .?'And we'll say, 'We *did* that in *On Her Majesty's Secret Service* . . .' Or sometimes we'll say, 'Uh-oh, that doesn't really fit with the character . . .' Obviously each film has to work within the context of the series. We have to all be on the same page, so that when you reach the point where the director starts principal photography *that's* the point where it becomes his movie and he's fulfilling his vision — because by then you have agreed what the movie is all about. Then, for us, the work becomes about helping the director get through the process.

MW: I tend to think of the structure of the movies in military terms; we're like the chiefs of staff, the organizers of strategic issues, and we handle the logistics. Then the director is the line commander, who makes it all happen in the field.

What impact has Pierce Brosnan had on the four films he's appeared in?

BB: What's brilliant about Pierce is that he has *so* inhabited the character that he instinctively knows what's right. That's very, *very* important. All of the directors have remarked when they come into the process that they feel very comfortable because Pierce is helping them, particularly when some of it starts getting difficult.

MW: It's the way he projects himself out there with his charisma, confidence and intelligence. People love him as Bond because he's romantic and tough, and when he says the lines people believe it. So you have sympathy when everything goes against him . . .

BB: I think it's hard for an actor who has to communicate so much when there isn't a lot of dialogue. Bond is a character who's very often in a situation where he doesn't have a side-kick to talk to and say, 'We've got to go and do *this* . . .' So there are many times in the scripts when he's solitary and creeping around and you think 'Oh God, how are we going to explain to the audience that once he's in the room he notices something strange, but he's able to put it all together in his head so that he's got to go and do X, Y, and Z . . .?' It's often difficult for audiences to follow action unless the actor can really take them through it, while the director explains the geography. Actors in these films have to do it all with a glance and body movements — and Pierce is great at that. Also, Pierce is very physically agile, which is great, because all the running and jumping is arduous but he does a lot of the action very well, and convincingly.

Until recently — say, the casting of Halle Berry in Die Another Day *— would you agree that there wasn't much of a tradition of leading actresses appearing in the films?*

BB: Casting Halle was manna from heaven . . .

MW: I think what's happened is that in the last ten years the perception of Bond amongst leading actresses has changed. So, for instance, we've had Sophie Marceau in *The World is Not Enough*, and Michelle Yeoh in *Tomorrow Never Dies*. We've steadily been able to develop those roles and raise the level of casting, so I think it was comfortable for Halle to come on board. Certainly, twenty years ago it was difficult to attract leading ladies — though we did early on, but then there was a period where it was difficult to get top notch people. Now, though, it seems that women feel more comfortable about appearing in a Bond film.

BB: When you go back to the early days of Cubby and Harry, when they discovered Sean Connery and cast him as Bond, one of the things that was so impressive — apart from the fact that he was magnificent — was that he hadn't really been seen before. So when he came on and said, 'I'm James Bond', everyone thought, 'OK, cool, you're James Bond.' They didn't associate him with anyone else — they bought him. Then, because these were films that were about a British character travelling to exotic places, you could cast exotic people who hadn't been seen before, and bring in European women as spies and so on. It made for a very interesting atmosphere.

We've always felt that because the films have always been successful, thank goodness, you can take chances on casting, and cast people who aren't big stars, which is fantastic. I think when people go to the Bond movies they have an experience that is different to a lot of other movies, where they're used to seeing the same people. Consequently we've given opportunities to a lot of actors, and that's part of the fun and excitement of discovering new talent — because as we discover them, audiences discover them too.

4. *A 'big mechanical fish'*

With many film franchises, the cost of each successive film increases. Is that true of Bond?

MW: They have to be profitable, that's number one. But then you can also destroy the series if you compromise too much on costs, and make the films look like they are running out of energy and not up to the level they should be. That's the challenge for us, balancing those two competing situations. The costs *have* increased and that's always foremost on our minds. But then these budgets are what we *do*. It's a full-time job controlling the budgets, and it's very hard to keep everything on schedule exactly the way it should be, because with so many units there are numerous situations when things can change. We also try to do things that have never been done before. So you are constantly challenging your ability to forecast what you can do with balancing how much it's going to cost.

If the Terminator *films are now costing roughly $170 million, and that's a relatively young franchise, how much do the Bond films cost by comparison?*

MW[*laughs*]: We're not far off . . . We're somewhere just over $100 million. Or the last few have been . . .

BB: For us it's all about knowing *where* and *when* to spend the money, and about trying to have it on the screen. Sometimes you can spend a hell of a lot of money and it doesn't look like it. Other times you can do something very effectively and not in an expensive way. It's about having people around you with the expertise to make the best decisions. It's a big responsibility when you have a studio financing a movie. I suppose my feeling is that when we are in charge of this stuff, we tend to treat it as though it's our own money. I fight more over construction costs on a film than I do over changes to my own house! It's just a reality, because when you're aware that every penny is critical you want it on the screen.

MW: Very often we have to make adjustments and modify the budget as we go along, because you have to be able to react to a situation as it comes up. If the director understands the script well, he can sometimes come in with a proposal for cutting it down and changing things that will keep us on track. In fact, most of the directors will participate in that way, to keep you on the right road.

Given the exoticism of the films — the locations alone — do you find yourself worrying about costs as you develop the script?

MW: I always laugh about this, because it's the little things the writers put in as dressing that, later on, can become major issues without you realizing it. Say a writer will put something in the script, some scene with a 'BIG FISH'. I'll say to them, 'You *know* what's going to happen. This is a detail we're going to ignore right now. Then we'll start shooting, and one day we'll walk into the art department and there will be a drawing marked 'BIG MECHANICAL FISH', or it'll be written down as a special-effects shot. We'll say, 'What the hell is that?' And the guy in the art department will say, 'Don't you remember? It's in the script . . .' And he'll show us the page where it says 'BIG FISH' and he'll say, 'Well, you want the fish to do *this* in the scene, and fish can't act, so we've got to make a mechanical one.' And I'll be standing there thinking 'Who put *that* in the script . . .?' So you end up shooting the 'BIG FISH'. And then, in the end, when it comes to the edit, *you cut it out*!

BB: My big bug is corridors . . . You don't think about it too much when you're reading the script and it says 'BOND walks down the corridor and goes into an office'. Then the *next* thing, a few months later, you're sitting there looking at the art department budget, the construction budget, the set dressing budget. And you realize it's going to cost £20,000 to build the corridor — it's going to cost £15,000 alone to dress and put down carpets, hang mirrors, paintings and lights . . . And I'm thinking 'We're never gonna *see* the corridor. Just have him walk in the bloody door!' Because the thing is, that's £20 or 30,000 of a budget that you're going to *desperately* need next week . . .

What about the logistics and cost of shooting on a frozen lake in Iceland, as you did in Die Another Day?

BB: The thing is, you read in the script 'A LAKE IN ICELAND' and you think 'We've *got* to have it, because it's spectacular, and it's going to be worth it. So how are we going to do it, effectively and safely?' You know right away that if you want to shoot on a frozen lake there are going to be a lot of dramas and problems and that it's going to be expensive. But you have to go for it wholeheartedly, embrace all the problems.

Is there anything you can't *do?*

MW: You can do anything. The question is, is it going to be convincing? And is it going to look good?

5. 'The car has got to fly'

One of Greg Williams's on-set stills from Die Another Day *shows you both with the director Lee Tamahori, the executive producer, and various heads of department, making the decision to put the production in hiatus for a week after Pierce injured his knee. How do you manage a situation like that?*

MW: The first thing that happens is you have to throw away the whole schedule. That means all the sets that you've built, all the locations you're going to — which means you've got to re-do the schedule so that when he *does* come back he does everything that doesn't require his knee. He was gone seven days, which meant we had to turn the whole thing around . . .

BB: It has a *lot* to do with the actor. Pierce was extraordinary. Once it happened, the decision was taken that he would go back to the doctor in LA. Most people take weeks and weeks, even months of recovery before they would come back, but Pierce was just determined that he would come back as quickly as possible. His whole attitude was 'Let's get on with this . . .' And he was so upset that it had happened . . .

MW: For us, the injury was not dissimilar to a super-athlete getting hurt.

BB: Making tough decisions like that is what we do. It's difficult and it's complicated and it involves a lot of logistics but, in a way, that one was a very clear-cut problem that had clear-cut solutions — you can't shoot on Tuesday, so you've got to do something else. Sometimes those decisions are easier than others, because it's just about doing something effectively. The biggest and most crippling problem on a film is indecision — that's one of the *worst* situations that you can have. If a director won't make a decision about something, even if it's a small decision, it can be quite crippling.

MW: Like 'What's the colour of Bond's jacket? Do you like this one or that one? Because we've got to have him in it, and then we have ten stunt-double jackets to make in addition. So if you don't like the blue, and you don't like the grey, choose another one . . .'

BB: The director is being hit with hundreds of decisions every day, so that's often a problem. Then someone will come up to us and say, 'We're trying to get the director to make a decision about this.' Those can be some of the biggest problems, just making choices — whereas with Pierce's injury, well, you just have to deal with the reality of the fact that he has a problem with his knee. The first decision was 'You have a week, let's get him better, and then let's address the damage-control.'

MW: What's so interesting about the film business is you always have to support the people you have working around you, and these are people who manage to do things that even *I* don't think are possible. Whereas our crew just go ahead, and it's quite amazing. Very often I get very frustrated in other areas of my life, say with contractors, because you can't get an answer out of them and it drives me crazy — whereas, very often, the people you work with in the film business just manage to solve things . . .

BB: The philosophy in film production is about '*How* can we do things . . .?'

MW: You call in a production manager and say, 'We want to shoot on the Thames. We want to go from MI6 at Vauxhall, past the Houses of Parliament, under Tower Bridge and down to the Millennium Dome.' And the production manager will say, 'OK, I'll look into it . . .' Then they call you back and say, 'We have to get permission from thirty-five agencies and you can only shoot when the tide is up, and it goes up and down by thirty feet per day and at different hours.' So I'll say, 'What are you saying? That we *can't* do it?' And he'll say, 'No, no, I'm just saying it's going to take a little time to arrange . . .'

BB: That sequence took six weeks to shoot and it was a whole operation, as you can imagine . . . The Thames is a very, very busy waterway, one of the busiest in the world, and with the tide there is an enormous discrepancy. Then we had many other things to deal with, such as environmental protection issues — because you have nesting swans, so there was a special grassy area that we had to protect. We were shooting this sequence in the spring but that's when all the nesting, hatching and laying of all sorts of wildlife goes on and you *can't* disrupt that. We had a similar problem once in Spain about protecting special eagles, vultures and lizards . . .

Then you have fish you have to deal with — so they had to put sonar devices down to send the fish away so they didn't get hurt by the charges. And then because we had some explosions we had to do, we found out that there were unexploded mines in the Thames from the Second World War. So we had to call a building contractor and inform them, and they had to do a mine sweep. Then you have to notify the Federal Aviation Authority and the waterways people, because if you're going to set off charges you've got to tell the Houses of Parliament — who were sitting at the time — so they didn't think it was a terrorist attack . . .

You must be a fund of specialist information . . .

BB: But that's what makes it interesting, you just don't *know* what's going to happen. You get up in the morning and you know you're going to be shooting a specific sequence, and you have a rough idea of what your problems are going to be. But then suddenly you'll get a call about some bizarre thing from a remote part of the world that you just couldn't have anticipated. And then that becomes your focus for weeks on end.

We have produced *Chitty Chitty Bang Bang* the musical in London, and it was extremely complicated but, because of the way we have been working all our lives, our first reaction was 'Well, the car has got to fly, and if we don't make the car fly we don't have a show.' So I think we apply this kind of philosophy to everything we do. We're currently thinking of producing another theatre show that has just as many spectacular moments.

6. The brand

What are your marketing responsibilities?

MW: As we go along we look at the posters and the artwork and we have our own head of marketing and publicity within our own company who liaises with everyone and supervises the enquiries during production.

Is it a creative process, re-thinking how to keep selling the Bond brand with each movie?

MW: That's primarily the job of the marketing-distribution company. But certainly we get involved.
BB: We get involved with promotions and we have a lot of tie-ins, because we need products and services on a very large scale, like with the cars. If we have a car sequence, we will need seventeen cars specially adapted to do specific tricks.
MW: That's seventeen cars of *exactly* the same model.
BB: We're very lucky to have a great relationship with Ford, but that means you've got to go well in advance, you've got to know exactly what's happening with the cars in the script, which means you've got to storyboard the car sequences for the company. And then you have got to get them to loan you the cars well in advance so you can work on them — change the engines or whatever — and have them ready.
    The cars we use are usually cutting-edge, new models, so they are hot off the assembly line . . .
MW: Sometimes, they're just off the design desk . . .

Do advertisers queue up to have their products in your films?

BB: Certain people do. We look at them as partnerships. The Aston Martin is synonymous with Bond and it's a big commitment on their part but I think it pays off for both sides. Obviously when we have big partnerships with products and services it's a big relationship, because they've given us those cars and a lot of support goes with that. When it comes to marketing the film, and the marketing of their product,

Ford want commercials they can use from our footage, so there is that aspect too.

MW: What will happen is that they show us their commercials and we can ask for changes. But there are generally only two or three trailers or TV ads that you can create using the car.

Is it a lucrative relationship with these kinds of partners?

MW: It isn't lucrative for us . . .

BB: We don't get cash payments. A lot of people think that we get a lump sum of money to put a product in the film, but it doesn't work that way. If, for example, we need seventeen cars then they are given to us for use in the production, but we destroy a lot of them.

MW: We have to give them back, usually with a *little* bang . . .

BB: It saves us a lot on the advertising budget to have products and commercials, so if Ford are going to do a commercial using the Jaguar or something, that's good for them — because they use clips from the movie — and it works for us because it means we're not having to buy those minutes on television to air a trailer. It's a benefit to the movie and it's a benefit to the product. The tricky part is having to give them the material ahead of the movie's release, because it's important the commercials are aired. So when you have complicated special effects to do in post which involve the car, because it's shooting or exploding — well, the commercial makers are going to want that, and quickly.

MW: We have to make sure that the material we deliver them works for us. We also have to be careful because there's a danger that you can go overboard with the advertising — and if you do, the public might get fed up with it. I try to tell people when they give us a product that if you make it *too* obvious, it becomes counter-productive because it takes people out of the story and audience end up saying, 'Look at that.' In those cases I think the advertiser gets negative feedback for their product.

7. Keepers of the flame

Do you know how much money the Bond films have made overall?

BB: It's hard to calculate overall from 1962 to the present, given the currency exchange . . .

MW: I think all you can do is look at the last one and say we're doing OK.

I have seen an overall figure of $25 billion . . .

BB: The last one grossed $425 million at the box office before you add on additional revenue from DVD, videos, et cetera.

What's your relationship with MGM?

MW: We have a reasonable relationship with the studio.

Could you take the Bond franchise to another studio?

BB/MW: No.
BB: I think the thing about movies — because they are so ubiquitous, and because everybody has an opinion about them, and about anything creative, whether it's a stage show or whatever — I think people always think they can do it better, no matter what —
MW: — including everybody at the studio.
BB: It's very important to us that we keep quality control on the movies. My dad said to me, 'Always remember, the most important thing is you don't let other people screw it up. You have to be the keeper of the flame. If you're going to screw it up, then screw it up yourself . . .' We can make stupid decisions like anybody else, but we don't let other people talk us into doing what they want.

Do you have the right to produce the Bond films for as long as you want to?

MW: Our company has the right to produce the films and we share the rights with the studio. So we are in a different situation to a lot of other franchise producers.

So you will carry on producing Bond films?

BB: I think so, for as long as people want to see the movies.
MW: We meet people who tell us that they went on their first date to see a Bond movie . . . It's part of the social history so we feel a responsibility to the series. There aren't too many brands like it.

So you're not done with it yet?

BB: I don't think so. As long as the audience wants to see the films, they will be made by us, or by some version of our descendants. Both of Michael's sons have worked on the movies. My daughter is a bit young, she's eleven, but she has asked me a couple of times, 'Am I supposed to take over from you guys . . .?' And I've said, 'You do what you *want*, girl!'

At the time of writing James Bond will return in *Casino Royale*, the twenty-first film of the series. The film will see Daniel Craig in his debut appearance as James Bond. Sony will be the releasing studio, having acquired MGM/UA in May 2005 and continued the Danjaq deal. The film is to be directed by Martin Campbell, from a script written by Neal Purvis & Robert Wade & Paul Haggis.

Part Two
THE BRITISH SCENE

No one hoping to produce movies in the UK can ignore Hollywood entirely, and none of the producers in this following Part have tried to do so — some, indeed, have openly embraced it. And some of their best-known productions have taken them far and wide around the globe. Yet each, in their own ways, have remained more closely associated with UK talent, UK subject matter, and the foibles of that particular industry.

Take 3

SIMON CHANNING-WILLIAMS

Simon Channing-Williams made his reputation as a partner in Thin Man Films with writer-director Mike Leigh, for whom he first worked as an assistant director at the BBC, and for whom he has now produced eight feature films, a sequence that began with *High Hopes* in 1988. No one makes films quite like Leigh, and Channing-Williams's wits are continually tested in the collaboration, as they have been by the challenge of securing funds down the years, first from British television, latterly from Europe and sources of 'alternate funding'.

Channing-Williams also develops projects outside of his relationship with Leigh through the company Potboiler, which in 2001 was signed to a three-year 'first-look' deal with the MGM-owned United Artists (Channing-Williams having long enjoyed good relations with the then UA president, Bingham Ray).

When I met with Channing-Williams he was preparing for 'Mike Leigh Untitled 03', and for a screen adaptation of John le Carré's novel *The Constant Gardener*. But first I was keen to go back in time and discuss his training as an AD within the studio-like environment of the BBC in the late 1960s and 1970s, a time when an enormous amount of single dramas were made on film and tape, considered by some film historians as a sort of 'golden age', analogous — at least in terms of its productivity, but also as a factory of talent — to the Hollywood of the 1930s.

1. *One of the very few people to be fired by the BBC*

SIMON CHANNING-WILLIAMS: I started at the bottom, as a runner at the BBC. Back then I was called a 'Call Boy', which of course you couldn't call people now . . . today there'll be some politically correct name for the job. But as a result of all my experience, I can pretty much do anything in production. I can't light or pull focus, but I reckon I'm a reasonably good grip, and I push a mean dolly. I've also done boom-swinging when the boom-swinger was ill. Being able to do most things on a set means that when I'm asking someone to do something, I know whether it's possible or not.

Back then, the BBC used to have two PAs or 'production assistants' for all the dramas they made — one was a production manager and one was a first assistant. Although I would do either job, to all intents and purposes I was a First. Mike Leigh still thinks I was the best, and I still get rolled out every now and again if our First is sick or away. I enjoyed Firsting because I enjoyed getting my hands dirty and being part of it, which I think you have to do as a good First. You have to know when to talk, when to cajole, when to bully and when not to.

HELEN DE WINTER: *Did you set out to become a producer?*

No.

Was there someone in the business who impressed you? Who made you think, 'I want to do that'?

I don't think I particularly looked up to any producer during my days at the BBC. There were some lovely people around, like Innes Lloyd,[7] and dear old Kenith Trodd.[8] But what I wanted more than anything was to work with directors of talent, and I think that's what spurred me on. What impressed me more than anything else was working with directors like Jack Gold, James MacTaggart,[9] Mike Newell, Mike Leigh, Stephen Frears — I did something like six or seven films for television with Stephen. And I think I decided, more than anything else, that I wanted to work with people like that — work with them and make things work *for* them — on ideas and scripts that really interested me.

Stephen Frears I remember very particularly. We were doing a film[10] about a man who was an Elvis Presley impersonator. And one day Stephen was really concerned — as, indeed, I was for him — that we couldn't make something work in terms of the shot. We had a

---

7. Lloyd (1925–1991) produced single plays and series from the mid-sixties to the late eighties, forming particularly strong partnerships with Stephen Frears and Alan Bennett.
8. Trodd, another strong BBC alumnus, made his reputation as the producer of all the major BBC plays and series written by Dennis Potter.
9. MacTaggart (1928–1974) also wrote and produced, and his untimely death was later marked by the naming in his honour of the annual opening lecture of the Edinburgh Television Festival.
10. Entitled *Long Distance Information.*

wonderful cameraman, Nat Crosby, and Stephen and Nat, with me a bit, were trying to work out whether or not we could do it conventionally, in single takes. Then Stephen eventually said, 'Leave me alone, I'm going to think about this.' So I left him alone for two hours, or probably more, and I asked the crew to stand down. Then he came back and he had worked out a fantastic single shot that would do the whole thing. Not only did it catch us up on the day, it took us ahead. It was quite simply brilliant.

So I was aware even in those days that — while I didn't have the ability to direct —I did feel I had the ability to be *really* supportive to directors. I also loved reading scripts and making comments. But, at that time, while I *sort* of thought I knew what was wrong with them, I didn't have the ability to express properly how to put them right. I believe I still have that failing today.

While you were at the BBC were you thinking about the possibility of working in movies as well?

It was very difficult to cross between television and films in those days. There was a really strict divide between the BBC union and the ACTT — the Association of Cinematographic and Television Technicians. I had done some third assistant directing on pictures, so I sort of floated in and out of freelance work. But yes, I very much wanted to do films and be able to realize what we were beginning to see on the little screen on a cinema screen.

How did you meet Mike Leigh?

I met him in 1979 on a BBC film called *Grown-Ups*. He had already got through two first assistant directors. I don't know if they were fired, and I genuinely have no idea why they left. And when Mike was then sent this bloke with a double-barrelled name, I think he thought 'Oh Lord, what's coming now . . .?' But we got on really well together and had a similar sense of humour — actually I had to ban myself from the set, because I couldn't stop laughing, it was so funny. So I ended up trying to first AD from the stairs outside the set.

Towards the end of production I became concerned, because I had made a promise to two sets of homeowners whose houses we were using as locations, next door to one another in Canterbury. One was a private house and the other was a council house, and I had promised both families that they would be back in their fully redecorated homes in time for Easter. As we had overrun by a week, this wasn't going to happen, and the local builders and decorators couldn't guarantee they could get the work done in time. So I did something I clearly shouldn't have done. I had a number of mates on the BBC workshop floor, so I paid for people from the floor to come down and do the work. I paid for the paint and materials — I ended up saving the BBC something like £1500, which was a lot of money in 1980. But the Corporation had a sense-of-humour failure, and I was summarily fired — one of the very few people to be fired by the BBC. The charge was 'Gross misuse of BBC funds', I think. My final notice of dismissal came on my birthday in 1980, so it was a fantastic thirty-fifth birthday present.

Interestingly, the other chap who was there with me didn't get fired, so I think I was seen as the ringleader, the mastermind — Mr Big. But the other chap is still there at the BBC, serving his days quietly . . .

Mike Leigh was incredibly supportive during the whole period, and sort of indignant and outraged for me, because I genuinely wasn't creaming money or materials from the Corporation.

Do you think that's maybe why you established such a good rapport with Mike?

It's very easy to say with hindsight, but working with Mike has evolved over the years, since 1988 when we did *High Hopes*. Mike had worked with a number of producers before — Tony Garnett, Margaret Matheson, Ken Trodd, and Graham Benson, who produced *Meantime* [1983] for him. Graham invited me to be associate producer on *Meantime* but I couldn't because I was doing Tony Palmer's *Wagner* [1984]. I was the associate producer and first assistant on that, which was fascinating. The production manager had left under a cloud just before we started shooting, and it fell to me to do all of the scheduling, over eight European countries, with six or seven months of shooting. I became associate producer along the way when Alan Wright, who was the producer, became ill. And it was an enormous job, because it was a six-hour drama, although it started off as a feature film.

Finally Mike and I were brought together again by Victor Glynn at Portman Productions — Victor had put *High Hopes* together, and he asked me to co-produce it with him.

2. *There is never a script . . .*

Given Mike Leigh's unique way of working, what's the starting point when he wants to make another film? Does he say, 'I've got an idea . . .'?

It starts with me going out there on my own — I don't need Mike for this, all I need is his name, to say that he and I are going to do a film. Then he and I will start to talk and I'll say, 'Well, I've been talking to X and I think I can get £800,000 out of them. And I've been talking to Y and they're probably good for £500,000. And there might be other money elsewhere . . .' Then we look at how it all might hang together.

*Back in 1988, was there a script for **High Hopes** that you could take out and shop around?*

There is *never* a script — there really isn't. Even now, people, financiers and heads of studios — some of whom I have known for a very, very, long time — say, 'Look, we *know* that you know there's a script. Just tell us a little bit about it.' But there truly isn't a script. In 1988 my pitch was exactly the same — 'We don't know what we want to do, but please would you give us £1.3 million?' Of course it was a monumental leap of faith by the financiers. And it continues to be.

How do you establish a figure of £1.3 million without a script?

It's simply a guess based on the largest amount of funding I believe I can achieve.

Does Mike say to you, 'Simon, it's going to be mostly interiors and one or two locations'?

No, because at that point, Mike doesn't know.

*So then — back in 1988 you went out and said, 'We're making **High Hopes** . . .'*

No, because until the film is finished all of our films are 'Untitled'. So that one was 'Untitled 88'.

How do you know what you are selling?

I don't.

What kind of questions are you asked?

All the questions you're asking me now. 'What's it about?' 'Who's in it?' 'Is there a script? And can we see it?'

In 1988 what assurances did you give to your investors?

None, really. But back then Mike had a body of work behind him which included *Abigail's Party, Nuts in May, Meantime*. And all of them had been made in that same way.

But what gave you certainty that you could persuade people to invest in a blank sheet of paper?

David Rose who started Channel 4 Films — now FilmFour — was somebody who was already aware of Mike's talent and ability. So, to a degree, I was preaching to the converted. We also had the support of Simon Relph when he was head of British Screen. So the combination of David and Simon meant that we had great, great support. In the early days it was literally those two partners — British Screen and Channel 4. They hadn't done anything like this before — whereas at the BBC, if you overran, it was fine. But we have always adhered very strictly to our budgets.

In general does Mike have an idea who he wants to be in the film?

Mike can't start casting until he knows how much money we've got. Having raised the money there will be nothing to the team except Mike, myself, and an assistant. So it's after this stage that Mike is really able to begin working.

Once I raise the money I will do a budget. The first thing we do is try to establish the number of actors Mike thinks he wants. Then I begin to build a budget based around a possible number of actors. Historically, the budget for actors comes out at about twenty per cent of the whole thing, so from there we work out what we will do with the rest of the money.

So your budgets are sophisticated guesstimates, starting with . . .?

The number of rehearsal weeks. I suppose what's so interesting is that I can prepare a budget in this way. Say we need twelve weeks of rehearsal — I can demonstrate . . . *[SCW takes a piece of paper on which he draws an inverted triangle and two lines that bisect the structure.]* Let's say we have twenty weeks for rehearsal and ten weeks of shooting, giving a total of thirty weeks. We have X number of actors and they come on for various lengths of time. Very simply, you have the actor whom the film is mostly going to rely on down for twenty weeks' worth of rehearsal and ten weeks of shoot. Then we begin to map out the number of actors who will come on during rehearsal, and the number of weeks they will shoot. Now we've become more canny, so we nominate weeks for each actor in the rehearsal period and then nominate the weeks of shooting on or before the first day of principal photography — so you can get more actors making better use of the available money. It's very selective scheduling and very precise economics, and we have to get it right, otherwise we're stuffed.

When Mike begins casting — do you then begin to have an idea of the film he wants to make . . .?

More often than not, Mike will not know what he's casting because it's out of the workshops that he does with the actors *during* the casting stage that ideas will come about for what he wants to do.

Do you suggest actors?

Absolutely not. That would be incorrect. Mike will discuss things with me, but casting is an entirely personal thing with him. Recently we have used a casting director, Nina Gold, who has been absolutely splendid, gets on fantastically with Mike and has transformed my life and Mike's as well, because she's so knowledgeable. She goes and watches everything, from the smallest bit of fringe theatre to all the big West End productions and, of course, more films than I've seen. In the early days there wasn't a Nina, so we would be doing the contracts for the actors. Hideous!

Do you go to rehearsals?

No, very seldom.

When do you start to know what Mike is doing?

Somewhere between four and six weeks into rehearsals. At that point we know what relationships the characters have together. We can normally establish one 'safe house', which is usually the key character's house, so we know that if we run out of things to do then the action can revert to that. The rehearsals continue during the shoot, Mike will rehearse with the actors after each day's shoot. We will then probably have two or three days off during the shooting period when we will lay the main crew off to allow Mike to re-define the script, the characters, and what happens next. Before we start shooting we do camera tests — for instance, we're doing tests on the new film next Tuesday and we will be looking at textures and colours. We know it will be set in the 1950s, so we're working towards that.

Does the rehearsal process yield a script?

No, it categorically does *not* yield a script.

Is there a script at the end *of the film?*

The truth of it is that there isn't a script until the film is cut together, because you could probably cut it together in a number of different ways.

At what point in the process of making a film with Mike do your shoulders start to relax?

They go down a notch after we finish shooting, and once I know what we've got.

I don't mean to be flippant . . . but when you produce films with scripts, they must seem like a doddle by comparison?

In many ways they are. Just today I've marked up a script and I've been able to know what's happening, and it's brilliant! But I enjoy working both ways. I've really enjoyed the challenge of *The Constant Gardener* and that has been every bit as hard as one of Mike's films.

So which is the most difficult time for you in the process with Mike? When you're raising the money, or when you're shooting the film?

To be honest, the most difficult time for me is probably on the first day of principal photography — because I don't have a clue what's going to happen on the *last* day of principal photography, or whether I have enough money to pay for it. I know that we have ten weeks of shooting and we will contract people for six days a week — although our mean average over the last fifteen years is that we will shoot for four and a half days a week and from that we can work out our requirement for stock et cetera.

A great deal of this was to do with 'Listen, trust me . . .' So people would trust us. And we have never, ever gone over budget. We continue to be bonded. Mike is an incredibly good partner to have, because he does listen. So if I say, 'Well, we have a problem', then we will talk about it. When we did *High Hopes*, it was a guesstimate, we had no idea — we said we would do it for X amount of money, and we did.

How did you survive?

With great difficulty . . . and it's still much the same today. If there is
a problem, Mike's and my fees will be the first to go. But we have
built up trust. After *High Hopes*, I'm pleased to say that Mike and I
decided to form Thin Man. We started the company with nothing. I
suppose we did have an office at the time, but it was funded entirely
by Mike and I, out of our own personal funds. The first film we made
through the company was *Life is Sweet* and there was a very, very
small production company fee available to us. Out of that, we set up
an office in Covent Garden, and when we decided we were going to
stay together we moved on from there.

3. Bigger numbers

*You played a very active role in encouraging the growth of distribution
of Mike's films in the US, didn't you?*

The release of *High Hopes* in the US was really interesting. Jeff Lipsky
was head of acquisitions at Skouras, and Jeff had always been passionate about the film, he was particularly keen to champion it.
However, I was aware that with a Mike Leigh film you were dealing
with only a tiny number of individuals — and not companies — that
actually *got* his films. So when Mike and I made *Life is Sweet*, it
became clear to me that we needed to look at North American distribution in a different light. Bingham Ray, then head of acquisition at
Avenue, was a Mike Leigh fan and it was through talking with Jeff and
Bingham that the idea of forming a new US distribution company
gelled.

Life is Sweet was presented at the American Film Market in 1993 in
order to get offers, although I didn't believe that any of the independents would give it a really good platform. I felt it was very much a
sort of 'scalp', rather than something to be taken seriously, and so I
persuaded Simon Relph and David Rose to give me the two weeks of
the AFM to raise the money for a new company which would be run
by Bingham and Jeff. I managed to raise $500,000 from a number of
UK investors within those two weeks, and so October Films was born,
and *Life is Sweet* was their first success of many.

Sadly, the asking price for our next film, *Naked*, was more than
October Films could manage, and with all the hype surrounding the
film at Cannes with both Best Director and Best Actors awards, Fine
Line eventually bagged it. We should really have followed our instinct
and let October Films take it for nothing, but we weren't to know then

that neither Fine Line nor First Independent in the UK either understood or cared for the film — so what I consider to be arguably Mike's
best and most challenging film failed to get the English language
release it deserved.

Bingham still regrets not getting *Naked*, but at least October Films
was up and running, and I had the pleasure of being part of the
creation of that company. October, of course, was subsequently taken
over by USA Films, and Bingham has gone on to be president of
United Artists.

After Naked *you also began to explore the possibility of alternative
funding sources, didn't you?*

After *Naked* I decided I didn't want to do another film where we were
at the mercy of financiers, and, very specifically, financiers in this
country — despite the fact that we had had great support from British
Screen and FilmFour. They were fantastic partners, but after *Naked*
I wanted to see if I could replace the foreign finance — or everything
except the UK — with another funding source. So the funding for
Career Girls was arranged through Matrix, Rupert Lywood's company, and I was introduced to David Forrest who ran Flashpoint —
either through Rupert or vice versa, I can't remember which. From
that, we managed to get three 'high-worth individuals' to come in and
back *Career Girls* to the tune of £500,000 each. The person who was
incredibly helpful at the time was Andrew Hildebrand, who was head
of legal and business affairs at Channel 4 Films. He and I spent days
— and I mean *days*, I think it was four — sat in his office just going
through the deal. If we hadn't worked that hard we would never, ever
have closed the deal. *Career Girls* was the catalyst that allowed me to
go on looking for further funding, because once we did it on *Career
Girls* I saw no reason why we couldn't continue to do it that way in
the future.

Between Naked *and* Career Girls *was* Secrets and Lies, *which won the
Palme d'Or at Cannes. How well did it do at the box office?*

It made a total of $53 million and it cost $6 million.

When the numbers get bigger on a Mike Leigh film, as they did with
Topsy Turvy *[1999], do you have a few more sleepless nights?*

Topsy Turvy was incredibly difficult, the organization was phenomenally tough. I think the first thing I should acknowledge is that we

have a line producer, Georgina Lowe — whom we are about to start crediting as a co-producer — and she is my and Mike's right hand. She is amazing, unflappable, and we couldn't do it without her. We also have a really good accountant, Will Tyler, who has been with us, again, for a long time, and he is incredibly pro-active rather than reactive. So in having Georgina and Will behind us, they have been incredibly helpful and survived with us during the process.

The problem with *Topsy Turvy* was that we reckoned we needed $20 million to do it properly. Uniquely on this film we knew what we wanted to do because I persuaded Mike against all the odds to do a four-page treatment, if you like, which roughly outlined what he wanted to do and told us something about the world of the film. But it soon became clear that I wasn't going to be able to get all the money I wanted, so with the help of Wendy Palmer and Fiona Mitchell at CiBy Sales, as it was then, and directly as a result of the amazing success of *Secrets and Lies*, we decided it was the right time to go and try and raise some serious cash. We got $3 million from October Films, and I can't remember how it broke down but Wendy and Fiona also pre-sold a whole load of territories — France, Germany, Italy, Spain, Japan and Korea, the UK to Pathe, and we had already pre-sold North America. Then there was a very small shortfall that we were able to gap-finance through a bank.

At that point, it was all slowly coming together. Jim Broadbent had especially kept himself free for us and I had a very small window from which to operate. But our window of opportunity coincided with the collapse of the Korean currency. At exactly the same time, Pathe decided the film wasn't worth the $3 million they had offered us in the first place, and they would only offer $2 million.

Because they thought they couldn't recoup that amount?

Exactly. So as Pathe reduced their offer, the financiers also said that the Korean currency loss meant that I had to lose $800,000 from my estimates. Suddenly, from one day to the next, we were $1.8 million short. The only way to get the film going was to go to Mike and say, 'We are short by this much. Any suggestions?' We decided to cut all of the exteriors except those we could afford to do, but we would only shoot them at the end of the film, when we knew how much money we had left.

What exteriors were you cutting? Were they specified in the treatment?

Well, I hadn't a clue how many, because we hadn't even started rehearsing. And I think it's the closest I have ever come to . . . well, at that moment the company could have gone bust. We were absolutely on the line, we were totally committed.

Did you tell Mike what was at stake?

Mike was far too busy, and I probably wouldn't have wanted to worry him. Neither of us had a great deal to lose, personally, and I thought we had a lot to gain. But it was a decision that had to be taken. Mike knew that I had pressed the button back in August, so when we lost the money in October he knew what was happening. But neither of us could possibly have known what that meant in terms of what we could and couldn't afford to do. So it was very weird . . .

Is there a budgetary ceiling for a Mike Leigh film?

We're actually at that ceiling at the moment. *Topsy Turvy*, unfortunately, didn't make money, nor did *All or Nothing*. And I think if we make another film that doesn't make money then I won't ever be able to get this scale of funding again. The new film is 6 million sterling, and it's absolutely at the edge of what Studio Canal think they can get back.

Don't awards, Oscar nominations, Palme d'Ors or BAFTAs add market value to films such as Mike's?

They do, but only if your figures add up and keep your financiers happy. You can make a critically acclaimed film — which *All or Nothing* was — but at the end of the day if that doesn't make money for the accountants then they're going to be looking at the bottom line and saying, 'Well, you didn't make X in this territory.' So when they come to do their sales estimates — and they do those before they offer you money — they will be saying, 'We can only go on figures based on your last film.'

Interestingly, although we made money on *Secrets and Lies*, because the film was fully funded by CiBy 2000 a deal like that means you don't make as much, because you are giving so much in exchange for the funding. But if *Topsy Turvy* had been successful, even modestly so, then the deal I had been able to do would have been much more beneficial for us because we were taking on more of the risk. I suppose if we were being hyper-critical, we could say that *Topsy Turvy's* release came at the time when October Films was in the middle of its acquisition by USA Films, and perhaps they took their eye off the ball. But, on the other hand, could you say that after we had won two Oscars?

In the UK we were really, really pleased with the way that Pathe handled the film and at the end of the day I think we were pleased with the way that October handled it. Unfortunately *Topsy Turvy* was seen as 'highbrow' — the Germans didn't like it because there was too much music in it and the Japanese didn't get it at *all*, so the film has never been released in Japan. But the investors all got out, and nobody got hurt.

You must have acquired substantial experience understanding how different financial structures can be made to work to finance films. Did you imagine when you started that you would be going down that road?

No, and for a chap who left school without even one O-level . . . I was an idle bugger at school, very good at sport, drama and skiving, but to this day I still don't have maths O-level. So, yes, it strikes me as amusing.

Have I got a good financial brain? I don't know. I suppose I must have, in terms of putting things together, but I would never, ever say I could do this on my own. I have been incredibly lucky. I think Mike would agree that we have both been lucky — he has got someone to produce for him who is prepared to look at anything and everything in terms of trying to make a deal work, because, as far as I'm concerned, everything is up for consideration. And I am very lucky to have a partner who is the UK's foremost auteur and who is prepared to be truly *collaborative* and totally supportive — even of some of my wilder ideas!

What's your corporate structure today?

I have two companies. Thin Man Films is the company Mike and I created in 1988. Then I also have Potboiler, my company with Gail Egan, which, again, we started with our own money. I would say that in the UK, probably ninety per cent or more of independent producers begin working through a company they've started at home.

Is a part of your job to go out and source funds?

It is, and that means networking and talking to lots of different people. I am very lucky in having Gail because she does that really well, enjoys it, and is incredibly well connected. I find it slightly boring because I'm not very good at suits and ties and things like that. I'm much better at lunches and jollies . . .

How did you meet Gail?

Through the ill-founded Alchymie . . . which was to do with a company called Flashpoint, who thought they had got money from an insurance scheme which would have allowed us to have $50 million a year over five years. Gail was introduced to me and we got on really well together.

When Alchymie was created, our aim was to become a mini-studio. We were based out of Cinema House in Soho, we had development, we had production, we were looking at sales, and we were going to look at distribution as well. Unfortunately, within months of starting — having been launched in October of 1999 by Chris Smith, the then-culture secretary, at the Oxo Tower amid much pomp and ceremony — the money failed to come through. It's still a mystery. The insurance-backed market didn't work. We were being offered up to sixty per cent of a budget, so the collapse of the company was a phenomenal disappointment. Gail and I, through our own funds, paid everyone's wages for the last two months, by which point we decided we couldn't go on. So we declared the company bankrupt and called in the receivers. We went away to lick our wounds, and then Gail and I decided that we still liked and valued the projects we had got, and decided we would keep going on our own. We formed a company called Cloud Nine and through that we made *Nicholas Nickleby* with the New York based company Hart Sharp. But we were then advised by a New Zealand company that they had the rights and trade mark to Cloud Nine, and even though they had registered the company and trademark in the US, somehow it had slipped through the net with our legal checks. So, from that, Potboiler was born.

4. *Allow the film to be British*

What does independence mean to you?

I consider myself truly independent — even though we recently signed a deal with United Artists. In *real* terms, I am a totally and genuinely independent producer. I think I can give you a very good example in terms of *The Constant Gardener*, which we got the rights to almost two and a half years ago. In fact, the rights are just coming to an end, but we've been given a free extension by John le Carré, which is wonderful.

I read it whilst it was in proof form and I thought it was a wonderfully angry book, incredibly political, and a real statement about the malpractices of the big pharmaceutical companies. In fact, the book was banned in Kenya, where it's set. So it's a very, very tough book, and I felt that a film needed to be pretty uncompromising, and that if it was left to the American studios it would be sanitized and mucked about with. I then wrote an impassioned letter to le Carré — David Cornwell, le Carré being his pen name — through his lawyer, Mike Rudell. My pitch was that I reckoned all his projects had been ruined — I didn't actually say 'ruined' in my letter, but I intimated that I *felt* they had been ruined — by the big studios. I certainly didn't feel that any of the films adapted from his books had fulfilled their potential, except, I suppose, *The Spy Who Came in From the Cold* [1965]. Now, that's a really dodgy thing for me to say, and I realize I'm putting myself on the line saying that we are transforming le Carré's book — a British adaptation — into a British-made film which I believe is going to be incredibly successful. But I was absolutely determined the book shouldn't go to a studio, and that if a film was going to be made it should be made by an independent out of Europe.

My letter was about a page and a half and Mike Rudell responded very quickly and said, 'David likes what you've written. He would like to meet and talk about it.' Rudell asked when I could come and talk to him in New York, and I said, 'Tomorrow.' I could have said, 'I don't know, I'm not due over for a couple of weeks . . .' But because I was prepared to be immediate about it, I think that tends to get you taken seriously.

When I met le Carré I reiterated that I believed *The Constant Gardener* needed to be an independent film without American involvement, and in terms of involvement I meant both creative *and* financial — because financial involvement could have given them creative control.

Often, the problem with studios is what works for them doesn't necessarily work for us. There is a studio mentality that lends itself to a lot of Hollywood pictures, where you end up having to 'tick their boxes' — so they want you to have an A-list star, an A-list director and an A-list director of photography. Then, invariably, they can end up saying, 'Well, couldn't the main character be American? Or couldn't he have an American mother? Or isn't there some sort of way we can put some Americans into this?' Then they would want a big name to play Tessa, the wife of the film's protagonist, and *we're* not looking for that — so we wouldn't have that box ticked, and hence we wouldn't be able to afford the biggest director of photography in the world, so *that* box wouldn't be ticked . . .

I simply felt that you had to allow the film to be British and you had to allow the *character* to be British, because the character *is* British and if you tried to make him anything other than that I couldn't really see the film working. We raised £350,000 through the Enterprise

Investment Scheme to acquire the option, get the script written, and have two and a half years of uninterrupted, un-Americanized development — which is where we are now. And we have resolutely stood firm on all of this. Our director, Mike Newell, has been great, and has been with us since we started looking at writers together. And we have just made an offer to Ralph Fiennes, so I hope we have secured a wonderful British star. And I believe we can pull it off so that it will absolutely be an independent film.

Are independent films more personal? Do they eschew commercial considerations?

Well, they're certainly less corporate. For us, *Constant Gardener* isn't one of five, six, ten or twenty projects sitting on the shelf that the big boys have at the studios. We have championed Ralph Fiennes and hope very much that he will do the film, but the studios wouldn't perceive Ralph as being an A-list star. In fact, interestingly, the sales people would argue that he doesn't bring a great deal to the table — for them he's more 'a name'. I sent the book to Ralph about four to six weeks ago, we had it delivered to him at the Theatre Royal, Haymarket one night and he read it overnight. We had a phone call from his agent the following day saying, 'Could you meet Ralph for lunch with Mike Newell?' Unfortunately this hasn't been possible because Mike has had to go back to Los Angeles where he is finishing *Mona Lisa Smile*.

We have shown the script at various stages very sparingly to people, simply because you have got to trust people and be able to send the script out. Quite often you don't get a second chance with a script, so you have to be very, very careful who you send it to, otherwise it can go to a reader and will only be read by that reader — and then the reader's comments will get stuck on a computer somewhere. So it's been building blocks from the very beginning, but we are convinced that now is the right time to send out the script. It's gone to Studio Canal, Simon Perry at Ingenious, Cameron McCracken at Pathe, and it's going to Constantin in Germany. Gail recently went over to South Africa to meet with the IDC, and we are trying to get funding in place through a company out there called ATO who are launching a production fund — so we're hoping we can bring them into the equation.

What's your estimated budget?

$22 to $23 million. It's a lot ... but we have to shoot in Africa, Canada, Germany and the UK, so it doesn't go very far. Our aim is to be shooting in six months' time.

In terms of scale, would this be the most expensive film you have produced?

It's difficult to know, really. I have no idea what *Wagner* with Richard Burton and Lawrence Olivier and John Gielgud would have cost now. Back in 1984 — I think about £6 million? And then *Topsy Turvy* was $17 million or $18 million. So I suppose the answer to your question is 'Yes'.

5. 'Dear man . . . absolutely bonkers . . .'

Does it get easier finding money now you have an extensive network of contacts and a track record?

I don't know. I suppose the trite thing to do would be to say, 'No, it never gets easier', and I'm tempted to give you that as an answer. But that's probably wrong. People will at least meet me, and I still go and see studio heads at Warners, Fox and Sony, and they are all absolutely charming — they take me in, and they're still determined to believe that I have a script somewhere . . . So after the usual pleasantries, the journey, the security at the studio, there's a sort of nod of the head and a sense of 'Dear man . . . absolutely bonkers, show him the door.' But that's sort of the story of my life with the big boys.

Would you consider a studio deal if it was offered to you?

We don't fit in under any circumstances. Neither Mike nor I would be studio fodder. In one of yesterday's Sunday papers there was a story about five hundred independent films among the different studios that have yet to be released . . . that's depressing. But, generally, I'm always interested in visiting the studios to keep up with who's doing what to whom and where.

How did you find working with Irwin Winkler on his Cole Porter musical, De Lovely?

It was a nightmare. We were asked to come up with a budget for doing the film at somewhere around $10 million. We eventually came up around $12 million. Then Ashley Judd came on board, and her very presence increased the budget by a minimum of $1 million — dogs, diet, yoga, all pandered to by sycophantic studio executives, with no one prepared to take responsibility. Then the music sort of had a life of its own, with Robbie Williams, Elvis Costello, Macy Gray, goodness knows who else, all coming to do their cameo bits. We ended up with a budget — that hasn't finished yet — of $17.8 million. It has been really, really interesting . . . quite horrendous.

Was De Lovely *your first experience of a studio film?*

It was my second, the first being *Greystoke* [1984, dir. Hugh Hudson] on which I was first assistant. I hated doing that because it was all to do with studios and egos and so on, and I said then that I never, ever wanted to make another studio film in my life — I wanted to be completely independent and make films with lower budgets. And that's pretty much what I've been doing.

De Lovely was very tough. I had Georgina on board and she was fantastic, she and her team took an unimaginable amount of shit. It was just the whole sort of uncaring attitude of 'I want it, so it's going to happen' and a lack of any awareness of the ethic of saving money. There was nothing involved in the making of that film which made any concessions to economy or people's sensibilities. But Kevin Kline was a joy, as were all the English actors, and Rob Cowan, the guy who really produced it, was great, and he cared . . .

What else do you have on the go at the moment?

We have a project which we're developing for Lee Tamahori — he's just read the first draft and there is an awful lot of work to be done on it, so it's just gone back to the writer for second draft. *Man About Dog* is a really good romp, it's not remotely politically correct, and I love it. We have a love story set between Middle America and Northern France in the time when Colonel Cody went to Northern France. *Hide* is an interesting script written by Matthew Thomas, set in America, about a serial killer chasing other serial killers. *A Taste of Rain* is set in Namibia, we hope to shoot that next year. *Brothers of the Head* is to be directed by Louis Pepe and Keith Fulton, who made *Lost in La Mancha* — this will be their first feature film, based on a Brian Aldiss science fiction novel. Then we have a wonderful thriller script by Jayson Rothwell.

I don't think you could put down on paper that we are after a particular look or feel — I think we've got reasonably eclectic taste. Sometimes 'eclectic' is defined as 'Can't make your mind up . . .' But these are all projects we really, really care about. We are very careful in terms of what we take on.

6. The unmentioned

Do you feel you get the right credit?

I don't. I got so frustrated at Cannes when *Topsy Turvy* was screening because the sound recordist and the make-up designer — and I'm not saying anything negative about those people because they, and everyone else, did a fantastic job — but they were all credited on the official brochure. And who produced it? Thin Man Films and CiBy 2000. I'm not mentioned at all.

Why not?

Because I'm a producer.

Do you think the industry doesn't value producers?

I do, but then I'm not a great self-promoter, I don't do party circuits . . .

Forgive me, but do you need to go to parties to be credited in the official brochure at the Cannes Film Festival?

That's why from that film on I have taken a possessory credit 'A Simon Channing-Williams/Thin Man Production of' . . . because it's the only way that I would get any recognition for the work I do, and the press and publicity for our films.

Is it important to schmooze?

It is, but I'm not very good at it. I enjoy socializing with friends, but the idea of a room full of blank faces is somehow terrifying. So I prefer to do it one to one. I think if you asked other people in the industry who I was, a lot would probably say they don't know me well, or they've never even seen me. I don't get out and about as I should.

Is London a schmoozing scene for producers?

I think so . . . Steve Woolley and Jeremy Thomas are people I consider to be *really* good producers, they have been at the cutting edge of filmmaking and they get out there and do it. Andrew Eaton, Andrew McDonald and Graham Broadbent are very good at it. But I don't mind *not* getting out that much.

How do you respond when you are on a plane and someone asks you what you do?

If it looks as though the conversation might go on for the whole flight, sometimes I say I'm a tea taster — that's a guarantee of being left alone.

'Mike Leigh Untitled 03', financed by StudioCanal, the Film Council's Premiere Fund and tax fund Inside Track, went before the cameras in September of that year, and was unveiled to audiences as *Vera Drake* at the 2004 Venice Festival, where it was awarded the Golden Lion. It was released in the UK by Momentum and by Fine Line in the US, where it was later honoured by three Academy Award nominations.

Bingham Ray was removed from the presidency of United Artists by MGM in January 2004.

The Constant Gardener was, in the end, directed by Fernando Meirelles. It was released in the United States on 31 August 2005 and was selected as the film to open the London Film Festival on 19 October 2005, and from two Oscar nominations, it garnered one statuette for Rachel Weisz as best supporting actress.

Take 4

STEPHEN WOOLLEY

Stephen Woolley — akin in at least one respect to Simon Channing-Williams — is best-known for a long association with a world-class filmmaker, for whom he has produced a sequence of acclaimed pictures. Woolley first worked with Neil Jordan on *Angel* (1982). His background, however, was not in 'firsting' for TV drama productions but, rather, in cinema exhibition and distribution — areas that were highly germane to his passionate love of cinema.

1. *Born into a cinema seat*

STEPHEN WOOLLEY: I'm not an archetypal producer, because I didn't think about it when I was a kid or a teenager, or even in my early twenties. But I started off loving films and thinking I had found a great job managing and running the Scala Cinema in London — I could see films by Herzog and Fassbinder, indulge myself in that way, and I enjoyed touching celluloid and projecting films because I loved movies. Then Nik Powell asked me to start a video company with him because he was impressed by what I was doing at the Scala, and he could see that I had balanced art with commerce. How else do you run a cinema where you have to make £3,900 a week — that was my 'nut', my break-even level — and at the same time show wild and wonderful films? In a sense it wasn't so far from producing, where you take ideas that seem bizarre on paper and turn them into something people will pay money to see — which is what we did at Palace Pictures with *The Company of Wolves* and *The Crying Game*.

But Palace Pictures didn't exist until our second year. I spent the first year going from festival to festival, acquiring films for the UK. Distribution is all based on judgement, but we worked out how many people we thought would go and see the movie, how much it could take theatrically and through video sales, and then we calculated backwards and worked out what we could sell the television rights for. We didn't have a lot of money, and we bought films that seemed obscure and not particularly accessible. *The Evil Dead* [dir. Sam Raimi, 1982] was a very low-budget horror movie that turned into a huge cult, and I was so impressed with it that I acquired the UK rights in Los Angeles for $75,000, which was a snip. Then we bought *Diva* [dir. Jean-Jacques Beneix, 1982] for what seemed like a huge sum to people around us. But both of those films were incredibly successful. Then the video market kicked in, and boomed.

But then in our second year, what started to happen was each time I bid for a film, another distributor with more money would come in behind my back and out-bid me. In other words, we were being gazumped out of the marketplace — we had become victims of our own success. At that point I had to think backwards. Instead of going to festivals I started buying films based on the quality of the screenplay, and we acquired *Nightmare on Elm Street* [dir. Wes Craven, 1984] and *When Harry Met Sally* [dir. Rob Reiner, 1989] on those grounds. But then we started being gazumped again . . . So our natural conclusion was that Palace should make its own films so that we could have complete control over the rights. We already had a distribution company behind us.

HELEN DE WINTER: *Were there any other spurring factors that made you consider producing?*

People asked me about it along the way, particularly John Boorman and Jeremy Thomas. I acquired Nagisa Oshima's *Merry Christmas Mr Lawrence* [1983], which Jeremy produced, and then Neil Jordan's first film, *Angel* [1982], which John executive-produced. After meeting me and seeing the sort of films I had acquired for video, I think both Jeremy and John encouraged me, because they could see that, while I loved films, I also had a business brain.

To secure the rights to *Lawrence* I had flown to Tokyo because I had read about the film, and I was a fan of the movies that Jeremy produced and of Jeremy as a person. He was one of the few producers out there making independent films, and I think for a producer to have gone off to Japan and put Oshima together with Laurens van der Post and then Ryuichi Sakamoto, Tom Conti and David Bowie was pretty outstanding. So I spent a week in Tokyo and saw the film twice and bid the most money our company had ever paid to acquire the UK rights. I was twenty-three or twenty-four at the time and it was a big risk — Nik was in London and no one had seen the movie, so it was quite nerve-wracking. But the offer was accepted. And during that week in Tokyo Jeremy quite casually said one day, 'Why don't you produce?'

I would definitely cite Jeremy as something of a mentor to me. There are people who feel a bit of rivalry with Jeremy, but I think he's an extraordinary individual who was busy producing in the late 1970s and 1980s when very few films were being made in the UK. Jeremy comes from a film family, with his dad and his uncle having made quintessentially British movies like the *Carry Ons*.[11] He was born on to a film set, in a way, whereas I was quite the reverse — I was born into a cinema seat.

In Europe there are very few ways that you can make decent money producing, but one of the ways to do it is to have a lot of titles behind you as a catalogue. The producer who has done that very successfully is Jeremy: if you look at the rights that he owns from his movies — as we speak, maybe the Australian rights to *Merry Christmas Mr Lawrence* have expired, or perhaps the German rights to *Crash* [dir. David Cronenberg, 1996] have expired — so they revert back to Jeremy. When we made *Company of Wolves*, Palace held the UK video and theatrical rights, and then as we went on we would try to keep more rights as part of the package, to build up the company. But if you go into producing just for the money then you would be an idiot to produce in Britain or Europe. If you want to make big money producing, you have to go to LA and do what you can to build relationships with the studios and talent. Studio rates are the only way for a producer to make big money.

You also mentioned John Boorman, whom you met through Neil Jordan's Angel?

Angel had been made for Channel 4 Television, and even though they had shot it on 35mm I discovered that they had earmarked the film for broadcast on television with foreign sales to follow. I realized that if they showed the film on TV first, it meant there wouldn't be a theatrical release, and we wouldn't be able to sell the video. I was so vociferous in my enthusiasm for *Angel* that I persuaded Channel 4 to let me release the film at the Scala cinema for two weeks, which was a very unusual thing to do, while they held back the TV rights. So we released the film with the British Film Institute, and then Palace

11. Jeremy Thomas is the son of director Ralph Thomas and the nephew of director Gerald Thomas.

released the video. This proved to be quite successful, and during the process John Boorman also suggested that I should produce. So with John and Jeremy and others encouraging me, the idea of producing gradually evolved. I admired Neil Jordan and Julien Temple as young filmmakers and I started trying to work out whether there could be an audience for the kind of films we wanted to make.

How confident were you about your skills in reading and developing scripts?

I was obsessed with books when I was a kid, and reading and going to the movies were the two things that I was always doing. So I took very naturally to the salient points of a story, and how to turn them into a good script. When I was buying movies from reading the scripts it became something that I not only enjoyed but felt comfortable with. This is what attracted me to Neil Jordan.

After I saw *Angel* I bought Neil's collection of short stories *Night in Tunisia*, and while his sense of story-telling was obvious from his first movie I thought he was even more interesting when I realized he had a literary background. And I could see that the imagination he brought to his stories and characters were the same as the visual elements he created in his films. Then when Neil and I met, we just sort of hit it off, and he was looking to come to London because *Angel* was being picketed at all the Irish festivals it was shown at. This was because Neil had been awarded the entire production budget from the Irish Film Board that year, so the other ten Irish filmmakers who were looking for small amounts of funding were understandably upset by this. Neil was in the strange position of having made one of the most impressive Irish film debuts for some time while simultaneously being criticized in Ireland.

Meanwhile I was thinking about producing films, whilst I was producing a documentary about the making of *Merry Christmas Mr Lawrence*. And I suppose I felt slightly confident about my relationship with Channel 4 because I had made a documentary for Jeremy Isaacs[12] called *The Worst of Hollywood*. I brought Neil over to London and he stayed at my apartment and I got him to come with me to Channel 4 to say why he wanted his film shown in cinemas, and how important it was to him. I think that by bringing Neil over and lobbying for his film I was, in a sense, already producing.

12. The founding chief executive of the UK's fourth terrestrial channel, served from 1981–1987.

So we decided to do something together through Palace. He wrote a script that later became *The Soldier's Wife*, and then became *The Crying Game*. But when he was writing it he could never think where the story should go after the soldier left Ireland and came to London. Then, years later in 1991, we were in a nightclub in Berlin at the film festival after a screening of *The Miracle* and Neil said, 'You remember *Soldier's Wife*? What if the soldier comes to London and the woman turns out to be a man?' Neil and I used to go to a transvestite bar in Soho called Madame Jo-Jo's, because it was one of the few places you could get a drink in London after midnight, and we were always completely amazed at how incredible these men-as-women looked, or rather how they looked as men and women. When Neil first finished *The Soldier's Wife*, I read it and thought it was the best thing he'd ever written. This was 1992 and I thought 'Great, I'll go to Cannes, raise the money, and we'll shoot in September.' Then nobody liked the script.

But back in 1986, when we made *Mona Lisa* and it was so successful, I was convinced that people would go for *The Solder's Wife*. They didn't. And instead we ended up making the big-budget comedy *High Spirits*.

2. 'Is this funny?'

One imagines you started out on the road of making High Spirits *in better spirits than when you reached the end?*

I was with Neil in a bar after *Mona Lisa* was finished, and we were feeling very good about the movie, and Neil started telling me about an article he'd read in an Irish paper about a down-on-his-luck guy who was running castle tours guaranteeing tourists that they would see a ghost. 'Apparitions Guaranteed' was the newspaper advertisement. And it killed us both, we thought this was a great idea, and I immediately thought of American films like *The Ghost Goes West* [1935], the Rene Clair film where a Scottish castle is moved to Hollywood brick-by-brick and its ghost goes with it. And there were touches of Clair's *I Married a Witch* [1945], with Veronica Lake. So it seemed that the script would work best if the story combined the comedic elements of witchcraft with a supernatural sex comedy, which is what I thought Neil wanted. I had recently read a wonderful funny ghost script called *Beetlejuice*, which was going to be directed by Tim Burton. Then I was invited to go to a meeting with an executive at

Columbia. At the time we were in the middle of cutting *Absolute Beginners* [dir. Julien Temple, 1986] and on the morning of the meeting I was totally hung-over because the night before we had had a fight with the completion guarantee company, and a drunken conversation with the distribution company — so I really didn't want to go to this meeting. I arrived at the guy's hotel suite and immediately laid down on the couch and said, 'Can you get me a big jug of orange juice and some fizzy water?' He said, 'Sure, right away.' Then he said, 'I loved *Company of Wolves*, what are you and Neil doing next?' I told him about 'Apparitions Guaranteed' and he thought it was really funny. It turned out that that this executive spent three months of the year writing in Ireland — big fat books that you'd see at airports — and enjoying his Guinness. He said, 'Let's do it, Columbia will commission the script.' I was stunned. Then I realized this guy was a pretty big cheese, and it turned out he was the *head* of Columbia — Steve Sohmer. I was so used to going to LA and hanging out with younger executives that I was expecting to meet Number Seventeen in the chain, someone with no power whatsoever except to buy you breakfast or dinner. But Steve was a real showbiz Hollywood type, and every time I saw him he would tell me to see the cashier on the way out . . .

To start with, the whole process on *High Spirits* was very seductive. We brought on Michael McDowell, who had co-written *Beetlejuice*, to work with Neil, and we took off on a four-day tour of castles in Ireland. Columbia paid for a chauffeured car, it was great fun. Neil and Michael wrote a very funny script. We met with Tom Hanks, who wanted to play the young lead, and then with Sean Connery who wanted to play the castle owner. And we had a vision about the film we wanted to make.

Then suddenly Steve left and David Puttnam was appointed Head of Columbia. And we knew David wasn't going to want to make the film — he doesn't really like comedies; *Local Hero* [1983, dir. Bill Forsyth] is probably the one film he's produced that comes close to being a comedy. *Chariots of Fire* is David's trademark movie. Our film was a comedy with a lot of sex. How much sex is there in a David Puttnam film?

So the day David was appointed at Columbia I rang him up, said, 'Look, we have a film in development with you. Will you give it back to us?' He didn't have to — the studios don't have to give you back a project even if they don't want to make it, because it belongs to them, it's their property. That's why Columbia paid Neil a decent fee to write the script and why they covered our expenses. But if they then put your project into turnaround, they can sell it to the highest bidder. So David could have said, 'We're going to think about it, give us a few months . . .' But fortunately he turned it around within a week. We then set it up independently, because we couldn't get another studio involved. That's the problem with going through studios, because if your project goes into turnaround other studios think 'Well it can't be any good if Columbia aren't making it . . .'

When we started pre-production on *High Spirits* I was producing a film in South Carolina called *Shag* [dir. Zelda Barron, 1988] and I was hoping to stay for the first few weeks then leave and go straight into pre-production with Neil. Kerry Rock was my associate producer and she was going take over *Shag*. But it was just horrible, because our financial partner Handmade didn't send the money, so everyone was very nervous. And I thought that if I left then they wouldn't send the money. By the time the money started flowing Zelda Barron had become very reliant on me being there in the US and wanted me to stay on for the shoot. So I got stuck. At the same time Neil was getting very upset with me because the independent financiers who were funding *High Spirits* had become concerned about whether it was funny enough, and they had brought another couple of writers on board to 'jazz up' the script — their idea was to make it more an *Airplane!*-style comedy. So, quite rightly, that pissed Neil off. When you are making a comedy the worst question in the world is, 'Is this funny?' And we were starting production, so it was crazy to start messing around with the script. Neil had to struggle with these criticisms all the way through the process. I utterly blame myself for that. It was the highest budgeted movie I had made and I should have been protecting Neil in pre-production. And it got so that the film turned into a culture-clash. The story was mainly about a young American married couple who come to Ireland for a holiday, until the American guy meets a ghost and falls in love with her. Neil took against not just the people who were making these suggestions, and the crassness of their approach to the script, but then he took against the crassness of the American *characters* and began to write more stuff for the Irish characters . . .

So it wasn't a particularly nice state of affairs with the financiers. Unfortunately, given the tensions and differing expectations when we went into production, I think that possibly what happened was that Neil became disenchanted with the *idea* of comedy, and certainly disenchanted with this particular film. Up until then, he had been quite appreciated by the people around him, both filmmakers and producers. *Angel* had got made through his relationship with John Boorman, and then it was a fairly painless experience making *Company of*

Wolves, and we had lucked out with *Mona Lisa* — originally EMI were going to make the film but when they collapsed we managed to pull off a deal with Handmade Films. So none of the projects had been sitting around in development for that long. By contrast, by the time we made *High Spirits* it had been in development for a while. And we were no longer making a film with Tom Hanks and Sean Connery but with Steve Guttenberg and Peter O'Toole. Both Steve and Peter are very good actors and artists one would give one's eye teeth to be able to cast. Daryl Hannah had just come off *Splash* so we knew she was perfect for the ethereal returning ghost, and she was terrific in the movie. The problem for Neil was that by the time we got into production we were not making the same film we had originally developed with Columbia. Neil reverted back to making the sort of film he knew best, and this wasn't necessarily the film the financiers wanted to make.

During post-production our difficulties worsened because our financing company started trying to interfere — which they had already tried to do while we were shooting, but luckily I had been able to push them off. We ended up with a massive post-production period and Neil felt, quite rightly, that we were forced into previews without the special effects having been completed, which meant showing the film to an audience with actors walking through green and blue screens rather than solid walls. Those preview results enabled the Americans to be very forceful with their ideas about what the film should and shouldn't become. It ended up becoming a strange stand-off where the financiers' attitude was 'Why don't you guys just go away while we fix this movie?' So Neil and I went on holiday, and they interfered with the film, and then we re-interfered, and then the situation deteriorated and became childish. It becomes extremely difficult to work on a film where people have lost their confidence and where a lot of money has been spent on the picture — the budget was in the region of $17 million, which is pretty high, with a long shoot and the cost of special-effects stages.

What affect did the experience have on your working relationship with Neil?

It was difficult, and afterwards I think he was quite relieved to go off to America and make *We're No Angels* [1989] with Art Linson. Meantime I made *Scandal,* which was fun. I enjoy making films about London, particularly films about the late 1950s and 1960s. I felt much more confident about what I was doing and how I was putting things together. I had a very good relationship with Michael Caton-Jones, different from the working relationship I had with Neil, plus I was very hands-on.

Neil and I came back together on *The Miracle* [1991], which was a small film. But it was so disappointing for me, because I thought Neil wrote a fantastic script and it was a really good movie, but it just didn't work. With *We're No Angels* and *High Spirits*, one could say they didn't work because Neil was taking a gamble with comedy, and you weren't going to get Neil Jordan fans to see them — they would say, 'Well we don't like these kinds of silly comedies.' And the silly comedy fans go to see it and it's too much like a Neil Jordan film for them to appreciate the movie. So it's caught in the betwixt and between. But also I think that Neil was feeling like 'I wish I hadn't gone to Hollywood, I wish I had done something else . . .' And after the disappointment with *The Miracle*, I think the reason that Neil made *The Crying Game* was because he'd had three films that hadn't worked, and I think he felt quite angry about the fact that people didn't take to the script for *The Crying Game*. I think part of that anger was directed at me, because I had been so enthusiastic about the script, but when I took it to Cannes and nobody wanted it I think Neil was as confused as I was.

However, after *Scandal* was successful across Europe and in America through Miramax, my stock rose within the banks. I had been able by hook or by crook to get finance for *Scandal* partly by being incredibly passionate about the whole thing. There was hardly any television investment, eventually the major financing came from Miramax, who nobody had heard of at the time. But without them the film wouldn't have happened. And it was only by pushing and pushing that *The Crying Game* got off the ground — making scary threatening phone calls to people, and taking money out of my cinema and threatening David Aukin with immolation in the Channel 4 lobby, because they were playing such a hedgy game with us about whether to do the film. And it wasn't because of me or Neil, it was because no one could suss out what the film was supposed to be. There were a few genuine supporters based on the script, and one of them was Simon Perry over at British Screen. But generally, it was incredibly hard to get going.

An awful lot of what a producer does is about balancing what is being said against what is not being said, just to protect the film. For example, on *The Crying Game*, when there was no money in the first three weeks, the biggest mistake I could have made would have been to say to everyone, 'By the way, I have no money, so instead of the £1,000 I owe you here's £300 and I'll give you the rest next week.'

Nor could I have said, 'I'm now going to my own cinema to take money out of the box office . . .' Although I knew the contracts *were* coming, I couldn't tell people that we didn't have any money, because everyone would have walked off and there would have been no movie. So that's an extreme example of when you are discreetly not telling the truth, because on a film set if people see that everyone is working they will assume that the money is there and the film is properly funded. Of course, it would have been *mad* to do that unless the contracts *were* completed, or on the point of completion . . .

3. *Virulently rejected*

STEPHEN WOOLLEY: Obviously there is a lot of rejection from the start to the finish, and it can be confusing. Channel 4 rejected *Company of Wolves* and *Mona Lisa*. When you get rejection, you look at the script and say, 'OK. I've got a project that nobody wants to make. Does that mean I have a bad script? Does that mean that I should still try to make the film? Or does it mean that we should just stop now, give up and find something else?' So you are constantly battling with your gut instinct, and believing that this might be something that people want to see, and if not *my* generation, then other generations might love it.

The irony is that every single US distributor rejected *The Crying Game* not once but twice, including Harvey Weinstein — and yet, apart from *Interview with the Vampire*, it's the most successful film I've ever produced in America; it took more than $80 million at the box office in the US and Canada.

The *Crying Game* rejection was really summed up by a senior studio executive who said that, firstly, Americans wouldn't accept the hero of the film being a terrorist; secondly, Americans would never contemplate or in any way enjoy a relationship between a white man and a black woman; and thirdly an American audience wasn't comfortable with homosexuality. He was very open — he said, 'You've got to be joking.' So it wasn't a gentle rejection — the script was virulently rejected.

The other side of that was the first time I screened the movie. I felt so strongly about it that I wanted to show it first to the studios. Jeff Berg, Neil Jordan's agent at the time, attended the first screening in LA and as he walked out at the end he said to me, 'This film will have the same effect in America as *Midnight Cowboy*.' Jeff doesn't drink but I thought he must be drunk. How could he say such a thing? Then at the first public screening at the Telluride Festival, an older couple came up to me on the street and shook my hand and said,

'Thank you for the film. Our son came out three months ago and we have been trying to cope with that, and this film has really helped us.' I thought it was great that the film had such an emotional effect.

After *The Crying Game* Neil and I were going to make a film called *Jonathan Wilde*, and then Neil was hired to write *Interview with the Vampire*, in the same way that he was hired originally for *Michael Collins*. David Geffen had seen *The Crying Game* and *Company of Wolves* and asked Neil to direct *Interview*, and Neil said, 'Well, I'm quite interested, but I'm making a film with Steve.' And they just said, 'Well, look, would Steve want to produce *Interview*?' Which I did, with David Geffen. There was no reason for Neil to have accepted that situation — he could have walked away and made a film without me for Warner but he didn't. And that is a recognition that *The Crying Game* worked.

Whether it's recognition that Neil liked to work with *me*, I'm not quite sure. I think Neil and I have survived partly by being slightly combative with each other. A part of the relationship is that of a warring couple rather than two content and complacent individuals, as I sometimes imagine Merchant-Ivory must have been. We never argue in public, but privately we can be quite aggressive with one another — though that's rare. Perhaps that's like most relationships, but we have been working together for a long time.

The creativity of producing is only there if you have a partnership with a director the way that I have had with Neil, and if you are making films outside of the studio. The classic example of an independent film that was made within the studio is *Interview with the Vampire*, because although it was shot for six weeks in New Orleans and a week in Paris, the rest was shot at Pinewood. And although on the surface it was a successful Hollywood film — two big Hollywood stars, Tom Cruise and Brad Pitt — it had an Irish writer/director, an Italian designer, a French DP, a British editor and costume designer and a British producer, shot mainly in Europe by Europeans, with a cast including Antonio Banderas and Stephen Rea. I had David Geffen as a partner, and because of that and because we had Tom Cruise, the studio actually didn't even come and see us that often. Because if Tom was happy and David Geffen was happy how could they not be happy? So it was actually a luxury to make that film. I thought it would be horrible making films for studios, but because of the success of *Interview* we were able to make both *Michael Collins* and *Butcher Boy* with Warner Bros.

Sometimes, though, I have felt that our relationship has been demonized by disappointment. And we have gone our separate ways for a while, which is a decision we made recently after our Borgia project fell apart — which has everything to do with the way that things are in European cinema at the moment. Neil's Borgia script is fantastic, but the film didn't happen because it became a situation of what we could afford, and pre-sales in Germany, Italy and Spain are not what they were.

My feeling is that, today, films like *The Name of the Rose* [dir. Jean-Jacques Annaud, 1986] or *Amadeus* [dir. Milos Forman, 1984] wouldn't be made if you tried to make them the way they were originally made — directed out of Europe, with a US pick-up or pre-sale, which is what we were trying to do with the Borgia film. No one would let us do it through a studio. We tried — Fox, who were closest involved, took US rights, and then I spent a horrible year travelling to every festival and market. We were going to shoot the film at studios in Berlin with exteriors in Umbria. Then two of the pre-sales companies pulled out, and Neil and I ended up losing quite a lot of our own money, because we didn't want people to be out of pocket so we paid them ourselves.

I read that you had Ewan McGregor attached?

For a while Ewan McGregor, then Colin Farrell. Not that we could get the finance in Europe without it, but we *did* have a fantastic cast — Christina Ricci, Angelica Huston, Antonio Banderas, Ian McKellen. Our budget was $55 million but we couldn't make it work, even though there was a lot of 'soft' money — money from government funds, and because Neil is from Ireland there were Irish funds we could access, and there was tax money in the UK together with sale-and-leaseback money. But, despite all of that, $55 million was too much. There had been a major crash in the marketplace in Germany; there weren't enough funds in Italy because Pay-TV can't pay any more and Berlusconi was busy reducing prices for satellite rights, and there isn't enough in Spain. There just aren't huge advances any more against theatrical and video rights, so even though we were getting good offers from these places, it just didn't add up. We couldn't make the film as a French co-production unless we shot part of it in France, and that would have meant losing the consistency of shooting the film in Umbria and forming an Italian co-production with Italian money.

Psychologically, what is it like working for a long period of time on a project that then falls apart?

It was horrible when that film collapsed — that Christmas was pretty terrible.

4. 'Was Al difficult, Neil?'

As a producer do you feel properly validated for your creative contribution to the process of filmmaking?

I know that some producers feel belittled, ignored, and sometimes forgotten, if not by directors then by critics. And that is part and parcel of the experience of producing. Most of the time a producer isn't viewed as a creative individual but rather as some kind of cowboy builder who turns up to put a piece of chewing gum into two bits of wood because you've run out of nails.

A producer does have to be creative in the manner in which they approach a director or writer with problems. You can't look at a screenplay and say, 'Can we lose these ten pages?' But you might lose two pages, and then the director or writer will point out that actually there are another two you can lose, though that means writing a new page of action to connect the scenes together. And then the producer suggests that the additional page could be set in such and such a place, because those characters are already on a particular set and as it's already built it won't cost the production any extra money. Generally there will be an eruption from a director that it's not possible, we can't do it, et cetera.

And often, even if a producer has a genuinely creative idea, the suspicion is that you are doing it out of an impulse to be cheap. That's the natural reaction of most directors and writers — that a producer is trying to shape the overall destiny of the film without having the emotional commitment and creative ownership of the writer and director. So feeling properly validated is a very difficult thing for a producer.

Neil is like all directors — once a director starts shooting a film, their brain takes on a whole other function. He will have a sense of everything that's in the script, and it has to stay as it is because now he's been taken over by the process. So once you have eighty people constantly demanding your attention and wanting to know what kind of dress? What sort of wall? Where should I stand, Neil? Do you want this in the scene? Is this night-time lit by moonlight or street lights? Constant bang-bang-bang, all day, every day — and the last thing in the world a director needs is for a producer to wander over and say, 'You know on page thirty-four? Do you think we could lose four paragraphs?' If you do that, the reply will be, 'No, I can't' or, 'I'll look at it at lunchtime.' A director will always be very defensive when confronted like that, because of the volume of thoughts and material they are holding in their head. A good producer will explain a predicament to the director, but you have to make your case very clearly. One great thing with Neil is that if you are clear and honest, I always know that he will take the problem home and come back and suggest we do something else, after he's had time to think about what changes he can make to accommodate the parameters of the film.

Then, at the end of all that, when the media are interviewing for the finished film, are they going to want to hear a story about how the producer sat at Cannes and talked to three different distributors, and finally managed to persuade one to back the film? Of course not. People are going to want to hear from the director about what it was really like working with Tom Cruise or Al Pacino. 'Was Al difficult, Neil?' If you've been a good producer and you haven't burdened the director with all the problems, then how can they remember problems that they didn't know existed, never mind the problems that did exist?

So while I understand that other producers don't always feel validated by directors or critics, I also think that a producer can't expect to be publicly acknowledged because it's not your role. If a producer gets upset or complains then perhaps they should direct a film, rather than pretending that their role is anything other than being the producer. I think the issue of acknowledgement isn't getting praise from a director, but rather respect and praise from within the industry.

In what regard?

Well, I had three producers on *The Good Thief*, including John Wells, a great guy who created *West Wing* and *ER*. John was the producer of the film inasmuch as he was keeping it going when it might have died. But then John actually didn't come to the South of France for the shoot. Alliance put money in and it's a Stephen Woolley/Alliance/John Wells production. On other films I have shared a producer credit with people who I haven't worked with that closely, in order to get the film made. Sharing credits at this stage in my career, I don't mind so much. I have no bad feelings about sharing a credit with John Wells. The point for me is that having a body of work behind me people in the industry would actually know that I was the producer on the show. We just have to be really careful that we try and not give the 'producer' credit to inappropriate people and keep some sense of respect for ourselves. We have sold it cheap.

But when you get to a certain studio level in America, the producer's role is pretty undervalued. When I think of the things I might do in producing — say, try to evaluate a movie and think 'This could cost X-amount' — they have a whole department that does that. Or work with a casting director — they have their own casting people in the studios, they don't need you to cast a movie. They have a whole script development department, they don't need you to develop the script. And they have a whole hands-on production department, they don't need you to make sure the film comes in on time and on budget, they can do all those things.

5. 'Walthamstow Beauty'?

At one time your company was supported by DreamWorks. Is that on-going? Or are you now entirely independent?

My last company with Neil, Company of Wolves, was set up to develop projects for DreamWorks, and they wanted us because Neil is a great talent magnet. But they weren't really interested in making films like *The Butcher Boy* or *End of the Affair*. So in the three years that we had our deal with them Neil and I made *The Good Thief* with Alliance, *End of the Affair* with Columbia, and nothing with DreamWorks. It was a shame that deal didn't work out, but we simply couldn't find a way of making a film together that they were happy with.

I think studios have an unwritten grid that determines what makes a film a studio picture. So you have 'A' list casts working with 'A' list directors and an 'A' list production team, which gives you an 'A' list budget of anywhere between $100 to 200 million. Then there are 'B' list casts with 'B' list directors, and 'B' list crews — these are lists that exist more mentally than on paper. But say an actor suddenly becomes hot — say it's Colin Farrell — you can't have an 'A' list actor like Colin Farrell on his own if everything else in the picture is just D. So the studio isn't going to be interested in your project. There are some actors — maybe Tom Cruise — who could go in and say 'I want to make the Yellow Pages' and the studio will say yes, but there are very, very few actors who can get what they want. If you are working with a studio you have to have a few other 'A's in there to get the budget and deals you want. It doesn't necessarily guarantee the studios a return on their $150 million investment but this is the studio mentality. To some degree I think that strategy has worked, which is why they stick to it. So no matter how drunk I try to get an executive or how far I try to persuade them that they are going to get x number of column inches in the media for their involvement in my film or how interesting this director is, the point is that the studios work in a unique and particular way, and they don't make one-off films that break those rules. Their philosophy is, 'We are a studio and we make studio films.' The irony is for me is that I love big movies, just like everyone else does. I thought that *Toy Story* and *Finding Nemo* were brilliant. When they can pull off good Hollywood pictures it's great. But there tend to be far more duds than hits.

It's not that DreamWorks don't want any part of successful films, because they do, but it's a huge studio, and they have got to make *Gladiator*, and they can't be doing things that Fox and Paramount and that the other studios don't. They are one of the riskier studios because they made *American Beauty*, but that doesn't mean that they are going to make 'Walthamstow Beauty' . . . But I believe DreamWorks have taken some interesting roads and I would like to think that they could go further down the Neil Jordan-and-Stephen Woolley route.

Doesn't your track record — ?

It means nothing.

Really?

Nothing at all. But, you know, my track record is quite bumpy, because if you just look at the films Neil and I have made together, for every *Butcher Boy* and *End of the Affair* and *Crying Game* and *Interview with the Vampire* — which are perceived as being successful — there's an *In Dreams* or *Good Thief*, which was commercially successful in Britain and Italy and Ireland and a few other places, but took no money at all in America.

Can I ask you how you keep your company going and being prolific?

Well, we have three films this year, and a lot of development stuff with some other companies. The reality of Company of Wolves is that Neil doesn't like producing — he's far too much of an artist to get his head round some of the basic things that producers have to do. We produced both *Intermission* and *The Actors* together, though we brought Alan Moloney on to *Intermission* and Redmond Morris on to *The Actors* so that we would have somebody who was hands-on. But I don't think Company of Wolves will continue in the form that it is now with Neil. He wants to direct films, and now I want to direct a film, so it doesn't make sense to have a company together where we're both producers. I can equally produce with my wife Elizabeth, who has her own company, Number 9, and we are developing quite a few projects with different companies, and that's how we meet any overhead until we go into production on something. Actually not having the DreamWorks deal is a great relief for us, because there was a huge pressure on us to produce, whereas actually since we haven't had that pressure it has been a lot easier finding material and just working with people.

Is it a friendly business? Have you made friends?

Yeah, loads of friends. I think the problem with films is that it can be too friendly — if you wanted it to be, it could be ferociously friendly. There are two sides to the friendships, one is the friendship of success, which all of us love, which is 'We made a hit movie, let's do it again.' Then there's the actual filmmaking itself, because if you go away for three months to another town or another country, then you are bound to build friendships with new people. Two things about film crews — one is that even though they may lie about it, most of them are drawn by the glamour of film — it's more glamorous hammering a nail into the wall of a film set than the wall of a house. And another thing is that crews are fairly nomadic and so they're used to pitching their tents and getting on with it, and there is a sort of camaraderie, the same as you would get with a circus or any sort of travelling bunch of players. So of course, over that period of time in the business you have made loads of friends, because the pressure of making films is long hours and the time off is spent eating, drinking, going out and having fun to make up for the tenseness of the week. It's very stressful, very, very stressful . . .

Have you ever felt that you were close to burning out?

There is a burn-out factor. The difficulty is recognizing it. I think I get it less than most, but a lot of people in the film business suffer massive amounts of stress. One of the worst things for a producer — and a director, I have to say — is when you're coming to the end of a long shoot and you begin to notice out of the corner of your eye people on their mobiles in the corner of the set, and a kind of general conversation of 'What are you going on to?' It means they're not concentrating. 'Come on, finish the film and then get another job, don't get another job while you're on this job.'

There are pitfalls and stresses in each of the areas that you have to go through that nobody on a film ever gets. You have gone through those lives of, first 'Can we get a decent script that everybody is happy with? Will anybody else like it when you send it out? If they don't, does that mean we have to change it?' Then you have the money in principle if you cast x, y and z so next you're searching for cast. Finally you get to day one — 'After all those months and years, we got there'. But you can't celebrate, because Day One is when the stress really begins. Can you make the film for the £3 million or £30 million that you said you'd make it for? How long is it going to be? It just carries on and on. Will the score be good enough? Should it be longer, should it be shorter? Why did we take that scene out? Why didn't we put that scene back in? The editing process is ferociously stressful. And the choice of composer. Then the preview process, which is the most stressful because finally you are seeing it with an audience and every-one who has invested money in you, all the bets placed on this film. I have to sit there, even on films that have previewed well, and I will be literally shaking. And every time someone laughs in the cinema or shouts or leaves to go to the loo or expresses anything, you just go out running after them, are you getting bored, or are you just going to the toilet? Can you just let me know, it's OK. And then when they fill the questionnaires in, and it's just not good enough, and everyone is very calm about it — 'OK, how can we make it better?' Or else the director becomes totally freaked and does everything that everyone says instead of holding his or her ground — they just lose it.

I remember going to New York three times for a post-mortem for a film, three times we all agreed to the changes that had to be made. The first time we came back to London the director froze. 'This film is a masterpiece, I won't touch a frame, my friend told me last night.' We go off to Manhattan again, exactly the same result. 'Oh my God, why didn't I make those changes? I'm so sorry to all of you, of course I'll make the changes now.' Two days later. 'I showed it to my friend from film school, she thinks it's a masterpiece, I can't touch a frame.' Back to New York for the third preview. By now I feel sick to my stomach, guilty about the flights and hotel rooms and the great meals they're taking us out to. And I know what's going to happen. Same result. So you lose your power because they say, 'Send the director on holiday, we are going to make the changes ourselves.' So they made complete and wholesale changes to the film which had nothing to do with what the cards said, because, finally, they had the power, and they had possession of the film — you had it for four months and you had three previews so how can you legitimately get upset? So it becomes a bun fight but by then you are on another picture . . .

So it's a life?

Yeah, the point for me is that my life is films — it's a horrible cliché, but life is films. It's not 'being a producer' — those are just are some of the skills I've been lucky enough to develop whilst I've been working within film. After I produced *Company of Wolves* I didn't consider myself a producer. It wasn't until I had made six or seven movies that I thought 'Oh, I suppose I'm a producer now . . .' I've been producing for twenty years and it's become the sort of natural thing. But I will do other things, I've always loved writing, and I will direct.

Why have you decided to direct a film about the late Rolling Stone Brian Jones?

Because the writer said to me last year, 'If you don't make *The Borgias* then you've got to direct Brian Jones. You've had two different directors, you haven't seen eye to eye with them, and you are so passionate about this that you should do it yourself.' For me this is a bit like the Jeremy Thomas/ John Boorman syndrome when they encouraged me to take a leap; I feel so close to the material, it's like I live in its skin. Having produced films for ten years, and at this point having gone through the script upwards, backwards, every which way, I have very firm ideas about what the Brian Jones film could be, what I can bring to it visually and what is required to make it work as a film. I've brought in a co-producer, Finola Dyer. I know Finola incredibly well from working on *Backbeat*, and I think she's going to be a good sounding board.

I will still continue to produce and think of myself as a producer until I've directed a few films. And while there isn't a decent lineage of producers becoming directors, I don't think it's impossible to become a good director having been a producer . . .

Woolley's directorial debut *Stoned* was released in the UK in November 2005. No.9 Films were awarded slate funding by the Film Council of Great Britain in 2004 in a deal that includes InTandem and the Irish Film Board. Woolley is credited as a producer on Neil Jordan's *Breakfast on Pluto* and he is developing a second feature film for himself to direct.

Take 5

Working Title

Working Title Films is one of the unalloyed success stories of contemporary British cinema. Its chairmen Tim Bevan and Eric Fellner each began their careers in the early 1980s while still in their mid-twenties, producing music videos, soon parlaying their way into features. Bevan founded Working Title in 1984 but grew to find the customary independent financing route creatively frustrating, not to say financially hazardous. Thus he went looking for and found a corporate backer, and at the same time made a new partner in Fellner. Their subsequent success has been founded on carefully nurtured and longstanding relationships with talent, as well as a refined and astute sense of how to work within the Hollywood system. I interviewed them separately and extracts from the conversations are interwoven below.

1. *This odd and very unstructured business*

HELEN DE WINTER: *What did you know about producing when you started?*

TIM BEVAN: Nothing. I knew that I loved the movie business, and it attracted me. I was an entrepreneurial character in that I was running a music video company, I had a pretty good grasp of economics and business, and I liked working with creative people, so that package seemed to be something that could lend itself to working in film. I had looked at the industry and considered starting as a runner — you can go the route of working your way up and doing those jobs. But when I looked at what producers were doing I thought their job seemed like pretty good fun. I thought 'Hang on, why not just dive straight in at the top . . .?'

I used the money we had made in promos with my then-business partner Sarah Radclyffe to develop some scripts, then it was from meeting a director on a music video, who had a film he wanted to make, that I produced my first film, *My Beautiful Laundrette* [1985, dir. Stephen Frears]. Luckily we were given all the money by Channel 4 Television, so that side of it wasn't very complicated. But I was very much a hands-on producer, and I learned how a film gets produced on-set. Then, fortunately, *My Beautiful Laundrette* was extremely well-received and became a hot property around the world, so I stuck by the movie and learned how the whole distribution machine worked, and how the money that you get from distribution by way of an advance should roughly equal what you are going to spend on making the movie. At the same time I found myself thinking 'Let's get on and make another movie, and not just sit on our laurels . . .'

What would you say were the most valuable lessons you had to learn in your early days as an independent producer?

TB: One of the mistakes a lot of people make in the film business today is the way they bullshit their way into things with no real knowledge. Right from the start I always asked questions, or I would say, 'I don't really understand that . . .' I was incredibly inquisitive in every area about how this odd and very unstructured business works. I wanted to know where the opportunities were, and how to *do* things. And the fact that there were no real rules was very attractive.

At the same time I learned early on that there are brilliant entertainment lawyers I could employ on my films who would know *far* more than I could ever know about how to put a film deal together. It was completely senseless of me to read through an agreement for finance or distribution from Miramax or whomever, because I wouldn't understand a word of it. All I needed to know was whether they were going to give me $3 million for the North American rights, then somebody else could sort out the nitty-gritty. Ultimately, anybody who's successful as an entrepreneur in whatever business they are in is a salesperson. I learned that, at the end of the day, trying to get an actor, writer or director to do a film or a financier to finance the film or a distributor to distribute your film is all about one's own charm, personality, and *modus operandi*. And, provided that you learned as you went along and didn't make too many mistakes, then you could progress.

I also learned immediately that the film business is a two-tier system and that if you want to have any career then you have to become Hollywood-savvy — because money, distribution and, most importantly, talent are controlled out of Hollywood. And with talent, that's something that you have no preparation for working in the UK, because British agents don't work in the same way.

In the UK there are very few good producers and, though I can't speak for the whole of Britain, I think it's to do with the times we live in. By the very nature of what you do as a producer, you are an entrepreneur and there is no getting away from it — it is an entrepreneurial game. And in a funny sort of way, I think we're over-protective towards new producers, and not tough enough. I do think that the dot.com revolution cycle, as it were, took people away who might otherwise have come into the business, because they were the sort of entrepreneurial characters who might have prospered.

I saw that the Hollywood studio system made films in a partic-ularly sophisticated way. But for six-to-eight years I was making films the independent way by packaging them up and multi-sourcing the finance from lots of different areas — distribution, private equity, tax breaks, or wherever. At the end of that time I decided that, actually, the independent way wasn't a particularly good one, because you're always under-capitalized and making creative decisions for financial reasons. I was basically trading at too high a level, and in that situa-tion the danger is you are pressing the 'Go' button on a movie as soon as you have the money, rather than when the script or creative package is right.

Were your early films profitable?

TB: They were, but not enough to sustain the whole company. Plus I always employed a lot of people. And we never took any money out of the company ourselves in those days.

How did you survive?

TB: I had enough to pay the rent. And at the time it didn't really mat-ter, because we had our independence, we were in our twenties, and I was just keen on learning the business. No one I worked with was buying fancy houses back then. But, oh, how times change . . . One of the things I can't stand about the younger generation today is they're more worried about their pension than they are about learning things. The most fun I have ever had in the film business was definitely in those years. We took risks — we robbed Peter to pay Paul, we bor-rowed money all over the place, we mortgaged everything and we were using any box of tricks we could in order to get our films made.

But we also realized that we didn't really want to continue in that way, and that, ultimately, what movies depend on most to get made is getting a decent script and — for want of a better word, and I don't like it very much — a 'package' together. We were lucky enough to come across someone from the other side of the fence who was looking to invest in films from a corporate point of view — Michael Kuhn from Polygram — so he invested in Working Title, and at that point I changed my business partner to Eric Fellner who I met in the early music video days.

2. *Lucky breaks*

How did you meet Tim?

ERIC FELLNER: He was just around, doing the same thing as people like Stephen Woolley, Nik Powell, me, Sarah Radclyffe and others. We were all independent producers, and at the time I was working out of Initial so we would bump into another. We all had a healthy rivalry and would try to get the same projects.

You started out producing music videos. Was that a natural step to then producing films?

EF: In the organizational aspect, certainly. But there are always exceptions. I know producers who are completely disorganized and completely incapable of being politically adept, and yet they are making huge, phenomenally successful movies. But I learned very early on that my skills were organizational and I was good at that. Making music videos and commercials, you are effectively a line producer, taking an idea that a director or an agency has conceived, and a lump sum of money from a client, and trying to make the two gel — which is a complete art in itself, but very much a mechanical role, rather than being the instigator, which is the next step up. A producer makes things happen from scratch rather than taking something that already exists.

Music videos and commercials taught me to be a good line producer so I had knowledge of how to physically get images on film, how to run a crew, how to run a budget, how to do a schedule — all of that. And I took those things with me into the second part of my career. But as to whether I knew or not if I could make films — well, I had no idea. There was very little that I knew about films. The first day I ever went on a set on which there was live sound and actors was the first day of the first film I produced.

But you had enough of a good instinct to get you through the film?

EF: I just think I was lucky enough not to fuck up. Some people say you make your own luck, and others say you exploit your own position to create luck. I think I was clever enough to exploit the lucky breaks that I got. It was just a case of grasping opportunities, running with them, and hang the consequences if they went wrong. Fortunately none of the *major* ones went wrong . . . *some* have gone wrong — *many* have gone wrong, along the way. But they've never been big enough to sink my career.

What was your first significant lucky break?

EF: It was being offered the opportunity at the age of twenty to produce two of the top music video directors, Russell Mulcahy and David Mallet. I had effectively been a runner or gofer, doing bits of everything for their company, then they had a disagreement with their producer and asked me to take over. I had been out of college for four-teen months . . . some people would have said, 'No, no, I'm not ready' but I said, 'Great, let's go.' I was nervous and scared but I felt I had nothing to lose. This was also in the days when there were no rules — music video was a new business, there was no real hierarchy, nobody knew anything. So I just went and did it. That was the first piece of major luck.

The second was, through a lady called Nicky Hart, meeting Alex Cox — a director who was a maverick and mad enough not to let anybody else control his material. I think other producers had offered to option his script *Sid and Nancy*, but Alex had told them to get lost. Most people would have said, 'Great!', then spent a year waiting for some guy to get the money together, and maybe it would never happen. But Alex was a maverick. And the fact that Nicky Hart intro-duced me to him — well, that was complete and utter luck. Alex liked the fact that I had never produced before, in the way that mavericks do, because they like to go with the unlikely.

But basically Alex talked to *everyone* about his script, and I was stupid enough not to know that that mattered, and just blindly went on trying to finance the film — not realizing there were two or three other people out there trying to do the same thing. Today I would never do that — I would make sure I controlled the rights before I put the time or effort into it. But again, through the naivety of youth, I didn't know, so I just went ahead and did it. And, thank God, I man-aged to put the money together through a fantastic lady, Margaret Matheson, who worked with Scott Meek at the production company Zenith. They loved the project and they supported and helped me.

They did something amazing — they didn't say, 'We want a proper producer', they let me have the opportunity of producing the film. And I think it went well for all sides. But that was another great piece of luck that came my way.

Tim and I started working together around 1991 to 92, and made two films, *Posse*, a black western that was rather good, and another called *Romeo Lies Bleeding* which didn't really work but taught us a lot. The script of *Four Weddings* had just come in through Tim's relationship with Richard Curtis, and it was starting to be put together while he and I worked out what we were doing . . .

3. 'Quality control'

TIM BEVAN: Within a year of restructuring the business we had our first very successful film — *Four Weddings* — but, luckily, during the early years I had made some reasonable movies and forged the creative relationships that have been the backbone of my career.

With whom in particular?

TB: Particularly Richard Curtis, because I made Richard's first movie *The Tall Guy* in 1989. We started working with the Coen brothers around that time too, and there were various other writers. But the relationship with Richard has been the most important commercial relationship for Working Title because, between us, we discovered a genre of movie that we could make outside of Hollywood that could make Hollywood money through distribution around the world. And that, in turn, has given us the financial clout and the creative freedom to do what we do, as well as a currency inside the movie business to work at the very top of the studio system.

On a Coen Brothers film or a Tim Robbins movie, we bring more of the marketing, money and distribution interface to the film than the creative side. And on a *Bridget Jones's Diary* or *Elizabeth* we bring more of the creative side to the picture. The Coens bring us a script with an entire creative package. That's their genius, and the thing about the Coens is that because they are true auteurs you just want to protect that. Whereas on a true Working Title film our creativity means that the film is something we have picked up as a good idea, developed into a cracking good script, and then put the right elements — principally the director and cast — into the package. Then we let the director go and make the movie. Then we get very involved in post-production.

On the whole, our films are character-driven rather than concept-driven, with a good story and a three-act structure and all that. I remember from early on in my career, people saying, 'It's not a script-driven business, it's an actor/director-driven business.' I don't believe that. I think it's all about the text, and if you have a good text that tells a good story with good characters then everything else will fall into place — including getting the film to an audience. Eric, myself, and all the people who work here spend a huge amount of time working on the screenplays, except that Eric and I do it in a more sophisticated way because we are working on everything else at the same time. Essentially I believe that as producers we are the custodians of the text, and what we have to ensure is that everyone is subscribing to making the same film. Quite often a director will want to make changes to the script on the day, and the pressures of a film set are such that often that director will get away with it. But he wasn't there two-and-a-half years ago when we made the decision to do it *this* way, so if I'm not on-set then I expect the development executive or the on-set producer to be the protector of the text day in and day out — because they know how it got there.

This is a lesson I have learned from working with people like the Coen brothers, and Richard Curtis and Rowan Atkinson. These are people who have what I call a very high 'quality control' which very, very few directors I have ever come across have over their own work. Richard will go on working on something and trying to make it better. And that's something here that we try and feed back into our own culture of making movies.

Can you describe the internal composition of your company?

TB: Eric and I defined the structure at Working Title, which is pretty much what we have today, and which, we believe, is a great machine for developing and producing films.

We have thirty or forty people working for us, ten or fifteen people on the creative side, as well as an office in Los Angeles. We do our own business affairs at every step, so we have a department and they do all the contracting work. They also handle our finance and distribution agreements. We have a production department that oversees films while they're in production, then we have a semi-in-house marketing and publicity department that oversees that side of our movies — which we believe starts at the moment when you may or may not make the movie, and goes all the way through to theatrical release. It's all very well making a decent movie, but ultimately you have to get it out to an audience.

People on the outside might think that Working Title have it easy because our films are incredibly commercial-looking, but the reality is it's a big and ongoing challenge to get the films to make proper money and do the business in the UK, America and around the world. So that's why marketing is so important. Actually, I think it's even more important now than when we started, because — without sounding imperialistic about content — the slightly dumb Hollywood film is the movie large audiences want to go and see. An English accent is foreign to an American audience, and a cut-glass English accent even *more* problematic, so anything culturally different is a challenge. Fifteen years ago there were ten or fifteen proper independent distributors in America in addition to the studios, and now there are no independent distributors at all — they've either disappeared or the ones that call themselves independent are owned by studios. So it's a very different landscape.

Parenthetically, is it true that the writer-director Christopher Nolan used to work for Working Title?

TB: He worked as a reader for us in America. And his wife used to work here.

Did he show you the script for Memento?

TB: No, he didn't. But he found a book that we have had in development for a while.

What's your annual spend on development?

TB: Several million dollars. Probably double-digit millions of dollars.

How much do you write-off?

TB: Probably the whole lot. Going back to Polygram days I realized that in the film business there is one really high-risk area and that's development. We can spend a million dollars developing something and then say, 'You know what? It's shit, it's never going to work as a movie.' So you have to write it off. But then it's better to do that than make a $25 to 30 million movie that's crap and then lose a whole lot more. That's our business — it's big bucks and it's scary and all the rest. But that's what it takes.

4. *Which film you're making*

Is there a particular way in which the two of you have divided the work of the company?

ERIC FELLNER: We work separately and together. In terms of any major decision about the company — employment, budgets, staff — we make those together, and then we split up the responsibility of who is going to deal with them. On projects, we make the major decisions together — whether we are going to do it, who's going to direct, who's going to produce, what the budget is and who's going to be in it.

The actual running of any one project we do individually, and that's for two reasons. Firstly, it's impossible to be passionate about everything. And secondly, individually, Tim could be running twenty projects and I could be running twenty, whereas together we could probably only run thirty. So the sum is greater than the parts.

TIM BEVAN: Every major decision about what goes on with the films we run past the other person, and that's always worked for us. And then any interface knows that if they have one conversation with one of us then they have to have the same conversation with the other. Consistency of information is very important.

Given the hours you work, do you see more of Eric than anyone else?

TB: Well, apart from my girlfriend, yes, possibly — though we don't socialize any more because we're working together day in and day out. But I would say that we probably trust each other more than anybody else. And we trust each other with personal things, because we know that in business the other person is one hundred per cent trustworthy. The only disagreements we might have are about how to handle a situation with the studios, because Eric might do it one way and I would do it another way. But we always work it out.

People are fascinated by successful working partnerships.

ERIC FELLNER: There's no great mystique or myth about it . . .

But Tim has talked about how you both evolved a corporate machine that has made Working Title so successful.

EF: I like the *idea* of the visionary status of that, but the reality is we stumbled along and it kind of worked and then we honed it as a result . . . so in retrospect, it looks like we're geniuses. There was no visionary planning and we never said, 'OK, year one — let's do this. Phase two, now let's do this.' It's just evolved.

But you were independent producers who . . .

EF: Wanted to make bigger films. We had an ambition that was greater than what we had already achieved. We wanted to make European films for a worldwide audience. It didn't really matter where those films were set but we wanted to imbue them with a European sensibility of storytelling and character, and we wanted those films to get out to a larger audience and have them successfully distributed. That then led us to Hollywood, because there's no way of doing it without the involvement of a major studio. But initially we had Polygram who were brilliant, but we were all blind and trying to see. Once we were able to see, I like to think at that point we did some intelligent planning. But up until the point when our eyes were opened we didn't know what we were doing.

There were many, many fantastic situations that arose that we had no idea about — like the success of *Four Weddings* that came out of nowhere. Or the success of *Fargo* — out of nowhere. Or the success of *Elizabeth*, although we needed that one to be successful because it cost quite a lot — but no one could have predicted that it would work the way it did beyond the accolades it had. The success of *Bridget Jones's Diary* — the project came with a great pedigree but there were many times during the process of making that film that I thought we wouldn't have a hit. Every time a film works, there is an element of luck involved, because it's such a complicated and difficult procedure. People liken it to getting twenty fairies to dance on the head of a pin. And that's what a producer is trying to do.

How would you describe your own instincts for material and talent?

EF: They have changed through my career. As you get to know more, you apply more rules and you then break those rules on a regular basis . . . But I know very clearly now that there are two kinds of films, whereas before — and this might sound very basic — but before I hadn't really realized it.

There are films you make with a passion and hope that they are a success, and there are films you make for commercial reasons that you hope will be really good. But you have to be very clear which of the two you are making right at the beginning, because that will set the tone in terms of who you cast, who you get to direct, how you write the script, what the budget should be, who distributes it, et cetera, et cetera. Tim and I have made films for business reasons — and if you look through our filmography it's quite clear which films those are — and, bizarrely, most of those films have worked. They may not have been the greatest films, but they worked as pieces of entertainment for people who wanted to see them, and they made their money back — whether they were small British movies, or something mainstream and bigger.

To what extent are you hands-on as a producer?

EF: Bizarrely, the one aspect where I tend to leave people alone — and some people will say, 'Well, that means you're not a proper producer', but I would disagree — is during the shoot. Other producers would say, 'That's the time when you most need to be present.' But I don't think that's the case, *if* you've done the work properly. If you've done your job in development and you've cast the film correctly and you've got the right director and you've put the budget together and everyone is making the same film — so long as you then watch the dailies and you know that the film you're actually making is the one that everyone *planned* on making, then there's not a lot you can do to steer the ship in a different direction once it's left the harbour, which was on day one of filming. I'm around — I'll get to the set if there are problems, and I'll visit, not every day. But I watch dailies and I will know — because I can't get rid of my old line producer habits — exactly what's going on every hour. I'll know what shot they're on, whether they're behind, how the day went, et cetera. For me, other big areas, which producers often don't get involved in, are the editing and marketing and distribution. I think Tim and I are similar in that matter because we view development, packaging, editing and post, music, marketing, and distribution as the key elements of producing.

How do you approach working with directors?

TIM BEVAN: It varies. For me you have to make a decision early on whether it's an auteur-type exercise or not. The Coen brothers are auteurs and in my opinion most directors are not — but it depends who it is. If we're working in the comedy or romantic comedy genre then most directors will accept that we probably know more than they do about that genre, and they will come on board the movie and collaborate accordingly. Film is a very odd medium because the director has a great deal of power in the process, and sometimes there can be a massive rush of blood to the head, so there are occasions where it can be combative when it doesn't need to be. What we seek is a real collaboration between producer, writer and director — between the filmmakers, basically. I think this whole 'A Film By' credit is much abused outside of the likes of the Coens or Richard, and it's an invalid credit that the film business could well do without.

What do you do if a director is having problems?

TB: Well, you just have to be all over it. And that's why cutting rooms can become very combative places. But fortunately it's usually down to the producers. At the end of the day there is no point having a bust-up on a film set, that's just counter-productive and expensive — unless there's a complete disaster going on, and that rarely happens. Once you get into the cutting room you have got all this film and you have to turn it into 85 to 110 minutes' worth of story that people are going to want to go and see. If at that point you don't have the director with you, then you've got to make the position very clear. We have final cut on all our movies and we absolutely believe in the testing process. 99.9 times out of 100 the audience will speak louder than anybody else. So, in a way, that makes it less combative.

It's a two-way thing now because, unfortunately, due to speed of information, after you test a movie it becomes public property — somebody will file a report about the test screening on aintitcoolnews.com. So ultimately a combative relationship with the director — where they think they've done the work and the film is the best it's ever going to be — is useless, because you have to listen to the audience. The audience will almost always be the producer's voice — that's just the way it works. So if you think the first forty minutes of the film are boring but then it takes off, and so-and-so is pretty good but such-is-such is really bad, you can almost guarantee the audience will agree with you. Then you can use that when putting your case to the director. One of the most amazing things about testing is its consistency. When we tested *Love Actually* [dir. Richard Curtis, 2003] in Bracknell in the UK and in West Hollywood, not only were the scores identical, but the percentage of people who didn't like certain things and liked others were identical. And this is a complicated, multi-stranded film.

Have you done re-shoots on the basis of test results?

TB: Yes. *Johnny English* [dir. Peter Howitt, 2003] was a straightforward English comedy — to some people's taste and not to others. But we were having problems in screenings, and we discovered that people were finding it difficult getting into the character at the beginning of the movie. So we went and re-shot the beginning of the film and worked on setting up the character. This worked very well, and the test scores leaped considerably.

5. *I would still be suing people . . .*

When Polygram was taken over by Universal in 1999 and dismantled, Polygram's deal with Working Title was the one element that Universal retained. So does Universal own Working Title?

TIM BEVAN: Yes, but it's a misnomer, because at the end of the day the asset of Working Title is Eric and myself. Inside of our relationship with Universal we have one hundred per cent creative autonomy, and we can green-light films up to $25 million. But it's not something that we use particularly, because you have to understand that the worldwide distribution of these films is everything. And we have believed since Polygram days that being part of a worldwide distribution operation is the beginning, middle and end of it, and that if you are not part of that then you are starting the race with your legs tied together. The film business, ultimately, is totally fucking crazy, and the only people who understand the levels of risk, the gambles and the rewards you have to pay creative people, are the people who run the studios. If I had made *Four Weddings and a Funeral* independently I would still be suing people all around the world, and I wouldn't have been able to pay Richard Curtis and everyone else their royalties from the film. And, in turn, we probably wouldn't still be in business. The studios are the only people who understand that if you have to make an $80 million decision on a Friday night, then once you have made that decision there's no going back and you stick with it. Then, on top of that, a studio understands that you are going to have to pay out fifteen per cent of your take on a film to some actor, because that's the way the business runs. Any new money in any way, shape or form that has ever come into the business doesn't understand its economics and can't live with it — so you come back to having a studio system that drives the business. At the moment our films are getting more expensive because the people we have worked with for years, their ambitions — rightly so — are getting bigger. And their appetite for what they get paid is increasing — and rightly so too, because they have been hugely successful.

How accountable are you to Universal, despite your considerable freedoms?

ERIC FELLNER: Tim and I come from the world of independent film-making where every pound or dollar was our own and we were responsible for that. Speaking for myself, I have never been able to get rid of that — so I always feel very, very responsible for every aspect of every film. I still feel the fear on every level, every project we green-light and every project we develop. Maybe when I stop feeling that then I won't be able to do it any more.

Has the experience of being part of one corporate culture at Polygram and then with Universal influenced the kind of films you make?

TIM BEVAN: Not in the least. Being part of a vertically integrated film structure is very important to us, but we decide what films we want to make. I think there is, in a funny way, a 'Working Title movie', and that's got nothing to do with what Michael Kuhn at Polygram or Stacey Snider at Universal or anyone else has said to us along the way. Because, ultimately, the movies we have made are the ones that Eric and I have a passion for. Put it like this: if we hadn't had the level of success that we have had from the start — and we were inside the studio system from the beginning — probably the only film we would have ever got made out of the many films we have produced is *Notting Hill*, because it starred Julia Roberts. Every other script we would have had to change. In *Four Weddings* we would have had to cut out the funeral because you can't talk about death. *Dead Man Walking* would never have happened because who wants to see a film about the death penalty? And everyone would have asked what we were doing making *Ned Kelly*? All the idiosyncratic bits and bobs that make these films what they are would have failed. Renée Zellweger as Bridget Jones — are you kidding? And don't forget, Renée wasn't very well known when we cast the first film. All of those films happened because we had the clout that came from the success of earlier films. And I would say that for a lot of other producers the experience is the same.

Do you have relationships with other studios besides Universal?

TB: We had a relationship with Touchstone when Polygram was in hiatus and Stephen Frears asked me to do *High Fidelity*. And then Touchstone came in on *O Brother, Where Art Thou?* With Miramax I have known Harvey Weinstein for a long time and I think they have a great deal of respect for us, but on the films we have made together we have only really had conversations in the editing room or after a test screening.

6. The Tim-and-Eric Experience

In 2000 you launched WT2 under Jon Finn and Natascha Wharton and immediately had a big hit with Billy Elliot. *What was your strategy for creating your smaller division?*

TB: Eric and I felt that we should have a forum inside Working Title to get lower-budget films made, and that maybe we weren't the people that other people who wanted to make those sort of movies would naturally come to. So we wanted to establish people inside the company who could do that. Secondly we wanted to provide an opportunity for an actor, or director to make a small film and then move on to bigger films — so Stephen Daldry or somebody like that could make a short here then a low-budget film, have a multi-picture deal and make big films too. That was never the case before.

Even though Billy Elliot *was a WT2 film, was it developed in the same way as projects on your main slate?*

TB: *Billy Elliot* was a script that we read because we had a deal with Tiger Aspect, which is Peter Bennett-Jones's company, and they had started developing it. When we read it we got it to Stephen Daldry. It was one of those scripts where there was no commercial reason for doing it whatsoever, except it was a damn good script and we all felt passionately about it. But we also put the Working Title quality-control machine on it.

Do you mentor producers within Working Title?

TB: I think that's a very difficult thing to do. If you like, the 'Tim-and-Eric-experience' is that you learn on the job. But we do mentor in the sense that we're always bringing new people on, we take on trainees. What we do on every picture is we bring another producer on board, and while Eric and I take a producer credit, whoever is actually running the movie will bring something else and live with the movie 24–7, which is something we can't do. Mark Huffum is a very solid line producer who is now learning a lot and working closely with me in the creative process, and I think he will definitely be a great producer. Jonathan Cavendish is working with us running the *Bridget Jones* sequel, and in the past Alison Owen worked with us on *Elizabeth*.

7. 'What have we done?'

Why was Bridget Jones *such a risk?*

ERIC FELLNER: It was more of a risk for creative reasons than financial reasons. You have to remember that, at the point we committed to the film, the book was biggish in the UK, but no one in America had a clue what it was. England was excited and looking forward to the movie, but for the rest of the world it was unknown.

My view is that making films at the $22-million mark is difficult, because you can't afford to cast Julia Roberts, but neither do you want to put Jenny Blow from Neasden in it. Renée Zellwegger was in a weird place where she was kind of known, but not really known. She had done some work that people weren't familiar with, but then most people had seen *Jerry Maguire*, so once you mentioned that film people would say, 'Wow, she was great in that!' So we thought the kind of level Renée was at was probably the right one in terms of star-power for a film of that size.

The big risk was that the British press castigated us for not casting an English actress. And all my English actress friends castigated me personally — they said it was a 'travesty' and 'the biggest mistake you have ever made' and it will be a 'disaster' — they were really quite aggressive. So, yes, that was a major risk, because Renée was a girl from Texas playing an English middle-class heroine. I remember being really petrified, thinking 'What have we done? We've ruined a piece of iconic popular fiction.'

But then when Renée walked into the room, and we took her out to dinner, and then I took her to meet Richard Curtis and we hung out — I thought 'Yeah, we should do this.' Whether that was luck or judgement I'm not sure, but it worked.

We take those risks all the time. Take the new film we're making, the follow up to *Bridget Jones: The Edge of Reason*. In the book there's no Daniel Cleaver — the Hugh Grant character — so we had to decide 'Do we have him in the film or not? And if we do, are we just shoe-horning him into a story that people love and want to follow, except he's not in it? But then if we *don't* have him in the film, then all those people who don't know the book but loved the movie will be disappointed.' So you have to make a decision and it's a big one, a high risk. And if it's the wrong one you can completely blow the movie. With every project, there is always a major decision that you have to make that could potentially ruin the whole project . . .

8. 'Chemistry'

Have you learned everything you need to know?

EF: I think often success happens for reasons beyond your control — whereas failure is usually down to having made the wrong choices, whether about the script or the way you made the film. There are lessons in both. I tend to look *closely* at our mistakes. Three successes gets wiped out very easily by one failure.

Why do you think Captain Corelli's Mandolin *attracted so much criticism? Are literary adaptations particularly difficult films to produce?*

TIM BEVAN: For me, literary adaptations divide into two categories. There are what I call 'pop literature' which is the Nick Hornby or Helen Fielding books. And we have produced quite a few of Nick's books and two of Helen's where the rule is the same, in my opinion — you want to see and hear the tone and the spirit of the book up on the screen. With those sorts of books the audience is far more forgiving if you're not too literal about it. Then there is so-called 'serious literature' which *Captain Corelli* would fall into.

In a way, it was a stupid film for us to make, because it's one of those books that everybody had a vision of in their head, so it was highly unlikely that we were ever going to satisfy that body of opinion. I guess Anthony Minghella managed to with *The English Patient*, but nine times out of ten, you don't. Also we made a decision, rightly or wrongly, that we wanted to make a movie of sufficient scale that would depict the impact of the Second World War on the island. And once we had decided to do it that way, our decision set the level of the movie, so we knew we were making an expensive film. Now it may well have been better to do all that off-screen and to have made some lovely low-budget movie that only told the love story. Nobody told us to take the politics out of the script — that was a creative decision that was made with the filmmakers early on. But, again, in retrospect it was probably a mistake, and you can't always get it right.

The other fundamental thing that went wrong with the movie is something I learnt back when I was making *My Beautiful Laundrette*, when we had cast Daniel Day-Lewis as Johnny and we were then looking for the actor who was going to play alongside him as Omar. When we found Gordon Warnecke we wanted to see the actors together, so we all went round to Stephen Frears's house and hung out together. And two hours later, when we left, we said, 'Yes, the chemistry is there.' The thing is, when you are casting big movie-star actors you don't have an opportunity beforehand to put two people in a room together to find out whether there is any chemistry. Very often you have to guess. I would argue that if there had been real on-screen chemistry between Penelope and Nic the film might have done better.

9. 'Traction'

Hugh Grant seems to be very aligned with Working Title . . .

ERIC FELLNER: Well he's been in six of our films — *Four Weddings, Notting Hill, Love, Actually, About A Boy* and both *Bridget Jones* films.

Are you developing other films with Hugh Grant?

EF: We're trying . . . he's busy . . . I would love to develop a lot of projects with Hugh, but he has a very, very high quality control of every aspect of every project, and, as such, it's hard to find things that are good enough to do with him.

Are you under pressure to carry on producing romantic comedies?

EF: It's a big issue. We didn't intend to become romantic-comedy pro-ducers because neither of us is particularly romantic or funny. It just happened through a relationship with Richard Curtis, and with a number of other people we have been very lucky to work with. We have *Wimbledon* coming out, but next year we won't have a romantic comedy in the marketplace — which is not *that* bizarre, because nor-mally we have one every two years, maybe three. We'll see. Richard Curtis may do another one, he may not. And we have a number in development that are looking very strong. It's a genre we understand and know how to make, despite having done some that have gone horribly wrong.

When your movies are released in the UK the poster often says 'From the makers of'. Do you see Working Title as a brand?

TIM BEVAN: Basically, you do anything you can to get a movie out there. So 'From the makers of' has been coined by a marketing person in order to get what we call 'traction', which is our term for getting the film out to the consumer. Nobody outside of the industry would know who Working Title is, and that's the truth of it.

Do you think that you and Eric get the credit you deserve?

TB: We get all the credit we deserve. Inside of the business, everybody knows who we are. But actually, it matters less and less whether I get a credit or not.

People know who Jerry Bruckheimer is.

TB: They do. But that's a conscious big-deal branding thing. I think Scott Rudin is the best producer in the world but I would argue that the man on the street wouldn't know who Scott Rudin is. People might know who Harvey Weinstein is because he makes a lot of noise. But personally that sort of credit doesn't really matter to us.

10. *A larger appetite*

How do you stay current?

TB: We consciously try to have new people coming up through the company. And we have a filter system in the company so there is me, Eric, Liza (Chasin), Debra (Hayward), and Natascha. So if something makes its way through the filter-system, then we're all pretty certain it has passed a test.

ERIC FELLNER: When I come to work on a daily basis, I don't know what I'm going to be subjected to in terms of opportunities. One of our development staff might say, 'I really love *this* idea.' Or *I* might have an idea, whether it's because I've been listening to something on the radio or just sitting in silence thinking 'Oh, what about this?' Or perhaps a director I've never heard of walks in with a screenplay. You just don't know, but your choices, I think, have to reflect what you or your colleagues are interested in. There are some projects that would not have happened if Debra or Lisa or Natascha hadn't looked at them and passed them on.

Today your slate is more diverse. Are you taking risks because of your success? And how much of your slate reflects your own taste?

EF: It's an amalgamation of a number of things. Right now we're finishing *Shaun of the Dead* — it's a romantic comedy-stroke-zombie movie. Now, did I go into the business planning to make a romantic comedy-stroke-zombie movie? I didn't think such a thing could exist. But when the script came in and we met the director I thought 'Ah! That would be great.'

I think what the slate represents is those ideas or people who have piqued our interest. One thing that is fantastic about Working Title — and we owe quite a lot of that to our partners at Universal — is that they have given us the opportunity and the ability to make *any* film. There are very few companies in the world that are given the keys to the kingdom to do whatever they want. It doesn't matter whether it's a £1-million film called *Thirteen* about a thirteen year-old who goes off the rails and uses sex, drugs and rock 'n' roll to define her life — in other words, an indie movie and a really hardcore story — through to *Thunderbirds*, a huge action-genre exploitation of a much-loved franchise with an $80 to 90 million budget, and the marketing muscle of NBC and Universal behind it on a worldwide basis. Those are the two extremes, and then we can do anything in between.

TIM BEVAN: The problem is there are a lot of shitty ideas out there. We have a competitive monitoring system that we update all the time, and there is never anything on there that I think we could have done. The only film that was made recently that I think we should have had was *Calendar Girls*, which I thought was a fantastic idea, and the second I heard that somebody had picked it up I blew the shit out of my development department.

We have made a lot of successful films, and I think it's a bit easier, but not *that* much easier, because it's still very difficult to get a film made. When we get something green-lit there is palpable excitement in the building, because everyone knows that happens only three or four times a year — and that's what you're aiming for all the time. But it's still difficult — even with the resources that we have, with the people we know and can phone up, the ideas we have ourselves and with every agent sending us stuff before they send it to anybody else. And yet it's still very difficult to make a film.

What are you working on at the moment?

TB: At the moment I'm working on a film called *The Interpreter* which is one that we had the idea for in 1992 and then commissioned a script. The story is set at the United Nations, and it re-surfaced again about three years ago just before 9/11 at which point we got an American writer to go out and reinvent it. Sydney Pollack is directing the film and he's a big auteur director but also an important commercial director.

Good ideas never die, interesting worlds never die, and we have about fifty or sixty projects on the slate. Then there are a couple of films that are slightly different. *Thunderbirds* is essentially a character-driven film but it was in development for about two years because our early script wasn't working. But now we're in post-production. We're also going to do a movie about the 1996 expedition to Everest which went wrong when a group of people died on the mountain — the film deals with what happened, and the tourism that has developed around Everest. Again that's going to be an auteur-type film and Stephen Daldry is directing. Those films are interesting for us because the visual effects you can create for a film mean that you can give an audience an experience and take them somewhere they might never actually go.

Is Everest *a deliberate decision to change direction?*

ERIC FELLNER: No, we had always wanted to do an adventure movie but never had the right script. It's true our films are becoming more expensive, but not by Hollywood standards. And some of our films are cheaper too. *Thirteen* was the lowest budget I have ever been involved with. It cuts both ways — films are becoming more expensive to make, stars are becoming more expensive, our ambition is greater. So we have a larger appetite for stars and bigger ideas.

11. *Mission accomplished?*

Do you feel you are fulfilling the ambitions you had when you first started?

EF: I didn't really have any ambitions.

That sounds very laid-back given all your hard work and success . . .

EF: I feel slightly different to quite a few people in the industry, because I don't like to put that much importance on what we do. And that's not to say that those who do are wrong. It's just I don't feel comfortable with it. I feel *more* comfortable thinking — and I don't want to sound like a moral crusader — that we are part of a wide range of cultural and leisure pursuits . . .

But at the luxury end of the market . . .

EF: Absolutely, but, as such, sometimes we can perceive our position in life and our role in society as *way* more important than it is. This is kind of irrelevant to what producing is about, and it's just a personal feeling — and sometimes it's confusing, because you *have* to have a total commitment and belief in what you do in order to do it well. And I think I do have that . . . But this is just entertainment. There are very,

very few life-changing movies. I think often people put far too much importance on what they do in this industry.

Still, it's a good life?

EF: Yes ... but right at this moment I'm rather jealous of Stephen Daldry spending three weeks walking to base camp at Everest ...

Is it a six-day week for you? Do you get exhausted?

EF: All the time, yeah, but it's not so much the time I put into it but the fact that since 1985 I haven't taken more than two weeks off work in a row. And even then, in those two weeks, with the advent of mobile phones ... I remember the first film I worked on, I had a mobile phone and it was the size of a brick. I think I was the only person on the unit to have one ... There is no such thing as 'time out', so your brain becomes more and more addled. And then you get into the addictive nature of this business, which is that if you are *not* running on empty at a thousand miles an hour, with twenty-seven unanswered phone calls a minute and five hundred emails a day and major decisions about multi-million dollar projects — you find it can be *equally* difficult to function without them as you do with them. That probably sounds like I'm having a mid-life crisis ...

Do you have a responsibility to carry on running this company for some time?

TIM BEVAN: Yeah, and it's a bit of a drag ... No, really, we like making movies, and it's fun making bigger movies — particularly in genres we haven't worked in before. I guess when you cease to be enthused about making movies then you stop.

Do you network within the industry?

TB: Not too much. I go to Hollywood every month for four days to see the studio, see the agents, meet with writers, and keep whatever we are doing moving forwards. One of the problems that a lot of UK producers have is that they are very mistrustful of Americans, and I think that's a mistake. At the end of the day, Eric and I have always felt that they are our friends and colleagues, and we have to work together. Hollywood is a crazy place and there are plenty of schmucks there, and sometimes you don't always repeat relationships. But we find most people pretty friendly.

Have you made good friends in the business?

ERIC FELLNER: Some of the people I work with, I genuinely adore.

Particularly the people you have worked with on your romantic comedies . . .?

EF: I would like to state for the record that I *don't* adore Hugh Grant . . .

Shaun of the Dead delighted at the UK box office in 2004, and the *Bridget Jones* sequel did good international business, though *Thunderbirds* and *Wimbledon* disappointed. *The Interpreter* was a success in the spring of 2005, and *Pride and Prejudice* and *Nanny McPhee* were further bright spots that year. In June 2005 Natascha Wharton succeeded Debra Hayward as Working Title's head of development while remaining in charge of WT2, with Hayward switching to an exclusive exec-producing arrangement. Stephen Daldry's *Everest*, meanwhile, remained on the drawing board . . .

Take 6

ALISON OWEN

Estimates vary, but ownership is widely thought to be nine-tenths of the law when it comes to producing: in other words, you must first acquire rights to the property you wish to film. If that property interesting you is an acclaimed novel, much the better the investment — or so you might think. But the odds are that Alison Owen already owns it. Owen's films have strong literary calibre. When I met with Alison she was managing the release of a much-discussed film about Sylvia Plath and Ted Hughes, and prepping an adaptation of Deborah Moggach's *Tulip Fever*. Like Bevan and Fellner, she is a graduate of music video, and served time at Working Title before producing her first movie at the age of thirty and marching onward to her own shingle.

1. *A Question of judgement*

HELEN DE WINTER: *How did you start?*

ALISON OWEN: When I was ten and at school in Portsmouth I read a book called *Clare in Television*[13] about a girl who went to work for the BBC, and it really caught my imagination. Later, when I was a student, the idea of working in television fitted in with my politics — I was a socialist and I felt that television was an arena where you could get ideas across to a greater number of people. But I didn't really know anyone who worked in the media, and having done an English degree, by the time I graduated I realized that I had become less politicized and more interested in story and structure. The idea of producing movies took shape, and I realized that was what I wanted to do.

13. by Pamela Hawken.

I started working in music video, and I was lucky because in the early 1980s MTV had just got going and music video was an incredible growth industry. You could literally walk into a record company and announce that you were a producer, and they would believe you — because they didn't know what one was either. So I invented myself as a pop video producer. At the time my then-boyfriend and soon-to-be husband (Keith Allen) was an actor in a group called the Comic Strip, and I thought it would be a good tool to sell comedians and actors as pop video directors — because people were quite interested in celebrity directors, plus they could appear in the video as well. So I set up a branch of the Comic Strip directors at one company, directors like Adrian Edmondson and Peter Richardson, and I made a few videos that way. Then I went to a bigger music video company, Limelight, and after a while I suggested to them that they establish a film-and-TV arm. It was through Limelight that I produced my first movie, *Hear My Song*, directed by Peter Chelsom. It was very successful for a first film, not so much in terms of box office but certainly in terms of profile. It was nominated for a Golden Globe award and selected for the Royal Premiere in London — the Princess of Wales came along. And I thought every film was going to be like that . . .

How did Hear My Song *come together?*

When I was at Limelight I rang up all the agents and said 'Send me everything', and they did, but for a long time I couldn't find anything that I liked. It was then that I realized I was pretty sure of my own judgement. And I think if you're a producer then you have to be *very* sure of your judgement. At some point, most of the agents got bored sending me material because I was constantly saying 'No' — even though I always replied. But one agent in particular — Elisabeth Dench at Dench Arnold — was really, really, tenacious and kept sending me stuff and we built up quite a relationship.

Then I went to a short film screening and saw Peter Chelsom's short *Treacle* and I thought it was the best short I had ever seen. I immediately rang up Peter and said, 'I'm going to be a producer and you are the person I want to work with, I want to produce your movies.' Peter said, 'You should speak to my agent', and that turned out to be Elisabeth Dench . . . Elisabeth told me that Peter had a project in development with Working Title but it hadn't happened, and he had another project with someone else but that wasn't happening either. And, also, that he had been writing a script. I think Elisabeth believed in me because I had spent a year writing these letters to her so she let me have a look at Peter's new script and it was the first draft of *Hear My Song*. Peter and I started working on the script together, but actually it was already in really good shape. Then I got the film funded really quickly, in about three months.

How did you manage that?

It was the halcyon days of Channel 4 Films and British Screen working together — David Rose at Channel 4 and Simon Relph at British Screen liked working together and would co-fund very readily. That brought two-thirds of the budget, then I pulled in some Irish tax money to get the rest.

That sounds very straightforward given the volume of scripts they must have received . . .

Yes it was, but I talk a good talk . . . I think a lot of producing is about inspiring confidence in other people. Some people bullshit, but I think I tend to be straightforward and honest.

Were you in any way daunted putting your first feature film together?

I found it exciting and challenging, but I didn't find making the film at all daunting. There is a lot to do, but it depends on your personality, and I am just a very, very determined person. I tend to work on films I feel very passionate about and get people to work with me who share that passion.

I also had some confidence about the process because, along the way, I decided to work on a film as a production coordinator, to get some experience. I thought that would teach me just enough to know whether everyone was doing their job properly . . . Then the film ended up being cancelled at the last minute. It amazed me that we had spent twelve weeks intricately making all these beautiful arrangements and then it took about half an hour to cancel it when the money fell apart.

After *Hear My Song* I produced *The Young Americans* with Harvey Keitel, directed by Danny Cannon. I thought it was OK but I didn't particularly enjoy the process of making it, and I wasn't that happy with the ultimate film. Then I realized it was because I had never really been that passionate about the film itself — because it was a theory. I was working with another producer, Paul Trijbits, we had a lot of visual ideas and we thought 'Let's see if we can make a glossy, American-style thriller set in London, because no one's doing that.'

But what I had forgotten was I wouldn't personally want to go and see a film like that, because I don't like glossy thrillers — so why on earth I was trying to make one, I don't know. Afterwards I thought 'I don't want to do that again.' So I set myself two rules: if I choose a project it has to be something I have a passion for, and then I have to be able to see an angle so I know how to fund and sell it. There have also been projects that I have been passionate about but didn't think through properly in terms of how to set them up and sell them. If there isn't an angle you end up banging your head against a brick wall for two or three years, which is a waste of time. So now I only take on projects that have those criteria. And it's amazing how that whittles down the field. There are only about two or three a year that pass both tests.

But the films you produce are always driven by your own interests?

Largely. I didn't develop *Proof* — the director John Madden asked me to produce it because I am going to be doing *Tulip Fever*[14] with him in the spring. *Proof* fitted into his schedule and mine, and we work well together. But I didn't originate *Proof* in the way that I did *Sylvia* or *Tulip Fever*.

2. 'Oh my God, that's Elizabeth.'

After Hear My Song *your next big success was* Elizabeth *which you produced for Working Title in 1998. How did that come together?*

Tim Bevan poached me from Limelight, he offered me a job at Working Title as soon as I made *Hear My Song*. I worked on staff there for a few years, and we made several films including *Moonlight and Valentino* with Gwyneth Paltrow. Then I left and had more of a satellite relationship with the company, but, as I was leaving, we had started talking about making a historical film. It's the only time I have ever done a movie where the idea came before the subject, which is an odd way to go about it.

Weirdly, our brief to ourselves was we wanted to make a historical film in the style of *Trainspotting* which meant we wanted to do a non-Merchant Ivory chocolate-box film, something gritty and muscular and more visceral than the sort of period films that usually come out

14. Deborah Moggach's novel, set in the 17th century, tells of a beautiful young woman who marries a wealthy merchant. She falls for an artist painting her portrait, and the lovers dream of a future together by investing in the market for tulip bulbs.

of the UK. I wanted to inspire people to look at historical characters in another way, rather than as myths and legends. We then looked for a subject to fit that brief, and we considered Boadicea, Cromwell, a few others. But I felt that Elizabeth I had a strong resonance for the modern woman — she had made great choices between her private and public selves, and we wanted to look at the juxtaposition of those personae.

Debra Hayward at Working Title was instrumental in coming up with the idea and we worked very closely on the development of the script. I also felt that we shouldn't just make a film that stuck to the facts but, rather, be faithful to the spirit of her life. Often, with facts, you have to change things around in order to be more faithful to the characters. Plus if we had just presented the events in a narrative order it wouldn't have made a very good drama, and we would have created the impression that it was going to be a long, boring reign — which it never feels when you read about Elizabeth, because her life was full of colour.

How did you find Cate Blanchett for the lead?

People kept trying to foist all kinds of stars on us, but the director Shekhar Kapur and I were really adamant that we didn't want a star. One has to be pragmatic about making films, and we realized there were some interesting names hovering around the part. But for us, it just seemed really important that we kept with the take on the story, which was about a young girl who grew up and decided to make herself into an icon. Therefore it was important not to have someone who already was an icon — it would have been odd to have Nicole Kidman, for instance. We needed someone who could grow into the role and, at the same time, grow into her fame. So it was a tall order. Our casting director, Vanessa Pereira, was absolutely brilliant — though now, rather irritatingly, she has become an agent. But Vanessa kept saying that she heard about a great girl who was acting in *The Seagull* in a theatre in Sydney and that if we were really up against it then we should go and see her. We were about to go into pre-production, so the idea of Shekhar and I getting on a plane to Sydney to see an unknown actress just wasn't going to happen. But Cate had just done *Oscar & Lucinda*, directed by Gillian Armstrong, and we were in our office at Working Title and among a pile of tapes that had come in was a trailer for the film. As soon as Cate came on screen we were like 'Oh my God, that's Elizabeth!' We still had to fly Cate over and persuade Polygram to fund the film with her . . . but it was just so obvious from the moment you saw her that she was Elizabeth that it didn't require any particular cleverness on our part.

What happens when, as was the case with Elizabeth, *you were nominated as producer for the 'Best Picture' Oscar? Does it change things?*

It does — it makes things easier. People return your calls quicker and take you more seriously, so that's really nice. In Hollywood if you have made a couple of movies and people think you have something to offer then they are much more receptive to you. Stars get films funded so, ergo, one has to be able to get hold of the stars, which means having relationships with their agents. Now I would say I'm finding it much better getting to the people I want to talk to. There was a time when people didn't respond, and some people were very rude — some people are *still* rude — but you have to learn to be thick-skinned and just get on with it.

The Oscar experience itself was great fun. I really didn't expect it — I didn't even listen to the Oscar nominations being announced because I was out at lunch with my daughter. When I came back along Oxford Street Eric Fellner from Working Title was waiting for me outside, and when he told me we both just jumped up and down like children on the street. I couldn't remember the last time I had jumped up and down with excitement. And then it was just such fun — people like Harry Winston ring up and offer to lend you diamonds, and designers offer you dresses. It was a laugh . . .

The nice thing about *Elizabeth* being successful was that once you have a little bit of status then people start to bring you fantastic material. My motivation is getting hold of the best material I can, and it's always a battle because every producer is after the same things, and working just as hard. As a baby producer, the way to build your career is by being able to recognize things that other people have missed. So it's a wonderful luxury, when people give you great books and ask you if you would consider producing such-and-such . . .?

But still you're always on the lookout for what is good material?

I try to be. I find that sometimes I get very absorbed with the film I'm working on and then when I come up for air I get in a panic and think 'Oh my God, I didn't get sent that manuscript, I can't believe so-and-so is making that movie, why didn't I get hold of that?' But I have become more mature about accepting that I can't do everything. I used to think that everyone else was much more successful than I am. So it was fantastic being nominated for an Oscar, not just for myself but it also calmed me down. One side of me is horribly ambitious and competitive, it's like having a dragon inside of me. So feeding the dragon with a nomination shut it up for a while and I was able to relax a bit.

After Elizabeth, *too, you decided to set up your own company, Ruby Films?*

Yes. Before that I couldn't really afford to. If you set up your own company you have to be prepared to work out of a shoebox and live on nothing for a couple of years, and because I had three kids I couldn't afford to do that. But after *Elizabeth* my kids were pretty much through their education, and I had enough kudos to be able to attract some investment. I had a first-look deal with DreamWorks for a couple of years, then a deal with Miramax.

You took on a partner, Neris Thomas. Why did that arise?

Neris approached me and, funnily enough, she used to be my assistant. So when she called me years later — and by which time she had done her own movies — to suggest we start a company together, I knew she would be the right person. Neris is a great complement to me in many ways. She's a great 'people' person — I've never met anyone who didn't like her. But she's also very good at blowing her own trumpet, or my trumpet, or Ruby's trumpet . . .

We don't have a studio deal at the moment. We're supported by the UK Film Council, and the company is myself, Neris, and our support staff. The company is mainly run out of our profits and production fees, and we pretty much stumble from production to production . . .

Is that your preferred way of working?

Not necessarily, and we're always trying to think of ways to make it more solid. But it's a tough industry. People always talk about supporting production companies with sales companies or television companies. We do a few TV projects as well, Neris is concentrating more on trying to build a television arm. Plus she's just had a baby two weeks ago, so she's fairly focused on that at the moment . . .

Would you say you are entrepreneurial?

I would like to have more financial stability for the company, but I would say I am better at funding projects than I am at finding money — and finding money for what you want to do is very much part of being a producer. I am pretty good at financing films but my strength is not writing business plans and doing flow charts to show how the business is going to be in profit in year two and yadda-yadda . . . so I need to work with people to do that.

3. *The vision thing*

I'd like to talk about how you work in specific areas of the process. First of all, what's your attitude to developing material and scripts?

That's my favourite part of the process. With *Sylvia* as with *Elizabeth*, we weren't basing the script on particular source material, we didn't option a biography, we just went out and did our own research, and I worked very closely with the writer John Brownlow in shaping the structure of the story.

By contrast, *Tulip Fever* has been tricky, a difficult script to get right. When I read the novel it struck me as the perfect film story, so it's been quite surprising that it's taken so long. Deborah Moggach wrote the first draft and then we had two other writers before Tom Stoppard came on board, and he's really got it right, he's written the most wonderful draft. Then latterly the development of *Tulip Fever* has been a process of getting the script to tally with the economics of the budget. They are inextricably linked . . .

Do you have a preferred style of working with directors?

It's different with each director. The more A-list the director, the more you hand it over to them. But that doesn't mean that there isn't a lot of creative collaboration going on. When John Madden gets going, he pretty much has a clear vision in his head of what he wants, and I'm just around to provide support. But on *Proof* and with *Tulip Fever* he likes to talk at length at script stage, which is fine by me, because so do I. With some directors you accept that they are going to realize their vision. With other directors, you take them on and you want them to realize *your* vision.

What is an example of 'your vision'?

Sylvia was very much my idea and a film I wanted to make. I decided how I wanted to tell the story — I knew I wanted it to start with Sylvia meeting Ted and end with her death. I also knew I didn't want the film to be a long bio-pic. So it's my vision that steered the project forward. But once the script was solid I wanted a director to come on board and make it their own. And *Sylvia* is very much a Christine Jeffs film at the end of the day.

How did you meet Christine?

Her debut film was called *Rain* and it's just a great movie, a coming-of-age story that did well at Sundance, Toronto and Cannes. When I needed a director for *Sylvia* I watched a whole bunch of tapes and after seeing *Rain* I literally couldn't speak for about half an hour afterwards. It made me weep, it was so affecting. In that moment I just felt that here was my director, someone who could produce the kind of emotion that I needed in the story of Ted and Sylvia.

To what extent do you get involved in post-production?

I tend to step back quite a lot. I don't think I'm particularly good in the edit because I lose perspective quite quickly. If I see a particular take of a scene five times and I'm asked which one works better — well, I don't know. I would know the first time I saw each take, but after a while . . . it's a skill I haven't got. And I find it amazing that editors can sit there for hours and hours and still maintain some kind of perspective.

But I find I am much more useful if I convert myself into a member of the audience at that point. So once we finish shooting I will go off for eight-to-ten weeks and let the director and the editor get on with the film, and then I will come back and watch the director's cut — that will be the first time I watch the film. From then on I'll start to work on a more intricate level. And you continue tweaking the cut until everyone is happy with it. Again, generally, in post every director is different. John Madden has a team of people he works with, but with *Elizabeth* and *Sylvia* I was a lot more involved in the directors' decisions, because both of them had come from abroad and they couldn't bring their creative team with them. It was great being able to help them make choices about their heads of department and with the music and so on.

Do you get involved in the marketing and distribution of your films?

That aspect of filmmaking is still a learning curve for me — how you select the poster and work on the tag lines and choose stills et cetera. The people dealing with it are usually experts in their field — I might choose an image and they will put it on a poster and immediately I will see that they were right and I was wrong. The paradox about being a producer is that you have to be a control freak with detail but also know when to let go and let people run with their ideas — otherwise you would never get good people to work for you, not if you were all over them the whole time.

But if the marketing isn't right there's not that much I can do. For example, Focus Features have bought the US rights to *Sylvia*. If I want Focus to spend more money on advertising, I can lobby them but I can't force them. So if Gwyneth Paltrow's agent rings me up and says, 'You're a crap producer. Why didn't you spend more money on advertising?' I can't be accountable for that because that's what Focus will have decided to do.

4. 'You haven't got the money sorted out yet, have you?'

What appealed to you about the story of Sylvia Plath and Ted Hughes? Why did you want to make it as a movie?

I loved Plath's poetry as a teenage girl. Like most adolescents I responded to the tragic death and the deeply felt emotions she had. Then when I read more of her poetry at university and got to know more about her relationship with Hughes, I found it very personally resonant. And I felt it was a fantastic love story — you could feel how deeply and passionately they loved each other, but their particular 'Can't live with you, can't live without you . . .' meant they couldn't find a way to make it work.

Did you anticipate the barrage of criticism you would get when you started to develop the story as a film?

You would have to be blind not to consider it. People got very heated about it. It's a minefield making a film about a real person, far more problematic than most films. In the beginning I was constantly reminded of that. FilmFour said, 'Ahhh, we made *Hilary and Jackie*, we don't want to go through that again.' At one point I was thinking of Frank Cottrell Boyce as the screenwriter, he wrote *Hilary and Jackie*, but he said, 'Don't make me go there again . . .'

The first thing I did when I knew I wanted to make the film was to meet with Ted's and Sylvia's daughter, Frieda. We went out for dinner and she was very straightforward — we got on well and I liked her very much. Frieda had liked *Elizabeth* and she sent me some of her poems. She was very clear that she didn't want a film to be made, but she also recognized that it was inevitable a film *would* be made. Then she indicated that if it was going to be made she was glad it was me who was going to make it. But she was always very clear that she wouldn't give us the rights because she would feel that if she did that then she would be complicit in the making of the film, and she didn't want to be — and that was fair enough.

It was Frieda who first suggested to me that I would be able to use a small amount of poetry under the laws of fair usage. So it was interesting because on the one hand she was saying 'I won't give you the rights' but on the other hand she was suggesting how we could use little bits in that way.

Frieda was recently quoted as saying that she would never, never, never, in a million years see the film. Did that surprise you?

I think the idea of the film was one thing, but the reality of actually seeing stills in the papers and people talking about her mother and father is very different. That she probably reacted differently to how she thought she would doesn't surprise me. When I first saw the still in the *Daily Mail* of Daniel Craig as Ted and Gwyneth as Sylvia punting down the River Cam, I thought 'God, I wonder what Frieda is going to think . . .?'

What did the film cost?

It was $13 million, which is not a huge budget, but quite big for a literary subject. I particularly wanted to keep the budget up so we could make the film on a good scale, so that was a big battle for me, with people asking me to make it more cheaply.

Was it a difficult film to finance?

Yes and no. The BBC backed me from the beginning and put money into development, which was great. Because it was such a contentious subject, it was good that the project had a home at the BBC because they have a reputation for being 'Auntie' so they gave the project a bureaucratic public stamp of approval that it wouldn't have had if it had been a small division of a Hollywood studio. I didn't want people thinking that we were going to make some sort of vitriolic, scurrilous bio-pic, which was never our intention. We wanted to make a balanced, beautiful love story. Then once we attached Gwyneth it wasn't hard to finance.

Was Gwyneth Paltrow a must for you in the same way Cate Blanchett had been for Elizabeth?

It was always obvious to me that Gwyneth would play Sylvia. I think star quality is always really apparent. I worked with Gwyneth a few years before on *Moonlight and Valentino* and at that point she was only about nineteen or twenty. We were in LA, going through boxes of tapes — because, you can imagine, in LA you have a lot of actresses — but as soon as she came up on screen we thought 'Hello, film star!' I know it's a cliché but a real movie star has an affinity with the camera, it's just there. It's interesting, because sometimes even after you've cast someone you don't always see it. So you might be watching them on set and suddenly you could be worried — I might go to the director and ask them what they think, because I think the actor looks a bit weak. And then the next day you see the dailies and think 'Oh my God . . . something magical has happened between there and here.'

Did having an American star increase the budget?

Not principally, though it contributed. But mainly it was expensive because we shot the film in lots of different locations. We filmed in New Zealand masquerading as America, and Cambridge and Devon in England. It gets expensive when you move around like that.

Was it cheaper to go to New Zealand than to shoot in America?

It was cheaper, but that wasn't the reason we shot there. It was partly because of the window of Gwyneth's availability, and partly because it was winter in Cape Cod when we were due to shoot, but those scenes were meant to be their honeymoon in the summer. So we had to look for somewhere in the world that would look like Cape Cod in the right season . . .

I'm wondering what is the worst problem you have ever had to deal with on a movie — and I'm guessing it might have been on Sylvia?

On *Sylvia* I made a huge mistake of not getting the insurance situation sorted out earlier. We had gone to extreme lengths to work out how to use small amounts of poetry under 'fair usage', but what I hadn't realized was that I still wouldn't get what is called 'errors and omissions insurance'. Without E and O insurance the finance contracts can't be completed. So at the last minute, really, we had the film financed, Gwyneth Paltrow and Daniel Craig were on set filming, we had a whole crew and cast in Cambridge, around two hundred people, punts going down the river, paparazzi everywhere, extras thronging the streets . . . the whole caboodle. And I was sitting in my trailer freaking out about how I was going to pay everyone on Friday. Some producers sail pretty close to the wind all the time, but I am decidedly not one of them, and in this instance it was genuinely unforeseen. The only person who clued on to what was happening was Daniel Craig, for some reason. He looked me in the eye and said, 'You haven't got the money sorted out yet, have you?' I shook my head and asked him to keep shtum, which he did. And luckily we got it all sorted out . . . but it was a terrible few days.

So on *Sylvia* I learnt about insurance. It's boring, I'm sure there are more interesting mistakes I made along the way . . . But I think that if you want to be a producer you have to accept at the beginning that it's all about accountability, and, as such, I am responsible for everything. The wonderful thing about filmmaking is that you learn an enormous amount with each film. Then later on you feel horrified by how much you didn't know — and how much you didn't know that you didn't know . . .

5. A bit manic

What are your ongoing aspirations?

I want to carry on making films from good material. I would also like to make quite big films, with big budgets and big names. When my kids are older I would quite like to go and work in New York or LA for a while, which I have never been able to do before.

As an independent or part of a studio?

I'm not quite sure yet, I just know in my bones that it's something I would like to do . . . *Tulip Fever* is about $40 million and if I made *Elizabeth* now it would be about $40 million. They are broadly the kind of films I enjoy doing. My projects tend to be very female-led. That isn't a particularly political decision, it's just the way it is — I feel I know more about female subjects and I'm more able to contribute creatively. But the budgets for those sort of films peter off at the $40 million mark . . .

Why?

Generally speaking, actresses can't carry films with bigger budgets than guys . . . You couldn't make a $100 million movie just starring a woman because it wouldn't work, the figures wouldn't support it.

Even though women account for more than half of the cinema audience?

Yes, and I think people are gradually recognizing this. Julia Roberts is as finance-able as a male star.

What are you doing at the moment?

My life is a bit manic. I'm currently heavily involved in the press and marketing of *Sylvia*. We delivered the film about a month ago, and it's just been released in America, so I went to the premiere in New York, and we had press for about two weeks leading up to the opening. The film is closing the London Film Festival in a few weeks, so now I'm making sure we have a print ready in time. I've been sorting out sound reels because we had a few problems. Yesterday we re-mixed. Some of my time is spent liaising with Focus, consulting about the figures and talking about what we can do. This weekend the film will go out to another thirty-two screens, and then more the following weekend, so there's this whole strategy about 'rolling out' the film.

Then we are in production on *Proof,* so my main daily focus is in making sure that's going well. Our shooting days run from 8 a.m. to 7 p.m. and then we have dailies to watch, so it's a long day. When I get home I do a few hours of the LA day, because Los Angeles has then started, so I'll have phone calls and emails regarding *Tulip Fever* — because DreamWorks are funding it and next week we're going into official pre-production. John and I will be crossing over between shooting and posting *Proof* with the prep and shoot of *Tulip Fever*.

Then I have a number of projects in development. This week I've been negotiating to buy the rights to *Brick Lane*, the novel by Monica Ali. I read it and loved it, then I called up the agent and he said, 'That's fantastic because you were on my list of people to call, so I'm thrilled you are interested and I won't talk to anyone else.' It was a very nice way for it to work out.

How do you keep all this stuff going?

I've got three kids, so I try not to work all the time, though it's easier now because the children are older — only one is still at school. So, actually, my life is less manic than it's been for years. For a while, being a single working mother with three kids was hectic.

Will you continue to do this?

I think there's probably a point when you don't have the same energy levels to do it in the way I'm working at it now. I reckon I have another ten years to keep at this pace. But I would like to think that even when I was in my seventies I could turn out a small film every three years or so.

What do you enjoy most about being a producer?

I can't think of another industry where I would get to meet so many intelligent people. Just yesterday I took a call between Monica Ali and Laura Jones, a fantastic screenwriter who wrote *An Angel at My Table* amongst others. Just being on that call for an hour with those two women was bliss. I felt like I was eavesdropping on a fantastic conversation, because I didn't really say very much except, every now and again 'Ah-ha', 'OK', or 'I agree . . .' But it's such a privilege to work with them, and with people like John Madden and Tom Stoppard. I can't believe I am allowed to do that.

Have you experienced disappointment? Is there a film you haven't been able to set up?

There was a project I absolutely loved, a book by Armistead Maupin called *Maybe the Moon*. It's probably the only project I have been incredibly determined to make and didn't succeed in making, because at the time I don't think the world was ready for a story about a dwarf who fucks a black guy. People have said it's about every non-PC joke in the world . . . The story is based on the real-life story of the woman in the E.T. costume. In the book she's called Cady, and she wants to be an actress and accepted for who she is, but she's doomed to be in the costume of a movie called 'Mr Woods'. I love Armistead's writing and I think it's a beautiful story but I have never been able to get it made. Perhaps I might one day . . .

Tulip Fever **was seven weeks away from production, Jude Law, Keira Knightley and Jim Broadbent cast, when the government shut down a tax break scheme, the budget swelled by $17 million, and the film was cancelled. But in October 2005 it was announced that FilmFour had acquired Zadie Smith's novel** *On Beauty* **for Owen to develop with Scott Rudin. They were also working on Philippa Gregory's** *The Other Boleyn Girl* **for Focus and Sony.** *Brick Lane* **was poised to shoot in 2006, Sarah Gavron directing a script by Abi Morgan and Laura Jones. And in November 2005** *Tulip Fever* **was revived at DreamWorks, Owen having convinced execs there not to put it in turnaround, the budget was scaled down to $25 million, Eastern European locations replacing London . . .**

Take 7

STEPHEN EVANS

Stephen Evans was apprenticed nowhere near the film business but, rather, at the heart of the City of London, in an era — the 1980s — when the City had lately been revived by deregulation and established itself once more as an entrepôt of international capital. So-called 'high-net-worth individuals' do not necessarily find film production the most rewarding investment, but a producer with an entrepreneurial bent always has the possibility of persuading them otherwise. Evans's spur came after his enthusiasm for books and plays led him to a serendipitous encounter with an actor who was then en route to becoming the foremost British film-and-theatre hyphenate of his time.

1. *Where angels fear . . .*

STEPHEN EVANS: I had no knowledge and no background whatsoever in film — I had worked in the City as a stockbroker for corporate and institutional clients. But by going to the wrong house, on the wrong day, with the right intentions, I met a young actor completely unknown to me. I financed his theatre company, Renaissance, and loved every minute of it. So now my new friend Kenneth Branagh wanted to make a film, *Henry V*.

We set up a film company together because I had access to money and stardust in my eyes. Because I was in a position to utilize friendships from my financial world to raise money, I said to Ken, 'If we're going for it, why not make *three* movies together?' My instinct was that investors would rather spread their risk. And I thought that if Ken was as talented as I imagined, then the first film, *Henry V*, would be our entry card to the movie world — commercial or not, at least it was Shakespeare, so it might travel internationally. In the end we had three Oscar nominations for *Henry V* and won one, so it was a great start — although initially the film lost £2 million. It has now broken even, seventeen years later . . .

HELEN DE WINTER: *How did you structure your finance?*

People have asked me that . . . and I couldn't do it again. There is no way of utilizing my blueprint. My first mistake was to try and use British film industry sources. Not for the last time did I realize that this was a cottage industry with very little cash-flow to support it. I tried the BBC, coincidentally meeting Jonathon Powell, then head of BBC1, at a dinner party. He was very supportive and liked the idea. I signed a deal for £400,000 for UK broadcasting. 'Hey this is easy' I thought. 'Where do I go from here?' Then I met a couple of sales agents who I'd been told might put up money. Delightful people, but when I mentioned *Henry V* the meetings finished quickly. 'Ken who?' tended to be the parting words. Their advice was kind, but their strategy was clear: 'Make the movie and then we'll look to sell it.' Everyone was Charm personified and little help.

Ironically, during that period the only encouraging remark came from a new-found film friend who had been dining in LA with Adrian Lyne, director of *Fatal Attraction* et cetera. On being told about the project Lyne remarked, 'It's such a wanky idea it'll probably work . . .' I immediately incorporated that into my new philosophy. Anyway, the strategy was now beginning to develop. I used a sales agent, Guy East, a man who could sell fridges to Eskimos. When he extolled the virtues of the film to my prospective investors, even I started to believe in it.

Back to the drawing board, I had to attack my high-net-worth playmates. I was in the City, I knew a lot of rich people, and at that point I was relatively rich myself — though after my film career I'm now relatively poor again. Every rich guy I came across, I would ask them to invest, and the majority of them did. I was promoting Ken on the basis that I believed in Ken and these people believed in me. Most of them had never heard of him, they'd never even seen his plays. But their thoughts tended to go along the following lines: 'Stephen Evans wants to make a movie, he believes in this guy Ken Branagh, it's tax-effective. Stephen's putting his money where his mouth is, so let's have a bit of fun.'

I couldn't do it now. I didn't know then what a dangerous game movie-making is. Unless you are doing it for charitable reasons or you are stupid, it is not logical to invest in a film as a private individual, unless you can get a significant tax break. Fortunately these tax breaks are now part of the UK film world. All the major tax funds have made it their number one objective to seduce high-net-worth individuals into the film industry through elaborate tax breaks, enabling them to invest with the minimum of risk. But at the beginning of my career those breaks barely existed. From a producer's point of view, unless you are unbelievably talented — which I wasn't — then to get into the film industry like I did mid-career, you have got to utilize rich people and bring in private investors. The rich are crucial to this industry.

What did you see yourself doing in your new career as a producer?

I didn't know. It was a case of fools rushing in where angels fear to tread. I knew one or two people who were big actors, because indirectly I had been their stockbroker. But the irony is that coming to it at forty was overall a blessing, because I hadn't been ground down by the industry — most producers are ground down to dust and few survive. When I started I had the energy of a thirty-year-old because it was all brand new.

Ken was lucky in the sense that I raised virtually all the cash to make *Henry V*. That $8.5 million seventeen years ago would be $17 to 20 million today. Equally *I* was very lucky because Ken delivered with talent and energy.

Then Ken wanted to do *Hamlet*, but I had loved Olivier's *Hamlet* and I didn't think Ken could improve on it, whereas I had thought he would give a very different slant to Olivier's *Henry V*. I said, 'Well, let's try to find something cheap and cheerful', and Ken gave me two or three ideas. I got *Peter's Friends* on New Year's Eve 1991. I endorsed it on New Year's Day. We finished the movie before the end of March. How often does that happen? The financing was not difficult, Ken's star was in the ascendant, and I was able to use the Samuel Goldwyn Company and Channel 4 Films, who I had met through the success of *Henry V*, and who subsequently had confidence in Branagh as a director. *Peter's Friends* was shot at one location and Ken was quite brilliant in how he put it together. I had my ups and downs with Ken, but when he moves he moves fast, and he made a *tour de force* of pulling it all together. Ultimately my decision to make three movies was proven right because both *Peter's Friends* and the third, *Much Ado About Nothing*, made a lot of money, whereas *Henry V* clearly didn't.

Essentially I was learning as we went along, and it took me about five years to begin to understand the business and have the contacts that are essential for survival. Without contacts in this business you are dead — unless you are a genius. Being an independent producer is something I wouldn't really wish on anybody.

What do you mean by that?

Well, it's such high risk. You can easily spend two years not making anything. There is no one in the UK making big international movies who is not owned by an American studio. Take Tim Bevan and Eric Fellner. They are part of the studio system, they get paid, they know they're going to make films every year. They've done very well, they have a great track record and they've got Richard Curtis. But for me and most others — there's no such certainty. What I try to do is to make movies between $6 to 15 million that can travel internationally and do well in Europe, Japan and America. I think I'm going to make two movies next year, but am I? Can I guarantee that to my bank manager? You only get paid when you make movies, and when you don't, not only do you not make money but you lose money on your overheads. Even the gestation period for seeing money come back on a successful film is about three years. You hang on in that period.

Fortunately *Peter's Friends* was quite a big success and in terms of a return on money it did brilliantly. Renaissance itself had put no money into it, and I think we made about £2 million out of it, which was all rather wonderful. But unless you're very, very lucky, being a British producer is not a great way of making a living. If you want to earn real money, don't go into it. I haven't made as much as I thought I would, but then I didn't realize how much I needed when I got into it. By the time I realized this, I had already made *The Madness of King George* and was full-time in my new career. Love it or hate it, I suppose by then I did have the bug.

2. 'Who can flourish . . .?'

How did you come to make the film of Alan Bennett's play The Madness of King George?

I had lunch with Alan Bennett's agent, Anthony Jones, at the Ivy — we're old friends. Neither of us seemed to have an idea in our heads. Boredom reigned. Towards the end I said, 'Is there anything remotely going on that I should be aware of? He said, 'There's a lot of interest in *The Madness of King George*.' I said, 'Oh, I never saw that, is it still on?' He replied, 'Don't be stupid, it finished ages ago.' I asked if it was on anywhere, and Anthony said, 'It's on at the Brooklyn Academy of Music' — a big two-thousand-seat theatre in Brooklyn, New York. I flew over that weekend. Before I saw the play I was determined to think it was good — and it wasn't, it was brilliant. As I knew the director Nick Hytner's agent, I arranged to meet Nick in the evening and got him on-side.

Did you want Hytner to direct even though he hadn't directed a film before?

Well, I had worked with Ken, so in a way I felt more confident than most about the idea of a theatre director as a first-time film director. Nick Hytner has a very powerful intellect and he is also a very powerful person, both of which are essentials for top class directors.

I rang up Anthony Jones the following Monday and told him I wanted to meet Alan Bennett and that I would like to make the movie. I had no money, though I don't think Anthony necessarily knew that, but I did, by this time, have the contacts and the knowledge of how to structure a commercial film deal. I met Alan for afternoon tea. He was delightful but didn't say much. I likened him to a teddy bear with a razor blade behind each ear.

What was your pitch?

I couldn't prepare one because I didn't know Alan Bennett. How many people do? But I told him I loved a line said by the king's doctor to the king's equerry: 'But who can flourish on such a daily diet of compliance?' I said to Alan, 'This is like Princess Di or movie stars or rock stars — most of them go mad in the end: if everyone fawns over you and tells you you're wonderful, even the most modest person starts to believe it.' I thought there was so much of this kind of psychology and natural wit in Alan's writing that if we set that against a rather grand, royal background and used the likes of Arundel Castle and Greenwich, and with Nigel Hawthorne as the king, then it could be a very interesting and quirky movie. Alan subsequently told Anthony that he would like to go with me on it. The deal I structured with Anthony Jones was weighted in Alan's favour, although it did Nick and I no harm — in fact, quite the contrary.

I then rang Sam Goldwyn in America and he immediately flew over with Tom Rothman, his number two — now Head of Fox. Richard Eyre gave me the VIP suite at the National Theatre for the schmoozing. They decided they wanted to do it. Just one problem. Sam wanted another actor for King George. The conversation went like this. 'We need someone bigger, Stephen.' 'But who could do it, Sam? I'll give you five minutes to think of two actors.' 'I don't need five minutes, Stephen. Dustin Hoffman or Sean Connery.' Picking myself up off the floor, I replied, 'Sam, I rest my case. Anyway, it's a deal breaker. Alan Bennett will only go along with Nigel Hawthorne and, for that matter, Nick Hytner, and I totally agree with him.' After ninety-odd performances of the role in the theatre, Nigel was word-perfect and he was steeped in the character. Perhaps George III was a combination of James Bond and Rain Man, but we wanted nothing of it. Finally Sam agreed — and as you could trust him on a handshake, that made it much easier to put together.

I found out later from Anthony Jones that he had used me as a stalking horse, because originally the project was with Working Title, who were procrastinating on certain aspects. The wonderful thing for me was that Alan wanted to go with me and not Tim and Eric. The pacemaker had won the race. You can imagine my pleasure when Tim wrote a vituperative letter to Anthony Jones asking what had gone wrong, and why haven't they got the movie? So that really cheered me up, it was a nice bonus.

Did the subsequent success of the film give you some stability as a producer?

Yes and no. As I said, it takes about three years for any profits to filter through. And as *The Madness of King George* was happening I had been developing *Wings of the Dove*. I fell in love with the book and was developing it with Eileen Mazel at Paramount, then they closed their London office so I was forced to option it. I had put up my own money for development and pre-production costs. It was a disaster. The film collapsed in pre-production because my director had what I will politely call a nervous breakdown. He accused my prospective female lead Uma Thurman of being a junkie, which she wasn't, and she rightly walked from the project. Lawsuits were due and the film collapsed. I lost a million dollars on that. Our house had to be sold.

After *The Madness of King George*, we did Trevor Nunn's film of *Twelfth Night* which was basically a film done to stay alive, and it was nearly a very good film but it didn't quite work. It played joyously at 140 minutes. However, we had to cut it to 110 minutes to meet with the American studio's delivery requirements . . . Meanwhile I was trying to get *Wings of the Dove* back on the road. I brought in a new writer, Hossein Amini and he did a great job — deservedly receiving an Oscar nomination. Harvey Weinstein, who had been very supportive throughout the demise, still wanted to finance it. However, he wouldn't accept any of the directors that I proposed. My last suggestion was Iain Softley. Harvey passed. It was all getting to a bad state.

The only alternative was to extend the overdraft and push off to the West Indies with my wife. The sun cleared the mind. I sent a fax saying bye-bye to Harvey and told him I was going to try to cut a deal with Fox who had earlier shown some interest. Then Harvey turned up on his white charger, because there is nothing Harvey likes more than not being able to do something — whereas if he *can* do it, often he's not so interested. He accepted Iain Softley, and paid $13.2 million having initially said he would pay no more than $10 million. Having spent half a lifetime in the City it just shows that, to get your best deal, you need two competing buyers.

After that, I had another barren period and couldn't get films off the ground. Money was haemorrhaging again. I had certain projects in development but nothing was coming through.

These are big personal risks. How do you keep going?

Well, the motivating force is that there's no real alternative. When *Wings of the Dove* initially collapsed I immediately had to look around for new projects while rescuing the old. Networking, in this business as in any other, is crucial — and to stand still is to move backwards. Much as I find making new contacts often a complete waste of space, it's very much part of the producer's journey, and sometimes it can deliver in spades. Maintaining appearances was critical, so after selling our house in the country we took a short lease in Eaton Terrace, London; ironically, it looked as if I was moving upmarket. Image is not everything, but it doesn't half help when you're a film producer.

3. *No pessimism allowed*

Your successes at Renaissance enabled you to produce bigger films. As an independent producer, what did you learn from the transition? And why have you since gone back to making smaller films?

In 1999 I raised $40 million from the Hermes fund managers who managed the Post Office and British Telecom pension funds. I knew the guy who ran the fund and I still had a lot of friends in the City so I got some of the great and the good on our board and brought in Angus Finney, a film journalist, who helped me develop the business plan. It sounds like a lot of money, but $40 million in worldwide movie terms is tuppence, really — and I soon realized how difficult it would be. At the time, the film sales industry went south, and we came to realize that we had an integrated model which was virtually obsolete as soon as it was set up. In the old days you could get forty per cent of your budget out of America and a load of pre-sales out of Europe, so you could make your movie. But that doesn't happen any more because most distributors have pulled out of the pre-sales market, and France, Germany and Italy don't pre-buy unless you have a big American movie star. So we were looking at the bigger international market, but we soon realized that we didn't have the resources to do it properly and I don't think we handled it very well. We probably passed on films we should have made, and made films that we shouldn't.

A movie we executive-produced which we were going to fully finance was *Confessions of a Dangerous Mind*. It was at Warner Bros in turnaround and we picked it up and developed it further. The budget was about $30 million but for us the level of risk was massive — to put that together out in LA with movie stars was just too big. The development costs alone were huge, even though we put about $1 million of our own funds into it. It was a very unpleasant-but-pleasant experience, but fortunately we managed to sell it on to Harvey Weinstein. It's another example of how, despite how difficult Harvey can be, independent producers are close to his heart. And amazingly this was one piece of development that we made a profit on.

We were also trying to work with Terry Gilliam on a screenplay called *Good Omens*. The budget was $75 million, and we were trying to get Robin Williams — we had believed we had Johnny Depp. But we could never really get it off the ground and therefore we were in development hell. In the end we lost a million, though we hope to get it back one day. Unless you are a studio like Universal with billions behind you, you can't put that kind of film together without tremendous risk. You probably have to make your stars pay-or-play, so $18 million disappears immediately, and at the same time you may have massive rewrites on the screenplay, so you're flying round the world and suddenly the costs are alarming.

I left Renaissance Films because my three-year contract was up. I decided I wanted to be a small production company, with a reduced overhead, and concentrate on development and production. I took with me a few of my staff and three or four projects. We have just finished *Dear Frankie* and that couldn't have been made without Film Council money, which came through Scottish Screen and more importantly Ingenious, the film tax investment company. It's clear that in the current arctic environment of the British independent filmmaking industry, the Film Council is very important. And tax companies like Ingenious and Grosvenor Park are becoming more and more friendly towards filmmakers. We could not have thought of making *Dear Frankie* without Ingenious putting up fifty per cent of the budget cost.

Do you think it's impossible to have a big UK-based production company?

Today the only people who can afford to make the *Harry Potter*s of this world and spend $100 million plus on it are the studios. When you add on the cost of prints and advertising there is no institution in the UK who can dream of doing that worldwide.

Apart from Working Title and, to a lesser extent, Jeremy Thomas's Recorded Picture Company, there is no big company in the UK. The lottery franchises have all relatively failed for different reasons. Civilian Content have now used up their money. Pathe — well, they're a big company and continuing to move forward and were a help to me, but their investments alongside the lottery haven't been a brilliant success. DNA spent very little, which is why they have been able to do their deal with Fox — if they hadn't, they would have lost what they didn't spend. You had the vested interest of the Film Council endorsing a 20th Century Fox/DNA deal, which I am pleased about, because it means for a producer there's somewhere else in town to go for money. People come to me for money, for goodness sake, and I've got very little. There's only one UK distributor who has any real money, and that's Nigel Green at Entertainment — and while he's been very supportive to me, he distributes mainly big international movies, because that's where the money is.

The reality today in the UK is there is very little support from the ITV network for film; there is a £10 million a year spend from the BBC on film and roughly the equivalent from Channel 4. BskyB have pulled out of movies. Quite frankly, apart from the tax funds and the Film Council, the outlook in the UK is so gloomy that I believe it's going to get better. It's so bad it has to turn. I'm not at all pessimistic. Producers are not allowed that pleasure.

Have you ever been offered a deal with a studio?

Yes, and if I hadn't have raised the $40 million I mentioned previously then I would have tried to use my friendships in America to finalize that deal. Studio deals often tend to be more trouble than they're worth in the UK, though naturally they can featherbed producers. They don't happen so much any more because the studios are bored by them, and the recipients are also bored with them, because it doesn't seem to help producers get films made. And you lose your independence. For example if Harvey Weinstein gives you $150,000 a year overhead — well, he's got you, hasn't he? You're his man and everything has to go through him. And if he doesn't want your product he'll probably take a long time *saying* he doesn't want it. Then when you go to someone like Sony, they'll say, 'Well, Harvey doesn't want it, and I suppose you want us to have it, but why should we play second-hand rose?'

4. *I could be totally wrong . . .*

Do you get involved in physical production?

In a word, no. I leave that to the line producer. On the film set my job is to make it a happy ship. If we have, say, an upset actress, or occasionally director, my job is to smooth them down. If the crew is fed up with overtime my job is to beg them to continue for the good of the film. Once we are in principal photography I hand over the baton to the director. My job is to protect him from the various elements when they are stormy, sometimes even from himself. All I ask for in return is at least he listens to my constructive criticism which ultimately he can use or discard. Producers may have a creative influence but you don't employ the director to override him or her on creative matters. If you don't like what he's doing then you just don't work with him again. In terms of production heads of department, the only person I ensure I approve is the editor, because, in the editing suite, I want the editor to like me as much as the director so I can put my point of view across and make sure I'm *au fait* with how the film is being put together.

Do you value the contribution you've made to the films you have produced?

My background was that I always had a great love of books, and in fact I prefer books to film. Certain books can make marvellous films, so in terms of contribution it's nice to know that on certain films, the only reason it's gone from the written word to the screen is because of you. If you hadn't started the process and kept with it then it would never have happened. Kenneth Branagh was the ultimate talent on *Henry V*, he did the creative work, but I hope he would be the first to say I enabled the written word of Shakespeare to end up on screen. I feel I am an enabler, and as an enabler, you can, if you get on with people in the right way, have a creative input. And then you can decide whether to get all bitter and twisted and try to have an even bigger creative input, or occasionally be told to sod off.

What drives you on?

It's my final job. I've got no alternative. If I had an alternative would I take it? Probably not. I think I've got ten or eleven films left in me, three every two years, so that would be about seven or eight years of work. But probably the biggest buzz that drives you on is to screen a movie that is really appreciated by the audience. If I like my idea or indeed someone else's I'll just push like crazy to make it. For example with *The Madness of King George*, people weren't falling over themselves to make the movie. In fact there is no movie I have made where people were falling over themselves to be involved. I was told by Sam Goldwyn, who I had worked with very happily, 'Don't even bother with *Wings of the Dove*, it ain't going to happen.' But that's just a point of view.

I'm hoping in the next year to raise £10 million from private sources, and if I'm lucky I might do it. We will then put this into our films, and one or two films from other people if we like their ideas. I want to make Lorna Sage's memoir *Bad Blood* in the next year and I think it's going to be a great movie, it's a story about a young girl who gets pregnant at school in the 1950s. The story of a young girl getting pregnant in *any* era is a major drama but in this story the girl overcomes her difficulties and becomes a professor. I think it's a really lovely, funny and dramatic piece and I have a great writer and director, and a great cast and I think it's going to strike a chord and do a lot of business. But I would say that, wouldn't I? I could be totally wrong.

What's the worst problem you have ever dealt with on a movie?

Whilst there are many problems which embarrass one — problems that cause loss of face, the direct results of a personal screw-up — by far the worst problem for me, and probably for all independent film makers, is when a movie you are making collapses. Apart from the loss of money personally, you feel terrible for everyone else who is working and relying on the film to pay the rent. You have to look yourself in the face and decide whether the film can be rekindled or whether you just close it down, take the hit and try and start again. *Wings of the Dove* is the only time it has ever happened to me, thank God. When my director made his appalling gaff, error or whatever, I had only three weeks to find another director. Despite the support of Harvey Weinstein it proved impossible. I called in the crew, gave notice, and wrote to or rang the actors' agents. People took it pretty well. My plan was to take it on the chin and try and regroup at a later date, say in six months' time. It took two years.

The day after the film collapsed I had already fixed to go to Paris with my wife to see our eldest son who was working there temporarily. We met up and sat down to lunch on the St Germain. Our son was admonishing me, saying I should sue the director and why should I always take all the responsibility if things really go wrong. He may have had a partial point, but I burst into tears and rushed out of the restaurant. Walking by the Seine to my hotel seeing Paris in all its glory, I saw it all in perspective. It's only a bloody film. I smiled to myself. 'It's only a bloody film' continues to lurk in the recesses of my mind. I find it helps.

You can't enjoy the whole process of being a producer every day. One of the worst things that has happened to me is the number of times when I bring on writers. I pay them, I cultivate them, I work with them, then it doesn't work out. Either the studio doesn't want them, the director doesn't want them, maybe I don't want them, or the work doesn't seem to work commercially. Having cultivated this person I then have to tell them that I don't want to work with them any more despite all the hard work they've done. Amazingly they don't like that. They don't think you're such a nice chap as you used to be. I find that difficult. Conversely there are many, many laughs along the way.

What would you say has been your best day in the job?

There have certainly been some wonderful ones. Winning the BAFTA for *The Madness of King George* was a fun experience but it didn't relate to watching the first rough cut, literally a day after finishing principal photography, and knowing that it was going to be a wonderful film.

If I had to choose one evening that shines in my memory, it would be going with a few of the crew and some of the actors to a remote Italian restaurant in Tuscany when shooting *Much Ado*. It looked to the Italian waiters that a coachload of loud-mouthed Brits had arrived to ruin the atmosphere of their little gem of a restaurant. The service was surly, and we were put in a corner. The wine flowed. Slowly, the mood changed. Pat Doyle the composer and Imelda Staunton the actress were at the front of the restaurant singing at the top of their brilliant voices. Others joined in. We were playing the Italians at their own game. They loved it. From then on grappa was on the house. I pinched myself. Here I am movie-making in Tuscany, my hard work has been done. Our completion bond had collapsed at one point, which meant that the film wasn't even insured for the first few days of shooting. Understandably, I kept this little secret to myself. That being sorted, little mattered, Ken Branagh was doing his normal classy job on the film.

I could relax and watch my friends put on this spontaneous cabaret for everyone in the restaurant. Weird, wonderful evenings like this are lifeblood for an independent producer. It's the bonus for all the hard — and not so hard — work.

So, is it a good life?

Yes, very much so, even including my involvement in the film business.

Dear Frankie was completed and received in Cannes in 2004.

Part Three

MID-ATLANTIC

The following group are British producers who have become perhaps even more familiar than those of the first Part with the London to Los Angeles flight schedules. That is to say that they are producers for whom the switch between US and UK production models (and even back again) has been decisive. JoAnne Sellar has traded London for LA but not her independence. Guy East and Nigel Sinclair are Britons who founded their own micro-studio spanning the Atlantic. Paul Brooks found the British scene too constrictive and made Hollywood his home. Barnaby Thompson went from UK TV to *Wayne's World*, but has lately devoted his energies to Oscar Wilde and the resurrection of Ealing Studios.

Take 8

JOANNE SELLAR

American cinema of late has produced few more admired auteurs than Paul Thomas Anderson, writer-director of *Boogie Nights* (1998), *Magnolia* (1999) and *Punch Drunk Love* (2002). His producer on those pictures was English-born JoAnne Sellar, who first found her way into the business through varied excursions into some edgy, off-beat and even ill-fated productions. Her experience on the abortive *Dark Blood*, a film beset by tragedy, might have been sufficient to extinguish the enthusiasm of a less hardy soul. Yet she persevered, with great reward. Her career in motion pictures began in London, under the sponsorship of a then-aspiring producer whom we have already met in this volume.

1. *'Queen of Gore'*

JOANNE SELLAR: I started out as an assistant programmer to Stephen Woolley at the Scala Cinema in London. Then Stephen left and set up Palace Pictures with Nik Powell. I continued programming at the Scala for about four years. I was into horror movies in a big way and I was nicknamed 'Queen of Gore' because I used to programme a lot of all-night horror fests. This was at a time when politicians were trying to ban what they called 'video nasties'. One night we showed Abel Ferrara's *Driller Killer*, which we got from New York, together with a whole programme of horror films, and sent out invitations to all the MPs who were trying to ban these films hoping that they would come and watch them. I don't think any of them had seen a horror film; they had based their arguments on hearsay. Obviously, nobody turned up — well, a lot of *people* turned up, but none of them were politicians . . .

It was really enjoyable at the Scala, finding films and coming up with fun programming ideas, but eventually I got bored and felt that someone new should come on board. I also really wanted to get into production, and by then Palace had set up a music-TV-video division. This was at the time of the music-video boom, so I went over to Palace and ran that side of the company. We had a sort of roster of directors, and we'd go out and sell them to the record companies. We produced videos for bands like U2, Elvis Costello and Fine Young Cannibals, and what we sometimes tried to do was to cross-over people and get film directors who Palace were working with to direct music videos as well. So Neil Jordan did a Pogues video, and Michael Caton-Jones did a video for Dusty Springfield.

In terms of producing, what was great about the music video experience was that I learned a lot. Often I would be producing two videos per month — they were always set up quickly, and so I was always dealing with different production nightmares. I would be given a week's or four days' notice and, for example, have to go and shoot the Pogues on top of a Gaudi rooftop in Barcelona . . . But that was a really good grounding in production. I would say the main difference between making films in England and America — or rather England and LA, because I think it's different in New York — is that in England, because the budgets are so much smaller, one really has to know the nuts and bolts of producing and be hands-on in order to be an effective producer.

I produced music videos for about four years, and then towards the end I was putting together a music television programme for Channel 4 that Roger Pomphrey directed, called *Beyond the Groove*. It was while I was getting the finance together for that that I came over to LA for an extended period, because the series was going to be shot here. And it was at this same time that the script of *Hardware* came to Steve Woolley and Nik Powell at Palace. The writer-director, Richard Stanley, had sent it to them, and they were interested in doing it. They knew I was a big horror buff, and because I wanted to produce films and not music videos, they sent the script to me. I knew straightaway that I wanted to make the film, even though they were making it on a minuscule budget. For me, it was the right time to move. So I got another producer on board *Beyond the Groove*, came back to London, and started working on *Hardware*.

HELEN DE WINTER: *Exactly how minuscule was the budget for* Hardware?

It was about $1 million. BSkyB, British Screen, and Miramax all put money into the film.

What was Richard Stanley's filmmaking background?

Music video — he was working with a company called Wicked Films. We shot *Hardware* on location at the Roundhouse in Camden Town, and we completely took it over, built all the sets there, and had our office in trailers outside. It was great — really hard but we had the best time making the film. We didn't have complete freedom because Miramax got very involved, though they were a very small company at the time. I was dealing with Harvey Weinstein the whole time, and it wasn't like it is now with all these other people around him — I think it was just Harvey and one executive.

   Given the budget we had, the film was pretty successful, and it got a proper US theatrical release and did well on video too. It also got Richard noticed, and we had some good reviews.

What was Richard like to work with?

Mad. He was the eccentric genius-type, with a crazy imagination. I thought the script was good, and his ideas were really good, but he was totally off the wall.

Had he storyboarded much?

Yes. He was obsessed with storyboarding and did the entire script — it was like his bible.

And did he follow those plans to the letter?

Pretty much. But we were doing some very ambitious stuff for the kind of money we had. The sheer number of effects . . . they were pretty sprawling and intense ideas. Most of it was shot in-camera, but we had Bob Keen's special effects company Image Animation on the film, and they did a lot of the gore effects. We had some great, great guys working with us — Steve Norrington built the machines, and we had the wonderful Chris Cunningham, who later directed amazing music videos for Björk and others. He would come in and work like crazy and draw amazing murals everywhere and then sleep at the Roundhouse. I think he was sixteen at the time — or at least it seemed to me he was sixteen. It was a really great group of creative people. And no one was doing it for the money.

Were you *paid?*

I got paid a pittance — looking back, it was a tiny amount of money. But at the time I didn't even think about it, I wasn't doing it for that reason.

After *Hardware* was finished I went back to the music side of Palace, and a woman called Leigh Blake came to me because she was putting a project together called *Red Hot and Blue*. It was an HIV/AIDS benefit record, using covers of Cole Porter songs. They had lost their financing so she asked us to help her produce a compilation of videos for the songs which were shown on Channel 4 and ABC. Then I went to Namibia to produce *Dust Devil*, written and directed by Richard Stanley.

Since Hardware *had made money, did you have a better budget for* Dust Devil?

We had a budget of about £2.5 million, maybe $4 million. So it wasn't like an automatic leap to £20 million.

But doubling your budget, that's pretty good. Did Dust Devil *attract the same financial partners as* Hardware?

Yes. Richard is South African, and he had grown up and spent a lot of his youth in Namibia, plus he had set the script quite specifically in Namibia, so that's how it all came about. Apparently Namibia is now a really up-and-coming location, I think they make a lot of car commercials there, but it's a beautiful country with amazing sand-dunes.

Was there an infrastructure there to accommodate a film production?

We took a lot of people from South Africa — Cape Town and Johannesburg — and people from England. Production went well, but during post-production Palace started going bankrupt, and things started getting scary because the company was falling apart and money was running out. Then Miramax didn't share Richard's vision of the movie. They saw the film as a more straightforward serial-killer movie in the desert, whereas Richard had a whole mystical/spiritual aspect of the story going on.

Were Richard's more mystical ideas for Dust Devil *scripted?*

They were, but I think you can read what you want on the page — particularly when you're in distribution . . . So inevitably Miramax were worried, because they weren't sure if they could market the movie. In the end it never really got proper distribution, so it was a shame.

Was Dust Devil *properly finished?*

It was, but only after it went through various post-production night-mares. I think Miramax had one cut of the movie, a shorter version of 88 minutes, which they released, and Richard had another cut.

How does a producer manage the situation when there is a critical difference of opinion between the director and a distributor?

One hopes that's a rare situation for all concerned. I think a producer will do everything they can to be the mediator or the person of reason, who goes to the distributor and tries to make them understand the director's vision. I see my role as being able to support the director and uphold their vision as much as possible, and get it on screen. But it's important when starting a movie that there are no grey areas. There has to be a happy medium at the outset between the distribution company and the director, and the distributors have to know that they can market the film to the public. With Paul Thomas Anderson, he's always made it clear from day one what he's doing — it was extremely clear what *Boogie Nights* and *Magnolia* were going to be. But these are the kinds of things you learn with experience.

2. Dark days

So in the wake of your first films with Richard Stanley were you also developing your own material?

I had optioned a script that I loved called *Dark Blood* by Jim Barton — interestingly, it was another film set in the desert. Richard Stanley went off to do *The Island of Dr Moreau* but I wanted to make *Dark Blood* and we got George Sluizer attached to direct. George had directed *The Vanishing* and at that point he was directing a remake of it in America, which I never quite understood . . .

Was Dark Blood *a horror film?*

No, it *sounds* like a horror movie, but it was a story about a couple who are on a second honeymoon, and the wife gets lost in the desert and ends up coming across a strange young kid living in the desert. The wife and the kid start having a weird sexual thing going on. Then the husband turns up, and it becomes like this bizarre *ménage à trois*. The script was set in south-west America, and at that point it was going to be a US production, so it made sense for me to come to LA, raise the finance, set up the production, and put the cast together — rather than trying to do it all from England. Palace had offices in LA, so I suggested I went over, and they were fine. And for me it was just like changing offices. So I moved to the US and I spent about a year putting it all together. I developed the script further, and then we got Jonathan Pryce, Judy Davis and River Phoenix attached. Then at Cannes in 1992 we put the money together, and got New Line to finance the film. So we went off to Utah, and shot there for six weeks, all of the location stuff. Then we came back to LA to spend three weeks shooting interiors that we had built on a stage. We had shot one day in LA, and then on the first night River Phoenix died.

It was a terrible, terrible tragedy . . . the most dreadful thing. He was such a lovely human being. River's death wasn't anything to do with the production — he had gone out and partied and stuff. But it was just an awful, awful thing to go through. It had been a fraught production, which it shouldn't have been as it was a simple script to shoot. But we had been in the middle of nowhere in Utah, and that kind of brings its own production nightmares — there had been a lot of flooding, and then some other fraught stuff that shouldn't have happened. But River was such a great human being throughout the whole thing.

I remember River's agent called me at four o'clock in the morning to tell me that he had died. And then, literally, within hours — I think by noon the following day — the insurance companies were calling me and saying, 'What are we going to do?'

Does production insurance cover a situation like that?

Yes, it does. There is a particular liability cover, one that not everybody takes out — and I had taken it as an additional liability, which was weird, a bit freaky. But we were completely covered.

I had to go to a lot of meetings, make decisions, be in complete business mode and keep all the emotion in check. We dealt with the situation as best we could, we went through different scenarios and conversations about re-shooting, keeping the stuff with Judy and Jonathan, but re-shooting the River scenes — which would have meant re-casting River's character and going back to Utah and starting again. What was so weird was there were mothers calling the production saying, 'If you're looking for someone, I have a son who looks just like River Phoenix' . . . these were pretty freaky phone calls, it was surreal.

So I was having to re-budget and work on all these different scenarios. Financially it seemed that the best thing to do was to abandon the film at that point, which was pretty awful.

Then the publicity was so intense and everyone wanted to talk about it all the time . . . and I just wanted people to go away. I went back to England for a while and, even there, people were still talking about it. So then I went off to Vietnam and Thailand for a while. At least if they were talking about it there then I didn't understand . . .

What happened to the rushes of Dark Blood?

The insurance company own the rights to the film, and I think George tried a few times to get the rushes back — but to do so he would have had to *buy* them back. For a time, George was trying to make a documentary, and then he asked me if I would like to try making the film again. Actually, other people have asked me several times if I would get hold of the rights and remake the film. But I just don't want to go there again.

Much later, people would tell me about the nightmares they'd had on different productions. Or I would get to the end of a shoot and think 'Well, no one's died, so . . .' But I think the experience strengthened me in many ways, as a producer and as a person.

After the Dark Blood *experience, how did you decide to carry on and keep working in LA?*

It was accidental, because when I came back from my trip after *Dark Blood* I heard that the director Clive Barker was interested in talking to me. I didn't know Clive, but I knew a lot of people who knew him through the whole Scala horror circle. And he said he was looking for someone to produce a movie he was going to do that was set up at Propaganda, *Lord of Illusions*, and he was interested in talking to me. So I met him, and he's the nicest guy in the universe, and I just felt like I should do it.

Clive is a creative genius and his ideas are his ideas — he has like a million ideas all the time — and that's what I get excited about, what's in a director's head and imagination. I like to work with directors who are really, really passionate about what they want to do, and then what spurs me into action is to find a way to make the process as hassle-free as I can, so that they can get on and make the film. It's the same with Paul Thomas Anderson — he writes everything into his scripts so it's all pretty much there apart from a few minor changes. This was particularly the case with *Boogie Nights* and *Magnolia* so when I read the first drafts I could see immediately what he wanted to do. I gave a little bit of input, and we had conversations, he asked me what I thought and changed a few things around but I wouldn't say I had a significant creative input into those projects. Though I remember him ringing and telling me about his idea to have frogs raining down from the sky at the end of *Magnolia*, and how it was going to be a huge scene . . . I said, 'You've gone totally crazy!' But there's the producer part of me that gets very excited. And with the frog scene I remember thinking 'How mad is that? And how brilliant would it be if we could pull it off . . .?'

Anyway, *Lords of Illusions* ended up with UA and it was a really good experience — we had Scott Bakula from the TV show *Enterprise*. And I think the experience of making that film really helped me get over *Dark Blood*, as much as I could.

3. Burt Reynolds didn't get it

How did you meet Paul Thomas Anderson?

I met him in LA through my husband, whom I had known for years before we married. He was the co-producer on Paul's first film *Hard Eight* and during that time I got to know Paul. Then when he finished the script of *Boogie Nights* he sent it to me. I knew the people at New Line and I also knew one of the other producers on *Hard Eight*, John Lyons — who at the time was primarily a casting director, though he's now gone on to produce a lot. John was going to produce *Boogie Nights* but because he hadn't done anything of that size, New Line wanted to have a producer on the film who had technical experience and confidence with that scale of production. So, since Paul and I had got to know one another, everyone thought it made sense to have me on board. Of course, after I read the script I put it down and said 'I *have* to work on this film' because it was one of those amazing, amazing scripts.

What was interesting was that Paul had written a short story about Dirk Diggler, and made it into a short film when he was twenty-five. So that's where it came from, and then the story just sort of escalated. Paul knew the world of the film because he had grown up in the San Fernando Valley and I think those films were being made all around him, so it was a fascinating arena for him. I was so inspired by the script that I just really wanted it to make it happen, so I got involved, and we made the film on a limited budget.

What's a limited budget in Hollywood terms?

We made *Boogie Nights* for $15 million, and that's tiny. I don't think we could have done it for less. It was a period film, a long movie, and it had all that source music that Paul had scripted. I would say ninety per cent of the music was written into the script, and that doesn't happen very often — usually a director will choose the music in post-production.

Boogie Nights was a big leap for Paul because *Hard Eight* had been made for $3 million. But Mike De Luca was an executive at New Line at the time and he was a huge, huge fan of *Boogie Nights*. I don't think Bob Shaye really wanted to make the movie. I mean, it's pretty out there . . . but Mike championed the movie through that company and protected Paul the whole way. Paul was so young and passionate, and as a director he really knows what he wants, which is great. There is nothing worse than working with an indecisive director, because that makes a producer's life very difficult and it wastes money. An indecisive director always wants to keep their options open, and so a producer ends up having to keep things on hold — locations, costumes, actors, whatever. And that means escalating costs. Whereas Paul knew exactly what he wanted, and I just had to go after it.

Did the completed film follow the script?

Yeah. Oh God, yes.

And how did you find working with Paul on this first occasion?

When I first started working on *Boogie Nights* I didn't really know Paul all that well, and I think he was very uncertain around me, because really I had come in to be the nuts and bolts and to get this project going. Paul had been burnt a lot on his first film, *Hard Eight* — he had various different producers, and at one point the movie had been taken away from him and he had to break into the cutting room to get his cut. So I think he was wary and very sensitive. Then during the process he saw that all I was interested in was the film, and that I didn't have a hidden agenda. Once Paul realized that my only agenda was to get this fantastic script up there on screen, and realized how excited I was to be making the movie — once he saw that I wasn't fighting with him and that I was trying to do my job and go out and get what he wanted to make his movie — then he completely trusted me. And with Paul, once he trusts someone you become part of his family. And then the whole relationship became really strong, we bonded.

On *Boogie Nights* we had a limited budget so there were a lot of compromises and we had to set parameters for certain things. Sometimes I'll have to fight with him and say, 'You can't have this because it doesn't fit in with the X-Y-Z . . .' If we have a fight he might see what I'm saying or I will try and find another solution to make it happen. But if we fight we make up. I can tell him how I feel and he can tell me how he feels. And since then we've really been a team.

How did you secure such an interesting cast for Boogie Nights?

A lot of the casting was due to John Lyons — we had a casting director on the film, but I think the strength of the cast came from John managing to pull in all those people. Also Paul writes with particular people in mind.

Did Paul have Mark Wahlberg in mind for Dirk Diggler?

No, originally we were thinking of Leonardo DiCaprio. And he had wanted to do the film but it clashed with *Titanic*. So he had to make a choice . . .

Is it true Burt Reynolds sacked his agent when he saw the finished film?

Oh yes, that's true. He totally didn't get the movie. Even when he saw it, he just didn't get it. So he sacked his agent, and then he went on to get all that acclaim . . .

What were your own feelings when you saw the finished film?

I remember seeing it for the first time with a huge audience, and people were really loving it. I worked incredibly hard on that movie, for eighteen months, so it's hugely gratifying to get that response. But when New Line tested the film, I think they had about five or six market research groups, and they were all appalling.

How do you test a film like Boogie Nights?

Well, it's totally the wrong film to test. I think the only films that test well are comedies and action films — so you can find out if a laugh is working here, or if the action is tense enough. But *Boogie Nights* wasn't that kind of film . . . Still, they tested it in LA and in the Valley. What made a difference was when the film got into the Toronto and

New York Film Festivals, because people loved it there — and that happened when they were doing all these test screenings and I think people at New Line were starting to panic, except Mike De Luca. We got very involved in the marketing, Paul was extremely involved — he designed the American poster. Then we worked with a guy that I know called Graham Humphreys who works for a big design company, and he came up with the cool 'Roller Girl' poster, which worked well in some international territories.

How successful was the film for you?

It wasn't hugely successful financially — it did pretty well. Once it was critically acclaimed it went on and made some good money — though I think it should have made more money. But because of the amazing reviews it launched Paul, in a way. So it was very exciting.

4. *A gi-normous script*

Magnolia *followed* Boogie Nights *pretty quickly. Was that the plan?*

Paul had told me about *Magnolia* and we had started talking about it when we were in post-production on *Boogie Nights*. He continued to talk about different scenes — including the frog scene — and we'd toss it around, and he'd been promising to show me the script for months. Then he delivered the script to me the week I went into labour . . . I received this gi-normous script that was about 190 pages long. When I read it I was very inspired by the story — in fact, it was like reading a novel. It's interesting because Paul made some adjustments but it wasn't changed in a major way — and the script became the film.

When the studio asked Paul to describe the film in two lines he would always resist, and instead he would talk about Julianne's character or Jason Robards's character, or individual scenes.

After *Boogie Nights* everyone wanted to work with Paul. There are many directors in this town, but not many have such a huge talent. And there are very few writer-directors, working from their own material, and here was this young kid . . . New Line obviously wanted to make Paul's next film and they didn't want him to go off and work with somebody else. Again, Mike De Luca was a huge champion so Paul wanted to stick with Mike but it was a lot of money for New Line to spend on a movie like *Magnolia* because it wasn't really a commercial movie. Ultimately it was all timing and we didn't intend for the film to happen as quickly as that. But what happened was that Tom Cruise had agreed to be in it, if we could film his scenes before *Mission Impossible* 2 started shooting. So, suddenly, we were like 'We have to do it now!' — we had to go into production straight away.

Had Paul written that part specifically for Tom Cruise?

Yes, and he wrote most of the characters pretty much for those actors who ended up playing them. Paul had met Tom Cruise when we had gone over to the London Film Festival screening of *Boogie Nights*. Tom was making *Eyes Wide Shut* and Paul went to visit him, and they talked about the possibility of working together, then Paul went off and wrote the part for him. I was thinking that Tom would never play the part — in fact I had convinced myself he would never do it — and then suddenly he was like 'Yeah, I'll do it.' I thought it was absolutely great that he agreed, because it was a pretty out-there role for him. Once Tom agreed the studio were more comfortable about giving Paul $40 million.

Did New Line ask Paul to cut the script down?

Well, they could have, but then he wouldn't have made the movie with them . . . There was definitely a lot of interest from other companies. But I don't think we really explored working elsewhere, because New Line wanted to make the film.

Did Magnolia *feel like an epic?*

Well, it was a huge production to put together. The frog scene alone was like a movie, it was $5 million-worth of computer and creature effects. I had my first child, and eight weeks later we went into pre-production, so in a way it was a horrendous production for me, because I had a new baby and *Magnolia* was such an enormous project. We shot the film for ninety to a hundred days. Then post-production was pretty quick for what it was, because we had to get the film out for Christmas time and for Oscar consideration. So I think we had maybe six months, which was pretty quick for a movie that felt like two movies. It was a pretty demanding year, to say the least.

5. *The English side of me*

Is Ghoulardi yours or Paul's production company?

It's a company for Paul and I to make his films. His father was a big voiceover artist in Cleveland in the 1960s, and he had a late-night horror TV show and his stagename on that was Ghoulardi. Paul is not into horror at all — which is ironic, given my tastes.

Originally Paul and I talked about putting more productions through Ghoulardi that he and I would produce. But ultimately it wasn't the kind of thing that Paul wanted to do — he wants to focus on his own projects. So after *Magnolia* I made *Anniversary Party* with Jennifer Jason Leigh and Alan Cumming. I had known Jennifer through Dylan, who was an ex-boyfriend, who was the editor on *Magnolia*. She brought the script to me and we made the film for $4 million with Fine Line. It was a really enjoyable experience and the first time I had done a movie that was shot on digital video. $4 million was a healthy budget for a movie on that format.

How does a co-directing team work? Did you liaise with one or both of them?

At first I thought 'Oh my God, is this going to work? It could go terribly wrong . . .' But it didn't. They had co-written the script and they were a collaborative team. Alan was away a lot during pre-production, so I would ask Jennifer a lot of questions about getting the production set up.

Then when both of them were on set, they were extremely creative. It helped that most of the cast were their friends, they had written the movie for them, so beforehand they had discussed the film with every-one. No one ever got into the whole thespy actor kind of thing, no one was improvising left, right and centre — they stuck very much to the script and they were very professional about it. They got the work done and were very responsible about the budget and schedule so it was great.

Right after that, Paul and I made *Punch Drunk Love* for Revolution. Mike had just left New Line and I don't think New Line got *Punch Drunk Love* so we went to Joe Roth who had shown a lot of interest in Paul and always has done. And Paul and Joe had a great meeting, so we decided to make the decision right there and it turned out to be a great experience — because Joe is hugely filmmaker-friendly and very, very supportive.

Do you have a deal with a studio?

We have a very loose arrangement with Revolution and they pay a very small overhead, for a small office with a couple of assistants, because that's how Paul wants things to be set up at the moment. I imagine he will take his next movie to them, but things change so much in this town, you never know. I have other things that I do separately from Paul, and then I have projects with him.

I'm pretty responsible to the people who have given us money to make our films, and that's probably one of my biggest strengths — in fact, I would say that one of the main stresses of producing is being fiscally responsible to whomever has given us the money. Paul is responsible in that way as well, but once a studio or company have committed themselves financially his big thing is 'Hey, leave me alone and let me go and make my movie . . . I'll make it for the money you've given me, but leave me alone while I'm doing it.' There are a lot of producers in this town who don't care about money or they don't care about their responsibility to the studio. I think there are some producers in LA who think 'Let's get some more money out of the studio.' Perhaps this is the English side of me — because it's so hard to get the money together and because budgets are so tiny in England, you can't go over budget. In England you have to be responsible to the bond company, and if you have a completion guarantor then you make sure the movie is made for within that price. I think that English sensibility has stayed with me, so no matter how big the budgets get I will always feel responsible to the people who are giving us the money.

Do you enjoy the producing culture in Hollywood? Do you prefer being in LA rather than England?

Pretty much. There is some back-stabbing and there are cliques of people, but there are also certainly producers and executives who are very supportive. If the opportunity came up to make a film in England I would think about it, but I enjoy having a bit more money to make movies — and the money is in the US. Having had some success here, there are people who are definitely more accessible. But, basically, you have to watch your back.

What do you mean by that?

I always feel that there's someone who wants to screw you over . . . there are a lot of people in this town who kind of, how do I say this . . . there are 'producers' who jump on to other people's projects and then suddenly become *the producer,* because they are a manager to an actor or this or that. I'm not saying this has happened to me, but I have witnessed it countless times. So the producer who has done all the hard work and developed the project all the way through and got the project ready for production suddenly gets shunted aside, because the actor — who is God, and who is worth millions and millions in box office receipts — comes along with someone who says, 'Oh I want to be the producer.' And then suddenly so-and-so needs a producer credit, and then you have all these people on board, and for the real producer it's like 'Well . . . yeah?' I think this happens a lot less in England — or perhaps it doesn't even happen in England. It doesn't happen much on independent films, it's mainly studio films where you suddenly have all these producers coming out of the woodwork. And it's kind of sad.

Do you schmooze and network?

Yes, but I don't do it enough. It's a side of producing I can't stand. I don't have to do it so much when I work with Paul, but I do on my other projects. Given what I've done to date, it's easier to open doors and I have connections with certain people, but it's still pretty tough being an independent producer out here. Having made *Magnolia* I don't sit around and look for projects that are more expensive — I'd rather make a $5-million movie written and directed by someone I admire, someone who I get creatively excited by, than make a big studio commercial movie like *Too Fast Too Furious* that I have no connection with, or ever will. I've been sent material like that in the past, and I was asked to come on to a big action project as a producer, but I couldn't do it . . . I couldn't go to work every day and work on that. I can only really do my job if I feel passionate about what I am doing. Otherwise I'd rather stay at home with my children.

If a stranger asks you what you do, how do respond?

I say I'm a checkout girl at Tesco . . .

In Spring 2005 it was announced that Sellar would produce Anderson's next picture *There Will Be Blood* adapted by the writer-director from Upton Sinclair's novel *Oil* starring Daniel Day Lewis. Meanwhile she was a credited producer on Neil LaBute's re-imagining of the horror classic *The Wicker Man*, starring Nicolas Cage.

Take 9

GUY EAST
AND NIGEL SINCLAIR

Esteemed ex-sales agent Guy East made his producing name with Majestic Films, in particular the successes of Kevin Costner's *Dances With Wolves* (nine Academy Awards in 1991) and Jane Campion's *The Piano* (Palme d'Or at Cannes in 1993). Nigel Sinclair represented the likes of Ridley Scott, Tony Scott and Sydney Pollack at the Beverly Hills entertainment law firm he co-founded, Sinclair Tenenbaum. Together, in 1996, East and Sinclair co-founded and ran the 'micro-studio' Intermedia Films, and went on a remarkable ride that included a merger, a huge flotation on the German Neuer Markt, and the auction of rights to *Terminator 3*, before they stepped down to 'retire' in 2002.

East and Sinclair are skilled executive producers, respectful of the specialized skills of the physical producer but no less proud of their own abilities as creative businessmen whose own skills are wrapped around the entirety of the filmmaking process, and just as essential to the film's ultimate success.

They are currently partners in Spitfire Pictures, Sinclair based in Beverly Hills and East in London. I spoke to them separately, and those conversations are interwoven below.

1. *Buy cheap, sell dear*

HELEN DE WINTER: *How did you get into the film business?*

GUY EAST: About twenty-five years ago I was a lawyer with a big City law firm, specializing in European law, and by chance I met Lew Grade. He suggested I leave the law and go and work with him at his company, ITC. I went to his office, and it seemed very glamorous and fun. And during the interview Lew said, 'Are you any good at buying and selling?' Well, since I was twelve or thirteen I had been buying and selling antiques, and when I was a student I started my own business. So that impressed Lew. In fact, I told him that when I was six years old we had a hazelnut tree in our garden and I used to climb the tree for the nuts, then weigh them on my mother's scales into half-pounds and pounds, put them into bags and sell them at the end of our road to passers-by, so I could use the money to buy tortoises. I was a lawyer with languages, but Lew was so amazed I had done that when I was six that that's largely what persuaded him to give me the job . . .

So I went to work for Lew and his team in international distribution, and I knew absolutely nothing about films other than that I enjoyed watching them. Initially Lew brought me in to do sales, so I was selling films to France, Italy and Germany. But I was their youngest chap, and Lew basically taught me how to sell films, he sent me off all over the world.

I worked with ITC for three or four years, then I joined Goldcrest and was responsible for all their international distribution. Jake Eberts was my mentor and he was very, very good to me. I spent seven years at Goldcrest and they were making Oscar-nominated films year after year. I worked on the distribution of *The Killing Fields* [dir. Roland Joffe, 1984], *The Mission* [dir. Roland Joffe, 1986], and *Hope and Glory* [dir. John Boorman, 1987]. Then as the production arm got into difficulties, I started to buy in films like *A Room With a View* [dir. James Ivory, 1985], *White Mischief* [dir. Michael Radford, 1987], and *Sid and Nancy* [dir. Alex Cox, 1986]. So I was buying blocks of international rights and then selling them territory by territory.

What skills would you say you developed as an international film distributor that proved useful to you as a producer?

GE: I have found myself becoming a producer by accident, but firstly I think the ability to buy and sell is crucial and because I have always instinctively been a buyer and seller, I guess that's my role as a producer more than actually physically organizing the film. Secondly, having 'people skills' is vital. Thirdly, having lived abroad in different cultures and speaking several languages has helped me choose films — I feel I know what people in other countries might like. From my point of view, how you present a film to the public in France, or why a German audience would go to see it, and how you persuade local distributors that you are going to do what you say you will with your project — all those things are relevant to producing.

I suppose the other thing I learned in distribution was the marketing aspect of a film. Can we actually sell this film? What kind of actors or director do we need to promote it? What tools can we give the local distributor to help him sell it to his audience? And how do we promote it in each and all of these countries around the world? I have always believed that in a production company you should have the influence of a marketing team helping decide what projects you make, because they are the people who are going to have to get the film into the cinemas, on video and on to television.

After Goldcrest I spent a year working for Carolco, learning how to distribute big action movies such as *Rambo III* [dir. Peter MacDonald, 1988] and *Total Recall* [dir. Paul Verhoeven, 1988]. Then I started my own company, Majestic Films.

Did you start Majestic because you wanted to produce as well as distribute?

GE: No. Having studied the industry very carefully, I realized that if you want to make real money in the film business then you need to be either a top star or a distributor controlling the rights and the cash, not a producer. In those days it was a fantastic business being a sales agent. You didn't have to put any money up for the rights. Producers would give you films they were producing for free, so long as you had the ability to travel round the world and persuade local distributors to give you a contract that said they would distribute the film. For example, a distributor would agree to pay you a $1 million advance and you could take that contract to a bank, who would discount it and loan you a little bit less than the $1 million, and you could use that money to make the film. I could earn ten to twenty-five per cent commissions for doing that. It was a staggering business.

When I set up Majestic, the bank could see that I had done this very successfully for Lew Grade, Goldcrest and Carolco, so they agreed to back me, provided I put up the overhead and showed them I was able to run the company for three years. I had built up a reputation that meant producers would bring me their projects they were trying to finance, so I would have a script with a star and director attached, and I would travel round the world pre-selling these projects.

2. 'More good' than you or I . . .

Is it fair to say that you developed a reputation for financing films that other people wouldn't?

GE: I just tried to do the projects I liked. So something like *Dances with Wolves*, which Kevin Costner had been trying to make for a number of years — well, when I read it, I believed in it fervently. I was also very lucky because my wife, Ruth Jackson, was a very successful filmmaker at the BBC, but she left to join me at Majestic, and she was a powerful creative voice in our decisions to go ahead on projects. Once we had committed, I would be selling the movie, trying to bring in the money for production, and working out how we could market and distribute the film. Gradually, almost accidentally, I found myself becoming a producer — because if you have sold your house to cover the overhead and have your own money invested, you do all you can to make sure the producer delivers the film on time and on budget — so you find yourself producing by default, not because you want to, but because you have to protect your investment and your business. You have distributors all over the world who are buying the dreams you are selling, because you are saying, 'We are going to make this film and deliver it in two years' time at a certain price.' They are paying you an advance. So in order to keep your business, you have got to deliver what you said you would deliver.

Why did you think you could finance Dances with Wolves *when no one else would?*

GE: Financiers perceived it as a tough call because it was going to be at least three hours, meaning fewer screenings than normal, hence fewer ticket sales. It was going to be directed by an actor who hadn't directed before.

And it was going to be subtitled, which is not something the US studios were fond of. But, coming from the European culture of filmmaking, none of that put us off.

I have always been fascinated with Native Americans. I also knew there was a script called *Geronimo* going around, and another about Cheyenne Indians being developed, so there was a mood in Hollywood. I also knew that the international market was intrigued by Native Americans — in Germany there is a total fascination, and there were several German cinemas that eventually played *Dances with Wolves* for a whole year without changing it. I also realized that Kevin Costner had the potential to be a huge star overseas — he had had hits in the US, but the international audience didn't really know Kevin yet. There was also a strong environmentally green movement at the time and I felt that *Dances* was a 'green' movie in the sense that it showed a successful native civilization which had been systematically destroyed by another. I also thought it was a fantastic love story with lots of action, and that it would be spectacular to look at.

So there were a lot of reasons which I thought could make this a successful film, and I was able to convince other people that this could be the case . . .

When I went to meet Kevin and his producing partner Jim Wilson, Ruth came with me. We were the only guests in a very old hotel in Cuernavaca in Mexico where Kevin was shooting *Revenge* with Tony Scott. The four of us spent an evening together reading through the script and projecting on to a white wall of the courtyard all the slides they had taken over the years of locations where the film was going to be shot, and some ideas for costumes. I don't think that anyone had previously sat down with Kevin and Jim for that length of time and gone through the details of their movie. Ruth was able to ask Kevin and Jim questions about how they practically intended to make the film, and how Kevin planned to direct it. At the end of dinner we were both completely convinced that they could make the movie.

There was one other interested financier, but when Kevin told me that he had pulled out, we immediately committed a large amount of money. Orion picked up the US rights and I asked my old friend Jake Eberts to come and help us with the financing. Then, as we now know, the film was very, very successful and it changed all our lives. It won nine Oscars, including Best Film, and I think at the time it was the fourteenth biggest box office hit ever.

So you bought back your house?

GE: No, I bought a much, much bigger house . . .

Presumably your pride in the film's success was based not just on the risk you took in backing it but also on the careful way you plotted its release?

GE: I believe it was the first independently distributed film to be released day-and-date across Europe and with properly coordinated marketing. For the first time, an independent sales agent set up a dedicated marketing team — led by Tristan Whalley — to supervise the booking of cinemas and organize all the marketing to support each territorial release. We had a print early enough to be able to privately screen it to the local distributors who had pre-bought it. They flew into LA, and they all agreed it was a sensational film. We decided to take the risk that we would win Oscars and planned the release dates very carefully around that happening. We had to get the film dubbed and subtitled ready for international release, and we had to think unusually carefully about how to do that because so many of the lead characters spoke in their native Lakota Sioux tongue and that would have been odd to dub. We also had to get all the posters ready, and the magazine and newspaper articles lined up, which are booked months ahead, with all the interviews done in order to get the film released at the same time.

The success must have made you a lightning rod for new projects?

GE: After *Dances*, lots of projects came to us, but at that point in my life I only wanted to help make films which I passionately believed could be successful. When the script for *The Piano* arrived at our office I gave it to Maggie Pope, who used to work with Ruth in development. Maggie came in the next day and said she had been deeply moved by it, so I immediately asked people in the office to stop work and to read the script. They all felt the same. It then took us nearly two years to convince Jane Campion and her producer to let us be involved. Eventually we made a deal with them to take on international sales. During production Jane wouldn't let anyone see the film, but she would send Ruth envelopes with tiny scraps of paper inside with 'Everything is OK' written on them.

Did that worry you?

GE: Well, Jane had persuaded the French financier CiBy 2000 to put up all the money and I was acting only as the sales agent on a commission, so our downside risk was very limited. I believed in Jane, she had great actors, and I knew the script was very powerful. One day a big envelope arrived and wrapped up inside in raffia were six photographs that were all absolutely beautiful. The first photograph I opened was of the piano on the beach, decorated with shells and Holly Hunter playing the piano with her daughter Anna Paquin doing a cartwheel. You may know the shot. I can be very emotional and I have to admit that I felt the tears run down my cheeks. I thought 'My God, this is going to be a beautiful, beautiful film . . . and a huge hit.'

How would you characterize the films you want to make?

GE: For me, the keyword is 'dignity'. I am really drawn to scripts where the characters show dignity. What I mean is that they are put in a situation where there is a tragedy or something very difficult happening around them— like in *Iris*, where Judi Dench plays Iris Murdoch, suffering from Alzheimer's. My mother died of Alzheimer's, as did the director's mother, as did Jim Broadbent's mother. So there was immense passion in the making of that film. But why I feel that film was so successful is that its characters find themselves in a very testing situation and they behave in a way which is 'more good' than you or I would be able to do in a similar situation. So Jim Broadbent's character, John Bayley, Iris's husband, has to look after her. And that's something that you or I might well run away from, but his love for her never wanes and he comes through adversity with great dignity. And Iris, one of the world's greatest users of words, handles her growing inability to remember words with the same courage and dignity. That, I think, is what can make an audience cry for joy, and I believe people yearn to see such goodness in characters.

3. The package

How did you first come into the film business?

NIGEL SINCLAIR: Initially I was an international business lawyer with Denton Hall Burgin & Warrens, the biggest entertainment law firm in London. Around 1987 I started focusing on the industry in California because it was the prime business activity, but when I moved out there I didn't practise as an entertainment lawyer — I was still a business lawyer. But I found that people would call me and say, 'So I guess you're a movie lawyer?' and I would say, 'Well, sort of . . .' and they would ask me to lunch and start talking about deals. So I started figuring out how to do deals, and that's how I built up an entertainment practice — just by going for it.

In 1989 I left Denton Wilde Sapte and formed my own firm Sinclair-Tenenbaum with Irwin Tenenbaum, who was Woody Allen's lawyer. We were a small firm of five lawyers that we gradually built up to sixteen. By 1995 Sinclair-Tenenbaum was the premier firm doing international and independent film deals.

Would you call yourself a creative deal-maker?

NS: I think I was an *original* deal-maker, by reputation, in the sense of coming up with innovative structures and ways for people to do things.

In the late 1980s and early 1990s there was a network of international companies that were heavily capitalized because of the privatization of European television. These companies had a lot of money, they were looking for films, and therefore the US studios were jamming them with packages. But many of these companies were trying to find other ways to secure major films — companies like Pathe in France, Constantin and Kinovelt in Germany, Entertainment in

England, and the big Japanese companies Shochiku, Toho Towa and Nippon Herald. These companies became the backbone of many movies. I would contact them and say, 'I have a client who's thinking of making a film. Would you be interested in being one of the founding partners in a package?' I would then bring two or three of the companies together. I worked closely with an agent called John Ptak at CAA, one of my best friends, and we teamed up with Guy East who at the time was my client. Together we became known as 'The Golden Triangle' because we put film after film together, and for many years at Cannes we were very present in the marketplace for high-end independent films. I had major corporate clients like Polygram and Village Roadshow in Australia, and the firm looked after lots of wonderful actors, including international stars like Anthony Hopkins, Mel Gibson and Gary Oldman.

The deals I made in the early 1990s were a very fertile time for me, and from that I got into being more of an entrepreneurial businessman, and that led to me becoming an executive producer.

Can you describe the process of packaging a film? In particular, what is the role of the actor/star?

NS: Film is big business, and successful actors have an agent, a lawyer, and sometimes a manager, who find their client work opportunities. Once the client decides they want to make a particular movie, the next question is 'What's the deal?' Making a deal for a superstar is a complex process because you're paying them $15 to 20 million per film. If you're a powerful star you may well be asking for more than just money — you might want some of the rights. There are all kinds of ways of being rewarded, and it becomes a lengthy negotiation.

Let's say you have a top screenwriter who's written a new script, in a similar genre to a previous hit, and they would also like to direct this movie. Say it's a project that could attract the likes of Jennifer Lopez. If I'm the writer's agent and I go to the studio, they will offer us a lot of money for the script up-front, but without a very good back-end for the writer — because writers don't get good back-ends. And they will likely pay *lip service* to the idea of my client directing but say, 'We can't guarantee it.' If, on the other hand, I can attach Julia Roberts by offering her the leading role — well, now I've got a script, a superstar, and a director — because Julia Roberts trusts the writer as the director. Then I will say, 'Well, I think I need a grown-up on the movie, so I will hire Ed Feldman.' Ed is a very famous line producer, a safe pair of hands who everybody trusts.

So, suddenly I've got a package that looks really attractive. But the studio is still going to give me a lousy deal. So say I go to Intermedia, as it used to be, and I say, 'Go raise the money by making pre-sales, I as the producer will go fifty—fifty with you, and you don't have to pay me anything up front until we've financed the movie.' Maybe we get pre-sales in France, Germany, Italy, Spain, Japan, and then we come back to the US not needing that much money, but we make a gross deal. So the jigsaw puzzle fits together. This way, maybe I've raised a hundred and ten per cent of the budget of the film, which means I've made a ten per cent profit going in, and as a result I've got much better deals in all these territories, and real ownership in the negative.

The disadvantages of this type of deal are that it's extremely high-maintenance putting the structure together — it's expensive with lawyers, you need insurance companies and banks, and you need to trust the people you're dealing with. You need to have the distributors, some of whom will let you down on the night and change the rules on the delivery elements. And you need to have Julia Roberts stay part of the package . . . All these different elements have to come together. But if they *do*, then you make *Braveheart*. The more upscale films have tended to fare better with independent deal-structures rather than the big popcorn films, because the popcorn films can take up to two years, just in the polishing and fixing of them for audiences.

What do you mean by 'polishing and fixing'?

NS: At Intermedia we made a film with Martin Lawrence called *National Security*, which turned out great — not a Shakespearean masterpiece but a really enjoyable movie with a great star. We set it up in a traditional studio way at Columbia, and they did $3 million of re-shoots. Every one of those films has re-shoots, the studio does extra work. And because it's their movie worldwide, they will keep on spending money. You wouldn't make *Bad Boys II* independently because you've got to meddle with the shot footage — it's got to be funny and hip and you've got to have those two guys looking good together and being great together, because that's what's selling the movie around the world. Whereas with the kinds of films I'm structuring, it's incredibly difficult to come back and say, 'The third act doesn't work and we have to re-shoot it tomorrow.' To make major changes would be very difficult and financially stressful. It's rather like building a house carefully priced to architect's plans. You can't change the house. Once we have designed the film to those specifications, *that's* the film we are making.

4. *Intermedia*

*Did your success with Majestic lead you to consider working for a
Hollywood studio?*

GUY EAST: No. I've always wanted to stay in Europe. Because of the
way I was brought up and my interest in languages, the market for me
is outside of North America — what the industry calls 'the rest of the
world . . .' However the big problem with being based in London is
how to get films made, so I realized that I needed to find a partner in
LA. It is surprisingly difficult to find a good partner because, generally, people who want to work with you are either effectively no more
than a post-box because no one is really going to take them seriously,
or they are using your contacts to increase their contacts and planning
to move on. So I was incredibly lucky, in that I was able to convince
Nigel to leave the law firm he had started and to co-found Intermedia
with me.

It was a very big, emotional and difficult decision for him, but
getting down to the bottom line, if you are a lawyer advising
entrepreneurs, you don't take their financial risks and thus you are
only ever going to earn your fees, however successful you are. I said to
Nigel, 'Look, I founded Majestic and now I have sold the company
and made an awful lot of money. You have been my brilliant lawyer
and with your advice I have made all this money and also got immense
satisfaction from the films we have made. Now you should come
round to the other side of the table and use your skills, contacts and
extraordinary ability to make and arrange film deals and actually earn
the capital you deserve.' Of course, you might lose everything, but
then you have everything to gain . . .

NIGEL SINCLAIR: After much heart-searching and agonizing I decided
to join forces with Guy and form Intermedia. But as we formed the
company together, we rarely disagreed over anything fundamental
so our relationship has been very . . . well, I guess apart from my
marriage, it's the best working relationship I have had in my life.

There is a certain energy that comes from having a partner in a
senior management team. If the two partners walk into a room, sit
down and say, 'This is the way it has to be, we both agree', then everyone knows it's checkmate — don't mess with it. Also, a lot of businessmen who have done what we've done go off the rails when they
get too much wealth and success, because this job is extremely intense
and it's extremely easy to be both flattered and humiliated on the same
day, and to lose your perspective. But if you have a partner who can

pick up the load or tell you if they think you're going over the top, if you have somebody you regard as your equal throughout that journey, then you have always got a counterpoint.

GUY EAST: I was confident from day one that we could be successful because we were skilled, we had the right relationships, we had good creative contacts who could supply us with commercial films, we had the right distribution contacts and we had the best banking contacts for private finance. I also believed that we would work hard enough to get ourselves out of any difficulty. What I didn't know was how successful Intermedia would prove to be.

With Nigel in Los Angeles and you based in London how did you build a company together?

GE: We had to work very, very hard. We worked twenty-four hours a day, seven days a week — and I mean twenty-four hours a day, because with the time difference, when Nigel was asleep I was working, and when I was asleep he was working. Email was invaluable, but we still spent hours and hours on the phone.

NIGEL SINCLAIR: We started the company with a couple of million dollars in equity that we both raised from connections and the strategy at that point was to spend some of our own money developing scripts to give us a power base within the talent community rather than just being a sales agency. I think our American-English connections enabled us to build a talent-friendly reputation and in the early days we had mainly second-look deals with Kate Winslet, Sydney Pollack, and Kevin Costner. But we were a small company living from hand to mouth, and in the early days we were producing four or five films a year ourselves and then distributing four or five more.

GUY EAST: I was able to concentrate on finding pictures in Europe and my wife brought films to us like *The Land Girls* [dir David Leland, 1998] and *Hilary and Jackie* [dir. Anand Tucker, 1998]. *Sliding Doors* [dir. Peter Howitt, 1998], the film that really got Intermedia going, was shot in the UK and was extremely successful.

NIGEL SINCLAIR: *Sliding Doors* was our first lucky break and came out of a deal we had made with Sydney Pollack's company, Mirage Enterprises. *Sliding Doors* did $50 million at the international box office and it cost $8 million to make, which is hugely successful. It took $21 to $22 million in the UK alone and that was just a great feeling.

Intermedia functioned like a micro-studio. We made high-end art films and occasionally crossover films. We made a profit every year, we paid ourselves. We were building up a library. Also at the same time we were a sales company, selling other people's films around the world, so for example we could sell Woody Allen's films — the whole run of them from 1996 to 97 onwards — for a sales fee. So we had that business to pay the overhead. By 1998 we were the premier independent sales company and, along with Summit, were probably the premier independent film supplier.

We developed a great relationship with Miramax — Harvey Weinstein really supported us. We made *Playing by Heart* [dir. Willard Carroll, 1998], *Enigma* [dir. Michael Apted, 2001] and *Blow Dry* [dir. Paddy Breathnach, 2001]. Miramax then got bigger and more complicated, but we owed a lot to Harvey in those years because he liked our taste and to him we were a very user-friendly group of people who tended to deliver quality films.

One of the key decisions we made was to start a marketing department under Paul Davis — it was unusual for a sales company — and actually spend a lot of money on marketing. We became known for marketing our films, for marketing our company — which is why, eventually, I think the flotation was so successful. So if you came to our offices in Cannes you would find lots of people there. Two-thirds of the meetings were with buyers who had already bought the movie and wanted to find out what the delivery and marketing plans were — an after-care servicing rather like buying a car — and only one third buying new movies. The effect of that for us was it made our clients very, very loyal to us because they felt that we had tried, and if the movie was a bit disappointing then we would give it the best position we possibly could. And if the movie was good then we really went for it.

How would you assess your ration of hits and misses commercially speaking?

NS: I think some of our films were disappointing. *Whatever Happened to Harold Smith?* [dir. Peter Hewitt, 1999] was a great idea, a great script — and you've probably never even heard of the film, right? I guess the most disappointing was *Blow Dry* [dir. Paddy Breathnach, 2001] because that was Simon Beaufoy writing about a national hairdressing competition coming to a small town in the north of England. Although it wasn't a bad movie it just wasn't what we all dreamed it would be, which was another *Full Monty*.

But others fulfilled their potential, such as *Up at the Villa* [dir. Philip Haas, 2000], *Sliding Doors, Hilary and Jackie*. They found the level of box office and distribution in line with their price. You expect those films to get an airing amongst a high-end theatrical audience, to have a very long TV life and a solid video life — which is exactly what happened.

5. *Flotation*

GUY EAST: Our belief was that if Intermedia proved to be successful for a period of time, then we would have to make a change to the company structure. You can't remain as a little company if you are building an inventory that needs exploiting. One of the lessons that I learned from Majestic is that if you want to get bigger you need more capital, because you must have more films, and that means taking on more development staff. Then, as the years go by, you have to reissue the films, and that means you need more distribution staff, checking the TV transmissions around the world and so on. At the same time, you still need to be buying and producing films. A film company that is engaged in all those activities has to grow. And Intermedia was doing everything. We developed scripts and financed films, we supervised production that we subcontracted out, we delivered and distributed all over the world, approved the marketing, collected the revenues and reported to partners. These are jobs that the US studios do with thousands of staff and we were doing everything with about a hundred people.

Was taking Intermedia public always part of your plan?

NIGEL SINCLAIR: Our plan was always to make some kind of re-financing in five years, except we did it in four. The flotation idea came along because everyone was going public in Germany and I was very friendly with Moritz Borman, who was an old client of mine.
GUY EAST: Moritz was a German producer living in Los Angeles, he was someone we got on with and he was also very clever at raising tax funds. The German Neuer Markt was buzzing and I noticed that several German film companies I knew well had gone public with high values.

We decided that we should merge with Moritz and thus form a new Intermedia which had offices in Munich, London and LA. We each had a track record of building up successful companies. We had a group of very successful producers who were attached to us through production deals, and Moritz had the tax fund that we had often used, so it was a natural fit. We made an attractive presentation as to how the merged company would be run and then later we had a very successful flotation.

NIGEL SINCLAIR: We were floated at a paper valuation of $1.3 billion on the terms of that exchange. We floated twenty-five to thirty per cent of our shares, and the price they have if you multiply by four comes to $1.4 billion. We raised about $160 to 170 million in cash equity. Then we expanded the company. We hired a lot more executives. Moritz, Guy and I were co-chairmen for two years. We had Basil Iwanyk from Warner Bros who came in as head of production, we had Jere Hausfater as head of distribution. It was incredibly stressful but very exhilarating.

GUY EAST: We built Intermedia into possibly the biggest independent film company in the world at the time. The other big 'independents' were New Line, who by then were part of Warners, and Miramax, who were by then part of Disney, so we were one of the only true independents.

NIGEL SINCLAIR: Once we went public, of course, it's another whole world of corporate responsibilities. You don't really own your company because it's owned by the public on the stock market, and you have all the challenges and tensions and so forth of a much bigger company.

GUY EAST: We had to make more films and increase our turnover and profit to sustain the growth that is required of a public company. That meant making bigger budget films. We had to make far more movies in LA because we couldn't make enough movies in Europe to satisfy the demand required by the market. So I couldn't, as I had wanted to do in the past, just make films about which I was personally passionate. We each had to make films that other people were passionate about, and films that hopefully made commercial sense. That's quite a difficult thing to achieve without the infrastructure of a studio. And that was a time when, in my opinion, certain films didn't work as successfully as they should have done.

NIGEL SINCLAIR: From 2000 to 2002 we made about fifteen big films: *The Life of David Gale* [dir. Alan Parker, 2002], *Terminator 3* [dir. Jonathan Mostow, 2003], *Adaptation* [dir. Spike Jonze, 2003], *K-Pax* [dir. Iain Softley, 2001], *K-19: The Widowmaker* [dir. Kathryn Bigelow, 2002], *National Security, Dark Blue* [dir. Ron Shelton, 2002], *Enigma,* and *Basic* [dir. John McTiernan, 2003].

GUY EAST: Sometimes at Intermedia we had seventy to eighty scripts in development, were being sent more than four new scripts a day to read and had several hundred million dollars worth of films in production in different parts of the world. I think at one point we started production on twelve films in a year. Effectively that means we had to have one film starting principal photography every four weeks. This was a staggering achievement for a company that had only about a hundred central staff.

In 2001 there was a huge amount of press that you were about to acquire Spyglass.

NIGEL SINCLAIR: In the fall of 2001 Guy and I decided that we had fulfilled our mission at Intermedia, should we say? And at the same time, Spyglass expressed an interest in acquiring Intermedia because they wanted our cash and our deals. The deal between Spyglass and Intermedia fell apart for a number of reasons — some of them to do with the change in the accounting rules that came about as a result of the controversies generated by Enron. The accounting principles for film are really designed for studios, and they don't take account of how independent film companies work with pre-sales. The accountants had all followed a certain practice, which we followed when we went public — which is that you recognize income when you deliver the film. Suddenly in 2001, faced with various scandals, they said, 'We can't do this any more, we're not going to recognize income until the first day of the film's release.' Take a company like Intermedia which has fifteen films to be delivered that year but which may not be *released* that year. Who knows when they're going to be released? *We're* not releasing them. They're going to be released by studios in the next twelve months. So it ripped all the income out of that year and put it in the ensuing years — which is why, this year, Intermedia is having a good year . . . But this happened to Constantin, and Kinowelt and every single company in the Neuer Markt and, by the way, a lot of other film companies in England as well. We didn't make our year-end numbers by a material amount, and our share price dropped. So the Spyglass deal collapsed.

6. *'We can't let this man down.'*

What was your role in bringing The Quiet American *to the screen?*

NS: Within Intermedia, the film was my personal project. It was something that Sydney Pollack had been working on from 1998. I remember meetings at Cannes, then it was going to get set up at Paramount. We had meetings when we were involved, then we weren't involved, then we lost the rights for a bit. Then there came a chance for us to get the rights and we went to Canal Plus. Buying re-make rights from a French film company is an epic process, because film in France has a precious value, sort of second only to human life. Canal Plus wanted to know what our credentials were, they were very sensitive about the terms, very concerned about making a short-term deal. And it's a Graham Greene novel — perhaps *the* Graham Greene novel. Eventually we managed to get these rights and go back to Sydney Pollack. Then Sydney got Philip Noyce interested, and it turns out that Phil always wanted to direct *The Quiet American* because fifteen years ago when he made a movie in Vietnam he bought a postcard in Hanoi and by mistake in the bookstore they put *The Quiet American* in his envelope. He went back to pay for it and they said, 'Keep it.' So he read the book and fell in love with it.

So we had a major director in Philip Noyce and major producers in Sydney Pollack and Bill Horberg, and a script that was a work in progress. Christopher Hampton then rewrote the script and we got Michael Caine and Brendan Fraser. What a great group of people to make a movie with. We started the movie before we went public, and without a deal. The budget was coming in at between $25 and $28 million and this was for a serious upscale drama. Then Phil Noyce committed to do the movie and turned down a huge offer for *The Sum of All Fears* before we had a business plan in place. I remember Guy and I saying, 'We can't let this man down.' So we went ahead and committed to make the film, come hell or high water.

Did you believe the cost exceeded its potential return?

NS: No. All financiers think all independent movies cost too much — it goes with the territory. But we had to balance the cost with the available finance. To the commercial movie business it's a Graham Greene novel, a period piece, plus the Americans were fed up with hearing about Vietnam, et cetera. So we had to get all these people to agree on deals. I got out all my old lawyer skills, got some high-priced lawyers together, and we said, 'Forget all the usual precedent deals. We're going to have a formula. Brendan Fraser got this much in his last movie, Michael Caine got this much. But everyone is going to be a shareholder in this money, pro rata, the rest of it is deferred, and then you are all going to participate in the movie on the same basis. Intermedia will pay our fees in exactly the same way and so will Mirage. This is the only way we can make this film. There is no other way, because there is no more money.'

Sydney showed great leadership. And eventually they all agreed. But I have to say that Phil Noyce and his lawyer Sam Fischer set the gold standard because Phil accepted much less than his studio deal. And then, of course, when we finished our job, Mirage's job began, which was to produce this movie in Vietnam. And I should say they did an unbelievably good job of bringing this film in on budget and on schedule.

What then happened was that Harvey Weinstein came back from his illness and became very focused on revving his company up and winning some awards. *The Quiet American* didn't test very well. It seemed to us at the time that, had it been five years earlier, Harvey would have spent a lot of time on it. But I don't think it was a case of Harvey not liking the film — I think it was a case of not quite knowing how to market it. That year Miramax had four out of five Best Picture nominations, so there just wasn't the psychological shelf-space to focus on it. And it wasn't until Michael Caine kind of claimed the film as his rightful ground that it received its due — because I thought *The Quiet American* was the best film we ever made. In the end it was a shame that Harvey didn't have more time to think about it, because I think if he had put his heart into it he could have made it do $45 million at the US box office, and he could have got a Best Picture nomination. Michael Caine got a Best Actor nomination, and I was very proud of it.

7. *Pay day for everyone involved*

Was the decision to make Terminator 3: Rise of the Machines *a creative or business decision?*

GUY EAST: *T3* was obviously part of a huge franchise and we needed bigger and bigger movies. Ironically, very big budget movies with a big star and a franchise are often easier to finance than very low budget movies like, say, *Iris*. So here was a company making *Terminator 3* and *Iris*, two films that couldn't be more different. We each had a good relationship with Andy Vanja and Mario Kassar. I had worked for them several years ago at Carolco.

NIGEL SINCLAIR: I also knew them from way back before Intermedia was formed. We persuaded Mario and Andy, who controlled the rights, that they would be better off making the film with us. We made a deal with them, and with Moritz Borman masterminded the deals with Schwarzenegger and the director, Jonathan Mostow. Then Guy and I left Intermedia, and Moritz took over and arranged the finance and supervised the film.

GUY EAST: Several US studios wanted to pre-buy the rights to *T3* because it's a huge tent-pole movie. We were able to successfully pre-sell the rights to Warner Bros in North America and to Sony internationally.

Why was Terminator 3 *so expensive?*

NIGEL SINCLAIR: I think it was properly priced. It was a $150 million-plus movie so that's a lot, even for a sequel to *Terminator*. But all sequels are expensive. This particular film was competing in a special effects world up against *The Matrix Reloaded* and all the other special effects films, so the effects had to be perfect. So you've got the most expensive special effects you can imagine. And the acquisition cost alone — there was $20 million sunk in this movie before we even started buying the rights. Then it becomes the pay day for everyone involved; everyone is expecting to get their cash up front this time. It's all about the star being in the movie. You get an expectation from the star that things have to be a certain way or the star will bail out.

Did you have to guarantee Schwarzenegger's fee up front?

NS: Yes. It's common knowledge now that the rate for top stars doing a sequel is $20 million. It's widely known that Tom Cruise has been paid $30 million in the past. So what would you ask for if you were Schwarzenegger? You'd ask for more than $20 million, because you would say, 'This is a sequel that is a guaranteed piece of business.' You know the film is going to do $150 million in the US and you know that in foreign it's going to go through the roof. Indeed, it went off the clock in Japan and Germany.

Can stars' fees keep going up in this way?

NS: Until it reaches a natural limiting point when the studios crack. I think that if you look at the business in the 1920s and 1930s, there is a comparison. The stars get bigger and bigger and bigger, then they over-price themselves, then they change the way they make deals . . .

8. Back to basics

So you created Spitfire to retire?

NS: No, to change hats . . . we've created Spitfire as a vehicle for Guy and I to produce films with a team of younger people. We thought 'Well, just for a few years, until our kids finish school, let's just focus on producing a few movies and lead a quiet life.' We left the board at Intermedia. We fulfilled our goals, we had a fascinating time and we had quite a ride.
GUY EAST: Now at Spitfire we have gone back to doing what we love doing which is trying to find the treasure, to develop ideas and screenplays about which we are passionate.

GE: The marketplace has been so difficult that our view was in the low cycle we should be concentrating on developing material. Then, as the market begins to improve, we will be in a position to go back in with some really good screenplays that we hope will attract interesting talent.

What's wrong with the marketplace?

GE: In the economic downturn around the world, the big companies who advertise on television have reduced their budgets. The result has been less and less money coming into commercial television stations, so they are short of funds. Parallel to that, there has been a proliferation of pay-television channels around the world, so now we have more stations but less money. This is why you have been seeing more and more reality television programmes, because they cost so little to make and get reasonable ratings whether they're about gardening, cooking or redesigning your home. Some of them like *Who Wants to be a Millionaire* and *Big Brother* are big hits. As a result, television stations have stopped pre-buying films because they're too expensive.

The cycle is beginning to change and advertising revenues are increasing. But whether it will ever really be the same, I'm not sure. The economic revival of independent filmmaking depends in part on whether audiences want to go back to watching films transmitted on television — which they are less accustomed to doing at the moment — or maybe buying DVDs to watch in their own time on the small screen will save the day.

But we have had to reduce our film budgets, so I think the industry is simply going to have to agree to earn less up front — particularly famous actors — and share more in the profit points of success, if any. I think also we will probably have to use more digital film processes and find cheaper ways to make films. It will be tough for a young producer starting out now, but I am feeling more optimistic than I did two years ago. Fortunately Nigel and I have made some money from the business and are able to invest in the development of ideas we feel passionately about.

NIGEL SINCLAIR: I'm producing *No Direction Home: Bob Dylan* with Martin Scorsese and Jeff Rosen of Grey Water Park, Susan Lacy of American Masters, and Anthony Wall at the BBC. At Intermedia I was introduced to Jeff, who is Dylan's manager, and he was looking for someone to finance the definitive documentary about Dylan's life. I have been a Bob Dylan fan since I was fourteen. So I was in New York and we had dinner with him and he was talking about this project and how he was looking for the production financing — this was after Intermedia had gone public — and I said, 'You're on, let's do it.' After I left Intermedia I bought them out of the project and took it with me.

How did you get Scorsese on board?

NS: He has always been a fan of Dylan's music and he's recently done a music documentary about the blues, plus he's a major documentarian. And Jeff was looking for somebody of sufficient stature that Dylan would trust and feel comfortable letting it be that person's film. Needless to say, Marty fulfilled both those criteria in spades. And I think dealing with a legacy like Dylan's, you couldn't have a younger person doing the film. You need to have somebody who is a veteran, who has been through the journey of being a creative artist and celebrity, and can bring a wisdom to that.

A lot of our projects now — unlike when we were at Intermedia and trying to feed a machine — are raw ideas, really early development. But we only get involved in projects that, frankly, we personally want to spend time on. We're not interested in making a film that has no clear creative purpose. It's about taste and interest. Making money takes care of itself. If you think about making money, you won't make money. If you focus on the work, the money follows.

No Direction Home: Bob Dylan premiered at the Toronto Film Festival in September 2005 before its broadcast transmission by PBS in the US and the BBC. In 2006 Sinclair delivered *My Generation: Who's Still Who*, a series of theatrical films and TV specials about the Who directed by Murray Lerner.

Take 10

PAUL BROOKS

British-born, Paul Brooks is now living and working in Los Angeles and London. He is of a generation of British filmmakers who emerged in the early 1990s and experienced a certain frustration at his native industry's struggles in — or perhaps indifference toward — making pictures that could satisfy the multiplex audiences. Now, as a US-based producer, he has certainly succeeded in that task. I caught up with him at his office in LA.

1. *Just do it*

PAUL BROOKS: My two great loves have always been architecture and film. I guess my passion for films started after seeing *Mary Poppins* when I was six years old — watching Julie Andrews slide backwards up the stairs and thinking 'How cool is that . . .?' After leaving London University, I first went into property development, made a lot of money, then contrived to lose it all . . . but I remember I ultimately reached a point that culminated in me coming out of the cinema after seeing *Last of the Mohicans* [1992, dir. Michael Mann] and finding myself feeling exhilarated but also incredibly depressed that I wasn't part of the world that had made that film. I realized I had reached a point where I *had* to make a film. I knew I wanted to produce and I figured that meant finding a script I liked and putting it all together.

HELEN DE WINTER: *Did you know anyone in the business?*

No one. But I started putting the word out and six months later I was shooting a film . . . I know it sounds a bit Californian but it's happened to me this way over and over again — which is that if you decide to do something and you just put it out there, then stuff happens. Logically, it shouldn't. But I was so driven and I realized if I didn't do it then I was never going to do it.

As it happened, someone in my office knew a producer called Gary Sinyor. I met with Gary and his director, Vadim Jean, and they brought me a script called *Leon the Pig Farmer*. I thought the maths looked OK, the downside was reasonable, and we went out and made the film for £150,000.

What were Gary's and Vadim's backgrounds? What convinced you, given your lack of knowledge about making films, that as first-time filmmakers they knew what they were doing?

Well, Gary had written the script and Vadim was going to direct and, very candidly, when I met them I thought that they were both so energized and bright that they probably had a reasonable shot of making something decent. I tend to take a simplistic view of things, which is that if someone has a lot of energy about what they are doing and they are bright and smart, with their ego reasonably under control, then they probably have a reasonable chance of success. I think Vadim had made corporate videos . . . but I don't think I even looked at them. Truthfully, I thought they had a funny script that was cheap to make and was going to provide me with a way into an industry I had wanted to be a part of my whole life. So it was simple, really.

How did you put the deal together?

Basically the money came from private investors — through personally knowing people who might fancy it as a fun business proposition. At the same time I did a little bit of due diligence; I dug around to find out what I could about the business and I realized the film was likely to have a limited appeal in the international marketplace because it was culturally specific — which did indeed turn out to be the case. But I believed it had a real shot at finding some success in the UK, relative to the cost of the film. *Leon* was a parochial Jewish comedy and in the UK the Jewish community is very assimilated and familiar — and the film was very funny. So that was how it evolved — we worked out a financial structure that was, I suppose, quite sophisticated for a little film — but it was the only way we could do it at the time. Then we made a very good sale to Channel 4 Television.

You got a lot of press attention when the film was in production. Were you thinking early on about the value of good publicity?

We didn't engineer that, but I think, given the collapse of film production in the UK at that time, people just responded to the fact that we had jumped in and were getting on with our film. The extraordinary thing is that there was a point during production where we realized we were the only film shooting in the UK. This was at a time, in the British film industry, when raising £150,000 was harder than raising £10 million.

When the film was released theatrically it took $1 million at the UK box office, which, at the time, for our little movie, was OK. Then we had healthy sales and rentals on video. So, ultimately, the film was successful relative to its cost. The investors got their money back, plus people got paid some of their deferrals. So, we got the job done successfully enough for a number of people.

So how did you build on your success with Leon the Pig Farmer?

Over the course of the next three to four years I was deluged with scripts and I developed and put together a bunch of similar low-budget films on the same basis. I had set up a company, Metrodome Films, with some partners, and we floated the company on the London Stock Exchange. It was the first time that a production company had been floated, even though we did so for a tiny amount of money. We sold off I think around twenty-five per cent of the company, and raised about 1.5 million, so it wasn't a great deal of money, but I think at one point later on we were capitalized at around £20 million.

How did the market find that value?

By putting a finger in the wind . . . At the time there were a few small production companies like us, but we were the only one that floated. We worked out what we thought we could raise and pushed ahead with it but ultimately our problem was that we were always under-capitalized, so we ended up turning the business from a production into a distribution business — where we were still under capitalized!

Production in the UK is a tough business and to be financially successful you need to blend distribution with production. We put money into the development of scripts and money into covering our overhead costs but gradually we became focused on turning the business into a distribution company. Truthfully, over time, I became increasingly frustrated with the way the British film industry operated. It was tough because we were always making films without enough money so there was never quite enough to get the right effects or to do the things

1. A band apart: Lawrence Bender (right) with Quentin Tarantino circa *Pulp Fiction* (top).
2. Cubby Broccoli (right), probably the most famous independent movie producer of all time, confers with his Agent 007, Sean Connery, c. 1963.

3. Bond co-producers Barbara Broccoli and Michael G. Wilson, here relishing the red-carpet part of their demanding job.

4. Stephen Woolley, expressing himself on set for his directorial debut, *Stoned* (top).
5. Working Title co-producer Tim Bevan and director Sydney Pollack on location for *The Interpreter* at the United Nations, New York, 2004.

6. Eric Fellner with Working Title colleague Liza Chasin on location at Lake Tahoe during the shoot of *Smokin' Aces* in November 2005. Photograph by Jaimie Trueblood (top).
7. Alison Owen on the set of *Sylvia*, overseeing the work of director Christine Jeffs and cinematographer John Toon.

8. Stephen Evans in conversation with Helena Bonham Carter and financier David Wickens in the penthouse of the Danielli, Venice, during work on *The Wings of the Dove*.
9. JoAnne Sellar with Paul Thomas Anderson on the set of *Magnolia*

10. Paul Brooks on the set of *Hellion*.

11. During the filming of *Fade to Black*, from left to right, Oliver Parker (director), Barnaby Thompson, Diego Luna
12. Mike Medavoy: The Man From Shanghai. (Photo by Gene Page)

13. Jennifer Todd (standing) and Suzanne Todd (seated) with John Cusack on the set of *Must Love Dogs*.
14. Robert Shaye in relaxed pose (left)
15. The Professor: James Schamus

we really wanted. And yet here I was in the business of trying to make commercial films.

I think it would be fair to say that at that particular time the UK film industry was not necessarily geared towards wanting to make commercial films — nor indeed is now — and I think that's one of the key problems in England. I believe there is a cultural predilection towards certain types of films, driven by what the critics think rather than what audiences want. For the critics, I think that by-and-large filmmaking and film-going in the UK is more of a culturally defined experience. I can't articulate it and I could ramble on about how it's got something to do with a difference between the generations, or class structure and I could come up with all sorts of sociological observations that might be complete nonsense . . . but at the end of the day, if you look at the reviews, I think there are critics in the UK who are very patronizing about commercial films. And I believe this has a negative impact, one that the British film industry could do without. Whereas over here, in the US — while one is trying to make films that one hopes one is going to be proud of — at the end of the day I don't run a charity, I run a business — however much I love movies. And I think that's the crucial difference between the UK and the US — not that the American critics are any kinder! Which is not to suggest that there aren't commercial filmmakers in the UK, because there are, but, rather, that fewer commercial entities and individuals exist in the UK while film continues to be perceived to exist within a cultural and not commercial framework.

If you look at those of us who started in the UK business at the same time, there was myself, Danny Cannon, Paul W.S. Anderson and Jeremy Bolt, Stephen Norrington, et cetera — and we all ended up making films in the US, because we either couldn't find the scripts we wanted to make at home, or we knew that, frankly, we were trying to make Americanized versions of British films and that was a mistake. So we all started thinking, 'Let's jump into a pond where we can make the films we want to make. We might get it wrong but at least this is a landscape that understands what we want to do and where we believe we can raise some money.'

So six years ago, on Christmas Eve, I said to my wife, 'I'm going to move to America in ten days.' I had to see if I could make films there. Ultimately I had to do it, I had reached a point where *not* doing it wasn't an option any more. It was that simple — though at the time I also saw it as part of an organic process that had started when I reached fever pitch and decided I wanted to jump into the industry in the first place. As I had grown up loving American films, ultimately I just wanted to try it here — plus I had to — this is where the industry is — full stop. I now divide my time between the craziness of LA and London when, frankly, I just need to be home and walk in the rain in Regents Park, or listen to some miserable cab driver whining about football and politics. I need to have that and without it I don't think I would enjoy this town nearly as much . . .

I love LA, but it can be a very difficult place in many respects. The business is brutal, attitudes are brutal, and you have to know how to deal with them. I think that to deal with them in isolation without being able to — and this is going to sound *very* wanky — *contextualize* one's life outside of LA is tough — and more than ever my Englishness is very important to me . . .

What's so brutal about the business in LA?

Well, everything in LA — or at least it *feels* this way — is about the film business. Which is great, and I'm not complaining. But, truthfully, when I'm here my weeks are consumed by, understandably, the film industry. Now, that's what I always wanted, but the reality of that is that even weekends — aside from going to the gym, spending a bit of time in the garden or having brunch with friends — are spent reading scripts; which I am absolutely not complaining about! So, it's really a six-day-a-week existence here and it's very, very cutthroat here. But the great thing about LA is that it's a town of possibility. Anything is possible here, and you can bang down any door and get in. Whereas, back home in England you can be whomever you are but it still takes at least five weeks to get into the BBC . . . I'm being flippant — and actually David Thompson is a terrific bloke and very accessible — but in LA people want to get things done — and that doesn't mean there aren't still politics or personality issues et cetera. But the fact is that I came out here and within six months I was making a film which, again, seems kind of impossible — because I didn't know anybody. But Vadim Jean and I had a project called *The Real Howard Spitz* and we wanted Kelsey Grammar for it, and we sent it to his excellent agent, Scott Lambert, and six months later Kelsey was doing the film.

2. *Outrunning the self-doubt horse*

Did The Real Howard Spitz *get distributed in the US?*

We sold the film to Live, who are now Artisan, and they flipped it to the Fox Family Channel. But it was a good start, because it meant that at least I had got a film made, and connected with a couple of agents, William Morris in particular, and this enabled me to start conversations. So when I arrived here it was just about getting the train moving. To me, that's what the film game is all about — from getting the film moving, getting other people to jump aboard, down to just getting on a plane and going to LA, while being as focused and strategic as possible in what one is doing.

There has to be an element of — not necessarily blind optimism but certainly a kind of misty optimism about what one is doing. I think that, like many producers, I am obsessively positive and will not entertain a single negative thought in any area of my life, particularly film — I simply will not do it. I have always had a capacity, which I hope will stay the course with me, to get up and get on with things and pull projects together and learn from setbacks or disappointments. I've always ridden my self-confidence horse just ahead of my self-doubt horse. The self-doubt horse has always nipped at the tail . . . but I am just brutally optimistic and I do think that is typical of producers in general because the game is so tough.

After *The Real Howard Spitz*, I put together *Shadow of the Vampire* [2000, dir. E. Elias Merhige] as an independent production using pre-sales, and thirty per cent of our budget was 'soft money', subsidy money. One of the benefits of coming from the UK is that one is used to utilizing soft money opportunities. Before I came on board *Shadow* there were people who had been trying to put it together for ages. Whereas I looked at it and felt I really knew how to put it together. I also believed that there would be a real appetite in Europe for the film, and thank God I was right, at least at the pre-sale level. Then Lions Gate came in and it was put together in the classic way.

Given the financial difficulties of financing films in London did you not come to LA and think 'I want a deal with a studio'?

No — although I would never have got one anyway. But one of the great things about being an independent producer is that at least one has more of an ability to influence what one is doing, whereas at a studio level, my observation is that increasingly a producer is looked upon as excess baggage. You get something started and then essentially you hand it over to them and their money pays for everything. The studio vetoes or approves the director and then often money is thrown at the problem. Whereas at an independent level, because there's never enough money to make the film, the independent producer is always trying to figure out ways of doing things — and that means having to be creative every step of the way. For me it's just a more stimulating way to work.

When I first arrived in LA I was then just trying to use or adapt the same systems I had employed in London. Not too long after arriving here, I came to Gold Circle — for a while they were one of my consultancy clients and then a couple of years ago I took them over. At that point Gold Circle were making different kinds of movies. The first film I brought them was *My Big Fat Greek Wedding*.

3. *My big fat hit*

Greek Wedding came about because, on the back of doing *Shadow of a Vampire* — which I had put together for Nic Cage's company, Saturn Films — the film had opened a bunch of doors, and one of those doors was to Playtone, which is Tom Hanks and Gary Goetzman's company. Playtone sent me the *Greek Wedding* script and I read it one Sunday night — which is when I end up reading most scripts — and I was crying with laughter off the page, I thought it was the funniest script I had ever read. So I met the writers and star, Nia Vardalos, and I thought she was an extraordinary personality and it seemed to me that this was a once-in-a-lifetime thing — which is a dangerous thing to think . . . Playtone had been developing the script for a little bit but, again, it was a tough one to put together for a variety of reasons. What happened, though, was that Playtone brought in HBO for fifty per cent of the budget, I brought in Gold Circle for the other fifty per cent, and we made the movie. And the rest is rather delightful history.

Can you account for the success of the film?

It was one of those extraordinary things where we got lucky every step of the way. To my mind it was a terrific script with a terrific actress that ended up being a terrific movie, and that doesn't happen very often. So from my point of view it was really an example of a kind of half-blind optimism that ultimately paid off. On top of that, I had a particular view about how to release the film. But what's remarkable is that to date this is a movie that cost $5 million to make that is going to end up taking theatrically something like $370 million worldwide. And that's just extraordinary.

Didn't the North American distributor lose out on a chunk of profits because they capped their revenue?

Gold Circle held the North American theatrical rights and the foreign rights. All that happened was that we hired IFC, for a fee, to book the theatres. Bob Berney was working for IFC at the time and I thought that Bob had done a very good job on *Memento*. Then we and Playtone put together the creative campaign, though Playtone really took the lead on that because I thought they had a great take on how it should be. Gold Circle put up all the P&A costs and we hired Paula Silver, ex-head of marketing from Sony, to be the grass roots' marketeer. The truth of it is that we very much distributed that film with Bob. We effectively took over the practical distribution some two months in when Bob left to join Newmarket. IFC did an excellent job booking the film into theatres and Bob had some excellent strategic advice at certain points but ultimately I was just so convinced that the film was going to work and so kept writing all the cheques.

What gave you that instinct?

At every test screening the audience reaction was huge — I mean, the scores were incredible. Twice the film tested in the mid-nineties, and you rarely see an audience react like that. So for me it was a bit of a no-brainer, it was obviously going to be huge at the box office — except when I say I *knew*, I mean I knew it was going to take $20 to 30 million . . . I had no idea it was going to take around $240 million theatrically in North America.

What happens when you are on that rollercoaster helping to drive a massive success?

The whole thing was fascinating. And so surreal when it happens to you, after you have stood on the sidelines watching other independent films take off — like *Four Weddings and a Funeral* or *The Crying Game* or *The Blair Witch Project* or *The Full Monty*. Suddenly, there you are, thinking 'Jesus, I'm in the middle of the biggest storm of my life.' And what was also fascinating to me was that at each step of the way I would have a particular point of view about whether we should do this, this, or this, based on what I thought was going to happen, and I saw it pan out as I thought every time; not as a function of me being brilliant, but rather I just had a very clear view of how it was building.

Such as?

Well, for example, I took the view that as long as we continued to aggressively support the film then we would withstand what I described as these tidal waves of blockbusters that were coming out every weekend and going up against us. We knew we would get splashed by them but we kept bouncing back and increasingly my view was if we could just get to August then we would have a huge vacation movie. I was convinced that *Greek Wedding* was the all-time family holiday movie and that's exactly what happened. Over one weekend alone in August we took more than $14 million, after being in the theatres for months.

How did you structure your advertising campaign?

We spent in an extremely focused way, but we aggressively supported the film. At the end of the day we spent over $20 million supporting the movie in advertising but that $20 million spend compared with our approximate $240 million box office take is nothing. The ratio was a staggering success.

How creative were you with the advertising campaign?

I can't over-emphasize Playtone's involvement in this but we were very well prepared and having done a ton of preview screenings we tried to be as imaginative as possible. We had some great sponsorship partners like *Brides* magazine and *Bed, Bath and Beyond* and so on and so forth. But the crucial thing was that we sent the actors, Nia and John Corbett, out to all the key cities to do intensive media campaigns. They would go in and do radio interviews in the morning, then television interviews, then editorial for magazines, and talk to newspapers. And that rarely happens on small movies. But we would bombard key cities with coverage. And when we saw any softening over the following weeks — I remember Boston was softening — so we sent Nia and John back out. Overall we refused to stop because we were so obsessed with the film and we refused to acknowledge that it wasn't going to keep on playing.

Is that the normal progress of a blockbuster?

Oh, no. It's completely contrary to it.

So your screen average kept on increasing?

Yes, or at least held, but everything about the film's success was completely atypical. We were always looking for ways of refreshing the advertising campaign. So we started off very much pushing the film as a 'family' movie, but then there was a point where we decided we should push it as a 'date' movie. And then it was the 'summer' movie. I was on the phone with the Playtone guys every morning of every single day of the week and we'd be asking each other what we could think of or try to come up with to keep the film going. We were absolutely obsessed with trying to make sure that there was nothing that we had missed.

The ride was extraordinary, because I remember doing the sheets — and at this point it was late spring — and I remember thinking 'We are going to get to $60 million on this film.' Then I thought 'We're going to get to $80 million . . .' And then, my God, watching it make $100 million was incredible.

Is the $100 million mark a symbolic number in LA?

Absolutely.

Your phone must have been ringing off the hook?

Well, the curious thing was . . . yes, people love to see success, because we are in the hits business and ultimately it's such a tough industry that despite all the jealousies people here actually enjoy and appreciate a successful movie — because it validates what we are trying to do. But the reality of it for me was that we were all so consumed by the progress of the film that to some degree other parts of the business got sidelined — or, to put it simply, they stopped. Because we never stopped. Once we crossed $100 million we were wondering if we could get it to $150 million. And then it reached $170 million and we thought 'My God, we could hit $200 million.' Then it was 'Holy cow, it's not stopping at $200 million!' I remember talking to HBO who are our domestic TV and video partners on the film and they were saying, 'Where do you think you are going to get to?' I said, 'I think we're going to get to $240 million.' That was when we had just got past the $200 million mark. When I considered where the trajectory was going to go, my feeling was that the film was going to trail off as gradually as it had built itself up. And again, that's exactly what happened.

Did you oversee the release of the film in other territories?

Yes, and the strange thing about overseas was that even when the film had taken $50 or $60 million in North America we never really had more than one serious bidder for the film in each territory — even up to the point where the film had taken $100 million. In the end we ended up with terrific distributors in all territories but it was certainly a curious process. For example, we didn't have a single bid in France until much later. There were buyers abroad who weren't interested at all. But in the UK we had Entertainment looking after the film and they are, in my view, probably the best independent distributors in the world. It took $22 million in the UK, a very decent hit. They knew exactly how to do it, when to do it. If they had delayed by even three months maybe the movie wouldn't have done half the business . . . they just nailed it, and that was very exciting. The thing is, at the end of the day, one is still a Brit, home is home — and for me it was huge and exciting releasing that film with Nigel and Trevor in the UK. It's terribly indulgent of me to say this — but there was something very exciting for me about going back to the UK and having a successful film. It was a nice thing to take my mum to the Odeon cinema in Swiss Cottage and see the movie with her . . .

It was a moment in time. The film worked out and there seemed to be an appetite for it. A year later, who knows? A different actor, who knows? Different films competing, who knows?

It wasn't like there was a war going on, and you can say, 'Well, people wanted to go and see a light film, a good piece of family entertainment.'

There were a lot of big movies around at that time, but not many romantic comedies — and so I think there's where the luck kicks in. In that moment in time all the planets aligned. That's where one has to acknowledge that good fortune plays a part in one's life. The trick is to make sure that one is playing the game sufficiently to take advantage of the moments of opportunity as they crop up — to recognize when you are on the lucky horse and keep riding it. And one thing that I think we did quite effectively with *Greek Wedding* was that we rode that horse into the ground. We rode it till it was dead.

But is there also a sense when you've had a massive success like that one that you might not have another one?

No, because I absolutely know I'm not going to have another one like that. There is no way that is ever going to happen to me again — that I can make a $5 million movie that is going to take $370 million worldwide. So it's quite easy for me to accept that. The challenge for me is to try to have other movies that are successful. Then again, if I had another success like *Greek Wedding* I would officially be the luckiest man on the planet . . .

Do you mind me asking if the phenomenal success of the film made you all millionaires?

It would be fair to say that Playtone, HBO and Gold Circle are all very happy with their respective takes . . .

When you have had a blockbuster, does that change things for an independent producer?

It actually hasn't changed anything for me in terms of the way I am trying to run the business. I have this concept of an independent multiplex model, of which *Greek Wedding* is an extreme validation. But I am really trying to do more of the same — make movies that I think are commercial but for low-to-medium budgets instead of making them under a studio construct. I am kind of still caught up with *Greek Wedding*. I'm hoping that there will be a sequel and we're going to try to do the stage musical, so ultimately we hope it's going to become a brand that will be around for some years to come.

Perhaps, ironically, I'm even more stressed than ever in terms of performance anxiety. I keep telling myself that I need to do more, because I need to establish a body of work and prove certain things to myself. Certainly all the pressure is self-imposed.

But there must be plenty of people you couldn't talk to before who you now have access to?

I guess . . .

So the success of Greek Wedding *must have transformed your working life?*

Well it certainly makes life a little easier in this very tough town although everything is temporary!

Hasn't there been a moment for you when you thought 'I've arrived'?

Not even remotely — I think producers are all absolutely riddled with insecurity notwithstanding their drive or maybe that's why they're driven . . . But people were very sweet and flattering, because I suppose there were a few people who knew that I put a lot on the line to release the film. And if the film hadn't worked, the company would have been shut down. So there were people who knew I had risked everything.

Was the risk at the outset or throughout the process?

The major risk was that the movie opened in theatres and took $2 million. But later there came a moment where we had spent $8 million on P&A and the film had only taken $9 million. So, quite rightly, my head office was getting concerned, and I had a job to do to persuade them to keep pumping money into the thing.

How did you assuage their fears?

I just managed to persuade them that we had something special and to look at where we were going on screen averages and consider people's responses to the film. And, thank God, they were brave enough to continue supporting it because that was an absolutely crucial moment. Then, fortunately, we started getting separation pretty soon after that in terms of spend and box office take.

So, I think a few people in town had heard and understood that I gambled on my instincts and that at a crucial moment it paid off. And while on the one hand people recognize, as I do, that the experience was lightning in a bottle, I think it's comforting for people to see an instinct pay off. That creates a hope that maybe it will pay off again in the future to whatever degree. So you start getting phone calls from people whom you would never have spoken to two years ago. It was very flattering. In the meantime, truthfully, I've probably got two minutes left of my fifteen-minute burst of success, so now I need to make sure that I push on and get other stuff done.

4. *O lucky man*

What is the corporate structure of Gold Circle?

We are a production, financing and distribution boutique, for want of a better word.

Do you read everything that comes in?

No, we have a coverage system, which is imperfect, but it is what it is.

Does your own taste in scripts drive the direction of the company?

Yes, absolutely, for better or for worse.

Haven't you now made about six or seven films with Vadim Jean?

I think we live in the kind of the world where there is the cult of the hot new director and everyone is always looking for that new guy to helm a film. There are also a lot of British directors who spend time on the golf course, if you will, practising their swings . . . and I am someone who happens to think it actually takes time to become a complete director although there are always talented exceptions. Vadim is someone I happen to believe in. I think that *Jiminy Glick in Lalawood*, the film we have just made with Vadim, is terrific — bold and different. Personally I like to work with bright people and I think Vadim is very bright.

But overall with directors I try to take a more measured view of the world. For example, we are doing this film *White Noise* with a Brit director, Geoffrey Sax, who is an absolutely first-class filmmaker. And while he might not be twenty years old he's been doing great work. He directed a contemporary version of *Othello* for British television with Christopher Eccleston which was astonishing. He's been a high-end British television director for years, and is someone who I believe is so ready to make a great feature film.

Are your projects still low-to-medium budget or are you planning to take a risk producing bigger films?

Generally I am risk-averse, other than those moments when you simply have to roll the dice. But I try and do it off the most carefully constructed foundation I can. Given my first career, my background in property, the key for me is if I'm going to roll the dice I have to know that if it doesn't work out it's not going to take me out of the game — although I broke my own rule here with *Greek Wedding*! As a producer I have got to be able to take the pain but it mustn't destroy me. Essentially I am in the low-to-medium budget game, so that's films that cost between $5 million to $25 million. We will do bigger films, but it's got to be the right set of circumstances. At the moment we are talking to studios about co-financing some bigger films but in the main my taste and interest is for comedies — any kind of comedies — and what I term 'adult horror', which are, I hope, like the smart, sophisticated and scary movies in the genre such as *The Others, Rosemary's Baby* and *The Sixth Sense*. I don't have a natural appetite for teen horror but I do like those movies where there is a compelling supernatural element because it's part of who we are. *White Noise* is without doubt the scariest script I have ever read. So those are the two genres that interest me, and I suppose in the middle of that I tend to like, and I am probably boringly old fashioned for saying this, but inspirational and feel-good stories — basically anything where I am fundamentally moved — because I love going to the movies and when I am a punter I like to laugh and cry. That's why I do this job, so that's my complete agenda.

So you don't have a desire to strike out and produce a $50/60 million movie?

Not at all. Or if I did then it would be using studio money rather than our own money or at least co-financing with them.

Is it a fraternal business? Do you know other producers?

There are good people and bad people, and truthfully I have always been a little bit of a loner, a little bit of an outsider. It's not that I mean I have never felt that I could have belonged to any club, but more that I have always felt that I was the guy knocking on the door to get into the club. That's just some curious childhood insecurity thing . . .

Did you think that while you were working in the UK?

Absolutely. But it's just me . . . it's a personality trait.

Do you network? Are you invited to premieres and parties?

Yes sometimes, but I tend not to do it to be honest. I don't get invited to that many! I know that's what I should do, but don't do here, is to get myself around a lot more. That's mainly because I want to spend time with my family. I know it's a fault on one level, but I am just not prepared to sacrifice family life for a faster track somewhere.

What is it that you particularly like about producing?

The biggest kick — and *Greek Wedding* is the best example for me — is having a point of view about something and then being right. Believing in a script — particularly when others don't — believing in a director when others don't, and believing in an actor when others don't. Believing in something and seeing it work out how you thought it would is incredibly exciting.

And now you are making deals with studios? Will that change or alter your position as an independent producer?

We're having all sorts of conversations with studios, but no, I'm not ceasing to be independent. It's more a case of continuing to feel my way around the business and trying to make decent films. That's my absolute ideal and sometimes you get it right and sometimes you get it wrong. In an ideal world I would make say six commercially driven movies a year . . . But ultimately it's a crap-shoot, it always has been and always will be . . .

Do you think the UK can ever have a sustainable film industry?

I think there is a sustainable industry there, but I also believe that people just have to have a perspective on it that makes sense — which is that the language of film is American. The world wants American films, full stop. That's the gig, that's the game. That doesn't mean people can't make terrific films in the UK, indeed they do, every year. But people also have to re-adjust their expectation levels. I think there is enormous pressure, with lottery cash, etc., and the idea that we're going to compete with America . . . Why say all of these things? The truth is the world is never going to want British films to the same extent that it demands American films — just as there is never going to be a huge demand for French or German films. However that doesn't mean that each of those local industries can't and don't produce strong movies that are sustainable in the market, and some of them have quality commercial lives. My point is I think that the UK shouldn't be trying to necessarily march to the beat of Hollywood's drum but do their own thing and that's to make films that are culturally relevant but also commercial. Ultimately, it's just about making good movies and realizing that we can never have a massive industry in the UK . . . we just can't, so it's pointless trying to build a huge building for which there are never going to be enough tenants — if you will forgive the rather obvious property analogy. The UK would be much better off building lots of really good little buildings each year that there will be a strong appetite for.

What about entrepreneurialism?

There are some very talented people working in the industry back home, but I think many of them are always having to work with one hand tied behind their back because the landscape doesn't provide for a particularly entrepreneurial approach. The size of the UK market indicates what sort of industry or landscape is possible, and the marketplace isn't there in sufficient size for the number of films that people want to make in the UK. I was struggling in the UK and I have had some success over here, and that's completely as a function of the different landscapes. LA is a place where there are, simply, so many more doors to knock on.

Are there any frontiers in terms of what you want to do?

Oh God yeah, that's why we set up an office in the UK. I'm trying now to get more access to a new generation of British writers and directors who have grown up with American films and who, I think, are capable of delivering more and more commercial material. I go back to London again next week and I can't wait, I love it. But if it all ends tomorrow it's been a great ride, and I can completely recognize how fortunate I have been.

Since *Greek Wedding* Brooks has signed Gold Circle to a two-year First Look deal with Universal Pictures. *White Noise* (which opened to $24 million) and *The Wedding Date* were released under this deal. Brooks has *Slither*, *Hellion* and *Griffin & Phoenix* in the can with *Because I Said So* (starring Diane Keaton and Mandy Moore) set to begin shooting in December 2005. The 2006 production slate includes *White Noise 2*, *The Waiting*, *My Sassy Girl*, *Seether*, *A Haunting in Connecticut* and *The Winged Boy*. The *Greek Wedding* musical didn't happen and a sequel is still being discussed. Paul now officially regards himself as the luckiest man this side of Primrose Hill . . .

Take 11

BARNABY THOMPSON

Barnaby Thompson began his career in the UK TV documentary sector, yet became an apprentice in screen comedy for Lorne Michaels, one of the contemporary legends of American television, who extended his *Saturday Night Live* empire all the way from New York to the Paramount lot in Hollywood. Thus Thompson became an integral part of a movie franchise machine that begat hits of the order of *Wayne's World*. Still, Thompson returned to the UK, co-founded Fragile Films, and made a wager on the appeal of an emergent girl band that paid excellent dividends at the box office with *Spiceworld*. On a different tack he has produced two well-received adaptations of Oscar Wilde with director Oliver Parker. Thompson has since gone further in reviving one of the greatest names in British cinema, Ealing Studios, not merely as a facility but as a fully operational production entity.

1. 'Wouldn't it be fun . . .?'

HELEN DE WINTER: *When you started out, did you have a vision in your head of what a producer did? Did you have role models in mind?*

BARNABY THOMPSON: Like all these things, when you start, you don't know anything. I think I was always naturally drawn to 'Old Hollywood', in the sense that all my references have tended to be shaped by the likes of Preston Sturges and Billy Wilder, *that* kind of world. And the kinds of producers I was drawn to were of that era too.

In other words, the 1930s and 1940s. What is it that appeals to you there?

The idea of the impresario, the showman . . . The fundamental role of the producer is to create an event, and those guys did that to the nth degree. It's about making the film that you are doing be the *most* important film that's going on at that moment. It's about making everyone who is involved in it feel it's important, then it's about making the audience feel that this is an event. That's a real trick. You see it today in guys like Scott Rudin or Jerry Bruckheimer, they are geniuses in terms of creating events. You can like their movies or not, but you can guarantee that everybody *knows* about them. You can talk to a distribution guy in France and he will be getting calls from Jerry Bruckheimer to find out what the weekend's grosses were, or what are his plans for the campaign. That level of attention to detail is what really makes a movie work, not just in terms of marketing but in terms of the creative side. David Puttnam, too, was very good at making people feel as though they were making a special film.

I remember coming into this business in the mid-1980s and my three heroes, as it were, were Jeremy Thomas, Michael White and Chris Blackwell because they were all guys who, creatively, had really put on a show. Plus, they were financially astute and they were impresarios. The one man who has done incredibly well in the independent world — even though the films he's made have been by no means commercial, and that's just his taste — is Jeremy Thomas. What Jeremy did with *The Last Emperor,* which was to take a fundamentally arthouse movie and put it together in the way he did and make it such a big hit, was a fantastic achievement. He owns all his films, he controls all his films. And I think that's what you try to do. That's what Goldwyn did, and that's what Selznick did. It's a combination of a creative instinct and entrepreneurialism.

When I first started I was like everyone else, I wanted to make a movie for creative reasons and I thought 'Wouldn't it be fun?' Then you learn that in order to do it properly, you have to raise significant sums of money, so you have to become a businessman. Because if, later on, you're looking at a statement and you see a lot of money go out in one direction and not much money coming back to you, then the next time you're negotiating those deals you've learned that much more about how to construct it so that you keep as much as possible.

2. *A Damascene moment*

How did you start?

I left university in late 1983 and in the summer I graduated I went to Pakistan and Afghanistan with two friends, a camera, and a book called *How to Make a Film*. This was during the Afghan/Russian war, and we made a documentary about Afghan refugees in Pakistan. It was an act of absolute madness, based entirely on naivety and ignorance. When I came back we put it together and sold it to Channel 4. I then worked for a producer in London as a runner-assistant for a few years and then in 1986 I started my own production company, World's End Productions, where I was making documentaries — they were my bread and butter — and trying to develop movies.

Then in 1990, more or less out of the blue, I got a call from Michael White who had become a friend of mine. Michael had been working with Lorne Michaels, creator of *Saturday Night Live* and Lorne had just signed a deal with Paramount. The idea was to take people from *Saturday Night Live* and build movies around them for Paramount. So Lorne had decided in his infinite wisdom that he wanted to hire someone who was outside of the Hollywood loop and Michael suggested me. So I was plucked from obscurity to go and run Lorne's movie division, in New York initially.

Surely you weren't that obscure? You had produced the short Dear Rosie *directed by Peter Cattaneo, who went on to make* The Full Monty. Dear Rosie *was nominated for an Oscar.*

Dear Rosie was a film I had finished just before I went to work for Lorne, so he hadn't seen it, he had no idea. A friend of mine, Peter Morgan, who was the writer, brought me an idea for a short film and back then British Screen, as it was called, and Channel 4, had a programme for funding short films. We interviewed a group of directors and Peter Cattaneo was someone who came in the door.

Why did Lorne Michaels want someone 'outside of the loop'?

God alone knows . . . and I didn't want to know! But when I met Lorne, we got on very well, he offered me the job, I moved to New York and spent two years there, then I moved to Hollywood and lived there for four years.

What were you actually doing?

Essentially I was a creative producer, because the business side of it was taken care of by the studio, so my job was working with the talent to develop and mould stories, and then make sure that we got it in the can. Both my parents are journalists so I came from a media background and I always felt comfortable with story and ideas — that was always the thing that drove me initially. So if I'm in a room with a writer kicking around ideas that's where I'm happy.

What made us unique was we were working from the power base of *Saturday Night Live* whereas most producers are out in Hollywood looking for ideas, or competing for the next big spec script, or wining and dining fancy directors. We were very much a producer-driven comedy unit. Lorne was, and is, a huge figure in American comedy, and for me it was a great playpen. The studio knew we would deliver a certain kind of picture and deliver it well, so they gave us an enormous amount of freedom. I had Alan Ladd's old office on the Paramount lot, and it was a fantastic experience because I got to work with some of the funniest people in the world — Mike Myers, Dana Carvey, Dan Aykroyd, Chris Farley, David Spade, Adam Sandler, Bonnie and Terry Turner who are now huge TV writers. We made a series of comedies, the first was *Wayne's World*, which was obviously a big success, then *Wayne's World II*, *Coneheads* and *Tommy Boy*.

So all in all the SNL/Paramount experience schooled you as a hands-on producer?

I have always been hands-on with everything. I'm training myself now to be less hands-on. But on a film like *Wayne's World*, I was in the room for virtually every word that was written, I was there every moment it was being shot, and I was there for about seventy per cent of the time it was being edited. So I was all over it. I'm not saying I wrote it or I directed it, I was just there.

It's very hard to make films and it's a lot more fun being in a full cinema than one that's two-thirds empty. I think if you have gone through the process in America for any length of time, when your whole future is defined by Friday night . . . My own road-to-Damascus experience was at a preview screening of *Wayne's World* in Manhattan. It was a cinema with about fifteen hundred people in Times Square and the audience was laughing and laughing . . . And the idea that we had created this thing that gave people so much pleasure was just fantastic.

In a funny sort of way, working for a studio was like working for the BBC in the old days because they take care of a lot of the detail. Hollywood is the club and because of who Lorne was, I was very lucky, because I was inside the club. It's very difficult to explain the experience of *being* or *not* being in the club, but you know it when you are in the club. In Hollywood there are about thirty people who really matter and it's about access to that world, and what you learn in that environment. Whereas I could have spent fifteen years working in Hollywood a bit further out, and never got the opportunity to see the machinations of power and learn what I did, so I was very lucky.

But you chose not to stay there?

My wife comes from New York — LA was never in the brochure for her. We were there for the riots, the floods, the fires and the big earthquake in 1993, which was very, very scary. We would be in restaurants afterwards and there were aftershocks and the whole restaurant would shake and there would be people running from the place screaming and others carrying on as normal; it was freaky how matter of fact some people were about the chaos around them. So coming home was a lifestyle choice. Hollywood is fantastic but it's a one industry town and it's a little bit like the court of the Borgias, it all gets exhausting after a while. So my wife and I were very drawn to return to England.

3. *What you really, really want.*

How did you set yourself up as an independent producer?

My friend Uri Fruchtman, who, like me, had a background in documentaries, was calling me up and saying, 'Come back to England, Labour are going to get back in, there are going to be incentives for the film business, it's all going to start booming here . . .' So Uri and I set up Fragile Films.

I think that in the UK the financing is more elaborate, and because you are putting a film together independently you are not just dealing with one person saying, 'Yes, we want to make the film.' But we were very lucky at the outset because Uri has a connection to the music industry and early on one of the people who called us was Simon Fuller, an old friend of Uri's, who had a band called The Spice Girls who had just had a number one hit with 'Wannabe'. Simon said, 'We really want to make a movie with them, would you be interested?' So we met with Simon and we met with the girls. I think as a filmmaker you are influenced by half a dozen movies, versions of which you want to make. One of the movies I wanted to make was *A Hard Day's Night* which was very much a part of the tone of *Wayne's World*, and when I met the girls it seemed like an opportunity to make that movie. We decided to make that film when the girls were one-hit wonders, so it was based on instinct, really. If they had crashed and burned after 'Wannabe' I suppose we would never have made the picture. But the important thing was that amongst ourselves, Simon and his brother Kim who wrote the script, we sat in a room and said, 'We're going to make this film.' And we set about to do it. And then every step of the way they got bigger and bigger, so it was lightning in a bottle really. The money came together incredibly easily because the budget was quite low and Stewart Till who was then running Polygram 'got it' immediately. So we did a deal with him before the script was even finished, which meant we were going to be OK in terms of covering the budget. In terms of our deal with the Spice Girls, we partnered with the girls and it worked out great for all of us, because it meant we all kept ownership of the film. It grossed over $90 million, so for a film that cost about $6 million that was a lot of money. For Fragile, on every level, positioning ourselves economically, it was a gift.

Is that how you have since proceeded? Has your company been supported by your own money or the profits from your films?

We've been lucky because we've had some hits, and we've made some money. So, on the whole, what we do is we plough some of that money back into the development of new projects, and hang on to the copyright of ideas and projects for as long as possible — because that's really what raises one out of the primeval swamp, one's ability to own one's own intellectual property.

So can you explain your connection to Ealing Studios?

Ealing Studios was bought by four of us — Uri, myself, Harry Handelsmann who has a company called the Manhattan Loft Corporation, and John Kao, who is a new media guru from San Francisco. We have now folded Fragile into Ealing so Ealing Studios owns Fragile Films.

Is it fair to say that the acquisition of Ealing is something to do with your coming closer to fulfilling your role as an impresario?

Yes. I had a moment on *An Ideal Husband*. Oliver Parker, who adapted and directed *An Ideal Husband* and *The Importance of Being Ernest*, is one of my oldest friends, we literally grew up together, and *An Ideal Husband* was a film we put together absolutely as a team, every step of the way. It was selected as the closing film for the Cannes Film Festival which was a fantastic thing. So you go up the red carpet, it's us, the cast, a sunny evening, there are thousands of people. And you get to the top of the stairs, and there is a moment when an arm comes down and the director and the cast go forward and take the applause of the crowd, and I found myself on the other side of the aisle.

It was in that moment that I realized that the nature of being a producer in today's world is different from what it was. You have a choice: you can make a career — and it can be a very nice career — aligning yourself to a particular director or directors, and you can be their guide. Or you can *build* something. I don't think I would have done it had Ealing not come along. But when someone came into my office and said 'You know, they're selling Ealing Studios . . .' it was such a marvellous, romantic notion, owning it — I went there on a whim. It was my dream, but it was really Uri who made it happen. He brought Harry in and made it real.

But it just seemed to be an opportunity to build up an English studio. There's never going to be a UK studio like the American studios, but I think that the idea of building something that becomes a home for talent and is already a name that exists in people's minds — and if it's a name that we can then expand and reinvigorate — I think those are exciting things, and that appeals to me in some empire-building part of my mind. It's no coincidence that the most powerful companies in showbiz are the studios. A studio is a place, a community, they have the facilities for production and distribution and they have the finance to do it. That system works. I think it's inevitable that to be a really successful and solid company you need all those things.

It would be great for us to get into distribution. Making sense of all that is obviously complicated, but I think that's where you want to be heading. We have set up two companies, a property and facilities company and a content company. We've set up a TV division and that seems to be going well, and we've now folded Fragile in so that becomes the film arm. I think, so far, so good. It's difficult to build companies, particularly in this country and this business but if the wind blows in our direction I think we have a real chance. The fantastic news is, people really care about Ealing Studios, and amongst people in the business there is a real warmth towards it, people are willing us to succeed. I don't know what is the exact science of building a studio but when you look at what Michael Balcon did when he started Ealing, that was to build a group of people who were there for a long time. My model is very simple — if we can have a group of directors, a group of producers and a group of writers who one gets on with, where you all see eye to eye, then that's the basis of a studio.

When I was working at Paramount, we would start with an idea, take it to the studio, and they would say 'Yes we can sell this', or 'No, we can't.' At that point, you are working together as a team to put together that idea as well as possible in the most commercial package so it has the best chance of getting out there. Often we were working to a set release date so you had a much stronger sense of the market and your place in it, and I think that's something, in general, that UK filmmakers have to learn. In England we make very good films but we don't often make films that are targeted for the market. Look at Richard Curtis — he has a supreme understanding of his market and that's what you need. There is a lot of talent in the UK but ironically I think there is a lack of good producers.

It's a very odd job description and because you have to be master of so many aspects, if you are weak in any one then you lose. It's very difficult. You have to be insanely passionate about the films you make but at the same time you have to have enough distance so you know that they have to be made for a price. You have to be able to nurture talent and make them feel comfortable, make them feel like everything is possible, but at the same time you have to make sure that you finish shooting at 7 p.m. It's an endless list of contradictions in terms of the skill-set you need to make the job work. I have been very lucky because of the people I have been able to work with, the fact that I was mentored by people like Michael White and Lorne Michaels meant that I was shown how to do it. But I think that if I hadn't been with them I would still be groping around in the dark. I think that's the problem: how do you train someone to be a producer? I think there are a lot of people who could be great producers if they were given the right kind of exposure and the right chances. That was part of the appeal of building Ealing up, to bring more people into the fold, because there are good days and bad days and there are days when you have to face an enormous amount of rejection. You have days when you feel that this film you've been working on for two years is a piece of shit. Sometimes you feel that five times a day, and it's all part of the process. But if you are doing it on your own and you don't have someone to share that with, it makes it very tough.

What's the basis of your partnership with Uri?

It's very different from, say, the relationship that Tim and Eric have where they very much do the same thing and put out their pictures. I always describe Uri as my bohemian rainmaker, in that he doesn't get involved in the day to day, but he will go out and occasionally bring in a big fish.

4. *The whole auteur thing*

How do you support a director?

It's always been very natural to me. I tend to think of filmmaking as a partnership between director, producer and writer so we're all in it together, and it's very much about teamwork. The films that I have worked on that had the most success are those where we have all been very much at one about the film we are making. I think that's what makes a good film and gives lie to the whole auteur thing. For me, the natural order of events is actually the relationship between the producer and the writer, with a director coming in — which is the complete reverse of how the process is perceived. And if you are Ridley Scott then you are probably not that interested in listening to producers. But I think that of a lot of those guys, maybe their films would be better if they did listen. The environment that I was brought into — which was Michael, and Lorne, *Saturday Night Live* — was very much a producer-led and writer-led environment. I'm not talking about the producer as dictator, but historically that has been the natural order, which in the last twenty years has been upset. I am not sure that it has been upset for the best reasons, or the best results.

A few years ago an agreement was made between the MPAA — which is the studios — and the Writers Guild that the writer's credit should go ahead of the producer's credit, which to me just seems an extraordinary manoeuvre. The producer credit in Hollywood has largely been discredited because a lot of people get credits who aren't really producers. Anyone who does anything on a film now expects some level of producer credit so I think that the way in which the role is considered has really suffered in terms of its perception.

What are you doing now?

I am making an animated film called *Valiant* with a friend of mine, John Williams, who produced *Shrek*. It's about carrier pigeons in the Second World War. It's a $40-million film, which is a lot for this country but not that much in the big wide world. Then I'm putting together a slate of movies — a teen comedy called *I Want Candy* about two guys who want to get into the movie business and decide the best way to do it is to make a porn film; a noir-thriller set in Rome that Oliver Parker will direct from a script he has written with John Sayles called *Fade to Black*; and a romantic comedy called *Kip*. I generally do comedy and that's what I am drawn to and my background, but I love the idea of doing a good thriller.

Does Ealing receive money from the UK Film Council?

We receive slate funding from them, and they put money into *Valiant* and into *The Importance of Being Ernest*.

The idea behind building Ealing is that we can give ourselves a certain level of independence and financial support and get on with making the films we want to make, and get out of that pattern of making them one by one.

The best thing that the Film Council have done is invest significant money into development, because that was the big hole in this country, and that's what hopefully will come back — that more people will write, and scripts will be developed further, and so help the writing talent. I think, in general, they have done a very good job, and they have a good record in the kinds of films they've invested in.

Fade to Black was shot in Belgrade in the summer of 2005, starring Danny Huston, Diego Luna and Christopher Walken and will be released in 2006. *Valiant* was released in the UK in March 2005 and became the highest grossing UK independent film for that year with a global cumulative box office of $70 million. *Imagine Me & You*, a romantic comedy directed by Oliver Parker, was released in 2006 as was *Alien Autopsy*, a sci-fi comedy starring Britain's TV duo 'Ant & Dec'.

Part Four

HOLLYWOODLAND

'Where any office boy or young mechanic can be a panic . . .' In this section we will meet movers and shakers at those fabled studios already spoken of with such mingled respect and resentment in previous chapters. To a degree that cannot be underestimated, today's Hollywood has been shaped by agents, and in turn by ex-agents who segue into production and executive jobs. Mike Medavoy is a distinguished pioneer of such a career move, while Gary Lucchesi is a member of a subsequent generation. Jason Hoffs is young for all his studio experience, and a firm advocate of the 'tent-pole' picture. Steve Golin and Jennifer Todd are associated with edgier fare, but they too know (to quote David Rabe's classic Hollywood play *Hurlyburly*) that the game in this town is not horseshoes . . .

Take 12

MIKE MEDAVOY AND ARNIE MESSER:
Phoenix Pictures

Former agent and studio head turned producer Mike Medavoy is proud to have been associated with eight winners of the Best Picture Oscar. But he has more exceptional claims than most: the son of Russian Jews, born in Shanghai, an alumnus of the Universal Studios mailroom who rose to be a top agent to the cream of 1970s talent, then, at United Artists, green-lit some of the blue-chip movies of that 'golden age', before carrying UA's flame onward to Orion. Medavoy has seen it all, and earned considerable kudos along the way: on the jacket of his memoir Marlon Brando describes him as 'a truly decent person', Sean Penn calls him 'a good man'. In the mid-nineties Medavoy went independent, in partnership with Arnie Messer, formerly a lawyer and senior business executive at Columbia. Their subsequent adventures at Phoenix Pictures have been instructive. I spoke with Medavoy and Messer separately about their work both at Phoenix and in the past, and their responses are interwoven below.

HELEN DE WINTER: *Where did your interest in movies begin?*

MIKE MEDAVOY: When I was a little boy in Shanghai and then Chile I saw some wonderful films — *The Searchers, Casablanca, Robin Hood*, and *Captain Blood* — they all became a part of my psyche, pictures in my mind. But I never dreamt I would have anything to do with movies. I didn't even live in the United States. I was born in China, and it wasn't until later — when my family moved to Chile — I became old enough to understand what America was, as seen through its movies.

I didn't really speak English and my Russian parents had started a life in Shanghai, China, then a life in Santiago, Chile, and then they had to start their lives all over again in Los Angeles, California. My mother was the fifteenth child of an arranged marriage, to two people who got married when they were fifteen years old. Seven of their

children died of starvation. So I'm the progeny of that kind of experience in life. It made me dream of better things, which was partly incul-
cated by them — life can always be better — and also influenced by
the mentors I met along the way. I went to UCLA where I discovered
an urge for both curiosity and learning. I was a history major, then
I got my first job in the film business mailroom at Universal Studios. I
was there for six months, I didn't learn much other than a bunch of
names. When I got there I thought I was the smartest guy in the
mailroom — though it turned out everybody was just as smart, if not
smarter. Some of them had doctorates in English and Math . . .

*In the mailroom were you thinking about where you were headed
next?*

MM: I wasn't thinking. I wanted to get into the international division
of the company and travel abroad, but it was modest thinking, certainly modest in terms of what eventually did happen. I then got a job
as a casting director, where I soon became bored and left to work as a
trainee agent, which I did for a couple of years, then I went to work
for CMA, a large theatrical agency and eventually became a big-time
agent at IFA. In 1974 I became the head of production at United
Artists on the West Coast. Here I met a group of experienced men who
literally changed my life — Arthur Krim, Bob Benjamin, Eric Pleskow,
and Bill Bernstein. Eric was president of UA, Arthur was its chairman,
Bob was co-chair, Bill was head of business affairs. United Artists had
a great reputation as an artists company and deservedly so, because
they respected artists and gave them a lot of free reign over artistic
matters. These were a group of very special people, with an enormous
amount of experience, and I was lucky to be in their company.

What were your responsibilities as head of production?

MM: To find movies to produce, put them together, and make sure they
were prepared in a manner that both Eric and Arthur could approve
their being done. Having been an agent for those years and knowing
most of the artists in the business, I found myself in a good niche. It was
an interesting kind of switch from seller to buyer and it took me a good
six months before I could get a feel for it. Producers were bringing
projects, writers were bringing projects and directors were bringing
projects. At first, I couldn't find anything that I wanted to do. I
was being either overly cautious or under-prepared. The good fortune
was that there were others in the company, and therefore it wasn't necessarily all about my taste, because there were many movies that came

out of United Artists I had nothing to do with — for example, Woody Allen's movies were originated out of New York, so were the Pink Panther movies, and the Bond pictures, I had nothing to do with them. But there were some I was lucky enough to have something to do with, like *Rocky* [1975], *Carrie* [1976], *New York, New York* [1977], *Coming Home* [1978], and *Apocalypse Now* [1979]. I brought the pictures to the studio, together with my staff and, of course, with the aid and encouragement of Eric, Arthur, and others.

How much of the business of backing pictures is about instinct?

MM: A lot. Part of instinct has to do with experience. Over the years I have had the foresight or luck to be able to say, 'Well, this is a subject matter that interests me, and I think it will interest everybody else, so let's make a film about this and buy this script.' But it's clear to me that films are on the whole a group effort.

Is that what you felt about say, One Flew Over the Cuckoo's Nest?

MM: Yes, and I think I was lucky that every other studio turned it down, but Eric encouraged me and the company to make the deal, and we did. This was probably a highlight in my career, and in my memory.

Of course, Cuckoo's Nest *was only the start of your relationship with Milos Forman, with whom you worked with again on* Amadeus, Valmont *and* The People vs. Larry Flynt.

MM: I just love the man, I think he's one of the great artists of film. I would do almost anything to work with him. There are so many similarities between us, in terms of our life experience. Unfortunately the last time we tried something together we got derailed by New Regency. It was a book called *Bad News* by Donald Westlake. But I never say die, one of these days we will get that one done too.

Looking back over some of the films and filmmakers you have championed, would you say that you have a European sensibility in your taste?

MM: Probably so. European sensibility, worldly sensibility . . . and for whatever reason I always got along very well with European filmmakers. I was an agent to the British contingent of the 1960s — Karel Reisz, Tony Richardson, and Lindsay Anderson, all of whom were considered to be the 'new wave' of British filmmakers. I was involved with Pontecorvo, Antonioni, and Truffaut. They liked me and I think they respected me, and of course, I learned from them, it was a real collaboration of interests. I introduced them to others, I would show up with Antonioni at events or small dinners and most people didn't even know him except for his reputation as a great filmmaker after *Blow-Up*. But they trusted me, trusted my taste, and my word. If I said something, I was going to live up to it, no matter what, so when I went to UA, it all came naturally from the people I worked for at UA; they were honest, straightforward people, and had similar backgrounds and experiences with foreign filmmakers.

I was at UA for four years, then in 1978 we all got into a tiff with TransAmerica and left en masse to start Orion Pictures. Orion was at Warner for four years, and then I was with Orion Pictures for an additional twelve years. I always feel sad about what happened to Orion — people miss that company.

In Medavoy's time Orion's successes included *Amadeus* (1984), *The Terminator* (1984), *Platoon* (1986), *Hannah and Her Sisters* (1986), *RoboCop* (1987), *Dances with Wolves* (1990) and *The Silence of the Lambs* (1991).

During your time at UA and Orion did you think of yourself as an executive or as a producer?

MM: I have always considered myself to be an executive, a facilitator. My main contribution is to know that people are talented, understand them, put them in a situation where they are comfortable, and protect them from being trampled. I think the creative business is mainly about writers and directors, not discounting actors — others who contribute to its success. Finally it's also about the editor, because most movies are made in the editing room. But if you really take the sum-total of it, it's about fitting together with the vision of the guy who says 'Cut' or 'Let's print that one' — the director. It's that vision that spells art or disaster.

Doesn't the producer have a vision in the act of bringing all those elements together?

MM: Yes, some producers do that and do it well. I always had the right to say no, and in some instances I did. 'No, I don't want that composer. No, we can't cast that person.' And sometimes I was wrong, sometimes I was right. No one ever has it right all the time, but finally you are in the hands of others . . .

Arnie Messer's career path first coincided with Medavoy during those Orion years.

What was your experience in the studio system prior to Phoenix?

ARNIE MESSER: I was at Columbia TriStar from January 1976 until March 1994. For the most part I enjoyed my time there, it was profitable, I learned a lot and I did almost every job in the studio because I rotated through the various kinds of departments. So I was very fortunate.

Did you have a mentor?

AM: I had several. I worked with Victor Kaufman for seventeen years, when I joined Columbia he was deputy general counsel. Victor was an extraordinarily smart guy, a businessman and lawyer. He was chairman of TriStar for a while and is now Barry Diller's number two guy. I also worked for Frank Price for four and a half years, and I loved Frank and learned an enormous amount from him.

How did you first meet Mike?

AM: I met Mike when he was at Orion, I knew *of* him when he was at United Artists. I was an admirer of his. Orion had always made wonderful movies — you look at Orion's pictures and the United Artist pictures that he did and it's hard not to admire that.

Mike had been using the old TriStar offices, and I was part of TriStar, I was head of business affairs, then president of television and various things. TriStar was formed in 1983 and I was part of the original category of people that formed it. We made a deal for Columbia to acquire some of the foreign video rights from Orion, so I got to know him a little bit through conversations there. Then in 1987 TriStar and Columbia merged, and TriStar in fact was a surviving entity, and changed its name to Columbia Pictures Entertainment. Then TriStar was re-formed as a division of Columbia, and was run by Jeff Sagansky, who continued there until Mike came in and replaced him.

Medavoy was chairman of TriStar Pictures from 1990 to 1994. There were prestige Oscar winners (*Philadelphia*) and hits (*Terminator 2: Judgment Day, Sleepless in Seattle*). But it was not a happy period, as any reader of Medavoy's 2002 memoir[15] can learn.

15. *You're Only as Good as Your Next One: 100 Great Films, 100 Good Films and 100 for Which I Should be Shot* (Simon & Schuster).

What's your assessment now of your tenure at TriStar?

MIKE MEDAVOY: One of the mistakes I've made career-wise — and I don't think I have made a lot of them — was to go to TriStar. I should have gone into producing four years earlier. My role at TriStar was pretty much the same role I had before, which was to run the motion picture division of the company.

How would you characterize your output at TriStar?

MM: I made some successful films, and the company is still there. But I probably should have started out on my own sooner: I should have relied on my own guile and intelligence. Instead, I made a critical mistake, I relied on a team of people who were at odds with me, who weren't *really* supportive — and I needed support. They probably see it otherwise, but finally it doesn't matter. I need to be on my own, reliant on myself and my hand-picked team, and not a bunch of people who are not on the same page, whose interest is themselves only.

Was it the corporate structure at TriStar that frustrated you?

MM: It was that, and it was also the relationships between the people. It would have been great if the guy who I went there for had been able to say to me, 'Hey, look, let me help you do this, let's talk it through, I'll tell you my feelings, you can tell me yours and we'll decide whether we want to do this or not.' But the whole thing was a sham game, a contract that was later changed, and a system of green light approvals that made it appear I had the authority. However, in the final analysis I had to get approval from a board of lawyers and accountants. Really, at that point in my life, I was too old for it. It's great when you're thirty years old, but you get to be forty-five or fifty and that's it . . .

Arnie Messer had separately been considering his own frustrations with the studio model.

ARNIE MESSER: At that time at Columbia I was running the television division and all the international divisions, both creatively and on the business side. The television division I had totally, and the international side was more about distribution.

What then prompted your transition to the independent sector?

AM: At a certain point in time, it's not about the money any more, it's really about 'What do I want to do with my life?' I don't like administration, and I don't like just sitting in meetings all day, or going to present budgets in Japan, or dealing with all the corporate politics. You get bored with everything except dealing with ideas. My dad had an auto-parts business and was very successful at it but it's tough to stay interested in auto-parts, tough to find things that fascinate you about them. When you are dealing with ideas, to me that's the luckiest thing you can do.

At the time I left Columbia I had thirteen hundred people working for me, and we were doing about a billion-and-a-third dollars of sales in the divisions I controlled. I don't ever want to do that again. It's a lot of administration and you're sitting in meetings with people whining at you about stuff. You wind up just looking at other people's numbers and trying to figure out how you can get those numbers up, and it's not a lot of fun. You're looking at the fundamentals of each division, and in the end it's real simple — you've got to get more in than goes out, so you try to maximize what comes in and minimize what goes out.

In the end Mike and I left TriStar about the same time because the group was sold, and we started talking about forming a company together. Then in early 1994 we founded Phoenix.

How did you raise the finance you needed to start up Phoenix?

AM: It was a terrible process. For every one guy who was real and useful, we met a hundred flakes. It's terrible trying to winnow out who is real from people who have agendas and are mostly just trying to create a middle-man role for themselves. There were people who didn't have money but who claimed to have money just so they could try and get the deal. And once they had the deal, they would see if they could go and find the money . . .

Were you looking for high-worth individuals?

AM: We were looking for sophisticated investors. The idea was we wanted to see if we could find people who brought something to the company other than just money. We had Onex and Pearson and a few others. Pearson owned the *Financial Times* and Thames Television at that point, and they were good partners. Greg Dyke was a very knowledgeable guy, and a good advisor, so it was wonderful to have him as part of the company.

Was the process of raising your funding like a road-show an investment bank might run on behalf of a client?

AM: Pretty much. And it took a good year to eighteen months, a year to raise the funds and another six months to close all the documents and get all the contracts signed. The idea was to have a company that would be truly independent, and you can't really be independent unless you control your own finances.

Were you trying to set up a micro-studio?

AM: 'Studio' is too big a word, because a studio has a huge distribution arm and a couple of thousand employees. I think what we were trying to do was position ourselves so we could take advantage of opportunities that came along. When a studio head is replaced, generally all of the existing projects are put in turnaround and they have to start all over again. So we thought that if we got really lucky we could be a unit with a development slate of existing projects in place. But the primary goal was just to create a flow of negatives that create assets — to try to do four or five movies a year and maintain the ownership of those movies. And after a while you've got a pretty nice library. We own seventeen negatives to our own films. It's a good income and a wonderful asset. I suppose if we retired, we can sell it, because there is value there. And if we don't sell then we will continue to license it.

   In the beginning we financed most of our own movies, but that turned out to be very difficult because it takes the cash a long time to circle back, even though we were successful. Now we vary our financing because you can't keep investing $10 to 15 million of our own funds into every movie. We still develop on our own nickel but now we've gone back to being a more traditional producing entity, either taking fees or packaging in the old negative pick-up style, meaning we control the production of the movie and the studio just buys the finished picture. We did a movie called *Lake Placid* that way — we made it and we had an agreement with Fox that when we delivered it they would pay X for it. In the case of very small movies, we'll still finance them. But it's a different business plan than when we started.

Did you structure the finance on the basis of a slate of films?

AM: The early deals were crossed in groups of five or so with Columbia. In the later deals we funded the slate on an ad-hoc basis. Right now we are doing a movie with Rob Cohen [*Stealth*] where we bought the project, laid it off on Sony, partnered with Laura Ziskin and Sony has the final controls, so we're really producers for hire and we are happy to do that. We made *Basic* that way, with John Travolta, and *Holes*. The idea was to increase volume by not having to use any more of our own money than we have to.

How have the movies you funded fared commercially?

AM: Some did well, some didn't. *The People vs. Larry Flynt* was a good movie, didn't do well. *The Mirror Has Two Faces* was a good movie and did OK. *Amy Foster, U-Turn* and *Apt Pupil* were pretty good movies but didn't do a lot commercially. *Urban Legend* made a lot of money, it was extremely profitable. We then made a sequel which didn't do as well. We made *The Thin Red Line* which we made some money on, *The Sixth Day* on which we lost some money. For the most part we have been able to keep the company afloat and we haven't gone back for additional capital since we raised the initial finance in 1995.

What is the internal structure at Phoenix, and how does it compare to the set-ups you had at UA and Orion?

MIKE MEDAVOY: We have a development department, a production department, and a publicity person. We're kind of self-contained, small, and nimble. But once we have established the team, we have to keep our head up and just keep going. In my opinion, this is the best creative team I have ever worked with. Basically five executives working on, say, forty or so projects. We have everything from drama to children's fantasy. We'll package them and we'll take it to a studio and find out if they like it or not. We still have to go out and pitch our projects to studios, and while I get a certain amount of respect, I'm considered to be a risk at times, perhaps not commercial enough — too up market. But I'm much more involved in the process than I ever was. To me, nothing has changed from the days of UA — the only difference is I don't have the supporting mechanisms I had there and we don't have our own distribution company. We have a lot less money and we have to do this on our guile and our relationships. In this business, nobody does anything only because of a relationship — they do it because they think it's to their economic advantage and because they like what they see.

Do you have a particular genre of film you prefer to develop?

MM: There are certain kinds of movies that I am drawn to and other kinds of movies that I am not. We're into making the kinds of films that I have always liked — stories with character that tell a story that interest me, I am completely aware that anyone who makes movies needs to make money. It's an expensive game, a low margin business, and it needs to be played by people who know that. I'm with that, but I still like taking chances. *The Thin Red Line* was taking a chance. *The People vs. Larry Flynt* was taking a chance. I think for me, a good producer is someone who does take risks. Making movies takes risks, living life takes risks, people make their reputations and make money by weighing risks.

Do you and Mike have a shared sensibility about what you like?

ARNIE MESSER: Not at all. I'm much more the philistine of the relationship. I admire the kinds of movies Mike makes and I enjoy seeing them, but as a business we are about selling tickets. So I'm more interested in the movies that are going to have a mass appeal — although Mike will tell you that good movies have a mass appeal and any subject matter that is good enough will work. *Amadeus, One Flew Over the Cuckoo's Nest, Rocky*, they were all subject matters that people didn't think were commercial. From my point of view, if you're doing the Kaiser Wilhelm story then you've just made your task much harder — you have to make a pretty good movie just to get people into the theatres, even if that material were wonderful. When people hear about movies their first two questions are 'What's it about?' and 'Who's in it?' So you want to have short, good answers to both those questions.

So The Sixth Day *is about a clone and stars Arnold Schwarzenegger?*

AM: That's it. Now there's no guarantee that's going to work, and *The Sixth Day* could have done better. But with the likes of *Urban Legend*, with interesting concepts and good execution, I think you have a pretty good shot at doing something.

Why in your opinion has The Sixth Day *been a commercial disappointment?*

AM: I think we tried too hard to be in the middle. When you do a movie with Schwarzenegger it has to be the best special effects. And a PG-13 rating is really *not* a good way to go.

Was an action picture like The Sixth Day *a departure, genre-wise from your usual interests?*

MIKE MEDAVOY: Every film is a departure for me. Every time you go out there, even if you're not the actor, your credibility is at stake. It's not all action, there is very little action. Actually, the mistake I might have made was I should have made that movie for less money. I think we made it for about $90 million. The movie will break even. We have a production department here who are really on the ball. We haven't had an experience yet where we have gone over budget. But the point is, we should have made the movie for less.

When the script is in development, are you reading it saying 'This a $90-million movie or does it become a $90-million movie because of the way you package it?

MM: The film itself has its own kind of rules and determines what kind of budget it's going to be. The question is, if you have a certain kind of action star, do you put more action in it? You can become a slave to that particular aspect of it, because you have to deliver on what he does. Maybe the movie should have been made for $120 million, and we should have put more action in it, or made it with a star who wasn't fading somewhat, but I'm glad we made the film and I enjoyed working with Arnold.

Has Mike made choices that you had questions about?

ARNIE MESSER: Yeah. I wouldn't have done *The People vs. Larry Flynt* — as much as I liked the movie, I wouldn't have done it. On the other hand I probably wouldn't have done *Cuckoo's Nest* or *Amadeus* either, so . . .

What concerned you about Larry Flynt?

AM: What happened was somewhat predictable — women just weren't going to go and see that movie because they were so turned off by what it was about. It's a shame because it was a wonderful movie, and it won the Berlin Film Festival. I don't know how we could have made it a better movie. But with hindsight maybe it could have done with a different title.

What's the process for Phoenix of putting a film together and taking it to a studio?

AM: I think those relationships are always in a state of flux. The studios are looking for successful projects, and there is always a notion of 'Not Invented Here'[16], it's never a totally objective filter.

---

16. A derogatory term in business, used to mock the tendencies of companies either suspicious or ignorant of any strategy or mode of practice that did not originate in-house.

Some of the stuff that gets made, everybody looks and says 'How could that guy have made *that*?' So there's a fair amount of subjectivity, and it's a function of what they think is going to work, the areas they want to be in — the producer, the director, the elements that are attached. The culture comes and goes with the head of the studio. Whoever is calling the shots basically creates their own culture because of their different tastes, interests and sensibilities. Of course any studio is going to do a Tom Cruise/*Mission Impossible* movie, but when it comes to the less obvious movies it becomes more a matter of judgement, where people see their niche. Some heads of studio see themselves more as programmers than filmmakers, and some see themselves as *purely* as filmmakers. So it's really a mixed bag, there is a whole myriad of factors that goes into how somebody makes a decision. One studio has a fairly mechanical process where everybody has to put in estimates and they go through it and they do what they do. But from my point of view — and I have seen that system both ways — it's impossible to do that. The distribution people can't tell you whether it's going to be a good movie or not, they can tell you that the elements are more or less attractive and that it's easier or harder to sell. But if it's *not* a good movie, then no matter what it's about, it isn't going to work. The estimates that you get from the distributors are either political — in other words, they are putting in the estimates that they think their bosses want — or they are reactive to the kinds of areas that have worked before. So, not *particularly* meaningful.

How do you interfere with that mindset? How can you change it if you think they're wrong when they turn down a movie you believe can be a success?

AM: You can't. What you can do is understand the process. At least if you understand what you're dealing with, you can kind of arrange the way you pitch things to fit in better with the process.

How do you and Mike work together on a daily basis?

AM: I focus more on the business side, and Mike's focus is the creative side. But we're both in each other's areas all the time, sometimes efficiently, sometimes otherwise. We're basically both on top of each other. There are certain things that I am more interested in creatively and he'll tell me what he thinks about it, and there are certain things that are really his projects that I'll give him whatever advice I can and try to cover his back from the business side. You can imagine that, with forty projects, everybody finds their own thing that they want to push.

Mike and I operate a little bit differently; Mike falls in love with projects; he loves them, they're his babies, he shepherds them through and Mike is wonderful in terms of protecting the director from the studio or other outside sources, he builds a little cocoon around there so everyone feels relatively well taken care of and safe and the director can do his movie.

Mike has a wonderful sense about screenplays, and even after nine years together I still like to watch him do things. I tend to be more interested in plots, the mechanics of plots, and he tends to be more interested in characters. I also enjoy the logistics of getting the movie on the floor and producing it. Mike likes post-production, getting into the edit with the director and working on it. And after three hundred movies he's extremely good at it. Mike and a director can argue over whether it's eight frames for a character's reaction, whereas I can't tell the difference.

MIKE MEDAVOY: I get more involved in the selling and in the editing process. But it's the director's vision. It's my sense that you have got to allow that person whom you have entrusted the work with to come up with his vision. I have always felt that unless you are doing something useful, it's a mistake. So I get as involved as I can without impinging on the director. I don't know what the director is thinking or feeling and it's presumptuous of me to intrude on that. If I were sitting on set and I thought 'It would be better to do this . . .', and I went up and whispered it to him, he would start to think I was nuts. As much as I think — and I said this in my book — that I know there are some really smart, communicative producers, I couldn't do what they do, certainly as well as they do, so why try it?

Do you like to be on set?

ARNIE MESSER: It depends on the need. Recently we had a movie shooting in Jacksonville where I was basically on the set the whole time, then we had a movie shooting in South Africa and I didn't go at all. If the director and line producer have it so well in hand that all you are is in the way, and you can see from the dailies that it's going well and no one is mad at anybody, then there's not much reason for me to be there.

What's the worst thing that can happen during production?

AM: The toughest movie I was ever on was *Tootsie*. The director Sydney Pollack was a wonderful guy. But Dustin was rewriting pages at night, and they would come to the set in the morning and they would argue, and it was a very difficult environment. You can get into really knock-down terrible fights and sometimes the movie gets better and sometimes it gets worse.

You need to have one uniform vision and everybody trying to get it off the page. If you have competing visions or ideas for a project *late* in the process, it's very difficult — it throws the director off if they're suddenly having to fight fires in other areas. That's not how you want everyone to be using their energy.

But the enjoyment for me is watching talented people solve problems, and the older I get the more fascinating it is to me how good people are at solving problems on the floor, given the enormous amount of pressure on them — that whole process of keeping the whole in mind while your concentrating on small details. When you're working with great directors it's just a joy to sit there and watch them own the set, making up shots on the fly that are fascinating, or teasing out performances from actors that you didn't know was there.

There are certain directors Mike likes to work with and directors I *don't* want to work with, and there are certain directors who I like that he would prefer not to work with. But we discuss everything and there are times when we will disagree, so it's sometimes a compromise.

Do you have similar conversations about casting?

AM: Sometimes we disagree on the *type* of cast. Sometimes he will try to cast it in a way that I think is more like an independent movie. For instance, the first time we looked at the casting of *Basic* it was Benicio Del Toro and Catherine Keener as opposed to John Travolta and Connie Nielsen. There are certain actors that the public is kind of accustomed to — and Benicio is a *really* fine actor. Sean Penn is a *wonderful* actor, an amazingly talented guy, versatile, enormous range but I think that when his movies come out people tend to associate those with art movies, they don't think commercial, and I don't think Sean *wants* people to think of him as commercial, I think he's very happy having people think of him as a fine-art performer.

Is that a Hollywood judgement based on the domestic market? Because in foreign markets, actors like Penn, Del Toro and Keener are highly regarded.

AM: The foreign markets are tending to be much more like the American market. *The Matrix* works well everywhere; *X Men 2* is working well everywhere, even *Urban Legend* is working well everywhere so I think that is to some extent the kids are kids, whether they are American kids, French, German or English kids and it's the special effects and action on screen that brings the kids in. The truth is, it is much harder to get adults — whether they are Germans or Americans — into the theatres than it is the kids. So those movies that appeal to the kids tend to have bigger grosses.

* * *

What's the first rule of producing?

MIKE MEDAVOY: The first rule is finding a good story to tell, then find really good people who can execute that story, and agree it's a good story, then find the money, then find a way to sell it. And make sure they don't put it on the wrong opening date. I thought *Basic*, which we did with Sam Jackson and John Travolta, was a really good movie. Not everybody agreed with me, but it was a really interesting movie. But it literally went out on the wrong date, the day the war started.

So at the end of the day, a good movie can be derailed by a bad release date on the part of the studio?

MM: They can make mistakes too — we all make mistakes. They didn't intend to do it with *Basic*, because they liked the film. Sometimes it can be the only date they can fit it in, it can be any number of things.
ARNIE MESSER: *Basic* was released the weekend that the war in Iraq started, so people didn't have much interest in a military film. You don't have any influence in that kind of situation. But then when the studio set the release date they couldn't have known, so it's just one of those really unfortunate things.

How far are you able to get involved in the studio marketing of Phoenix movies?

AM: There is an old saying, 'Half of the money spent marketing a movie is wasted, you just never know which half . . .' And it's true. The two elements that people look at with marketing are, one, making people aware of the movie and, two, making those people have an interest in actually *seeing* it. It's easier to do with some movies than it is to do with others. And there's a lot of competition for leisure-time activities, so just to bring the guy in the street who may go to two or three movies a year is extremely tough. The studio will traditionally pay for the P&A, and there is a fairly constant battle between producers and the studios, with the producers trying to get the studios to spend more to buy television spots, to do more electronic media, to put on more events. With several different producers competing for resources, you have to keep pushing the studio to do it.

Often the bulk of the money is committed before you know it. There's a lot of testing, a lot of research screenings and there is a lot of other kinds of useful information about how a film is going to do. But an audience reaction to a film is palpable, it's really instructive to see how an audience perceives it, and then to have focus groups afterwards where they take twenty people and ask them questions about the movie. If you have a movie with a complicated plot and fifteen of the twenty people are shaking their heads figuring out what happened, then you have some work to do . . .

* * *

When you meet people, how do you describe what you do?

MIKE MEDAVOY: I describe my life as I make movies, I co-chair a think-tank on international relations at UCLA, I'm on the Board of Advisors at Harvard's Kennedy School, and on the Council of Foreign Relations. Also, I have been involved in presidential politics. At this moment, there is my family, but after the years I have been doing this, there are times when I feel really exhausted, and I probably take my eye off the ball because I'm really more interested in doing something else at that moment. This is a lot of hard work, it takes a lot of thinking and concentration. It's exhausting and you do need to get away from it once in a while just to get some perspective, and that's a good idea for all corporations and all people.

Do you feel you still have the stamina for the business?

MM: I do. I'm sixty-two now, I'm not the thirty-four-year-old guy who took the job at UA.

Of all the movies you have been associated with, is there a particular one that stands out that you are particularly proud of?

MM: Sentimentally, *Cuckoo's Nest* is the film that got me going. But there are a hundred other films that I feel are worthy of being remembered. Now, with *All the King's Men* and *Zodiac*, I feel like I'm hitting another stride.

Do you think it would be possible to make those films of the seventies today?

MM: They are harder to make today, probably almost impossible. Times change. This is the year of the comic book. Somebody once said to me, 'The problem with you, Medavoy, is your pictures are too intelligent.' Well if that's the worst thing they can say about me then I am a happy fella. Somebody said I might have taken too much credit for things, and I know that I didn't, but what I said was, did they feel badly when I took blame for things? Did they say 'You deserved the blame?' I also know that in the grand scheme of things, I'm unimportant. What's important is the work itself. Nobody's really going to give a shit about me at the end, except for my family and a few friends. And other than that . . . *Apocalypse Now* remains, *Amadeus* remains. I know that I had something to do with it, and that's all that matters. As far as movies are concerned, we have a wonderful relationship at Sony, but also work with other studios — we like our freedom.

* * *

Is Hollywood a friendly business?

ARNIE MESSER: It is and it isn't. Having been doing this for twenty-six years, I have a lot of friends now and we all grew up together through the business. But people are extraordinarily jealous of other people's success. One of the really fun things to do, if you are perverse, is to go out and start saying really nice things about one studio executive in front of another studio executive, particularly studio heads . . . You'll see them slowly becoming uncomfortable, and sooner or later they can't stand it any more and start trashing the guy.

Because everything is so subjective, except for grosses, there is an enormous amount of jealousy and fear and envy of all sorts. But it's part of the dynamic. There's a real competition and a real sense that everybody wants to come to the fore, so there are a lot of people bumping elbows and stuff. But in any business you have the same kind of thing. Here I suspect people are just more articulate, a little cleverer in ways of showing it.

Would you say you have a particular philosophy or credo for how you work at Phoenix?

AM: We have thirty-five employees here, and other than those mandated by law we have no policies. We try to be bureaucrats as little as possible, and we try to take each person as they are and maintain the maximum flexibility and function in a comfortable fashion as opposed to a formal fashion. It's nice, it runs well and it's a good way to live.

Every time you work with someone you learn something. You try to learn what their thought processes are – how are they getting the results they want? Today, I see the opportunities to learn from younger people. We have a couple of guys in their twenties here who view the world very differently to me, but that point of view is useful and keeps you fresh. And they're *much* closer to the age of people who buy cinema tickets today.

We have a partnership with one of the large hip-hop managers and I know *nothing* about that world but we are going to do a couple of movies in that area with them, and it's a whole new powerful dynamic for us that I had no idea about. The merchandising power of that — these guys all have their clothing lines and they're doing $300 million a year in sales, and they're making rims for SUVs . . . It's become a whole, cultural phenomenon. And that's the kind of thing young people can bring to you.

In 2004 Phoenix co-produced John Boorman's *Country of My Skull* and in 2005 Rob Cohen's *Stealth*. Their production of Steve Zaillian's *All the King's Men* is eagerly anticipated for 2006, as is *Miss Potter* with Renée Zellwegger, and *Zodiac,* directed by David Fincher also to be released in 2006. On 19 September 2005 Mike Medavoy was honoured with a star of his own on the famous Hollywood Walk of Fame.

Take 13

GARY LUCCHESI

Gary Lucchesi is among the more established of the many ex-agents who have taken the path into producing, from Paula Wagner to David Hoberman. One-time William Morris agent Lucchesi cut his studio production teeth at TriStar Pictures, graduated to president of production at Paramount, then segued into a production deal there after quitting the executive job in 1991. After several successful producing credits, in 2000 he became president of Paramount-based Lakeshore Entertainment, joining chairman/CEO Tom Rosenberg. Their biggest success of late has been *Million Dollar Baby* (2004).

Why the career move? In Lucchesi's case he wanted a bigger share in the creative process. 'It's all been a learning experience,' he told me, 'but I can say quite frankly that prior to becoming a producer my experience in terms of understanding production was quite limited — and this at a time when I had a position of incredible responsibility as president of production at Paramount . . .'

1. 'What are you going to do about it?'

HELEN DE WINTER: *Was it a love of movies that brought you into the business?*

GARY LUCCHESI: Growing up, I went to the movies, but on reflection here's what I really liked — I liked *stories*.

My father served in World War Two and most of his friends were Italian-Americans, all of them born here but their parents had been immigrants. Most were drafted at the same time, and all of them, for some strange reason, were recruited to the Army Air Corps and sent to Italy. After the war my father drove a bread truck. He would go to work at four-thirty in the morning and be home around three in the afternoon. And at five-thirty, religiously, we would have dinner, my mother and father and sister and I. After dinner, maybe four out of seven nights a week, the doorbell would ring and it would be one of my father's friends coming over for a coffee. They would sit around the table talking, and I listened to them. 'Did you hear what happened to so and so? Oh, do you remember him?' They were telling stories, about characters, and they were human, funny, emotional and scary. And I think it's that side of film, the characterization and story-telling, that I like the most — because when I was a kid I listened to stories . . .

How did you get into the entertainment industry?

I went to UCLA, and I was a history major. For a while I thought about academia, occasionally I thought about being a lawyer. But there was also a side of me that felt, after studying for four years in college, that I didn't particularly feel like studying much more . . .

In my senior year someone in my class said, 'What are you doing next period?' and I said, 'Nothing.' He told me that David Geffen was teaching a class in entertainment, and that two weeks before Bob Dylan had been there, or Joni Mitchell, or someone like that . . . At first I went to the class and just audited it — I didn't enrol. But there were forty kids sitting there, mostly motion picture/TV majors or theatre majors, and they were excited because this was their vocation. My girlfriend — who later became my wife — was a film/TV major and she wanted to be a producer-director, so no one thought of *me* as the person who was interested in film. But I sat in the class and I was intrigued, because Geffen brought in studio executives, agents and some of the most powerful people in Hollywood.

Whom in particular?

I remember he brought in Lew Wasserman, Sid Sheinberg, Steve Ross, who was head of Warner Communications. People like Lew and Steve were titans. Mike Medavoy came in, Sue Mengers came along and she was a very powerful agent at that time. This is the absolute truth, but it was the first time in my life that I had ever been witness to rich people. Since my father drove a bread truck, you could call my back-ground working class, though it felt like middle class in San Francisco. But where I came from, the people I knew were wealthy if they owned restaurants. None of my friend's parents were lawyers or doctors or white-collar professionals. And all of a sudden Geffen had brought in these captains of industry. Of course, when you're twenty-one years old you can be completely naive, but what I knew about all of them was that they were making a lot of money working in the entertainment business, where their skills were handsomely rewarded.

Can you remember what was the content of their lectures?

I don't remember exactly — running studios, or just how much it cost to throw a party . . . But they were guys in suits who got to make movies and they were talking as casually to the thirty or forty of us as I'm talking to you. Then at a certain point, David Geffen said, 'OK, so you've sat in this class for ten weeks, what are you going to do about it?' And I don't know why but he pointed to me and said, 'What are *you* going to do about it?' So I said, 'Where do you go if you want to get into the business side of entertainment?' And Geffen said, 'I *talked* about this. You go to the William Morris Agency and you start in the mailroom and work your way up. I did it, Barry Diller did it, Mike Ovitz did it, Irwin Winkler, Mike Medavoy . . .' So I said, 'That's what *I'm* going to do', and Geffen said, 'Great!' And that was absolutely a seminal moment in my life, because suddenly there was a plan.

Have you ever met David Geffen since?

Yes, I have, and I've told him this story. I credit him all the time.

2. At the Supreme Court

So you went to the William Morris mailroom. Were you confident there?

I had no doubt about my abilities, especially when I saw the people I was competing against. But I was rather unique because I had no connections to Hollywood, and I wasn't Jewish. I had sales skills because I had worked in a grocery store all through high school and I basically put myself through college by working. I guess I thought I could become a talent agent, because I felt fairly confident about selling — that meant being able to approach somebody and say, 'I know you don't know me but there is something I would like to talk to you about. This is what it is, and this is why you should consider it.' I didn't have much fear about that.

In the mailroom you started by sorting mail and then you went through Dispatch where you would deliver items to studios. So you're running all over the place all day, and you have to make sure you don't get lost. Then you're promoted to secretary. I had been reading screenplays and writing coverage for Steve Reuther — now a producer —

and Steve was Stan Kamen's assistant. And at this time in the late 1970s Stan was the most powerful agent in Hollywood. This was just when the power was moving from Sue Mengers to Stan — before it moved again to Mike Ovitz. But between 1976 and 77 and 1985 and 86, Stan was the top guy. He represented Jane Fonda and Jon Voight on *Coming Home* and Michael Cimino and Christopher Walken on *The Deer Hunter*. He had tons of clients — Robert Redford, Burt Reynolds, Al Pacino, Jimmy Caan, Diane Keaton, Goldie Hawn. And directors including Franco Zefferelli, Fred Zinnemann, Alan J Pakula, Norman Jewison, Karel Reisz, Jack Clayton — all big filmmakers.

How did you get your big break?

The guy behind Steve Reuther was promoted, and Stan Kamen's desk opened up and one day he said, 'You're the guy we have chosen.' So all of a sudden I went from being a kid in the mailroom to basically clerking for the Chief Justice of the Supreme Court. I was terrified. But I knew I had plenty of skills, particularly 'people skills'.

Enough skills to succeed in the job?

I had worked in San Francisco in a mom-and-pop grocery store for ten years as a clerk and delivery boy. There were three cash registers, and what you do in a store like that is, you problem-solve and you sell. If somebody comes in and says, 'I bought a dozen eggs and two of them are broken', you say, 'Fine, I'll give you another dozen.' And if you tell somebody it's the peaches or the grapes today, they might buy some peaches. That's pretty much what you do as an agent. You problem-solve and you sell. So that was never complicated for me. But when I started working for Stan I needed to overcome one last hurdle, which was my anticipation for the worst.

What do you mean by that?

I had a stomach-ache most days and there were a couple of months when I thought 'Jesus I don't know if I'm going to get through this.' It was so rough. Stan was always so busy, and it wasn't that he was a difficult man — well, he was a difficult guy, because he was capricious. At first I would only really get a good night's sleep on a Friday or Saturday night, because I didn't have to go to work the next day. Monday mornings were always the worst because the phones would be ringing off the hook and there would be a ton of work to do. I would get to the office at 7.30 a.m. Stan didn't arrive until 10 a.m.

so I would make sure I got there early and psyched myself up for everything.

One morning I was talking to my mother, I said, 'Jeez, I just don't know if I can do this any more', and she said to me, 'Gary, you're anticipating the worst. You're thinking that the sky is going to fall on your head, and sometimes it's not going to.' And that day was a tough Monday, but I thought 'Fuck it, I'm just going to get through it.' And I did, and I felt at the end of the day that I was able to master this. Then it got to the point where I wasn't afraid of any day and I would just think, 'Throw whatever you've got at me, I know how to deal with it.'

There would be times when there were certain phone calls Stan wouldn't want to return and if I mentioned one of them at the wrong moment, he would blow up. But then there were times when he would say, 'What do we have?' and I would say, 'You don't want to know . . .' and he would say, 'Yeah, go ahead and get them . . .' I learned that it was about picking your spots. Funnily enough, all of that served me very well as a producer, taught me when to say something to somebody. If you pick the wrong time everything can go wrong, but if you pick the right spot you're OK.

I started on Stan's desk when I was twenty-two and the theory was that all the good young guys got promoted quickly, but you would be happy to be an assistant for three or four years. I was an assistant for less than two years and became an agent at twenty-four.

What was the decisive factor?

Stan liked me, you know, he and I were very much in synch. I realized that I was basically Stan's agent to Hollywood and he was my client, so I had to figure out how I was going to represent myself both to Hollywood and to Stan. Sue Mengers was his rival, though they would talk on the phone and they used to go out or have dinner parties or smoke dope together occasionally. I had called Sue's office one day and said, 'Is she there for Stan Kamen?' and her assistant said, 'No, she's out of town.' I asked where? He said, 'Oh, Las Vegas.' I walk into Stan's office and say, 'She's in Vegas. I wonder who's playing in Vegas . . .?' He looks at me, and I said, 'I'll find out.' So I come back and I said, 'Barry Manilow is in Vegas.' At that time Manilow was a Morris client, making $14 or 15 million a year — he was valuable. Stan says, '*That's* where she is.' And he loved that I was thinking ahead. The next day Sue calls back and Stan says to her, 'How was Barry?' She says, 'How did you know? There's a leak in my office . . .' Stan laughed, he thought that was great.

3. 'Did I do that well enough?'

What then was the push that took you out of agenting into producing?

I left being an agent because I saw the work as a vicarious endeavour. I loved my clients, but my work was basically behind the scenes — I was living vicariously through their craft, their efforts. So I became a studio executive to get closer to the creative process — though still living somewhat vicariously. Today I'm a producer, I don't live vicariously any more — my name is on the film, I'm on the set, I'm producing the movies. And I like being part of the intimate group that makes the movie.

Another reason why I stopped being an agent is that there weren't any role models for me, not really. I was married, I wanted to have a family, and hardly any of the agents were married or had families. Mostly they were single men or they were gay, and their lives were the business. So I left being an agent aged twenty-eight, and went to work for Tri-Star.

In your early days were there particular projects that you lobbied for?

The first movie I worked on at Tri-Star was *Places in the Heart* with Robert Benton, who later directed *The Human Stain* for Lakeshore. I loved that. John Malkovich, who had been a client of mine, was in it. After that came a movie called *About Last Night* which was originally called *Sexual Perversity in Chicago*[17] and it starred Demi Moore and Rob Lowe. I was integral to getting that movie made, without question. I was its champion. I thought that movie was about me — it was about young love and commitment, I was twenty-eight years old, I had been married for five years at that time. But what did I know? It was Ed Zwick's first feature, he was great and he's gone on to have a great career.

Peggy Sue Got Married [dir. Francis Coppola, 1986) was mine, *Blind Date* [dir. Blake Edwards, 1987] was mine, and *Nothing in Common* [dir. Garry Marshall, 1987]. I was there for four years, I was a VP, then a senior VP, then an executive VP. And I pretty much knew that I was going to be hired by some studio to be head of production — I was on that track and those jobs would open up, they always did. So I went to Paramount, and it was *Fatal Attraction* [dir. Adrian Lyne, 1987], *The Untouchables* [dir. Brian De Palma, 1987], *Hunt for Red October* [dir. John McTiernan, 1989], *Ghost* [dir. Jerry Zucker, 1990], *Shirley Valentine* [dir. Lewis Gilbert, 1990] — I worked on all of those.

17. An early stage play by David Mamet.

You had hoped for a closer involvement with movies. When did you feel that you really began to understand the process of how a film is made?

Once I finally became a producer. The first movie I worked on as producer was *Jennifer 8* — I was brought in on it, Andy Garcia was playing the lead and he was a friend of mine, and I took over from another producer. It was a difficult movie, complicated. Bruce Robinson directed, the movie wasn't entirely successful, but it was good, and critically successful.

If, having since produced, you could have your time as a Paramount executive over again — do you imagine it would be different?

Oh, yes, oh my gosh. I would be a much better executive now.

Why?

Because I understand the filmmaking process much better. When I left Paramount, I was thirty-six, thirty-seven — and I hadn't produced a movie. My knowledge of film production was really based on talent, and as a studio president the thinking was 'Hire the right talent and let them do what they're supposed to do.' That's not a bad theory, and it's the way most people do it. But I think, in hindsight, that the studio executives who are the most capable are the ones who have actually spent time producing movies, and know how hard it is. You can work just as hard on a flop as you can on a hit. In fact, I almost believe that you *have* to have had a flop to be a good producer.

Have you had a flop?

I have had movies that should have been better . . . One movie that still bothers me is one I made at Paramount called *Virtuosity*, starring Denzel Washington and Russell Crowe. I couldn't have cast better, because those two actors went on to become Oscar-winning movie stars, worth $20 million per picture. And, ultimately, we went with a director who, without question, had the ability to convince both actors to star in the movie — so he served a tremendous function there. But at the time I questioned whether or not he had the right artistic sensibilities for the movie.

The experience of making *Virtuosity* taught me that you have to be real careful about whom you hire as the director. It's one of the critical decisions — or perhaps *the* most critical decision — that a producer has to make in the entire process, because the director has extraordinary power. It's difficult for the producer who sits behind the director to interfere with that director's vision, or with the relationship between an actor and director. Actors want to listen to a director. They say all great players have great coaches, and actors want their director to say things to them that will add to their performance.

But there is nothing more satisfying than hiring a filmmaker who actually brings more to the film than even the producer has imagined. That has happened to me on occasion, and it's very rewarding.

Have you ever been in the position of having to replace a director?

Not as a producer, but when I was running Paramount there was a director on one particular film, and we realized he just couldn't do it. The producer was the one who first came to me about replacing him, and I agreed. But that is absolutely the last resort. And it's terrible, because it means you made a mistake in the first place by hiring him.

The director Greg Hoblit once said to me that a director has to know two things — what he wants, and how to get it. A lot of filmmakers have an idea of what they want, but then they don't know how to get it. Sometimes they will imagine a scene a certain way and then have no idea how to stage it. Or they have an idea of how they want the performer to act but no idea how to communicate with the actor to get that performance. But good directors know what they want and know how to get it.

You don't get to know until you start shooting how well all of that will go. Some people are very good talkers and then don't know quite how to get it. Or they doubt themselves.

Don't all directors doubt themselves?

Absolutely. Why wouldn't they? At a certain point they're committing a moment to history. The moment a director says, 'Cut! Print that, let's move on' — he or she is not going to get a chance to shoot that moment again, it's just sailed off into celluloid history. So of course it's got to be really difficult — 'Did I do that well enough? Can I do that better?' But at the same time they must be responsible to a clock.

If the director is shooting and shooting and afraid they've got what they need, does there come a point where you say, 'No, I think that's great'?

I think what you say is, 'You've done eight takes. I think you've got it. And you've got a lot more to do today . . .' And as long as they know that you're not trying to form the movie, then that's one way of doing it. But there are moments there when they *don't* have it, and they have to trust you to know that you'll let them have longer . . .

4. 'Who the f&!k are you?'

Your early producing credits were shared, but Primal Fear *[1996] was your first solo credit.*

Primal Fear was really the first one that I did sort of entirely on my own. I developed the project and the script, I called in every favour I had all over the place. It was Greg Hoblit's first feature, though he had done great TV — *NYPD Blue, Hill Street Blues, LA Law*. So he understood narrative. And he wasn't afraid to shoot. He was fantastic, a lovely man. And I still think *Primal Fear* is his best movie as a director — that's my prejudice . . .

And you brought him on, you hired him?

Yes, and I hired him because *Primal Fear* was a courtroom drama and he certainly knew a courtroom from *LA Law*. Then in terms of casting, I had a relationship with Richard Gere from *Internal Affairs* [dir. Mike Figgis, 1990]. I had been the executive in charge of that picture at Paramount, it was my project, I developed the idea. And I loved that picture.

A great film. And clever casting to have Richard Gere as the crooked cop at that point in his career.

That was me. I went through shit for that initially . . . But it was a great movie. So I knew Richard, and I introduced Richard to Greg, and Richard liked the script and he liked Greg. Then we wanted Leonardo DiCaprio for the other key role, but he turned us down. Our casting director Deborah Aquila found Edward Norton — and that was really the best piece of luck, because not only was Edward fantastic, but since no one knew who he was, you watched the movie and you didn't see the whole con of his character coming. Had it been Leo, he would have given a great performance, but you might have started suspecting something.

Did you get hands-on with the making of Primal Fear?

Very — I was there every day and we were rewriting the script throughout the whole process. It was driving everybody nuts, but we ended up changing a big reveal as to when Richard Gere's character finds out that Edward's character is a multiple personality. Originally that came later in the picture, but we moved it forward, and it really played slightly different.

When you're watching dailies, do you feel you can tell whether the film is in good shape — or not?

You can feel comfortable that it's reaching your expectations, but I think most producers know that with every project there is a gamble that you won't truly know about until you've seen the finished movie. On *Primal Fear* we knew that Edward Norton was giving what we thought was a very credible performance, but, frankly, until the entire movie was cut together and put in front of an audience, we didn't know whether that audience would see it all coming and suspect that he had conned them.

I remember sitting in the first test screening. There was a scene where Aaron/Roy comes out as a multiple to Richard's character, Vail. Vail pushes him and says, 'Who the fuck are you?' and Roy says, 'Who the fuck are *you*?' Basically Vail's saying, 'You're Aaron', and Norton's character's saying, 'I'm not that little pissy guy, I'm *Roy*.' And the audience started laughing. We didn't know if it was a good laugh or a bad laugh. They were howling, we didn't know why, and we thought 'Holy Christ, is this a disaster?' Then you realize 'No, it's just that the audience doesn't know what's happening. They anticipated *something*, but this is off the charts, it's a misdirection of the nth degree.' It actually elevated the movie significantly to something more profound and interesting. And at the end they cheered, and afterwards in the focus group when they were asked, 'Which character do you love?' they all loved Richard Gere, but they were saying, 'Who is this guy Edward Norton?' They just couldn't figure out who he was. And we knew at that moment we had a good movie. We had a couple of cocktails that night . . .

So the risk you took in casting paid off. Is that harder to fight for outside of a studio?

It's always the same fight, but it's the best fight. And, quite frankly, a lot of films ask for that. Movies aren't that unique, you know, and every year there is one where somebody does something a little bit different. Take Russell Crowe, he had done a lot of movies but the one that I think set him apart was when he played that older man in *The Insider*. You said to yourself, 'He's thirty and he's playing a convincing fifty-five-year-old.' There were probably fifteen movie stars who could have played that part and they went with Russell Crowe — what a daring choice.

It sounds like you had a positive experience in the case of Primal Fear, *but are you generally positive about the process of audience testing and marketing?*

It's a necessary evil. But it's also a very peculiar dynamic, because I find that with many marketing people and studio executives, their days are so busy that they do lose sight at times of what's happening to real people. If you're taking private jets all the time and if you don't really go to the movies, if you're not around young kids — because that's your audience most of the time — you don't know how they're really feeling. We had a situation on a movie where the studio executive saw it and knew it was good but he just said, 'I don't know how to sell this.' And he would talk to the wife of another executive who would say, 'What? Are you nuts? This is the easiest thing in the world!' A lot of the time, the wives are at home with their children, and they are the ones who know what their sixteen-year-old daughter is really thinking. So they can say, 'Are you kidding? My daughter and all of her friends are going to see this, it's the easiest film in the world to market, don't even worry about it.' But somebody could still say, 'Well, will the young males like it as much?' Or 'Do we sell it as a thriller?' And they really work themselves up into a frenzy about it. I think a lot of it comes from the fact that there is a tremendous amount at stake, a lot of pressure, and most people don't want to lose their jobs.

5. *Good shepherding*

When you're producing, what do you actually do on set?

I use a religious phrase, just because I went to Catholic schools and I know the Bible a little bit. In the New Testament Jesus gives the parable of the good shepherd. 'I am the good shepherd, I know my flock, and my flock know me.' And I think the producer is the good shepherd. You have to know the personalities of the people on your crew — your director, your cinematographer, the actors, the production designer, the script supervisor — also the grips and the gaffers, the video-assist person. It's very important. Because you can walk by the hair and make-up trailer, and if there's a problem with the actors, you're going to hear it from them. OK, if there's something going on with the director you may hear it from the first AD. But you have to know all of those sheep and those sheep have to know that you're paying attention. So on set I'm accessible, and I've got my eye out.

When it comes to post-production, and the director is working toward their first cut, what's your general attitude? Are you content to wait and see what the director comes up with?

According to the Director's Guild, the director has ten weeks to prepare his cut. But what I've quite often found is that there's a cut that exists around the fifth, sixth, seventh week — and it's going to be a little longer, but it's fun to be invited into the cutting room at that point and to sit with the director. He says, 'Of course this isn't my cut', and I say, 'Of course not . . .' But we look at the movie when it's twenty minutes too long, and we just see the direction it's going. Tom Rosenberg and I had the best times doing that on two movies in particular, *The Human Stain*, which Robert Benton directed for us, and *Wicker Park*, which Paul McGuigan directed.

Is editing rather like development in that respect? Refining or honing the story?

I once heard an editor say that the editorial process is the final draft of the screenplay. And I think that's exactly right.

Have you ever had an instance on a film where you felt the cut was completely different from the screenplay you started out shooting?

Yes, there was a movie I made for HBO, *Gotti*, about the life of John Gotti. It ended up with seven Emmy nominations, and Armande Assante won. But the director was so afraid of HBO — who had a rough reputation at that time — that he undercut the movie. It ended up at two hours and seven minutes, but his first cut was like an hour and forty — so there were twenty-seven minutes that we added back into it. When it was shorter it wasn't as good as it should have been, it lost the bravura of Gotti's ranting and raving, which was actually powerful, and slightly more performance oriented. And I thought the character needed that, it was part of who he was.

When HBO did *The Sopranos*, they used half of my actors from *Gotti*. I made a terrible mistake in not thinking ahead, I should have gone to HBO and said, 'I want to do a mob series, here it is . . .'

6. You want friends

Since 2000 you've been in the post of president of Lakeshore Entertainment. How do you operate?

The company is owned by Tom Rosenberg, and we develop, co-produce, and produce movies. Sherry Lansing actually suggested that we work together. One of the reasons why Lakeshore works so successfully, for me, is that Tom and I aren't really that dissimilar — he's from Chicago, he grew up in the city and he's a lawyer, but he's also a guy who likes human stories, as I do. We're very much cut from the same cloth, we hardly disagree with each other creatively at all.

Are you in a 'first-look' deal with Paramount?

We are. Our primary relationship is with Paramount, but if Paramount turn us down we can go someplace else, so that's good for the people who bring us material — the screenwriters and actors and so on. Usually one of the hurdles that you face working with a studio is that even if *they* don't want to make your movie, they won't let the picture go, for fear that if the movie is made by somebody else and it's a hit, then they will be corporately embarrassed. So we're able to get around that situation . . . and it's nice to have a few more roads to travel down in the process of getting a film made, as opposed to being an exclusive producer in just one place.

Whereas many producers in Hollywood are dependent on a studio's money to get a movie made, we usually look to outside sources to raise more than fifty percent of the negative costs of making the film to add to our domestic deal — so, consequently, we have more viability as producers, because we're bringing more of the money.

How do you raise your outside finance?

We have an international division that pre-sells the rights to our films to foreign territories. Then it's our discipline that forces us to make the movie 'inside the box' — in other words, we must then manufacture the product for that total amount of money. Hopefully, from that we can then take a small percentage for ourselves so that we can continue to survive. That discipline is essential to our operation, because if we go over-budget on the money raised, then the cost of the overage comes from us.

In recent years a number of companies raised part of their budgets from foreign pre-sales, and with the heavy influx of money from

Germany, producers realized they could make movies with a 'gap' — which is where the budget exceeds the size of the box. But these companies were relying on the profitability of the movie to sustain their enterprise. And if that doesn't work, then you are gone . . .

If Paramount gives producers one hundred per cent of their budgets, are they less disciplined about 'staying in the box'?

Well, no — because there are *many* producers who are completely funded by studios, and if the studio president says, 'We are going to make this movie for x amount', then they are determining the size of the box and that's how the movie will be made. But the irony with studios, sometimes, is they have a tendency to be much less disciplined and will throw money out, so studio films can then go over-budget. Whereas if, as a producer, it's your own money you're spending, then quite often you have to find creative solutions to budget problems.

Do you have a remit to produce a certain number of movies a year?

On average we have to make four or five movies a year. This last year, we produced three and we've picked up two that we sold foreign on, so it's been a good year. Sometimes it's a nightmare . . . I don't have next year's slate put together yet so I'm not taking a holiday this summer — I don't have the time. The usual problem with producing isn't finding the money, it's finding material that's worthy of it. We have our own development, but we certainly rely on agents to give us material.

How do you fit all the reading and thinking about new projects into your working day when you also have films in various stages of production?

Right now I have three films in post, two with release dates — one on September 19 and one on September 26. I tend to read better in the morning — I have a wife and two daughters, so when I get home in the evenings I like to spend time with them. Then it gets to 9.30 and I am just not so alert as to open up a screenplay and read it properly. Truly, it would put me to sleep. My clock is just better oriented to read in the morning, so that's when I read.

Does the job give you enough time with your children?

I think they think it's OK, my wife seems to think it's OK, nobody gives me a hard time about 'Dad doesn't spend enough time with me . . .' And when I go on location, I call them all the time.

Do you tend to go away for the entire length of shoots?

Sometimes. Most of the time Tom and I alternate every other week, or one of us goes for two weeks and the other for a week.

Is there anything you really don't like about producing?

Everything is difficult, but I probably *like* the difficult — it's probably a sickness. Even when I was a studio executive — after I got past the Stan Kamen nervousness — there were times where there was a crisis, and I loved it: I loved having to put on the fireman's hat, and go in and try to resolve something that nobody else could. I was excited — that's sort of sick, but it's true.

How long do you envisage yourself in the job of producing?

There is a side of me that doesn't think I'll retire, I'm not the retiring type. But I do look forward to a day in my dotage, where one of my daughters has her own family and calls up me and my wife and says, 'Dad, do you guys want to come over for dinner Sunday?' I think my parents like coming and visiting me and their grandchildren, and I absolutely know that there is a sense of accomplishment when you see that your children are OK and they have grown up to have some sort of productive life. I can produce a lot of movies, but you want friends and family when you're old . . .

Lakeshore's recent credits include *Suspect Zero* (2004), *Million Dollar Baby* (2004), *The Exorcism of Emily Rose* (2005), *Aeon Flux* (2005) and *Underworld: Evolution* (2006).

Take 14

JENNIFER TODD

Sisters are doing it for themselves. Producers Suzanne and Jennifer Todd formed Team Todd in 1997 and made a two-year, first-look deal with New Line and top gun young exec Michael De Luca. In 2001 they moved from a two-year, first-look deal at HBO Films to a multi-year deal at DreamWorks, reuniting them with De Luca. They won't be pigeon-holed, as a track record boasting both the *Austin Powers* pictures and Christopher Nolan's *Memento* would attest.

1. *Fighting fires*

JENNIFER TODD: Suzanne and I both went to film school in LA and then we started working. For a time in the late 1980s both of us were working for Joel Silver — Suzanne was an associate producer, and I was Joel's assistant. What was interesting for us is that we built up a lot of experience on the production side by working on big movies like *Die Hard 2* and *Lethal Weapon 2*. As we were lucky enough to be in a company that was busy making films, we learned how to be very hands-on, and got to know quite a bit about budgeting and the physical and logistical side of film production.

Then we both worked our way into different companies. I worked as a junior executive at Miramax for a year, and Suzanne got a couple of movies produced on her own at New Line. Then she partnered with Demi Moore in a production company, Moving Pictures, and I ran Bruce Willis's production company Flying Heart at the same time. Once Demi's company got busier with their slate, I switched over and produced *Now and Then* for them, which was a little movie for New Line in 1995. Then, around 1997, Mike De Luca — who was head of production at New Line and is now at DreamWorks — offered us our own company deal, so we moved to New Line and we were there for four years.

Presumably being a hands-on producer is a much harder graft than being a packager?

Production is physically exhausting because the days are longer — anywhere from twelve to eighteen hours — and then you are on your feet all day, dealing with problem after problem. But, personally, I think physical production is very exciting . . . it's the bit of the process that is like running a race in the Olympics. You've done a huge amount of work and training to get to the first day of shooting, and it's a moment where the producer thinks 'I can't believe I have pulled this off . . . the movie is now about to be made and everyone is here working on our film.' It's a great moment.

As a result of your hands-on experience, do you find that when you read a script you have a good idea in your head of how much it's going to cost?

You can tell whether it's going to be expensive or not. But the funny thing is that people immediately say, 'What's the budget?' And you think 'Well, there isn't just *one* budget, there are a million ways to make this movie.' So I will say, 'Well, these are the possibilities for doing it *this* way. Or we can do it like *this*. Or we can do it like *that* . . .' The true cost of a film depends on so many factors — like who you cast in the movie, and who you hire to direct it, or where you're going to shoot it. A studio has physical production executives who you do the budgeting with, but then when you get a budget the figure is always ridiculously high and they say, 'Oh, your numbers are high', and then you say, 'No, no, we'll get it down.' Then you have to talk to everyone involved and find out how you are creatively going to get the numbers down so you can get the budget signed off. This is done in correlation with hiring a director and figuring out who the cast is going to be. You don't always have what you want in a budget for the cast. Then the studio might say, 'We will make this movie if you can get Brad Pitt to do it. If not, forget it.' So, often you will have done all this work and you still don't know whether you are going to be able to get the movie made. And then everyone is trying to get the most popular actors out there.

Once you cast the movie then you're not the architect any more, you're the chief fire-fighter, because you find that often you show up on set and there are huge crises going on. It might be 'There's a problem with the location', or 'We've lost this particular actor today', or 'The make-up girl is sick.' And you have to deal with all those problems. And it's not only the producer's job to crisis-manage situations as they come up — you're also trying to protect the director, who's busy figuring out where the camera is going to go and what the actors are supposed to be doing. So the last thing you want to do is to go over to him or her and say, 'Look, we need to be out of the building by four o'clock today, so you are going to have to shoot this as fast as you can . . .'

Do you choose the people you want to work on the film or is that the studio's prerogative?

You choose in conjunction with the studio. And often it's a horse-trade — it depends on what level of producer *you* are as to what *they* think. A studio will never let a producer just hire who he or she wants. For example, the accountants have to be hired by the studio, because they are dealing directly with the money. But the creative people, such as the cinematographer or the production designer, usually are agreed on between the studio, the producer and the director — unless you hire a very big director, and oftentimes the studio will relent because a big director will prefer to use his own crew. If you are a newer producer and you are producing your first couple of projects for a studio, they tend not to defer to your opinion so much. But, for example, for a long time there were a few people that we worked with regularly, such as our casting director whom we worked with on seven movies. So it wasn't difficult for me to say, 'I would like to use my guy if you're OK with that. He's really good . . .'

2. *Not a movie kids would want to see*

When did you meet Mike Myers and how did Austin Powers: International Man of Mystery *come together?*

In the beginning Suzanne and I were friends with Mike and knew him socially. Then he kept telling us about a Bond spoof he was writing. When he gave us the script to read we thought it was very funny, but at that point it was more Bond-oriented and had a lot less of the 1960s 'swinger' side to the character. We then heard about a Leslie Nielsen vehicle that was coming out, a spy spoof called *Spy Hard*, so we went back to the script and worked with Mike to develop more of the sixties ideas. In fact, Mike kept on working on the script right up until we started shooting . . . We set the film up at New Line — we had already made a couple of movies there before we got our deal. And Mike De Luca gave us $16.5 million to make the first film.

As we were making it we had no idea how successful it would become. Mike wasn't as big a star as he is now. *Wayne's World* had come and gone. He had made a movie called *So I Married an Axe Murderer* about two years before, then he had purposely taken time off to write *Austin Powers*. He had written a script based on one of his *Saturday Night Live* sketches, and that was based over at Warners, and it's a very funny script but they couldn't get it made over there. So, really, nobody saw *Austin Powers* coming . . .

I think we thought we were making an adult or college-age spy spoof. We weren't thinking it was going to be a movie that kids would want to see. But when it came out we were very surprised that it was a hit with young kids.

If a film is a hit does a studio automatically push for a sequel?

Not at all. The domestic take on the first movie was very good, I think, it made about $55 million in the US, but while that was good, it wasn't necessarily a figure where anyone would turn around and suggest a sequel. What changed was when it came out on video, the video numbers were very strong. Comedy tends to do well on video, and this film did *extraordinarily* well. I think it was so off the chart and so unexpected that that's when they decided to make the sequel. Ultimately both sequels made a lot more money domestically than the first film.

3. As long as there's a plan . . .

How do you support a director during a shoot?

You try to take care of everything you can for them so they can just focus on making the best of their shooting schedule. My main focus is to deal with whatever the logistics are. The studio will call me every day to discuss how the production is going and how the movie looks. So the producer's job on set is a combination of production and creative issues. If the producer wasn't on set, you would have other people like the line producer telling the director whether they can or can't have a second camera — and those are creative issues that need to be managed properly. I think that, as the producer, you have to be there making the decisions. So you might say, 'OK, we only have X-amount of money. Should we spend it on a second camera? Or should we spend another three hours at the location?' You've got to think about what's best for the scene, what will work best for the movie overall. Those are the sorts of logistical issues that you confront every day, and that's why I think it's such an interesting job. I don't think all producers are like that, but that's how I like to look at it. I enjoy helping directors make creative decisions, and I couldn't imagine putting a movie together and then not being there while it was being made.

Do you insist on storyboards and shot lists?

On the day, a shot list is very important — just so that in the morning when you get to the location there's a plan for the day ahead. Whereas storyboards are really only important for specific sets or locations. It's very hard to storyboard a movie until you have all your locations, and often you don't have them all until just before you shoot. Plus a whole bunch of different things happen everyday, so often by the time you come to shoot something you're looking at it differently than you did before.

What's important is that your director has a plan so that you can say, 'OK, by lunchtime we want to be out of here and set up to shoot over there.' But very often it's not that the director arrives unprepared or doesn't have a plan, but that plans have had to change. So the director arrives to find that the schedule for the day has been changed because there's a construction unit based across the street, which means we can't record dialogue unless we move inside the location. Or we have to change locations altogether. Or an actor is late, or it's raining . . .

Do you discuss dailies with the director during the shoot?

You talk about the important stuff — but it's also important to give the director time with the footage. Of course, if there's a problem with something then you talk about it. But if the dailies are looking good, you just want to tell them that and let them get on and do their thing. When the movie wraps, a director has a period of time as set out by their contract — ten weeks per the DGA — to produce their own cut, and that is a time when you have to be really respectful of them and let them have their own time with the material.

Are first cuts often disappointing?

Sometimes. Then again, often they're great. But the truth is you just don't know. It's such a weird process when you are making a movie, it's as though your face is pressed up against the glass, and because you are so close to it you lose your perspective. Then the shoot wraps and you come home and for ten weeks you don't look at anything while the director works on it. So by the time you see the director's assembly there is a lot tied to it emotionally. You are looking at your footage again, and sometimes you have to go through it a few times.

Other times you see something that's missing, which means you might have to re-shoot a part of it.

4. *A certain amount of movies*

Is there a financial limit to what you can develop at DreamWorks?

If they don't like what I take them, then my deal allows me to set the project up with another studio. They don't usually do 'smaller' movies, meaning anything under $15 million. So films such as *Memento* or *Boiler Room*, which we made elsewhere, don't really fit into their scheme — which is the good and the bad of it. And that's a very funny situation because you have to adjust yourself to wherever you base your company, just as you have to adjust yourself to the ebb and tide of the business. There are times when it feels like, all of a sudden, movies have got very big, or then they're small again . . . But very often it's the middle ground that is a lot harder to tread in terms of movies we might want to make.

How many projects do you have in development?

We have about twelve to fifteen projects that are set up at studios, and then we have other stuff that we are working on internally — ideas that aren't set up anywhere out in the world. We spend time working on one project for a while, then another, then writers will be off working on a script, so there will be a period of time where you're not doing anything on it. Then a script comes in and we will write notes. Every day is different, which is a great part of the job.

Now that I've produced a few films, I feel a little bit more secure in my taste, particularly as some of the movies were well-regarded. Overall I think I have my own taste in movies. I grew up liking certain types of movies. At the same time I have great respect for people who make other kinds of movies that maybe I wouldn't have read or seen. But I think all producers have a certain amount of movies in them. The trick is, I believe, that producers have to be very smart to recognize what really speaks to them. Sometimes I read something and think, 'I don't know if this connects with me but it seems like it *should*, because it's a teen horror movie, and maybe that's what kids want these days . . .' But that's the biggest mistake a producer can make. If I can't actually *see* what the movie should be or have an idea about it in my mind and connect with it at some level, even if its going to be the next *American Pie* and make hundreds of millions of dollars, it's not going to be the right movie for me to make. Whereas when I read *Boiler*

Room as a spec script I really loved it, and what fascinated me was this Wall Street world with all these kids running around trying to sell stocks. So I talked to the writer, and he wanted to direct it, so I tried to find financing for it. But my studio deal had already passed on it, so I set it up with another company and we made a bunch of offers, and got some cast interested. Then that company figured that the movie was too expensive for them, so I went back to New Line and they took the movie back, and we set it up and made it there.

Every movie happens differently, and it's a crazy process, a real lottery. You work on a lot of other projects at once and only a couple of them ever get made. I have spent hundreds of hours on projects that will never see the light of day, because at the end of the day I couldn't get them through — either I couldn't find the right director, the right cast, or the studio changed their minds. So you have got to feel something about the material and connect with it, because you have to be so diligent in your effort to get a movie made. Every single day, just when you think you've got somewhere, you look up and the rock is coming back down the hill . . . so you have to keep pushing and pushing it back up until finally you get it into production.

5. *The King Arthur movie*

Do you have preferred habits in working with writers at script stage?

Suzanne and I don't work with readers. We both read the scripts ourselves and make all the notes. A script has to be something that I can see very, very clearly and give good conscious thought to, or I'm not going to do a good job helping the writer to bring the script along.

Boiler Room and *Memento* were both writer-director projects and it's a very different journey working with writer-directors. And I love working with writer-directors, because it's easier. If you agree with what's on the page and you can see from your notes of the conversation that you are moving forward together, then there is a consistency and you can tell your future meetings are going to be the same.

Often a large part of our job is waiting for new drafts to come in, but when they do Suzanne and I get very involved in turning the script around and giving the writer notes and suggestions about how to fix things. Working with writers on a script all the way through is a very different experience to when you are just selling ideas. Sometimes you sell a basic pitch to the studio and then you have to work with the writer on getting the pitch to a story, and then to a script of a hundred and twenty pages. Then you have to go back out, try to set it up, find a director and so on. Usually if you sell the verbal idea or the pitch, then that person writes at least the first draft. But sometimes it doesn't go that way. We have a movie that we sold as a pitch to one company and we got to a first draft, but neither we nor the company were happy with it, so we got another studio to pay them back, moved it elsewhere and got a couple more drafts with the writers. Until the studio said, 'Look, we want to bring in some new writers just for a couple of weeks, to kind of punch it up and get it ready to shoot' . . . And that's quite common. Personally I like to stick with the original writers for as long as I can, and I think it's a bad trait in Hollywood when people are constantly saying, 'Let somebody else do it.' Unless you can be very specific about what you want from another writer, then I tend to think it's the original writer or writers who have the movie in their head that you should be thinking about. And if you are not quite sure what it is you want from the new writer, then you shouldn't keep trying to throw new people at it.

Often projects just die, that's the crazy thing. Sometimes as a producer you go in really hard with the studio to sell a project, and then the writer writes it and rewrites it, and it comes in — and no matter how hard you work on it, you know that it's not in a good enough shape. And that's when the studio decides to replace the writer — or sometimes they will just say, 'Let's just forget about this project, move on and find something else along the road.' For the producer it's a terrible loss. Anything you don't get made is very, very hard, because you spend such a long time working on these things. Even if the writer got paid for writing it, when you don't see the movie through to fruition that part of the process is really tough.

So much of the job is actually out of your control, and I think that's the hardest thing for people to understand. I didn't really understand it when we first started. I kept thinking 'I *have* to get this movie made' and I thought if I had tunnel vision that would make it a little bit easier. Until finally you realize that you can have a great piece of material with great people who want to do it, and still it won't get made, no matter how good you are as a producer. It always depends on a number of different things. For instance, sometimes you sell a project to a studio, but then the person who loved it originally leaves. A lot of producing has to do with timing, luck and perseverance.

If a project fails can it be regenerated or developed again later on?

You always hear stories from people who say, 'I bought this book ten years ago and it's taken us all this time to get it made.' So, yes, it can take ages. Sometimes it's hard if a movie is on the point of being made and then for whatever reason it doesn't happen — so you have to go back out there again and try to get the agents to pay attention to the material and give you talent and so on.

Do agents send you material?

They do. Tuesdays are a big day for submissions because if they send out material to producers on Tuesdays, producers read the submissions that night, then they call the agents back Wednesday, and then if the producer likes something they will submit it to the studio and the agents will hope that they can sell the material by Friday. Or if the studios don't read the material before the weekend, then it goes on their weekend read and hopefully somebody will buy it on Monday. So it often happens Tuesday is a busy day for submissions and we read between five and ten scripts or books. My sister and I divide it all up, I'll read two or three things and Suzanne will do the same.

That's a lot of material to read in one night.

It is, but, you know, you only keep going if it's good. I will always try to read as much as I can. But if it's bad, you quit after thirty pages. And sometimes a script is *so* bad . . .

Do you read unsolicited material?

The only material we look at is stuff that comes from the agencies, or scripts that come from writers with some kind of track record. Often agents will call and say, 'We have this new material and it's from so-and-so, you're not familiar with this writer but he has two projects with Paramount.' Or the writer might have written a spec script and the agent will give it to me usually with the idea that I'll take it to DreamWorks. But the agent would have also given the material to other producers around town, hoping that they will also take it to *their* studios. And then sometimes you read something that's really great, and you'll call the agent, and if it's something they have sent out to a lot of other producers you say, 'Can I have this if such-and-such doesn't want it? Or can I have any other territories?'

That said, I think we read a lot of stuff 'in the middle', and we find ourselves thinking 'Is this a really good idea for a movie? The idea is good but it's not that well executed' or 'I liked the first act but then the rest of it falls apart.'

Often agents are just trying to sell spec material, in which case they are not going to let a producer stop and work on it, and that's not an ideal situation. Often you're not given the opportunity to try and improve the script before you have to shop it to the studios. A lot of times an agent will say, 'Do you want this? Yes or no?' You might like it but you think the ending could be better. But you have no choice but to take it to DreamWorks right then and there and say, 'I like this, I think it could be better in places, but do you want to buy it?' Sometimes they say no, sometimes yes.

The other side of development is when you wake up in the middle of the night and think 'Right, I want to make a movie about King Arthur and I'm going to find a writer and come up with the idea.' And sometimes you get lucky when you originate ideas.

Recently there was a funny script that Suzanne read about a young woman who was scared of her mother-in-law — it was called *Monster-in-Law*. The script was sent out a few months ago, and it was a spec, written by Anya Kochoff. There was a huge bidding war between all the different studios, and we didn't get it. Then immediately the deal was done, they started casting and negotiating with Jennifer Lopez to be in it. That's a very valid way to get a movie made. But you only get serviced with that kind of material if you have a deal with a studio. So it's much harder for producers to have access to scripts if you are not set up somewhere.

If you want some particular material very badly, will a studio go after it on your behalf?

Sometimes, but I have to work hard to convince them to do it. They will ask you why you want the script or the book or whatever it is, and you have to be able to explain to them why it is a valid piece of material and what kind of movie it is going to be. And you have to go over it again and again . . .

Who do you present your projects to at the studio?

The first tier of executives is a team of vice-presidents and creative people. Then you have the president of the studio. I don't really know how many people it takes to get a 'Yes'. And it's an interesting thing inasmuch as who has the power to actually *say* 'Yes'. A studio doesn't like you to actually know that . . . so there is a kind of mystery about it.

Do you have to lobby hard for your projects? Is it political?

It can be. I've never worked at a studio as an executive, so I don't really know what their mindset is — only that it's a very different job to mine. I suppose when you're a producer you are pretty much a salesperson — you are constantly setting out your wares to the studio: 'I think this is a great story and we should make this into a movie' or 'Do you want this movie with this actor or director?' or 'I've got a comedy as well . . .' But if you're the executive then not only do you have a slate to fill, but in addition to making creative choices you have to choose movies in a way that is financially responsible. Executives have to deliver on a corporate level which means they make their decisions with a different mindset. I don't think I have drastically un-commercial tastes, but sometimes the films I find aren't necessarily *Spider-Man* and yet I still want to make them.

6. *'I will never get another movie made . . .'*

Do you ever feel overloaded or exhausted by the process?

I think it's a crazy job. When I started I really didn't know, and when you're young and innocent you think 'It's OK, I went to film school, this all makes sense.' But actually I think there are probably more satisfying ways of being in the business, because it's a difficult job. You spend your day at the office constantly making calls and trying to get your material out, read and seen, and thinking 'Well, I have this script but can I get this particular director to read it?' Or 'Can I get the studio to say yes or no?' You may have a project and be trying to grab an actor that everyone else wants.

Then you go home at night and you have piles of reading to do. And if you don't get it done and someone else buys the script the next day, it's your own fault. You also have to keep current on everything, you have to know what material is already out there, which is tough when you're busy. You have to *see* movies too, because you need to be aware of who everyone is in the business — you have to know directors, writers and creative people, you have to know what projects everyone is making, and you can really only do all of that in your free time. You have to be aware of what projects people are working on, because if you and I decide we want to make our King Arthur movie and we sit here working on it for two months and then I go to DreamWorks and they say, 'Oh, didn't you know that Touchstone just went into pre-production on a King Arthur movie? So we're not going to make one as well' — then you're screwed. All this means having your company track what everyone else is doing in case there is an overlap.

On top of that, the business changes a lot because people just want different kinds of movies. And there are days when it feels very personal, there's no doubt about that . . . There are plenty of days when you think 'I will never get another movie made again — it's just impossible and I really don't know how it's all going to work out.' What people find so hard to understand is that no matter how good you are, so much of the process of getting a movie made is out of your control. Really, there are lucky days and unlucky days.

Do you have access to a studio information network?

There are a couple of websites that give all that information and you have to pay to access them, but then you can look up people's projects. The site we use has a section called 'Aggressively current status of development' which is important — because say you go on to the Internet Movie Database and look up somebody's credits: it only identifies what that person is attached to and you don't always know what they are working on right now. But on the site I'm talking about, if you want to see if a writer is available, then you can click on their name and go in and look at what they are doing. It also gives you a lot of the information that the industry trade magazines cover, such as which projects have been sold or which movies have been green-lit. At the studios they handle this information differently, because all the executives go into these big staff meetings every day and go over every project.

How many phone calls do you take in a day?

A lot . . . and the volume goes up and down because it depends what you are doing. My job is very different if we're not shooting. But if we are in pre-production — and I have a movie that is casting right now — then seventy per cent of my calls are about that. Then in-between that there are all the specific calls relating to other projects. So, for example, I'm sending a script out today so most of the calls are about that. So much of the job is about your relationships with people, whether it's the studios or with agents, because if someone sends me a piece of material I want to pay attention to it and at least be polite — even if I don't like it, I will always call them back and be conscientious, also because I want them to send me the next script. And it's important to have a reputation as someone who is honest. But it's a twenty-four-hour job, it really is.

Do you find the job easier working with your sister?

Absolutely. I feel very lucky to be working with Suzanne because it's such a rollercoaster of highs and lows, and for every movie you get made there are some really hard days getting there. So it's nice to have somebody whose shoulder you can cry on. Then you pick yourself back up and go 'OK, what's next . . .?' We work on everything together but we try not to be repetitive. So usually one of us will make the majority of phone calls on one project and the other will look after something else. We share the responsibilities and we talk throughout the day. I think it's nice to have that sister thing because it's hard to be a producer on your own. And thankfully for now I don't have to think about that because it's working well.

7. *Will people in Kansas show up?*

How did you meet Christopher Nolan?

On *Memento* we worked with a company called Newmarket, who financed the picture, and I was introduced to Chris by the executive producer Aaron Ryder who worked at Newmarket. We got very lucky because Aaron had this interesting piece of material. I thought it was amazing. I can't say whether I thought *Memento* was going to be successful or not, but I know I kept thinking what a cool exercise it would be to try and pull it off. I thought that being associated with it would be interesting, and, if nothing else, I knew my friends would like the film. When I'm thinking about making a movie, I often ask myself, 'Do I want to see my name come up on this when I'm channel surfing at 3 a.m?' And, 'Will my friends like it?' It's all you can really ask for, because I really can't tell you if people in Kansas are going to show up or not. Perhaps it's not the most perfect example of how to choose a film but again, it's all about going with your instincts and sticking with them.

I was given Chris's first film *Following* to watch which I thought was pretty cool, and then we had a meeting. Guy Pearce has a great agent, who flipped over the script early on and was really helpful, and it was a testament to Guy that he understood the material and wanted to do it — I think it's why he has such an interesting career. Some actors just want to stay in the mainstream and do the big stuff and some of them really love to mix it up and Guy is one of those, a chameleon.

It was clear on the page that Chris had a very specific idea in his mind about what he wanted to do, and that's the brilliant thing about him. It was a lovely experience making the film, everybody just came together and worked really hard. We shot *Memento* in twenty-six days. My job was to try and help Chris get the most out of his days, but I think when we were shooting the film that things were straight-forward for him because he had planned the film so well — he had storyboarded a great deal, and then most of it was in his head already.

The script was shot out of sequence according to the locations, and all the black and white scenes in the hotel room were shot at the end of the shoot. It was a really funny, crazy shoot. The crew loved how complicated it was, and key departments like the art and wardrobe departments rearranged the script from back to front so they could get the chronology of the story. Then, once they understood that, they could put the script back into its shooting order. It was funny to see everyone figuring out how to make it work. I remember standing with Carrie-Anne Moss and Guy Pearce looking at all the Polaroids — there were piles of them everywhere — for Guy to keep writing on in the same way.

When we finished *Memento* we couldn't get anyone to distribute it. No one would release it. When you make a film with a studio you have your distribution already set up with them, so this was hard. I remember thinking 'We're never going to make another independent film again.' The original plan was to sell it to a studio, but after we couldn't find a studio to buy it Will Tyrer and Chris Ball, who financed the film, paid for the distribution themselves. They hired a brilliant independent distributor, Bob Berney, who was here on the west coast but who had worked at Miramax a long time ago, and he understood the movie and got the film released in cinemas on eighty prints. After releasing *Memento* he went to work for IFC and distributed *My Big Fat Greek Wedding* and *Y tu mamá también*.

Once the movie was released in theatres it started to do well and played for quite a long time, so they spent more money on its release and it went out to more and more theatres. At first it was difficult and frustrating, because I believed in the film so much. Once it was out there it was easy to push. Newmarket paid for the marketing but it was a small release. At most, and at the widest point of release, we were only filling a couple of hundred theatres as opposed to a big film like *Too Fast, Too Furious* which was released in maybe 2,500 theatres.

Were you surprised at how well Memento *was received?*

I could never tell *anyone* what's going to work or not work. What I feel is that if I like something then other people might want to see it.

Producing *Memento* got me to the point where I felt validated, but the success we had with the film doesn't mean that I know how every movie is going to turn out. I am not the producer who can make *Too*

Fast, Too Furious and that film made a ton of money. I wouldn't know how to make that kind of movie because I don't know anything about cool cars, I wouldn't know what kids want — that's not my arena.

I saw *Memento* mostly as an art-house movie, and I thought it was the kind of movie my friends would really go for. But, you know, it's funny, because it came out in Europe before it opened in the US and I was on safari in Kenya and I found myself sitting next to a sixteen-year-old French girl, who told me she had seen a movie she loved so much called *Memento* and had taken her whole family to see it, and her twelve-year-old sister really loved it. I remember thinking at the time 'Oh, she's French, they're so much more avant-garde and they love cinema — thank God!' It was cool that they loved the movie, but I was still wondering whether American teenagers would respond like that. And then, sure enough, when the movie came out my friend's teenage kids all wanted to talk to me about *Memento* and they were all so appreciative and savvy and up to date with it all. So it was great that it became something bigger than even I had imagined.

Will you work with Chris Nolan again?

I would love to work with Chris again. I don't have another project with him at the moment, though we have been trying to find something. But he's very busy because he's doing the next *Batman* movie and that's going to take two years out of his life.

8. *In the club*

To what extent would you say that commercial success has enhanced your standing in Hollywood?

There's no way of knowing how you are perceived in the industry because it's not like there is a big chart on a wall somewhere where someone is saying, 'Oh, it looks like the Todds are moving up today.' I think if you have some success with a movie you produced then people listen to you a little bit, but not nearly as much as they will to directors. Chris Nolan proved himself on *Memento,* then a studio offered him *Insomnia* and he proved himself with that and now he's directing *Batman.*

Is the bottom line that if your movies make money then you carry on?

Having a successful film doesn't mean anything other than you have a *slightly* better chance of getting your next movie together. The bottom line is if a studio hates the script, they are still not going to make it — even if you've proved yourself to be right about other films. I guess if you show up to a meeting with Jim Carrey then you get a little bit of support . . . but it's not like they hand you the money to make another movie. Producers have to prove themselves over and over again — particularly in our case, as we like to make movies in different genres, so it's not like I can say I specialize in comedies or thrillers. I really enjoy producing, and the thing is you never know how long it's going to last. But I hope to keep doing it until they don't let me do it any more.

Do you make time for vacations?

Well, it's funny, but I've just decided to go to London for a wedding, but when I was thinking about it I thought 'I can't stay long . . .' Except I probably could. It's just that I worry too much about the projects that are going on. So I don't really take long vacations. But it's my own fault.

What kind of people make good producers?

You have to be so committed. My sister puts it well: she thinks there has to be something a little bit off the wall about someone — you have to want to do this so badly. It has to be about more than money. There has to be this thing in you where you just want to make movies *no matter what*, so that you live and breathe it every day. If you don't have that passion you'll never get through all the difficulties. And then even if you do get through it you still have to be lucky to get a movie made. It's competitive and hard and you have to live it one hundred per cent. And then on top of that you have to have a lot of luck.

Would you say producing is financially rewarding?

It depends on the movie, and on what kind of deals you make. You are not going to make a lot of money on the first movie you produce. But then your deals get better. Obviously, the guys who are at the top of their game make a great deal of money — the Brian Grazers and Jerry Bruckheimers. But to make a lot of money you have to really prove yourself. If you're the one putting the financing together or you have ownership of the film, then the financial upside can be huge.

Is being a woman in Hollywood an issue any more?

Yes and no. It's an amazing time in the business, there are women as chairs and/or presidents at all the major studios. As far as industries are concerned, the film business must have one of the strongest success rates for women.

That being said, I still find there can be a boy's club mentality from time to time. It's hard because often men have more disposable time to network and form relationships, where women usually spend any non-work time on children and family.

I read that you and Suzanne organize a women's networking club for fun?

We socialize, and it's fun for women to do things in the same way that men have their golf outings and so on. I find some of my friends in this business are so amazing — the way they are so good at their jobs, and keep their lives together, and also have to run their households and families. So every once in a while it's good to get together and sort of burn off steam and do something fun.

In 2003, Team Todd signed a deal with Revolution Studios. *Must Love Dogs* and *Prime* were released in 2004, and for 2006 they produced *Zoom* and *Across the Universe*.

Take 15

JASON HOFFS

In one of those occasional pieces of Hollywood reportage destined for future anthology ('Boss-Zilla!', 24 September 2005), Kate Kelly and Merissa Marr of the *Wall Street Journal* anatomized the hiring practices and management style of super-producer Scott Rudin. 'Mr Rudin', they wrote, 'holds the unofficial crown of Hollywood's most feared boss.' His office, they claimed, '. . . has become a modern equivalent of the William Morris Agency's mailroom . . . a proving ground for would-be moguls.' There were, however, caveats. 'In Mr Rudin's office, caustic rants, shrieking threats and impulsive firings are routine. Mr Rudin hires the young and ambitious who flock to the movie industry, testing their mettle in an intense environment . . . The result is a revolving door that never stops spinning.' The piece claimed that Rudin may have gone through at least 119 — maybe 250 — hirings in the space of five years. But the testimony from all ex-hirings was respectful.

Jason Hoffs has been through the Rudin experience and survived. From a pupillage at Scott Rudin Productions while Rudin was at Paramount (and there was, Hoffs recalls, an 'intense level of turnover in the operation'), Hoffs became a VP at Steven Spielberg's Amblin Entertainment. He was then a DreamWorks senior production executive, and supervised development and production of features including *The Peacemaker, Deep Impact, Mouse Hunt* and *Meet the Parents*. In 2000 he had a run in New York at the Internet firm Kaufman Patricof Enterprises (KPE) before returning to Hollywood.

1. *Big budget B movies*

HELEN DE WINTER: *Did you set out to become a producer?*

JASON HOFFS: It's always been my aspiration, but it's taken a while . . . Early on, I spent time working an apprenticeship for people who were great producers and executives, and finally that gave me the confidence to go out and do it on my own.

A lot has happened by accident. But in the early days and then along the way I acquired some producer-type credits on a couple of low-budget movies. One of them was a movie called *Red Surf* that I made with a friend in 1989, starring George Clooney.

Were you a writer on that as well?

My friend and I came up with the original idea, and I have a story credit. The script was loosely based on some surf kids in Newport Beach, California, who got in over their heads when they started dealing drugs. They used to surf the drugs in hollowed-out surfboards . . . The idea for the movie was to take a group of fun-loving kids who were a little bit punk and nihilistic, but who were essentially comfortable in their own world, until they took the experience further by moving to another turf — which, in the case of our movie, was some Mexican coke-dealing gangs in East LA.

We were very young when we made the movie and didn't really know what we were doing, so it was a film conceived with a lot of bravado. In the writing we would try to put ourselves in the mindset of these characters and come up with scenes. So we hung out in Malibu with a bottle of Jim Beam and some punk rock music, and tried to figure out what the characters would do next.

So, in other words, it was a kind of Method screenwriting.

It was, kind of . . .

*How was **Red Surf** funded?*

I left as the film was being financed, but it was funded as a direct-to-video project, and it cost about $1 million. In the late 1980s you could make these B-genre titles. At the time I was working for a producer called Gregg Sims, who was a classic independent producer, mostly making genre movies by trying to put together theatrical, foreign, and videocassette money, and producing movies in the $1 million to $2 million range. But there was something about making *Red Surf* that made me want to work in a bigger studio sandbox, because it felt like there weren't the proper resources in the low-budget or independent world to make genre or action-adventure movies for these budgets. It's one thing making low-budget *art* movies, but we were working in a B-movie paradigm. Starting from the time of AIP and

Roger Corman[18] you had had low-budget movies that were what we would call 'independent films'. But by the late 1980s, it seemed to me that the studios were co-opting B movie franchises and making them for enormous budgets. And I realized I wanted to move in that direction.

Did you know people in the business when you started out?

I grew up in Los Angeles and Santa Monica, and I have an aunt, Tamar Simon Hoffs, in the business — she's directed a couple of films. Growing up I loved movies but I had no idea about auteurism or anything like that. I knew who Humphrey Bogart was from watching old movies on television, but when I was younger I was never looking at who directed or produced the movie. It was only later when I went to University of California at Berkeley and started taking film classes that I was introduced to how movies were made.

In college, two films really excited me. One was a movie called *The Stunt Man*, directed by Richard Rush, about a convict who wanders on to a movie set and becomes a stunt man. Watching that movie I felt there was an intoxicating dialectic between what was happening in front of the camera and behind it. It showed me the process of movie-making for the first time, and I thought it painted a glamorous and fantastic world. After seeing the movie and hearing Richard Rush talk about it I thought it would be great to do that. Also while I was in college Werner Herzog was a romantic character on the world stage, and he would go and do things in his sort of Germanic and iconoclastic way — so I was watching movies like *Aguirre, Wrath of God* and *Fitzcarraldo* and thinking that there was something about Herzog's style of movie-making that I found very appealing. *Aguirre, Wrath of God* was really stimulating to me in that I felt immersed in an almost intense and heroic environment, akin to a lot of western movies, where characters are forced to make important, primal and elemental choices. I realized that the films that appealed to me were where characters inhabited hyper-real worlds where they often had to make those really difficult and heroic choices. These weren't movies with a literate appeal, but true spectacles where I could be subsumed into a complete environment.

18. AIP (American International Pictures) was masterminded by producer Samuel Z. Arkoff (1918–2001) who from the mid-1950s turned out innumerable pictures aimed at the nascent 'teenage' audience, from horror and sci-fi to beach movies and biker pictures. Roger Corman (b.1926) directed many pictures for AIP prior to founding his own legendary low-budget company, New World.

After college I started out doing physical production work, but I wasn't good at it because I'm not good mechanically or with my hands. As I had studied literature and read thousands of books in my life I was drawn to script development and the process of analysing story and character and looking at what makes a good script. After I stopped working for Gregg Sims I wanted to work in the context of a bigger company, so I became an assistant for a friend of mine who was head of drama development at the Fox network. After being an assistant for a year I was promoted to being the lowest level of executive. Then we were both fired, and I didn't know what to do. I decided TV wasn't for me, the low-budget film world wasn't for me, so I was going to try and make it in the movie business.

Then in 1989 through a mutual friend — an agent who was a close friend — I met the producer Scott Rudin. I had one meeting with Scott and he hired me and became my first real mentor. So having been fired as a low-level executive in television, I was taken on by Scott to be his vice president of production at Paramount.

2. *That might not make everybody happy*

What did you do for Scott Rudin?

I spent nearly two years in development. That meant tracking material and collecting an enormous amount of intellectual property from all over the world to assess what could be developed into films. For example I would look at plays from London or New York, published articles, books and screenplays. At the time, I would say Scott had become renowned as a commercial film producer with very elevated taste; he had a very high level of talent relationships, a knack for what was commercial, and an ability to find source material that other people might not recognize as having box office potential. Often Scott would put together the appropriate elements or even fashion the story himself, so it could become a motion picture that he would then get financed in the studio system. He had enormous energy, worked twenty hours a day and was tireless and relentless. There was also an intense level of turnover in his operation, but I managed to stay there for what was a comparatively long period of time.

Did you work twenty hours a day?

I worked about sixteen hours a day, seven days a week . . . Scott would scrutinize my schedule and encourage me to have breakfast, lunch, drinks and dinner meetings every day. Then we would frequently speak at night, and if he had any questions we would go through my follow-up on things. It was a relentless job.

If you consume that volume of intellectual material does it destroy your instinct for what's good?

It can kill off your instinct. And it can make you not want to read books for a number of years. If there was a manuscript that came in from New York I would work an eleven-hour day, then I would go home and try to read 350 pages of a 600 page book by 11 p.m., write an opinion about whether it could make a movie or not, then get up at 6 a.m. the next morning and do it all over again. We had about twenty-five projects in development all over town and I was required to find writers and directors for those projects. Even though there were a number of people working in development, sometimes it was just me — because of the aforementioned turnover in the office.

What projects did you have a particular proximity to?

I worked superficially on a bunch of things while I was there: *The Firm* and *Sister Act*, and we made *Searching for Bobby Fischer* and *Little Man Tate*.

During this time were you thinking, 'This is what you have to do to become a successful producer in Hollywood'?

I saw in Scott many of the elements that a successful producer has; an ability to charm people, not to be intimidated by anybody — and to run over people or through them when necessary.

What do you mean by that?

A lot of the time, people have their own agendas, or they're going to say 'No' to you. You need to find a way to get something done, and that might not make everybody happy. It didn't seem like Scott was that concerned about people being temporarily unhappy if the outcome was for the greater good of the picture. I certainly learned from him that you can't keep everyone happy all of the time — and I'm sure he would say that. Personally I have more of a people-pleasing personality, and it's harder for me to do that — though sometimes I wish I had more of that kind of thing.

3. *Steven's movies*

Why did you leave Paramount?

I was unbelievably burned out. And Scott and I mutually felt like
the relationship had gone as far as it would go. But the fact that I
had survived in the job for a year-and-a-half caught the attention
of some people around town, whom I then discussed working for. I
was approached by Don Simpson and Jerry Bruckheimer and by the
Amblin people. At Amblin I initially met with Deborah Neumayer,
and then with Kathleen Kennedy, Spielberg's then producing partner
and then with Steven Spielberg. Working with someone of Steven's
talent would be appealing to just about anybody, and I really wanted
to go and work for him. I joined in January 1992 and they became a
new series of mentors.

I felt at the time that I wanted to make the kind of movies that
Steven directed and his company produced, and I really wanted to
learn how those kinds of movies were made. *Close Encounters of the
Third Kind* is probably my favourite movie, but I didn't mention that
at the job interview because I didn't want to suck up. But when talking about influential movies, I often refer to that one because for me
it's a template of the things I want to be developing and producing
myself. I think of *Close Encounters* as the story of a particular person
who finds himself in absolute overblown, outrageous circumstances.
On one level it's a character who has the first contact with extrater-
restrials, but on another it's like the story of Job — a man who believes
he is going crazy, leaves his wife and family, and is then tortured by
demons until his nightmares are ultimately proven correct. For me
that's a perfect template of a classic heroic story. A lot of Steven's
movies have those elements and that's always appealed to me and
I wondered how he kept doing it so well and hoped it was something
I could learn.

When I joined Amblin it was a relatively small group of people
but there was a very advanced filmmaking infrastructure there with
some tremendously talented and experienced people. Even on the
technical level they had been doing extraordinary things with new
technologies years before I got there. When I arrived they were working on the first *Jurassic Park* that at that time had the first advanced
computer-generated characters. At Amblin there were always exciting
and groundbreaking things happening.

Did you continue to work in development?

I worked in development and production, because it blurs a bit, and I stayed there until 1995 when DreamWorks was created and Steven said, 'Do you want to hang out and continue working at DreamWorks?' I said, 'Of course.' DreamWorks was in transition from being a large production company to becoming a studio. It was a little bit different, but I certainly enjoyed being a studio executive — and it was about as busy or more so than it had been with Scott.

While you were an executive were you thinking about the films you wanted to produce?

It was always in my mind — and maybe I always felt more of a producer because of that. But because it takes years to develop and produce a movie I wasn't really thinking about that, or planning on leaving the company for a while. When you're a studio executive your job is gathering ideas from other people, be they producers, writers or agents, and you find yourself acting as a gatekeeper to a flood of material that just keeps coming in. You are basically so busy trying to sort through the material that there isn't time to pursue and generate your own ideas quite as much.

DreamWorks was probably a little bit different because it's a production company, a studio hybrid run by creatives and producers like Walter Parkes who is now Steven's producer. Back then, the volume of submissions wasn't quite what it was at a studio like Warner Bros where there might be four hundred projects in active development at any given time and an executive might have seventy projects they were working on. For a while it wasn't quite that busy at DreamWorks so they might have had a total of a hundred projects in development, spread across five or six executives. Being a little different, there was probably a bit of time to be thinking more personally about things. What I found incredibly satisfying was trying to bring in an idea or generate an idea and work on things that I had originated rather than, say, something that one of my bosses had put together where I would be support staff. What appealed to me was helping to initiate something, whether it was my idea or somebody else's, and then ushering it all the way to being made and released — that's definitely a more producer role. Traditionally a typical studio executive will want to work on as many successful films as possible at *whatever* stage the project is at. There is less ownership if you are the studio executive because your name is not on the movie, but instead you're getting a guaranteed pay-cheque. So there is less risk upfront. The studio executive becomes more the manager or administrator of the creative process and represents the financing entity. Whereas being a real producer is somewhat different in that you generate material more directly.

As an executive how did your days go?

There are a couple of staff meetings a week and you usually discuss a project when an executive wants to buy or pursue, and it's usually discussed around the table. It's either consensually decided upon or sometimes the executive will have the power to buy a project — less so nowadays. In my case I would need the OK of Walter and Laurie MacDonald — who ran the movie division at DreamWorks — to say whether we should move forward.

4. *Basically homeless*

How did you find the idea for The Terminal?

I had heard the story a long time ago about a man who had been living in Charles de Gaulle airport in Paris for ten years, and I thought it was an interesting idea and started to think about it as a movie. I remember making some progress and talking to my colleagues about it, and to some degree I recall hearing from them that there was *something* there — but the question was, is there enough in the story? And are people going to want to see a movie that takes place entirely in an airport? What was interesting was the real character I had read about could have left the airport at any time, he could have escaped. And I felt that made him less sympathetic. My wife is an agent and she put me together with a client of hers, a writer, Andrew Nicol, who was also interested in the story. And Andrew suggested that the character should be trapped behind Customs — trapped like McMurphy battling Nurse Ratched in *One Flew Over the Cuckoo's Nest*. And that made it possible to create more of a dramatic context. Once Andrew came in and there was an element that is known as 'Talent Attached' I think Walter Parkes and Laurie McDonald, who had always liked the idea, were more inclined to feel like there was a starting place. Walter and Laurie also wanted to work with Andrew because of his extraordinary work on *The Truman Show* [dir. Peter Weir, 1998]. At the time Andrew was writing and directing *Gattaca* [1999] so we went out and found a screenwriter, Sacha Gervasi, who did an amazing job. Andrew then came on board to supervise the screenplay and the creative process, and for a time he was attached to direct. Later he stepped off as director and went off to make another film so we hired Sacha.

Cut to a few months later: I had got caught up in the internet boom and had a cool offer to go join a company, so I left DreamWorks and the movie business for about nine months. But I asked them if I could stay on board one of my projects which was not yet in script form, as producer, and Walter and Laurie very generously said yes. And thankfully that movie has now become *The Terminal*, which they are producing and Spielberg is directing and Andrew Nicol and I are executive producing. When I was at the Internet company, our production executive Adam Goodman assumed my role on the project but I stayed very involved in the creative process. We had Sacha and he wrote a couple of drafts, and then the script started to get the interest of some talent and various directors became aware of it, and Tom Hanks became aware of it, and obviously Steven had been aware of it and liked the idea from the beginning. In the very early days we talked about Roberto Benigni starring in it, and we had some conversation with him and he thought it was a really great idea.

Why were you so passionate about The Terminal?

You always need a solid reason to stick with a project, and when I first read the article I became extremely emotional for reasons I couldn't comprehend. And it was because I would get choked up about the story that this suggested to me there was something in the kernel of the idea — something about the character and his situation that resonated with me like nothing else did. I don't know if that's a good reason to pursue an idea or story, but at least that feeling was there. I had an emotional connection to the story that frankly I didn't understand, and that doesn't happen on every project. What appealed to me about the story was that it was about a character who was a victim of circumstance, trapped in an alienating environment that nobody would want to be trapped in, and who has basically found himself homeless. This guy is looking around his environment, he's not supposed to talk to anybody or touch anything and everybody around him is either having a loving or tearful hello or goodbye, or they're off to make a big business deal. The people in the airport, the janitors and workers may not love their jobs but at least they have their lives. By contrast our guy feels pointless and purposeless and as he looks out and sees limos waiting outside JFK — he might even see Manhattan in the distance — he dreams of escape. It's only later when he has a chance to leave that he realizes he has built a life for himself. It's the John Lennon line, 'Life is what happens to you when you're busy making other plans.' That's what happens with him — he has this quiet, indomitable spirit and he ends up winning over everybody in the airport and becoming the soul of it. And surprisingly he creates a whole life for himself in this most unlikely environment. An aspect of that resonated with me, because in terms of my life I sometimes look around and see all these people who seem to have a good life, more so than me, and then I'll look at my own life and think of Viktor Navorski living in the airport and realize that I *do* have a good life. There are projects you might do for purely commercial reasons because you think you can sell $80 million worth of tickets — there are different reasons for developing projects — but for me this one came from some strange emotional connection. Luckily it's now in pre-production.

It must have been a great moment for you when Steven Spielberg decided he wanted to direct the film and Tom Hanks was attached to star?

Pretty amazing. I had worked at the company for a long time but hadn't had an opportunity to work on any of the projects that Steven ultimately directed, so it's very exciting to be affiliated with one that he is directing. Frankly, a part of me just felt vindicated that it was a good idea for a movie and I was glad that they shared the excitement. Will it change my life? I don't know. I still have to go out and find great things. I don't feel like it changes my life much at all frankly.

But you are one of the producers of a film directed by Steven Spielberg.

Yes, that's amazing and of course it's a thrill to be working with such talented people — that goes without saying. But while it's a once in a lifetime experience and this might sound strange to people, I don't really see it the way other people might because I have spent almost twenty years of my life doing this. With the film in pre-production it validates the work. But then I like a lot of the movies I have worked on because I think they have brought something to people and it feels like this could be one that does that plus a little bit more. If people see this movie and it makes them look at their lives in a different way, then that would be incredibly satisfying.

Now that The Terminal *is being made do you consider yourself a producer?*

Yes, absolutely, because this helps me get *perceived* as a producer. Before *The Terminal* I had worked on a lot of movies and had some equity around town, but it will help more when the movie is in production.

5. 'An installed audience of 100 million'

What are you doing now?

I am currently based in a first-look deal here at Sony Pictures with John Baldecchi who has been a friend for a long time, we've probably known each other about fifteen years and stayed in touch over the years as our careers progressed. So we've known for a while that we wanted to work together. Now we are in a first-look deal at Sony mostly looking to do the kind of elevated genre movies I have mentioned that inspired me in college. There is a movie that we're developing and trying to launch that is very time consuming, it's a movie based on the Mattel toy franchise 'Hot Wheels', which may seem like a strange place to generate a movie from . . .

But it sounds like a very commercial proposition.

Mattel sell 250 million toy cars a year, and they do close to a billion dollars in revenue with their Hot Wheels line a year, so it's a significant operation. Mattel have zealously guarded what they would call their 'IP' or intellectual property over the years, and were approached in the past by producers with a track record much longer than ours, but they had declined to sell. They had also been approached by Columbia TriStar but they hadn't been ready to sell it.

Did the success of Spider-Man *change things?*

It may have, but I can't say exactly what did. Mattel did indicate to us that sometimes when they had been approached in the past filmmakers had a pre-existing script and had said, 'Why don't we put the Hot Wheels name on this?' When we approached their management we approached them from our understanding of the brand — which, frankly, I had studied a bit.

So you made a personal pitch?

A pitch always has to be personal. So part of our proposal was about our childhood experience with their cars and play-sets. We believed that for Americans of our generation, you aspired to be in that world. There was a strong sense of you having one foot in fantasy and one foot in reality and that you were the driver of that car in a world you could create in your living room. Everybody did it — they built these enormous orange track sets. And they were always more ergonomically designed and much better than any twin-set. Mattel said the reason they never put a driver in any of their Hot Wheels cars is because *you* are the driver. And we felt like even though this wasn't a comic book in the way that *Spider-Man* has all this story, there was something in that world where if you took the very essence of it, it could be translated on to the big screen. We felt there was an aspect of the excitement that they had consciously built into it in 1968 when they created the line that hundreds of thousands of people had kind of nuanced and husbanded along up to the present. Now people like me in my forties and my two-year-old daughter who loves Hot Wheels share that common feeling about the essence.

So you are developing something you hope will become a franchise?

I sure as hell hope so. We have enormous enthusiasm and excitement about the project.

Because you're taking a brand and maximizing its commercial potential?

We think so. Cynically, we think everything about it is cool, from the cars to its logo, but what we're doing, I feel, is that if we succeed we are creating a world where, when the lights go down, for two hours the audience will be immersed in a world that is designed by car fanatics and car-creators. It's all 'car-chitecture'. So when people come out of the movie and get into their cars to drive home there is going to be this sense of disappointment because driving a real car can't compare with the experience you have had in the movie and it doesn't matter whether that person is my age or an eight-year-old so if we do our jobs properly we will create a powerful yearning to go back into that world. In terms of brand identification I would liken it to what Nike has, because when I look at my Nikes in the closet I actually believe I am going to be able to go out and slam dunk — even though it's not true.

Is this the high end of commercial film production?

Budget-wise this would be up there with the biggest films ever made. And most of the things that we are pursuing are on a tent-pole level and now would be considered movies that are being made in the $150-million range, plus $75 million for advertising, so you're looking at a $200-million investment. There's a lot riding on that with thousands of people working on the movie. So the challenge partly is to take something where there are many elements involved and to give the project a sense of the complexity as to what those elements are. In terms of the commercial complications we've got a studio that's looking at spending $150 million just on the budget; we're looking at working with a company that has a billion-dollar franchise and wants us to respect its integrity. We're also looking at potential tie-ins with automobile companies. We're meeting with some of the major automobile companies about creating a brand identity tie-in and what you get from that is potentially extraordinary — both in co-promoting car brands in our movie but also we might be able to get access to the top designers at these companies to help us build the cars in the movie. I'm not given to grandiosity, but I do feel very grandiose about this project. I'm a slight student of the world's fairs and before television became the biggest world fair of them all, the 1939 World Fair in New York was an event dedicated to the future that changed people's ideas for the next twenty years. I feel like our movie could change people's ideas of what cars could be — though I'm not saying that this is for the better.

How do you persuade a studio to spend $150 million on a movie?

It will help if the studio's advertising partners offer $50 million of co-branded TV commercials, that will help on the advertising budget. This is a property that Sony have always loved but were told in the past that the copyright holder wasn't willing to exploit as a motion picture. Another example of our commercial approach is we are negotiating for a video game that is considered by gamers to be one of the top five games of all time. The studio didn't know this, and there are at least three studios bidding, so we went to Sony and showed them part of the game, but crucially we showed them the sales figures. The game has only been barely exploited and sold eight million copies, and the sequel to the game which is going to be even more groundbreaking is about to come out and is estimated to have an audience of *twenty* million. So the studio said, 'Wow, we think that not only is the game a good basis for the movie but we appreciate that we can be on the ground floor of launching a franchise that, as the game franchise grows, will enhance the value of the movie franchise.' We won't pursue big games just for their own sake, but if that game happens to be around it becomes valuable for the movie.

What's to stop the movie from turning into a commercial for Mattel?

Obviously you have to stay within the story, and you can't deliver something that is just a hollow Hot Wheels commercial. We have an opportunity to be much bigger, bolder and more operatic with our characters and storylines and to have *Star Wars*-type moments where, for example, a character might fight against his nemesis only to discover that this person is his father. In other words, we are entitled in a movie like *Hot Wheels* to tell stories that are almost biblical and mythical. The risk is these movies require tremendous finesse, and to do it really well you have to get inside the story. To take a familiar story and a familiar brand takes a lot of skill and you don't generally get the credit that you would if you had made *American Beauty* or *The Terminal*.

Doesn't your credit for a movie like this come at the box office?

It does, and if a six-year-old comes up to you and tells you the movie was cool. The credit also comes when you're driving away from the movie and you see some forty-five-year-old guy you saw in the movie theatre and he's pulled off the freeway and is sitting there illegally by the shoulder in his car looking at the off ramp and imagining there is a loop in the middle of the road because he wants the damn *Hot Wheels* movie to be reality . . .

Would you say this is a very businesslike approach to producing a movie?

It's the opposite of my feeling about *The Terminal* because I didn't know at the outset if the idea for *The Terminal* could make a whole movie. All I knew about the idea for *The Terminal* was that I would get choked up and cry if I talked about it with people. There is a big difference between that and coming in with a pie chart and saying, 'You've got an installed audience of 100 million people.' So these are definitely opposites.

Is there a danger that the commercial preoccupations of developing a franchise movie can override the development of a good story and characters?

This is going to sound absolutely terrible, and maybe it won't even make sense, but the studios are certainly much harder on the scripts that are — and maybe this is obvious — much more execution dependent: in other words, scripts that are very high concept or that are based on franchises where the movies are going to be more expensive. But often the studios are so excited to get going on a franchise movie that they will offer less notes on things, so you could argue that's why sometimes the movies aren't better. The best of the franchise movies tend to be those that come from a single author. James Cameron's *Terminator* movies are quite elegant, as are the *Matrix* movies, because they've come from one person's head, or a duo. If franchise movies are made by a committee then they tend to be less successful, but I would say that any way you can do it is the best way. Every franchise producer would rather stick with one talent if they thought that person could deliver. I don't believe that this should ever be an assembly line process because it's not, it all comes from inspiration; that's why I think it's often a thankless job because if you do a great job making one of these big summer movies people will say, 'Well, it's a factory process and it was managed well.' That's not necessarily true, and I believe it takes the same creative investment as a film like *American Beauty*. Steven's movies *Jaws* and *Close Encounters* and George Lucas's *Star Wars* were blockbuster movies but they have a very strong, specific authorial and creative imprint and it's our goal to do it that way. We have a tight schedule that means we hope we'll shoot *Hot Wheels* in May 2004 and see the movie on release in the summer of 2005. Also we're working with a great director, McG, who just did *Charlie's Angels* and he has a great passion for the project.

Are you developing films exclusively in this genre?

We have a project of equal scale at DreamWorks called *Argonauts*, about a group of modern-day hi-tech treasure hunters searching for the wreck of Jason's ship, the *Argo*, and for the golden fleece, but who end up passing through a portal to another dimension, into a world of Greek mythology that exists now and always has, but in another dimension. So our contemporary Argonauts, if you will, pass through that portal twelve minutes into the movie and find themselves in another land where the technology doesn't work, where none of the rules apply, and they realize, 'Oh my God, did Greek mythology really exist? Perhaps Jason really was there three thousand years ago, came back out into our world and told these stories that we know as mythology.' So these characters ask, 'What are we doing here and how can we deal with these extraordinary creatures, and how can we get back home?' And they become a kind of heroic team. There's a mystery around Mount Olympus and what happened to the Greek gods, and they come to realize that the fleece — which is not a golden ram's head — is their key to getting back. So that's another high-concept summer tent-pole movie that again will be in the same budget-range. I heard this story as a pitch and bought it for development at DreamWorks but we never got the script right and it went into turnaround. Then DreamWorks got back ownership of the project and when I hooked up with John Baldecchi a couple of years ago I said, 'Here are my opinions of some of the greatest ideas of all time for a tent-pole movie, because it enables us to do Greek mythology without doing just a certain sword-and-sandal movie. They can be modern characters in that world.' John's old pal Steve Sommers who has done the *Mummy* movies has always been interested in the *Argonaut* movies, so we've brought him aboard as a producer, and possibly to direct. There is also a young writer who's becoming very accomplished, called Simon Kinberg, who I have been following since film school who we want to write it, and he is very adept at writing these movies. We think Simon is an extraordinary talent and his senior thesis at Columbia Film School is now being made as *Mr and Mrs Smith* with Brad Pitt, shooting this fall. So we felt like we were bringing DreamWorks a very compelling project. We didn't have any claim on it and we didn't own it, but we felt we were bringing the right elements that would bring it to life. You have to stay current, and it's harder and harder as you get older, but we probably have about fifteen other projects in development that are like that.

The Terminal was released in 2004. *Hot Wheels* remains in active development with John Baldecchi at Sony. In 2004 Jason returned to DreamWorks and set up Jason Hoffs Productions where he has ten projects in development, including *Argonauts* which, he hopes, will be included on the 2006–2007 DreamWorks slate.

Take 16

STEVE GOLIN

Steve Golin co-founded Propaganda with Joni Sighvatsson in 1986 as a film, commercial and music-video production company. Top-gun young directors David Fincher and Dominic Sena were among a group of others who also came on board. The company made its name with some exceptionally hip flicks: David Lynch's *Wild at Heart*, *Madonna: Truth or Dare*, John Dahl's *Red Rock West*, and Sena's *Kalifornia*. Propaganda became one of Polygram's key labels and along with Golin left Propaganda in 1999, struck out alone with Anonymous Content, and has continued unabated with his backing of cutting-edge talent.

1. *Incredibly dreadful*

STEVE GOLIN: I went to NYU film school in the mid-seventies, and then came out and got a job as an assistant to a stills photographer — except I realized that wasn't what I wanted to do. In 1981 I decided to go to the American Film Institute and do their producing programme and that's where I met Joni. I was at the AFI for two years until 1982, and I produced a little film while I was there. After I graduated I got hooked up with Joni Sighvatsson, he and I became partners and basically started out together, working on low-budget movies. There was a big video boom in the early eighties, companies like Cannon and New World were making movies that went directly to video, and Joni I worked on a few things like *Hard Rock Zombies*, *American Drive In*, and *Nickel Mountain* . . . and they were *incredibly* dreadful.

HELEN DE WINTER: *What exactly were the two of you doing on these films?*

We were basically hired as line producers. It was really hideous and we didn't like it but at the same time we were developing some movies with friends we had been to film school with, who were now at the studios. But we had no real experience in that so we didn't really know what to do — it was all just kind of a mystery to us.

How were you funding the development of your own movies?

Just out of the little money we were getting paid for line-producing. Literally we paid a writer $1,500 to write a script — we were friends, and it wasn't like they were getting hired by the studios. Everybody was just starting out.

Hadn't film school given you a practical training?

NYU was both theoretical and practical. I was also an AD so I had pretty much been around the block. I could break down a script, and Joni and I could do budgets — we used to do *everything*. On those low budget movies you *really* did everything, from driving a motor-home to writing up call-sheets, doing the cost reports, organizing all the equipment — as well as scheduling, making sure that the director was making his day.

Where did the financing come from for those low-budget pictures?

They were independently financed, two of them by two Indian guys, and then *Nickel Mountain* was actually financed by a computer guy who had quite a bit of money. I also worked on a movie for *Playboy* . . . When Joni and I started developing movies on our own, there were a number of people we'd been to film school with who were pretty good writers, like John Lafia and John Dahl. John Dahl and another writer called David Warfield were in the class of 82 and Joni and I were in the class ahead of them, in 81, but we were friendly with them and they had been working on movies as grips and all this nonsense . . . So we hired them to write some scripts for us. They wrote one called *Private Investigations* that we made in 1984 to 85 for Polygram, and we sold it and made quite a bit of money, in a very long-winded way . . .

So you took the script to Polygram, they agreed a budget, and off you went?

Yeah. It was around $400,000. Then they sold it for a million bucks, so they were very happy with that experience. Then we started getting into business. What had happened — just to go back for a second — was that while Joni and I were doing all those crappy movies and developing our own movies, we continued getting offered a lot of *other* crappy low-budget movies to line-produce, because we knew how to do it. But we didn't really want to do that any more. We kept thinking that all the movies we were developing were going to get made, and so if we had worked on another movie it would have taken four months of our time or something. So that was a problem — we were really caught between a rock and a hard spot.

Then John Dahl and Dave Warfield came to us and they said did we want to produce music videos? We were like 'I don't know. What's that like? Can we get paid?' They said, 'Yeah', so we said, 'Great.' So we produced some music videos for them, and Joni and I quickly got into a cycle of producing music videos — I think we did the first one in 1983 or 84 and then we produced a *lot* of them. First we produced for individual companies as freelancers, then we made *Private Investigations* in 1984 to 85.

We went back to making music videos because we didn't have any money and it was then we realized that if we were going to be movie producers we needed some kind of revenue. Joni and I devised a plan to start a company that would make music videos and with the extra revenue start making commercials and the profits from that would enable us to start developing movies. So we started Propaganda in November 1986 and the company became a launch pad for our ambitions.

2. *Then there would be no shitty movies*

Was your ambition to get your projects set up at the studios?

Not really . . . We had *some* development deals with the studios so we would come up with an idea, and a writer, and go and pitch it; we had a project in development at Paramount and another in development with what used to be MGM. But Joni and I felt like we were outside the studio system — we really had no idea what we were doing.

When we started Propaganda, our original partners were the directors David Fincher, Dominic Sena, Nigel Dick and Greg Gold. We had gotten to know them because we were working on their videos, and it just kind of took off. We became very, very successful very quickly in music videos — we did music videos for *everybody*, we were the dominant company of the eighties and nineties. Right after we started, we immediately got into TV commercials too, and built up relationships with directors like Michael Bay, Simon West, Gore Verbinski, Antoine Fuqua and Spike Jonze. And, obviously, Fincher and Dom became big directors. So we had a constant cash-flow that we could use to develop our movie slate.

A whole bunch of other historical stuff happened then. Joni and I sold Propaganda to Polygram in 1992, then Joni left in 1994. In 1999 Polygram got sold to Seagrams, then I got fired, and started Anonymous Content that year. Many of the original directors are here at Anonymous — Fincher is here, Gore Verbinksi, Antoine Fuqua, David Kellogg, Andrew Douglas, Malcom Venville. We make movies in a variety of ways. Today fifty per cent of our movies are made at the studios so it's a combination but we always initiate our projects and of the thirty-five projects we have in development nineteen of them are with studios.

You are known for distinctive and risky films —

I'm trying to wean myself off those.[*Laughs*]

— But what sort of climate enabled you to put together John Dahl's early films at Propaganda, Kill Me Again *and* Red Rock West? *How alive was the independent sector at that time?*

Actually Polygram gave us the money to make both those movies. *Red Rock West* was RCA-Columbia video and Polygram foreign, *Kill Me Again* was MGM and Polygram foreign. Joni and I really had to cobble together our movies in a whole bunch of different ways back then, but Polygram funded a lot of the movies that we did. *Wild at Heart* was Goldwyn and Polygram, it was all these different pieces of the puzzle. Recently I have made movies for Miramax, Focus and Sony . . .

In a way, you make it sound very easy.

It's not easy, it's *torture* — it's very, very hard to get anything going, and for any one that gets made there is a sense of disbelief that it's actually happening. It's a lot of effort and a lot of time — on average it takes three to four years before anything happens.

You have worked with some distinctive and risky filmmakers. What is it like to produce David Lynch, for example?

When you're working with David, you support him, you hang around a lot and talk to him, watch what he does, see how that brain of his works — and it's really, really interesting. There are other filmmakers who are equally creative who you can be a lot more collaborative with. But David always listens to your ideas and will talk to you — he has a very distinctive view of what's what. With *Wild At Heart*, we found Barry Gifford's book and gave it to David and then David wrote the script. So, in that sense, we married the material and the voice of the writer-director. I've done that a lot — I gave the book of *Sleepers* to Barry Levinson and he then wrote and directed it and did a really good job. A big part of the job is knowing what is going to appeal to directors and why, what they might be good for. That's not to say directors don't bring me material, because they do. With *Eternal Sunshine of the Spotless Mind*, Michel Gondry had an idea and he and Charlie Kaufman started collaborating on what that was. Then they brought the idea as a pitch to me, and I bought the pitch while I was still at Propaganda. Now the movie is coming out at the end of the year.

Would you say that your own tastes as a producer have helped to drive surreal and quirky films into the mainstream? I'm talking about the likes of Being John Malkovich *and now* Eternal Sunshine.

I don't know . . . The year that we made *Being John Malkovich* was the year they made *American Beauty*, which I think was also a very tricky picture, a picture that you wouldn't predict would do the kind of business it did or touch that much of a nerve in the mainstream because it was quite a dark picture. Sam [Mendes] did a really sterling job of walking that line and it's hard to do that. Making a movie that can touch a nerve in the mainstream and be satisfying while *still* having another level of quality to it, is tricky to do. I was just reading Peter Bart's article in *Variety* today about *The Hulk*.[19] Is it worth trying to make a tent-pole movie today that has more intelligence and integrity? I'm not sure that they're more successful that way, but I think it *is* worth doing that. A lot of movies could be better and less pandering to the audience, and might be less satisfying but might make more money ultimately. But a *lot* of really dreadful movies have made a lot of money — I don't think anyone would argue with that. And there are a number of really good movies that don't make any money. I think the integrity and quality of a movie and its marketability are two different things. The big questions now at the studio are 'Who is the audience?' and 'Can I market it?' Not 'Is it any good . . .?'

19. Bart's column ('Is "brainy" a box office turnoff?') ran in the weekly *Variety* of 23 June 2003, citing the hiring of Ang Lee for *The Hulk* alongside those of Christopher Nolan for *Batman Begins* and Alfonso Cuarón for *Harry Potter and the Prisoner of Azkaban*.

But you're not operating in quite that arena.

I can and I would like to. I would *love* to have a big hit movie, I really would. I think a movie I'm involved in now, *50 First Dates*[20], is going to be a big, big hit but I think that Adam [Sandler] and Jack [Giarraputo] deserve most of the credit for that. I can identify a commercial movie, I *think*, but they really pushed it in a direction to make it more commercial than I would have. I think that's my sensibility, but it's not really my strength. I want to make commercial movies and I'm really trying. But I learned a lot from that experience, which is good. That's what's great about this job, every project is different — the sensibilities are different. You could put the same team together on three different movies and get three different results. There's an alchemy that goes into it that's very hard to quantify, and it would be amazing if you *could* quantify it, because then there would be no shitty movies . . .

3. 'If this movie bombs, you're fired'

Is it true that **Being John Malkovich** *was difficult to get into production until Spike Jonze kept coming back with amazing actors, so that finally no one could say no?*

No one wanted to make the movie. It was a script that had been kicking around for a long time, and it was an extremely *odd* script, with a first time director. Michael Kuhn, who was my boss at the time at Polygram, didn't really want to make the movie . . .

Because . . .?

Because he thought it wasn't commercial, he didn't get it, which is entirely understandable, based on what the script was. Everybody used to laugh at me all the time. And we put a lot of effort into getting the movie made.

How had you met Charlie Kaufman?

Charlie was around — it wasn't like anyone didn't know Charlie. I had read the script *years* before Spike gave it to me, and I was like 'This guy is really talented, he has got an amazing imagination.' Then Spike came into my office one day — we were looking to do a movie together

---

20. This project, which began as a spec script by George Wing bought by Columbia, reached the screen in early 2004 and marked another hit for star Adam Sandler and his producing partner Jack Giarraputo at Happy Madison.

because I had been representing him for commercials, and I knew he was going to be a movie director so I said, 'OK, let's find something', so we started developing a dare devil movie type picture, with a friend of his. Then he came in and said he wanted to do Charlie's *Malkovich* script, but I said, 'Forget it, I'm not doing it', so he said, 'Let me bring Charlie in.' So he did, and we started working on it, and started talking about what would change. They had some great ideas, and from there we developed the script and reached a point where I thought it was pretty good and I really wanted to get the movie made. Obviously we needed John Malkovich, so we went after him. I already knew him because we had done *Portrait of a Lady*. But it was tricky because a lot of people were telling him it was a bad idea career-wise for him to do the movie, then we didn't have any money, which was a problem but when John signed on he was an amazing sport.

How did John react when he first read the script?

John knew about the script already because it had been going around, and he had read it and thought it was entertaining. But Spike charmed John eventually into doing the movie. It was an extremely pleasant experience on the movie, really a lot of fun. There wasn't any friction — once we got the money.

Was it a small budget, relatively?

It was $9 million. Originally we wanted $13 million but we couldn't get it, so we just had to beat everybody down and make it for $9 million.

Is that a lot of money for a 'low-budget' film?

It's not a lot — a relatively low budget for a big independent movie.

How supportive were the talent?

They came later. The thing was that we green-lit the movie when we got Malkovich. Cusack had always wanted to play the part of Craig, we knew we would get him and he decided in about thirty seconds — Cusack and Malkovich had done *Con Air* together and they were friendly and had wanted to do something together, even though they're not in that many scenes together. Spike wanted Catherine Keener and she gave the script to Cameron Diaz. Actually Spike was a bit dubious about Cameron playing the part because she is so pretty but she came in and read for it and he loved her.

Were you under a lot of pressure?

Everyone was under a lot of pressure. Michael Kuhn was like 'If this movie bombs, you're fired.' And I was, 'OK, so be it.' We wanted to make a good movie, we wanted it to do well, and we wanted people to see it — so you can't put more pressure on yourself than that. But I was spending a few years of my life working on this project so I didn't need pressure to motivate me — I was motivated on my own.

Despite having worked with Spike Jonze previously, did you have any concerns about him as a first-time feature film director?

You always have concerns about a director, particularly with first-timers, and if it's a first-time director who has come out of videos and commercials you don't *really* know if they are going to be any good until they do it. There are plenty of video and commercials directors who are working in feature films and are not very good just as there are a lot of feature film directors who have tried to work in the short form medium and can't. Just because you are a director doesn't necessarily mean you are going to be good at both things. I always knew Spike was the real deal. I had believed in him for so long, I liked him as a guy and I had sat side by side with him on commercials and videos and seen his thought process which is really interesting. I had also seen how commercial Spike is without trying to be, simply because his *instincts* are commercial. So I already had a lot of admiration for Spike. And he made it work.

4. Marriage guidance

Is it true that you can't really know a director as closely as you need to until you're out there shooting?

Everybody's different in pre-production — different when they are trying to get a job or get a movie made. If you're a big director, and I'm trying to convince you to do my movie, I'm going to be different from that once you've got the job. People are different on the first couple of dates than after the first few years of marriage, and that's how a relationship is . . .

How do you collaborate with directors during development and pre-production?

It's really a whole process where you work extensively on the script so that you familiarize yourself with the director's thinking, then by the time you start production you *know* you're on the same page because you've already talked so much about the movie. The development of a script is really the foundation of a lot of pre-production — we spent two years working on *Malkovich before* we started production. I'm very much involved in talking about the characters and understanding what it's going to take to do the movie. You have to try and find solutions to a lot of different problems like 'What's the character about?' and very often you end up throwing away a lot because it's not working or it's not interesting. This morning, I was talking to a director about some characters for three hours and that's just about the treatment. Sometimes the process is a little different if a director brings you a script that's already developed and says 'Do you want to produce this?' And because you haven't been through that whole environmental process where you see the development of the characters and the story you don't always know what the director has in mind and you can be less emotionally invested. The process is different with every project.

I have made movies where once the process starts you wish you could get out and it was like being in a bad marriage and having to stay through the whole thing to the bitter end. But you can't leave because no matter what, you're in it and that's it, you have to be professional.

Were those relationship problems or a realization that you weren't making the same movie?

It could be a relationship problem, it could be a creative problem, or what they call 'creative differences' out here. There are certainly movies I wish I could take off my résumé. When you make a movie that loses money you just wish you could get the money back. I made a movie with Todd Solondz called *Fear, Anxiety & Depression* which is completely dreadful, just crap.

What did you think at the time?

I didn't realize until two weeks into the movie that I had made a mistake. It took me a bit of time while I was making the movie, with him acting in it too, to realize I was making some bad decisions. But I had to stick it out until the very end. I have tremendous respect for him creatively and for his intelligence, but we did not have a pleasant experience, either one of us. After our movie I never thought he would make another movie. He didn't make a movie for five years until *Welcome to the Dollhouse*, so when I saw that film, I felt vindicated that he had talent.

5. *You can't not look at it*

What are you doing day to day when you have a film in production?

As little as possible, in a sense . . . If it's going really well then you kind of just hang around watching dailies. You're being supportive and you bullshit with the actors and watch the cost report and make sure that everyone's getting along well. Then the minute there is a problem, you are *completely* on the line dealing with the problem — it could be a weather problem, or a scheduling problem, or a money problem, or an actor problem or a creative problem because the scene doesn't work. When circumstances occur outside a director's control or when stuff goes wrong on a movie — and things go wrong on *every* movie — then a director needs your help so you are there to help find a solution that gets them out of a bind, or at least put a Band-Aid on it and try to figure it out further along. The job of the producer during production is really to be a problem solver and to make sure things go smoothly.

Have you had a situation where a script is being rewritten during production?

Obviously you try to avoid that — you try to have the script in the exact, perfect shape. But you don't want to stifle ideas if the actor or the director or the writer have them — particularly Charlie, because he is very involved in the whole movie, and he was on set a lot with *Malkovich* and now with *Eternal Sunshine*. He's in the cutting room a lot too . . . On *Eternal Sunshine* Michel Gondry would come up with an idea, or Kate Winslet or Jim Carrey would come up with an idea, then we would call Charlie up and say 'Here's an idea' and he would rewrite the scene and email it to us. There were a couple of scenes in the movie that were very tricky, and sometimes on the set we would tweak the dialogue and make it better. Charlie is a *genius* in post-production, and he comes to all the screenings — in fact, I have a conference call with him in fifteen minutes about a decision we're making because we are showing the movie to the studio later this week. So we'll get on the phone and talk about the pros and cons. At this point, ultimately, it's Michel's decision. But Michel is very open and listens to everybody, and he *really* listens to Charlie. I would say he's a little bit more hesitant to listen to me because of that authority thing, which is total bullshit as far as I'm concerned but he's a little bit like that, which is just the nature of it. But he is extremely close and respectful of Charlie.

Do you find post-production exciting yourself?

A lot of big decisions get made in post, and I really enjoy it, and I think I have some good ideas and often a good sensibility in the edit of what will work. The edit is a place where a producer can play a very, very important role in post-production. It's an interesting process because the director will be in the cutting room trying five hundred things, and the producer isn't there when all that's happening and so sometimes I'll ask 'Have you tried it that way', and they say 'We tried that' or sometimes I might look at it and see a way through. I always enjoy the screening process and seeing what works with the public, particularly on a movie like *Malkovich* where the film was tremendously complicated. We know everything, logically, about why something does and doesn't happen, but if we were in a screening there might be something that we take for granted, then when we put the movie in front of several hundred people, if they are confused, we have to look at it. A lot of directors are hesitant to listen to that, but you can't *not* look at it.

And having been there during production and seen dailies you know what the director has and hasn't got?

Yes, because as you go through the different cuts sometimes you can forget that you have the shot you need that helps explain the scene, if there is a difficulty in understanding. I like that part of the process a lot. A producer's role in development *and* post-production is crucial whereas in production you are kind of there helping but sometimes you're not doing as much.

6. *It's all about the money*

What are your aspirations going forward — is your life in movies?

They'll take me out of here in a box ... No, really, I like it, every experience is different, you never stop learning and I don't have any aspirations to do anything else.

Art Linson has talked about the producer not being sufficiently respected or acknowledged creatively. How do you feel about that?

It's frustrating. The director still gets all the credit. I think the value of producers, or *good* producers, is dramatically undervalued in this town. That's not to speak of Bruckheimer, Joel Silver or Scott Rudin. Their contribution *is* valued, but I think the next tier of producer — people who are good, working really hard, initiating and developing good projects — are treated like shit.

What's your profile, do you think? Are you perceived as an independent producer?

I really don't know. I don't have that much of a profile, I just get on and do my thing. I think most producers couldn't care less about their profile . . . Really, it's *true*!

Has it become easier to finance edgier, more challenging films?

Today I think the market is tougher. Even the art divisions of the studios — Paramount Classics, Fox Searchlight — I think they are looking more for genre pictures that can make a lot of money, like thrillers or romantic comedies, which are not necessarily the pictures that they started out making. They are still making interesting pictures, but things have definitely changed. Everything is so corporate and so much about money — *it's all about the money* . . . The thing of it is, it doesn't matter if your film cost $3 million or $30 million — if you want to release it in the same way, it costs the same to market it. And each film is an individual transaction. I could produce a thousand movies and every one of them could be a bomb.

There are three questions that a studio asks. How much does it cost? Can we sell it? and Who is the audience? If they can answer those questions they make the movie, even if they don't think the movie is any good, because they are in business.

Eternal Sunshine of the Spotless Mind **proved to be another bold success for Golin and the film's creative team, not least Charlie Kaufman, who claimed the Academy Award for Best Original Screenplay. 2005 saw Golin engaged in another brave and fascinating endeavour,** *Babel*, **with the talents behind** *Amores Perros* **and** *21 Grams*, **director Alejandro González Iñárritu and writer Guillermo Arriaga.**

Part Five
NEW YORK, NEW YORK

The Bronx is up and the Battery's down, for sure, and New York's resident movie producers also tend to take it as gospel that theirs is a hell of a town, sufficiently so as to view Los Angeles with suspicion, resignation, or outright disdain. Still, the two must coexist. But the producers in this Part are emphatic New Yorkers, and there is an edge to what they do, whether it is bringing to the screen *The Last Temptation of Christ* or *American Psycho*, bringing out of the closet *Reefer Madness* and *Sex Maniacs*, or producing the first Oscar-winning gay cowboy romance.

Take 17

BARBARA DE FINA

Barbara De Fina was from 1987 to 2003 Martin Scorsese's partner in the production company Cappa, and the two were also married from 1985 to 1991. De Fina first joined forces with Scorsese creatively in the early 1980s and proceeded to work with him through a remarkable period as his career recovered from various setbacks and was blessed by a sequence of artistic and commercial successes, with a few prime controversies along the way. De Fina's interest in strong dramatic material is also borne out by the pictures she has produced for Stephen Frears, John McNaughton and Kenneth Lonergan. But her work with Scorsese necessarily makes her a producer firmly associated with New York City rather than Los Angeles, CA.

1. Gated communities

HELEN DE WINTER: *Why do you choose to be in New York, and not LA?*

BARBARA DE FINA: I have always lived here, and I like the fact that while there is a film community here the city itself is home to many industries. In LA everybody seems to be part of the film industry, and I'm not sure that is helpful creatively. I honestly feel that I wouldn't do well in that environment. I think LA is so much about where you live and what you drive and where you park . . .

Really? Where you park . . .?

Where your parking space is on the lot. You get sucked into it so fast, and so much energy is wasted. Then every day in LA you have to go to lunch for business, and it becomes an event. Whereas in New York we might have lunch occasionally, but generally we don't do that, it's not like trying to work your way up with lunch partners. It's just a different way of life here.

We don't live in houses with gates . . .

Do you network in New York?

I go to parties and screenings, and I like seeing people I know, but we're not all in a studio. What I like about London is that people are more accessible. Even the agents, if you meet with them, will actually offer you their client list which is unheard of in LA — they keep their client list to themselves like they're guarding Fort Knox.

Are you friends with other producers?

I think more so in New York, people aren't quite so aggressive . . . I think it's a little more laid back here, just generally because we're not all locked in the studio. In NY it's very competitive in a different way. In LA nobody will ever say anything to your face, it's very strange for someone to be confrontational. The betrayal is more about backdoor and cutthroat tactics. On the surface everyone is kiss-kiss friends . . .

2. Working to numbers

How did you first find your way into producing?

I worked my way into it — I came from a physical production background and gravitated towards producing. I was a production assistant, then a production manager, then a line producer.

As a result of that background, presumably you can look at a script and know how it's going to break down?

Yes. For instance, right now I'm working with a director and we have just been talking to a French financier. But because the film is in the early stages we don't have an assistant director or a production manager, so we have been breaking the script down for the financier. That's when it's very helpful for me to understand how a script breaks down into a budget and a schedule. It's interesting, too, because once you have broken it down, then the director — especially if he's also the writer — will suddenly see the movie in a whole new way. He starts to see how many locations there are, or how many times we have to go back to the same location, or how something he has written might be confusing. So it becomes a time when the director can cut or trim the script.

When you work on the development of a script, must it accommodate the budget you have in mind?

You never want to shoot the budget — you want to shoot the script. But there are times when you have to work to a number. Sometimes in that process the script actually gets better. So the constraint can be helpful and make the material stronger, because it gets more controlled and condensed.

What were your first credits as a producer?

I did some associate producing and co-producing on small low-budget movies and television movies, and then I started doing features. I did two movies with Sean Cunningham, who produced and directed the original *Friday the 13th* [1980]. After that, he got a deal at Columbia to make a $3-million movie called *Spring Break* [1983] and we did that together. It was a sweet story, and we spent eight weeks on the beach in Fort Lauderdale, so that was a great place to start. The budget was good — this was $3 million fifteen years ago, and we're still making $3-million budget films today. And it was a negative pick-up, so we didn't have studio people watching over us, we just made the movie and delivered it. I was his associate producer but he was directing too so I did most of the producing, and that was the first time I actually had hands-on control of the production. *Spring Break* actually made a lot of money for Columbia, then they asked Sean to do another movie in the same budget range, but it didn't do so well.

What came next for you?

I started line-producing bigger movies. Even though I freelanced, I always worked steadily. Once you learn any craft the basics are fairly simple but as it gets bigger and more complex, it costs more, and I think that's the next step for a producer. It doesn't take that long to move on and up, so long as you have done a good job, not made too many mistakes, or upset too many people . . .

3. *Marty does go in prepared*

How did you first meet Martin Scorsese?

It was after I had made one of those movies in Florida and I had just got back to New York. Marty was in post-production on *The King of Comedy*, which had gone on for ever — I think it was a couple of years. Arnon Milchan was the producer and it was the first movie he had ever produced. And Marty was not in great shape at that moment. So he had been editing for a long time, then he would put it all together and screen it, and each time Arnon would think 'Great, it's done!' But before he could physically get the film, Marty would take it all apart again. Really he just needed to finish it and re-shoot a little bit of footage for the end. A friend of mine was called first but he was busy, so he called me and said, 'Would you mind covering for me?' It was a two- or three-day shoot, then Arnon Milchan asked me to stay on and help finish the movie.

Wasn't it rather a delicate process coming at that stage when the director had been at work for so long? Generally how do you manage a situation like that?

I am sure there are directors who can just finish a movie and put it away, but if a director has worked on it for a year or more it becomes a very emotional thing. There's an issue about separation — you realize that once you have made that last cut and sent it off to the lab, the movie is going to be that way for ever. Directors are always looking at their mistakes and deficiencies, and from the first dailies to the very end they will be saying, 'I wish I'd done a little more coverage . . .' or 'I could have done that another way . . .' So it's hard to let go. I think sometimes what it takes for a director is a combination of exhaustion, pressure, and ultimately knowing that it's as good as it's going to be, even if they don't think it's perfect. But movies don't have to be perfect. The audience forgives a lot . . .

You presumably knew Scorsese's work already. How was it actually working with him?

It was a great experience, it wasn't nerve-wracking. I had worked around a lot of other directors before and I had a vocabulary. And we were there to do a specific job — it wasn't as though we were meeting to develop something, so it wasn't about 'getting to know you' and 'What are you like?' We were there because there were scenes to shoot. So we sat down, went through the scenes, and talked about how many extras and how long it would take. I think in the end there were two or three scenes towards the end of the movie when Jerry Lewis is running down on the street and he sees Rupert Pupkin on all those TVs . . .

After that we didn't actually work together again for about a year. I went off and did a TV movie in Nashville which was a horrible experience — not Nashville, but the movie. We were staying in a motel in the middle of nowhere, and I had the crew from hell, the worst crew I have ever had. It wasn't that they lacked experience, they just weren't into it. And you really want to work with people who want to be there, rather than a crew who are just putting in time. The weather was awful too. I liked the director, but there were people with substance problems, and the actors had issues . . .

Did you have to deal with that?

Yes, because you would never know if they were going to show up. And if they showed up, you wouldn't know what condition they would be in. The whole shoot was a combination of all the worst sort of problems.

Someone once said to me that movies are 'a people business' and that's true, it's about relationships and getting along with each other, as well as ultimately delivering. Every day is problem solving and a lot of it, it turns out, is about people. Some days, I go home and I feel like I am a psychiatrist because I have been sitting there talking to people. Every crew member, every actor comes to the set with some personal issue.

Subsequently to the Nashville experience, though, you teamed up again with Scorsese?

Yes, then I did my first studio movie with Marty, *The Color of Money* [1986], which was a sequel to *The Hustler* [1961]. I was working with Marty, and he developed the script with Richard Price. The producer was Paul Newman's lawyer, Irving Axelrad.

Were you involved in the development of the script?

I was. As development periods go, it wasn't all that long — I think Richard wrote two drafts. But for me, it was the beginning of learning about story. You can learn three-act structures and so on, and I think some of that is valid, but I also think a lot of good storytelling isn't about what happens on what page, but that it occurs in a place that is satisfying to get you to the next place in the story. I think there is an over-emphasis on issues like 'character arcs'. Some characters have arcs, but some don't, and that's OK. I do think the best writers — and this makes a lot of studio executives crazy — don't know how a script ends until they get there. And often studio people just don't want to hear that. But I believe a lot of good screenwriting has to do with creating good characters who really do lead you on a journey. To some extent I believe that the first two acts you can plan out but I think the third act takes a lot of work, you really have to get there and I think that's very frustrating for a lot of people when they are working on scripts.

So for me *The Color of Money* was the beginning of learning how to do that and acquire that vocabulary. I think the big story issue was about the Minnesota Fats character. In the first movie, *The Hustler*, it was basically his movie, and he was in the first draft of *The Color of Money* but they could never make it work. So it was a big step not to have him in the story: here was a sequel without the main character from the first movie. But instead it became more about the spirit of the game, and the young man, Vincent, teaching the older man, Fast Eddie.

How did the production period go for you?

The budget was modest, it wasn't tiny, but for a studio movie it was quite small. There weren't any action sequences. It was actually a fairly small and contained movie, with a fairly small cast. It had one big star and one actor we didn't know was a big star until afterwards . . . We made the movie with Tom Cruise just before *Top Gun* opened, so he started out as a really good young actor and then by the time the movie was finished he was a superstar. We shot it in Chicago and there weren't that many locations, it was all pool halls, hotels and apartments. When we got to Chicago I got to work with a production manager, a woman who I knew from before, so she was helpful in helping me learn the city and the crew.

And how was this experience with Scorsese, working from the top for the first time?

Marty does go in prepared, and on that movie he was *very* prepared. There are other directors who walk on to the set and don't have a clue, but Marty really knew what he wanted, and he would discuss that with everyone — he would talk to me and the DP, Michael Ballhaus. Marty tends to work with a lot of camera movements so that aspect is pretty well planned and there isn't a lot of room to improvise within some of the complicated shots. But there's always room for change and for something to be different as Marty does give the actors a lot of space and lets them improvise, sometimes with dialogue — he is always listening to their ideas and lets them try things. Then the joke is he uses *his* ideas most of the time . . . Occasionally he does use actors' ideas, he always likes to make them feel that he is listening to them.

Scorsese is not the only director with whom you've worked on more than one occasion.

I have done a couple of movies with Stephen Frears — *The Grifters* and *The Hi-Lo Country*. *The Grifters* was a smaller independent movie, and we got to do what we wanted. It was dark and crazy, none of the studios would even touch it.

Does working with a director repeatedly make things easier for you as the relationship goes along?

With Marty there will be a shorthand, and a lot of that is about making it possible to have what he wants. With Stephen Fears I think it's more helping him focus. Usually there is such a lot of pressure and a lot of work for a director to do day after day that it can be hard for them to finish their day. Directors get tired, and having time to think and rest is very important. I have worked with directors who at the end of the day are prepared to say, 'Let's just drop it here and come back tomorrow.' Then I've heard them say, 'Thank God we stopped, because if I had kept shooting I would have got into so much trouble . . .'

But most of all it is about getting the right crew in order to get the support the director needs and the right atmosphere. The industry draws certain people . . . you're not dealing with people who would be happy working in a corporate atmosphere. You're dealing with people who are freelance or creative, so there is a great mix of personalities, and part of it is casting — trying to put people together who can get along, at least for twelve weeks, and actually come up with something interesting.

4. *Theatres would burn*

The second feature you produced for Scorsese turned out to be extraordinarily controversial — the film of Nikos Kazantzakis's The Last Temptation of Christ. *How did you manage the demands and complexities of that production?*

In some ways it was difficult, but in others very simple. Marty had tried to put the movie together before at Paramount, on a much bigger budget, and at that point the actors were all meant to be getting their quotes. So eventually we said, 'The only way we can make this film is to do it on a small budget and everybody just has to work to scale.' Almost all the original actors who had said they were going to do it agreed to do it for scale, so we cut the budget down.

What was a small budget in this case?

About $7 or 8 million. Though, now, we're making movies for $3 million. And budgets, oddly enough, have got smaller since then.

But didn't you have to virtually knock on doors to secure the finance?

It was one of those things that could only happen once, and never again. After *The Color of Money* we got an overall development deal at Disney. Marty had signed with Mike Ovitz as his agent, and he was then pursued by Universal. Tom Pollock became the head of Universal, he had been a lawyer, he hadn't really come through the usual studio executive route. He believed in free speech, and he decided he was interested in making *Last Temptation* as long as it was a very small budget. So we said, 'OK, we'll do it.' I think Tom suggested we shoot in Morocco. I had worked there and had some problems getting things done, but we said we could make it work. Then part of the deal was that Marty would then have a deal with Universal.

The other piece of the puzzle was that the reason that Paramount wouldn't make the movie in 1983 was that all the exhibitors said they didn't want the movie in their theatres, because they were afraid there would be violence and their theatres would be burned. Garth Drabinsky at the time controlled the Cineplex Odeon theatre chain, so he put money in, and Universal put in money, and Garth guaranteed that there would be theatres to put the movie in. So that's how it got made. I don't think that would ever happen today. I'm not sure after that, whether any studio executive would take that chance any more. None of us realized that further down the line it would become a nightmare.

We shot on location in Morocco and we had a great Italian line producer, and an Italian and local Moroccan crew. Our resources were low and in some ways that was difficult, but in others it made things really, really simple from a production standpoint, because we didn't have that many choices. And sometimes that makes the movie more about the story and characters than a situation where you are worrying about digital effects. Morocco was really simple to shoot in, there were no distractions, there was no traffic — we would go up on the side of a mountain and shoot for the day, and we would have somebody who would bring us our food, and that was it.

What was your perception of the movie you were making at the time? Did you have any sense that it would provoke the reaction it did?

No. When the book was published there was a lot of controversy but now it's respected. I thought there would be *some* controversy, we knew there would be criticism through articles and reviews, but not the hysterical reaction that followed. But the most shocking thing is how it was used by the Moral Majority in the US. They sort of latched on to the movie and used it to get people motivated and get support. Even though they were invited to see the movie, they never saw it, but they used it to rally their troops.

Meanwhile there was a whole other component of anti-Semitism against people who were involved incidentally, such as Lew Wasserman and others, because they happened to be executives at the studio. So the protests were, 'These Jews have made this blasphemous movie about Jesus.' None of us expected that. We were completely shocked. It was totally illogical because it wasn't *about* the movie. They hadn't seen it. There were a lot of countries where the movie was never shown. A theatre was burned down in France. It was one thing for people to be marching, but when they start burning theatres? Enough!

Making the short project New York Stories *with Scorsese after* Last Temptation *must have been a relief?*

New York Stories was one of my favourite experiences because it seemed like a perfect format, a forty-minute film, one of three. It was an interesting experiment because all three directors were given the same amount of money, about $5 million and told to make a story about New York.

Then of course you returned to Morocco a decade later with Scorsese to make Kundun [1997].

Kundun came out of nowhere. Marty was given the script by his agent and Melissa Mathison came in and there were a lot of rewrites, but Disney funded it and then we made it in Morocco.

You must know Morocco pretty well?

I know Morocco *very* well.

5. *They bled to death and died*

What brought Scorsese and yourself to the material for Goodfellas?

There was an excerpt from Nick Pileggi's book *Wise Guy* that appeared in a New York magazine while we were shooting the *The Color of Money* and we thought it was really interesting and very funny. We always loved the humour. We thought it was dark and violent, but there was something very comic about the way these people lived — they prided themselves on never having a job but they were working twenty hours a day. I think Warner Bros. never really understood what they were getting, and when they started looking at the dailies I think they got quite scared.

Then the previews were just horrible. There were two in LA, the first one was in Redondo Beach and the projector broke and the audience started getting really agitated and angry so we abandoned the screening. Then we had a second preview in California but closer to LA. At a certain point in the movie a lot of women would walk out because of the violence. And then at the end some people got really agitated and wrote 'Fuck you' all over the cards. I think the audience got into it, but it was kind of frightening and scary because I don't think people really understood what was going to happen.

Finally the movie opened and there was only one bad review. Every other review was incredible. It's become a classic and is probably the first mafia black comedy. It turned out that teenage girls liked it and were renting it, so what was *that* about? It touched some sort of nerve. I think it's been overdone now and has been imitated to the point that it's time to move on. But at the time it was a pretty crazy experience.

Did the violence of the film concern you?

It didn't concern me because, as real as it was, you saw the consequences. I think the reason it was so upsetting was that it was so raw but there is much more violence, actually, in a movie like *Terminator*, because you never see the aftermath, it's like a cartoon. In *Goodfellas* people got shot or stabbed and they bled to death and died. It has a certain morality to it.

6. *It's not like real estate*

Is your speciality as a producer lower budget films?

I would love to have more money, but I do like character-driven movies with strong narratives, and those movies tend not to be studio movies. The studios are into franchises, sequels and big action movies. It has to do with studios guaranteeing that they can get their money back. So there aren't that many real story-driven movies. Lately we have had the huge movies, the big summer blockbusters, and then there are the small independent movies and it seems to be that there isn't much in the middle. So unfortunately all the movies that might have been in the middle have become independent movies, and the budgets have gotten smaller.

Producing an independent movie is not as guaranteed financially because on a studio movie you're getting your fee whereas smaller movies are a little more erratic. And with *really* small movies sometimes it's like roulette. It's very hard to gauge what's going to work or not, but everybody still works just as hard. And when you take the trouble to make a movie you want a distributor who is going to spend money promoting it and keep it in the theatres. On the other hand the money spent on marketing and advertising is going against the negative so it makes it harder to break even. On *Goodfellas,* for example, the perception is that the movie made a lot of money when, in fact, it never did. I think eventually it broke even and made a profit for someone but certainly not in the way that it was perceived to have done.

Have you become more involved with independent financing? How does a producer become a deal-maker and financial negotiator?

In the independent film world the financiers are always changing and companies come and go. There will be rumours that so-and-so has equity and then everybody attacks that source — you want to be the first one in before other people catch on. I don't know why people invest in movies. Unless they really have serious tax issues and they want to write off money for a long time because there is very little guarantee of a return. On very small budgets, if you are lucky to sell it then the investors get paid off and there is some money for everyone, but that doesn't happen that often. Today pre-sales are difficult, and foreign isn't worth as much as it used to be. The so-called German money is almost gone. At the beginning of this year I was in England looking at tax shelter opportunities.

Is it as time consuming working on the finance as it is focusing on creative issues?

It is, though lawyers do a lot of the work. In this country there is no government funding. It's very complicated when you are raising money from tax funds abroad because each fund has a different back-end, and then the money comes through at different times. So I very much rely on the expertise of my lawyer.

Have you been approached by high-worth individuals offering to fund your films?

Occasionally, but a lot of the time the people who come forward are not real. They say they have money when in fact their intention is to go out and raise money. I have become more and more adept at figuring who's 'real'. The problem is everyone wants to be in the movie business, but when you finally explain it to them, it's really not a business they want to be in. A lot of people think financing movies is like real estate, so you build a house and sell it, whereas often the reality is you build a house but you *don't* know if you are going to sell it. Then, when an investor finally realizes they might not get their money back or they might only get it back over *years* then they're not terribly interested any more.

People perceive film producers as being fantastically wealthy. Is producing a business where you can really make money?

Some producers are wealthy but I think the people who make huge amounts of money are the A-list actors and A-list directors. But I think that for most producers — unless you are like Bruckheimer and you have these huge franchises — you can make a good salary compared to the real world but you are not fabulously wealthy.

7. *One big guy*

Would you say there are particular kinds of talent you like to work with?

I enjoy working with writer-directors because I like the singular vision, and also because I think you're also closer to actually getting something made. If you start with a book or an idea and then you have to get a writer, a director and a script together, it's a long process. Whereas if someone comes in with a good script and it's something you can work on with them, then you're so many steps closer to having something that could get made.

Collaboration and openness to creative suggestion are important. If somebody is not open to that and the script just doesn't work, then it's not worth going there. A lot of it has to do with focusing the writer. I find in a lot of scripts that it's all there but it's not focused, and too subtle sometimes. The emotional moments are there but they're too hidden. With a lot of writers, if you say, 'I missed the moment when he really realizes that . . .' then the writer will say, 'Oh it's there, it's there!' And they will show you it's there. But only they know it's there. So it's not about changing writers' ideas but making them work better for the audience.

Do you have an instinct for talent when it comes to casting actors, in the same way you would feel excited about a new writer or director?

The problem with that is, unless it's a really small independent movie, you are a slave to a list. All the actors have values, so you have to cast someone from a certain group . . .

Do the studios have lists?

There are actually lists of actors with numerical values. So somebody is a 99 and somebody else is an 18, and unless you're making a movie for 10 cents you can't cast the 18 actor. It's like a game of putting the pieces together. If it's a bigger movie they will have a list of about five men and then there are five others who are almost as good. So you don't always get to choose the best actor for the part, and everyone is competing for those top five actors. And if you don't have the funding your script is going to go to the bottom of the pile. Meanwhile, there are thousands of actors who might be better.

How do you persuade a studio executive to let you have a '50' actor instead of an '80'?

You always have to get the *one* big guy. On *Goodfellas* we got to work with Joe Pesci and Ray Liotta because we had Bob De Niro, though he had a much smaller part. This is why European funds are so interesting, because it's less about who the actor is. If you have British or French money you have a lot more leverage about who you cast so long as their nationality is where the money is coming from. So you actually get to cast the actor you want.

8. *New York was closed*

What are you working on currently?

I am doing a movie now in Greece called *Brides* with a Greek director called Pantolis Voulgaris. I was a bit frightened about it in the beginning because I didn't know what I was getting into, but it's turned out to be a really great experience. Pantolis has directed a lot of projects but this is his first English language movie, with British actors. We're working with Steven Berkoff and our lead is Damian Lewis who has been around since *Band of Brothers* and is really interesting. The shoot has gone really well and it's been a good experience.

Generally, what are you doing during a shoot?

I like to be on set and see what's going on, but the nuts and bolts of production, managing a lot of detail and people asking for things tends to be time consuming so I work with the line producer because I have other scripts and projects going on at the same time and I like to be able to work on those. I am going back to Greece to finish off this movie — I spent a couple of weeks on set with the director, sitting next to the monitor, which was fun.

Do you have a preference for a particular part of the job?

Production, shooting, is still the part I really, really love because it's so immediate. Every day there is such a sense of accomplishment — we got it done and we've got something we can look at because there's a piece of film. I enjoy the development stage too, but it tends to be frustrating and take a long time. Shooting is exhausting physically and emotionally, but during development just the phone-time is exhausting. In New York you start making phone calls early in the morning to Europe and then you can still be on the phone at 10 p.m. talking to LA. When I was working on a film in Vegas, the one thing I couldn't get through my head was that after 8 p.m. I couldn't talk to anyone, because it was too late, Europe was closed and New York was closed.

Post-production is interesting and a little more relaxing, but it's so much about the director and the editor sitting in a room. The whole process seems to take for ever, and then it's finished overnight. It's a strange emotion, letting go . . .

Do you enjoy post, the various elements, sound design and so forth?

I don't dislike it but it's not my favourite part of the process. It used to be that you could understand what was going on, but in the last five years or so it's become very technical with all the digital processes, new formats and constantly upgrading the technology so it's more and more this language that only *they* understand. So that kind of work I don't particularly like. But I like the final mix when all the pieces come together, and I love recording music. I know nothing about music but I have a little bit of a vocabulary, I know what works. And I really enjoy listening and watching how the music really does change the picture.

Of course, so much of Marty's music is licensed music as opposed to score, which is incredibly expensive . . .

Were all the songs in Goodfellas *scripted?*

A few pieces, but not many. If you are working with a studio then you have access to a music department who budget it out for you. Whereas if you are making an independent movie, you have to do it yourself.

With *Goodfellas* people expected the music to be expensive, but it got bigger. Then with *Casino* the studio anticipated that the cost was going to be significant, but these things always grow. It's always a negotiation.

Do you shudder at the costs for the music in a picture like Casino?

The people paying for it did . . . but then I don't think the movie would have worked as well without it.

Brides premiered at the Toronto Film Festival in September 2004.

Take 18

BOB SHAYE

Bob Shaye is a true pioneer of the independent scene. The son of a Detroit wholesale grocer, he founded New Line in 1967, and went on to build it on horror/exploitation, art-house and whatever else he could find, from John Waters to Freddy Krueger and Teenage Mutant Ninja Turtles. New Line's diversification with the Fine Line Features division has further muddied the question of what defines a New Line film? Is it *Dumb and Dumber, Hoop Dreams, Shine, Seven, Boogie Nights . . .*? For the time being, New Line are immortalized as the backers of *The Lord of the Rings* trilogy, a risk that was also pure New Line — a fantasy franchise with edgy appeal, one that paid off in spades. New Line remains small, with offices on both coasts. I met Bob Shaye in July 2003 at 116 North Robertson Boulevard in Los Angeles.

1. *From hand to mouth*

BOB SHAYE: I started out wanting to be an actor, then I directed some short films. One was shot on 16mm and very much an 'experimental movie', as they were called in those days, made with $3,000 that I had saved from taking souvenir photos at school dances. The film was kind of an 'epistemological parable', as I snootily liked to call it, but it won some awards and it was well received.

I had lived in Sweden for a couple of years and when I moved back to New York I asked everyone I met whether they knew anybody in the movie business. I had written letters to people like Sam Arkoff at AIP, but I hadn't heard from anybody, and I didn't really have the fortitude to just pack up and move to Los Angeles — I had only ever visited the place for a couple of days, and I didn't like it very much. Then somebody said, 'Why don't you call Willard Van Dyke' — who was head of the Film Department at the Museum of Modern Art — 'because he might be able to help.' It turned out that Willard knew of a job running the film stills archive at the Museum of Modern Art. That was two steps closer to the film industry than where I was, which was nowhere. And that's how I got started.

One of the conditions of my job was that I would be invited to all the parties that the Film Department gave at MOMA. Not long after I started, there was a Czech festival going on so I went to a party and met some people who said they knew how to distribute films on college campuses. My family was in the wholesale grocery business so I knew what distribution was about. And through a Czech contact I discovered some films that were available for distribution. Plus, friends of mine were short filmmakers, then there were my *own* films, so this became our first programme. There were feature films by directors such as Jan Nemco, Jan Schmidt, Graham Ferguson and Sheldon Rocklin; and we had eight short films, two with each programme. We put together programme notes, posters and trailers — a whole marketing campaign to go with the films, and we rented them to student activities' offices on college campuses. My belief was that these were films that people of my generation would find interesting, because they were not available from regular art-house distributors. I thought renting films to college campuses could be a new way to get a distribution system going, as opposed to just going to movie theatres.

HELEN DE WINTER: *Did you make money from this?*

That would be an overstatement . . . We survived from hand to mouth. The girlfriend I was living with — and ended up marrying — was a systems analyst at TWA, so she paid the rent. But we were living modest lives. We created enough cash-flow to pay printing and lab bills, the rent, and people's modest salaries — though sometimes not my own. But film societies were making money from our films, and they were telling other film societies, and we were getting interest from people. At the time tax shelters were very popular, and one of their plans was buying films for distribution. So we were contacted by various promoters who either had films or who asked us if there were any films we wanted to buy that they could finance in return for us distributing them. And that gave us access to films that went beyond Czech art-house movies.

What did you learn from this?

I realized that there were people who were sincere about making films and not just avaricious about earning money and grabbing power, but people who really *do* enjoy making films that entertain people. For them it's not like they *just* want to make a personal statement, but that they understand that film is a business and it's a business that one has to understand and appreciate as *a purveyor*, and as *a creator*, as opposed to simply being a business where you are selling shoelaces. There's something a lot more rich and satisfying about it. So that was something that I realized I enjoyed doing.

Were there more exhibitors for art-house films in late sixties New York?

Quantatively I don't really know. I thought it was pretty defined, which theatres showed art films and which theatres showed commercial films, but there seemed a greater interest from people who were going to see art-house films. We had major competition from Don Ragoff, and Cinema 5 in those days.

Why didn't you take theatrical rights?

We started out not having theatrical rights because it was part of a trick we had going. We didn't have any money to pay the producers so we said we would split the rights with them and that all we wanted was the non-theatrical rights to get the film going; then when the film made it we said we would try to buy the theatrical rights from them but that was just a ruse really to get them to give us the film for the marketplace we were working in.

When did you start distributing films for paying audiences?

We didn't really jump into theatrical distribution for three to five years. We found a film that Jean-Luc Godard had made called *Sympathy for the Devil*, which was very successful on college campuses, and we eventually got the rights to show it in theatres and that's how we crossed into being grown-ups. The success of Godard's film convinced us that we should try to distribute films theatrically.

Who were you working with at this time?

There was me and six or seven employees and we worked out of a loft on 13th Street and University Place, which was downtown New York. We were based in New York until after we made *Nightmare on Elm Street* when we opened an LA office.

How did you raise money to start New Line?

I started off with $1,000 but after nine months to a year we had raised about $80,000 from a bunch of investors, so that was our seed money.

I found the investors through a girlfriend of my sister's, whose husband was a lawyer and a friend of a venture capitalist — this was the late sixties when people were making a bit of money on the stock market, so we raised $3,000 from one person, $5,000 from another and $10,000 from someone else and that's how it came together. They invested in the New Line Cinema Corporation and we had a business plan and sold them privately held stock.

Do the original investors still hold stock in New Line Cinema?

No. They betrayed the company when we eventually went public. But that's another story . . .

Did you start out with a vision about what you wanted to achieve?

We developed a business plan that wasn't very sophisticated, I'm embarrassed to say, even though I'm a business school graduate from Michigan University. But it was definitely ambitious. It was a plan that began with distributing films to colleges and then went on to detail how much money we needed and how we were going to recoup it and create cash-flow and then eventually distribute films to theatres, *buy* theatres, and produce movies of our own that we could distribute. So it was a big plan — and actually we have pulled off some of it.

In the early days we had a theatre for a while on the West Side of New York. This came about because we wanted to go into partnership with the guy who owned the Elgin Theatre, a guy named Ben Barenhott. We were showing *Pink Flamingos* [1972, dir. John Waters] at midnight — it was one of the films we had got the theatrical rights to, and we found a guy who was a lawyer who owned this theatre who was going to go into partnership with Ben. Then Ben decided that he didn't want to be my partner, so we went into partnership with the guy who owned the theatre instead. Originally we thought it was going to be a kind of real funky, cool, art-house theatre, selling home-made cookies in the lobby and the kind of stuff that never works but we didn't know that then. Then, over the first eighteen months, the projector was stolen and guys started getting mugged in the hall and the men's room, so it got a little dicey but we were theatre operators for a moment in time. One of the wonderful things is our theatre manager back then in 1972/73 is now the head of marketing at New Line.

We managed to survive for perhaps too long a time, though at least it meant that we were working and we had enough to keep going. But we never really had a film that made millions or tens of millions of dollars. I was constantly trying to raise money even though I had a bank line of a $200,000 overdraft. I would go to Cannes every year and buy little films and talk my way into things. Then we started getting films to sell and I took *Reefer Madness* [1936, dir. Louis J. Gasnier] which I knew was in the public domain and we distributed that very well and licensed the film to other independent distributors. Then we discovered that the Beatles' *Magical Mystery Tour* was in the public domain. And we pretty much distributed any weird little film we could get our hands on. We distributed a couple of Warhol films, including *Women in Revolt* [1971, dir. Paul Morrissey], Werner Herzog's *Fata Morgana* and *Even Dwarves Started Small*, and another Godard film, *Wind from the East* [1970].

How did you meet John Waters?

One day I got one of those 16mm board containers with canvas straps on it at our office on 13th Street in New York, which was a loft above Smiths bar and grill. I opened this thing up and it was a film called *Multiple Maniacs* and it was a black-and-white movie that was pretty awful. Well, I sent the film back with a note saying, 'This is not quite up to distribution quality but you're such an off the wall guy, if you do anything else you should send it to me.' About six months later I received a bigger package and inside was a 16mm print, of *Pink Flamingos* so I put it on the projector and this time the film was in colour. I remember at one point thinking that the film was so mind-boggling I had to stop the projector and run it back to make sure that what I had seen was actually on the film and not something I was making up in my head. Afterwards I rang John and said, 'This is pretty interesting. What do you want to do?' And he said, 'Well, the guy who is showing *El Topo* [dir. Jodorowsky] at midnight has seen it and he really wants to have a midnight showing and I'm going to get out there and help promote the film.' So John came down with some of his friends and we hit it off pretty well and I liked the guy a lot. So that's how we met. He did *Female Trouble* and we distributed that, then he did *Desperate Living* and we distributed that, and then he did *Polyester*, which was co-produced with us and Michael White, the English producer. Last month we won eight Tonys which is the American Oscar for theatre for the Best Musical on Broadway which is the stage version of the movie *Hairspray*, and it's currently the number one theatre event in Manhattan right now. Sometimes things take a long time . . .

2. No one was rolling in dough

At what point did you think about producing?

I would say it took about fifteen years, until I went to Los Angeles. I came out with an American living in England, Mark Forstater, who had co-produced the *Monty Python* movies with Michael White. Mark and I got to be friends and he said, 'Why don't you go to Los Angeles and meet filmmakers who are making interesting films and see if we can get some projects together?' The plan was I would guarantee the distribution and we would raise the money together. So we came out for a week and hooked up with Joe Dante, Tobe Hooper, and Wes Craven. At the time Tobe had made *The Texas Chainsaw Massacre*, Joe had made *Piranha*, and Wes had made *Last House on the Left*. Nothing came out of it initially. But I stayed in touch with them . . .

How did you produce your first film?

At the Cannes Film Festival in the late seventies and eighties there was always a carnival atmosphere, people were always doing crazy things to get attention — so there would be aeroplanes flying around and blimps in the sky and people dressed up in kooky outfits. One year I was sat having a cup of coffee with a guy who was hustling films, and it turned out he used to be a stunt man. I said, 'That's really interesting . . .' So this guy starts telling me about all the different types of stunt men and different gags — water gags, horse gags, fire gags, high fall gags . . . I thought this was a fantastic idea for a movie, something that people could get really excited about because we could have all these terrific stunts in a movie and this is what audiences wanted. Also at the time I thought it was a way to get a film going and get some international buyers on board. I was an experienced buyer but now I wanted to be a seller — except I didn't have much money in my pocket.

A couple of months later I went on vacation with my family and wrote a twenty or thirty page treatment for a story called *Stunts*. The plot was about stunt men who were being murdered on the set of an action movie. It was basically an action/mystery story with a whole bunch of stunts and things in it. Once I had the treatment, a friend of mine knew a guy who was in the advertising business who was a real hustler and he said, 'I can help you raise some money but I want to rewrite the treatment.' So he did, and then it was a question of how were we going to find the money to hire a screenwriter to write the script? Well, it turned out that the guy who said he could raise some money couldn't raise *any* money. And somehow, as people do when they have an enormous amount of talent, he got himself attached to our project in a way that I didn't really know how to get rid of him. But I thought at least he knew how to produce things, because he was a commercials producer. The way a lot of films used to get financed back then was from storyboards and treatments. We had a treatment, so I got a storyboard artist to come in and do six 16- by 20-inch renderings of some of the big action set pieces in the movie. The guy who was in charge of our sales pitch got very excited about the action in the storyboards, so a year after having the idea, we went back to Cannes and I got a Japanese distributor whom we had done some business with before and a distributor from Hong Kong interested in buying the rights based on the treatment. The distributors gave us letters of credit based on delivery of the movie that I could take to a bank, and then I got a completion guarantee and a lot of other rigmarole, and discount to make the movie — so we were on our way. Then a girl working in our office who was a political fundraiser decided she wanted to raise money to make movies, and she knew a wealthy lawyer who had just made a movie who said he would be interested in investing in the film and that he had a friend who he wanted to be a producer on the film. But it turned out that the lawyer's friend and the commercials producer were very good friends and they had both produced commercials together so it was kind of like synchronicity in a weird way. The lawyer put up almost $400,000 or about half the budget of $750,000 and we cast Robert Forster as the stunt man and Fiona Lewis as the investigating reporter. Joanna Cassidy was in it as well. The director was Mark Lester, a guy I knew because we used to rent him films when he was head of the film society at University of California at Berkeley; he had also made some films for Roger Corman.

How did production go?

After the enormous struggle of pulling the film together a whole bunch of awful things went on. We started principal photography early because for technical reasons we had to get started by a particular date or our line of credit was going to expire. So we had the whole company out shooting second unit until the lead actor arrived. But unfortunately while he was on his way to the airport he got into a car crash and was in hospital for eight weeks. Then, a week into principal photography, the completion guarantor sent in a guy from the mafia to take over the film. So for a while it was one thing after another . . . but when the film finally got finished it came off really well. In fact we took it to Cannes the following year. I think the idea was later ripped off by the television programme *The Fall Guy* with Lee Majors.

Were your commercial instincts right? Was the film successful?

Well, the film had a downside because the guy who put up $400,000 in cash made a totally outrageous deal with me where he got to triple recoup his investment before anybody got anything. We managed to sell the film to NBC for $700,000 before it was released theatrically, and then we sold it internationally for $1 million, so this guy was way ahead of the game and we didn't make anything from it. But I got him on his next film. At the time I didn't think the film was a particularly ambitious first film, I just thought the idea was good. And ultimately I was right, because the film still kind of stands up and remains in television syndication.

How did New Line survive financially prior to the big breakthrough success of Nightmare?

They made dollars and cents, not huge amounts of money, but they helped pay the overhead. No one was rolling in dough at that time. I was just very glad that my wife had free flying privileges because she was working with TWA. In fact I was once with Michael White and we were going to Baltimore together because he wanted to see them shooting *Polyester* and meet John Waters. We were at the airport and got to the gate and I had one of my wife's spouse passes, and we had bought Michael a ticket for about $110 — Michael didn't know what was going on. So they check Michael's ticket and he's allowed to get on the plane, then they look at my ticket and say, 'You can't get on.' And the reason was that if you were travelling on a special pass then you couldn't wear blue jeans. Michael was completely astounded and kept saying, 'What's wrong? Why can't he get on?' Finally I reached into my pocket and managed to pull together $110, using all my cash and credit cards to buy a ticket.

3. 'People don't like movies about dreams'

How did you end up producing Wes Craven's Nightmare on Elm Street?

About two years after we first met, I called Wes and asked him what he was doing and he said he had a fantastic idea for a movie — it was about a guy who killed you in your dreams, and the only way to avoid being killed was to stay awake. I said I thought that was fantastic and would he send it to me? But he said it was being considered elsewhere. At the time his agent was a guy working on his own and they were shopping the script around. I think they went to every place in the whole world, and six months passed and nothing happened. Then one day I got a phone call from the agent to say that Wes was going to send me the script. We were obviously the last place in the world they wanted, and we didn't have any money, so it was a desperation call. But I knew that, it was OK. And we loved the script. So then we got into a long development process. The story is painful to tell . . .

A Swedish friend of mine introduced me to a Yugoslavian guy who had made a lot of money. This Yugoslavian wanted to start packaging movies, and his girlfriend loved the script of *A Nightmare on Elm Street*, so he decided to put in some money. Then an English producer was going to put in a certain amount of money, but the English producer lied to me and instead of giving us the money he had promised, he put it into an Australian movie instead. I had a deal to sell the home video rights to a guy in Los Angeles — based in the very building in which we're now talking — and *he* was going to put up a certain amount of money, but once the English producer had betrayed his investment the home video guy said, 'OK, I'll put up what's missing, but I want to have double recoupment. And if you don't finance the remainder of the movie in sixty days I'm going to take over the whole film . . .' Meanwhile Wes was ready to start shooting because the film was supposed to be ready for a Halloween release and I was funding the production with $10,000 from here and $15,000 from there, whatever I had, including all my savings and all the money the company had. And we weren't supposed to be using our company money to produce films because it went against the covenant of our bank loan. Then, when we came back to this building to make the presentation to the production people, the Yugoslavian guy decided he didn't want to be involved any more and refused to put up the money. So suddenly the whole thing seemed like it was going down the drain. I kept on trying to persuade the Yugoslavian guy, and at the last minute I got him to agree. In total, it was about $1.2 million. Eventually I got a bank to finance the home video contract, and we made the movie.

Did things get better when you started production?

Oh, it was a complete crazy mess. One of the problems was that Wes wanted to end the film on a happy note, with the Nancy character waking up in the morning and it's a wonderful day and the whole thing has been a bad dream. I said, 'I hate that. And the audience won't want that ending, because it's a horror film — they're going to want one final shocking thing at the end.' But Wes said, 'No, I don't want to do that', so we had a big war about how to end the movie. Meanwhile we were running out of money and we were over schedule and the director of photography was a militant unionist who said, 'I'm walking off at midnight if you don't finish this whole thing, I don't care.' So we had to beg him to give us six more hours but he said, 'No, midnight is it.' So we were shooting every goddamned thing. I was shooting and everybody was shooting scenes from the film, just to finish it. And the end continued to be a big issue and Wes refused to direct the ending where the car pulls up and Freddy is in the car. Wes said, 'If you want to do it, you direct it, I'm not going to do it.' I said, 'Come on!' but he didn't want to do it. So I directed the sequence where the car pulls up and the top goes up and Nancy gets into the car but it's revealed that it's really Freddy Krueger who's in the car, and the dream continues. Wes thought I was being cynical because I wanted to make sequels, but I didn't have any vision of sequels, I really wasn't that sophisticated. I just wanted the audience to walk out thinking about how good the movie was.

When we finished shooting we didn't know what to do. We had three different endings — Wes's ending, my ending, and a compromise ending. So we had some test screenings in New York and invited thirty or forty kids to a screening room to try them all out. None of the endings really seemed to work on their own, so we thought, 'Why not use them all?' And of the three suggestions, that seemed to be the best one. I said to Wes, 'Do you want to do something else? Because I don't have any solutions here. Yours didn't work, mine didn't work, the mother in the house didn't work.' So we let the kids see everything, and that one worked the best. So we added all the endings on. Nancy comes out, everything's fine, then the car drives up and it's got Freddy in it, then the mother is standing there calling for her and she gets sucked back into the house. Wes was kind of in agreement about it, though I wouldn't say that he was ecstatic. But by then we were all so tired, and, frankly, Wes just wanted to get the film finished.

Did you have a sense the film was going to be a hit?

As soon as the film was finished, the lawyer who was representing Sean Cunningham and Wes Craven on some of their other films including *Friday the 13th* suggested we try to sell the film to Paramount. I said this would be fantastic and he thought we could probably get $2 to 2.5 million. We set up a screening for Mike Mancuso and the Paramount people on a Saturday morning, and we had our editor in the auditorium mixing the sound live on four tracks because we only had a temp mix. Then about an hour into the film the editor comes running up to me and says, 'Oh my God we've got the wrong ending!' Fortunately the cutting room was across the street so the editor forgot about the sound mix and ran across to the cutting room, grabbed the right ending, ran back to the projection booth and while frantically watching the film we spliced on the right ending. Well, we made it in time, but in any event it didn't matter because later that afternoon Paramount called and said they weren't interested. When I asked why, they said the reason was because about six months before Joe Ruben had directed a movie called *Dreamscape* and it hadn't been successful, so they said, 'We've decided this movie is about dreams and people don't like movies about dreams.' Well we ended up distributing the movie ourselves and every time I see Mike Mancuso I say 'Thanks a lot' because *A Nightmare on Elm Street* took millions of dollars at the box office.

4. *All of my good friends*

Did the distribution of this film properly launch New Line?

It was a mess, but it really got us started. We certainly had problems and there were a lot of crooks and a lot of cheating and a lot of stuff along the way. We had global sub-distributors who were representing the company who I think were skimming all kinds of stuff off, and people taking bookings and not reporting them. When we made the second *Nightmare* film we changed our sales staff and hired a new guy from Los Angeles. He said, 'Why don't you start an office out here?' Interestingly, the office we ended up renting was the very same office we went to when I was begging and pleading with the home video guy to give us more money.

Did box office success make it easier for you to grow and develop your company?

Some wonderful things *did* happen along the way. Just as we were starting to shoot *Nightmare on Elm Street* I began a negotiation with another home video company, RCA Columbia, for the international home video rights to films even though I didn't yet know what they were going to be; I made a deal with them, a $15-million deal for ten films for the international home video market. Little did I know that this was the most important market, and it was very hard to sell the films internationally without the home video rights. But it was great to walk around with a contract that said $15 million on it, and that helped us get more bank financing.

After *Nightmare on Elm Street*, a guy I had gone to law school with came to me and said, 'Would you like to raise some *real* money? There is a fantastic company called Drexel Burnham that's raising money for all kinds of people.' They were investment bankers and junk bonds was their big deal and it was run by a guy named Michael Milken. I was introduced not to Mike Milken but to a young guy, a very bright Harvard-educated lawyer. I tried several times to get them interested in putting up money for us, and he didn't think much of us initially but after the second *Elm Street* movie I went to see him again and showed him our business plan and he said, 'I think we can do something.' Eventually we got Drexel Burnham to do an initial public offering for us on the Sinericon stock exchange.

Eventually we had our initial public offering, then those people who had invested with us at the beginning took all of their stock and threw it on to the market. The investment bank, because they sell the stock to their customers they can't let the stock go down in the first few days, so if there is an imbalance between selling versus buying, they come in and buy back stock for their own account, just to keep the share price up. The price was originally going to be $11 a share. They couldn't sell it at $11 so ended up selling it at $8 a share. But the stock was going to go down to $4 unless they came in and bought shares. Then all of my good friends dumped hundreds of thousands of shares and stock into the market, and Drexel Burnham went completely crazy; these guys were raising money for big shots like Ivan Boesky and Ted Turner, and here's this little company that they decided to take a shot with and it was causing them incredible aggravation so they threatened to withdraw. There is a rule in the American Stock Exchange that it takes three days from when a sale is made to actually consummate it and close it, and in those three days if there was anything wrong you could stop the sale. So in the first two days they said, 'We're stopping the sale.' So that was another little learning curve . . . Just as I thought things were going OK, I would wonder, 'Why are these things happening to me? Why can't it just be the way it's supposed to be?' But we ended up fixing it and it all worked out. We got money to make more movies, and we expanded our distribution operations and started opening our own offices in a very careful way.

5. *Not making art movies per se*

Would you say you have had a strategy for the films you have produced and distributed?

We were more distributors than producers, but we wanted to make both more cutting-edge films — but not art films — and entertaining films. We made films for the dating crowd. We thought with scary films if the girl grabbed the guy and the guy grabbed the girl it would be a great way to start off an evening. And that was the kind of film we specialized in.

How did you grow from a small distribution company into a bigger entity?

There were other people like Canon, Cinemation, AIP, Roger Corman and New World who were much better financed than we were and much better involved in the Hollywood community. We were just mostly upstarts from New York and I wasn't even living out here in Los Angeles. I would come out for a week or ten days every month. We had a little bit of development money in New York. Mike De Luca was working as an unpaid intern. Sarah Richer was our head of production — she used to be my secretary, she liked movies and was good friends with John — but she hadn't a clue about production. It became a task to understand how to develop movies and how to market them. It's a long process and we're not finished yet. We're just at the beginning of the learning curve and the company is thirty-five years old.

The distribution organization was essentially based out here in LA but everything else was in New York and there were guys who I used to sell college films with who were suddenly involved with producing movies and coming up with ideas. It ran on instinct. None of us knew how to really do it. It wasn't like we were independent producers who just went to a big company. We ended up doing the whole thing ourselves and that actually was the good part of it because that's what gave the company viability. Eventually it made us attractive as an acquisition candidate as opposed to just being a little independent producer with a production deal for some big studio, which is not what I wanted to do.

What's the difference between New Line and Fine Line?

When we started off, New Line had a Fine Line sensibility, then as we segued into more commercial films . . . actually, the time when the separation really came about was when *sex, lies and videotape* showed up at Sundance in 1989. Sarah saw it and said, 'We had better try to get this film.' I knew one of the producers, Nick Wechsler, very well and Miramax was after it and I said that I was going to get this film but the guy who was head of distribution had a much more commercial perspective plus our marketing was much more commercially orientated at that time, so we had kind of evolved. Then the price got so high, I decided I didn't want to . . . I wasn't sure we could market it as it was more arty and needed to be handled carefully so we let Miramax take that film, which I was pretty irritated about. And that's when we decided to start Fine Line.

It took a long time to figure out what we wanted to do and how to do it. There is no question that good taste and marketing expertise are good for both things. Fine Line ended up with *The Player* and *Shine* and *Hoop Dreams* and the concept was correct, but it still needs some kind of integration into the overall company; it's a little awkward to be running a whole distribution organization for art films. So we have what we think is the right mix right now of shared marketing to some extent with managers who work exclusively with Fine Line and a head of distribution for Fine Line who really understands that the art exhibition marketplace is different. And people are different and attitudes are different and the direction and philosophy is different and there are a whole bunch of things that are different. So there needs to be a discreet branch that handles that without a large overhead. There are more and more films being developed by Fine Line and distributed by New Line. Because there has been this merging of art theatres and cineplexes, that means there are few theatres showing these sorts of films. We've just finished this film *Birth* with Nicole Kidman directed by Jonathan Glazer and that's a Fine Line film that will be distributed by New Line because it's a bigger movie. And in a way that's what some of the other companies like Miramax and to some extent Sony Classics and Focus are doing; they have turned the art film into the mega art film. It's hard for traditional art-house films because for really tiny films, if they do a million dollars at the box office you're jumping up and down, but the reality is that's so small that for us it doesn't really get you anywhere and there's no particular reason to do it. You start using up too much manpower and too much administrative time. If you don't have any films and much to do then all you have is administrative time and manpower so there's always an opening for new films that come along that a new young, ambitious, aggressive distribution organization can find and begin the process of creating a cash-flow. There are new companies like New Line was thirty years ago, that are just starting up now and I think that's great because they offer an opportunity for filmmakers to get their films distributed.

Do you remain intimately involved in the running of your company?

Very involved. I spend most of my time out here. Our corporate head quarters are in New York but since the inception of the company our lawyer ended up becoming my partner and he is very much more involved managing the administrative affairs, although we share cre- ative and green-lighting authority. In terms of developing stuff I read a lot, we have two or three meetings a week plus informal meetings with all of our key people. By the time I read script notes we're on our way to committing to it and then I definitely give script notes and I hope they will be adhered to. Sometimes they are and sometimes they aren't but I am very much involved in the process. There was a point in time when we were just letting our production people produce, but I decid- ed that was kind of a stupid thing to do, firstly because I wasn't having a good time, and second of all I think the company was not benefiting from a certain amount of value that comes from experience and travail and also development at a certain kind of pace which has proved in one way or another quite valuable to the corporation. I usually send over my notes to our head of production and there are production executives and teams to whom they are assigned. But nothing gets approved without me reading it, or Michael Lynne, my partner in New York, reading it. Then we do a set of financial scenar- ios based on what our marketing and distribution and international licensing people and everyone else comes up with, so they have their input which yields a much more commercial version, but that's fine — because we're not making art movies *per se*, we're making movies that are going to appeal to people and be stimulating and *maybe* they will evolve into art too . . .

6. *Just too long*

You have released a lot of risky films, risky not least in terms of length.

What catalysed *Magnolia* for me was the cast. But what bothered me about *Magnolia*, and *Boogie Nights* too, was I thought they were both too long and could easily have been shorter. Not for the sake of it, but because of the attention span of the viewer, and the sort of skill a director should have in knowing how to shape a film so he keeps the audience on the hook, so to speak. That also happened with *Short Cuts* — we ended up with films that were just too long. And that's what disappointed me, and in conversations subsequently with the directors of those movies they kind of admitted that I was right, but it's too late. One director who I had a similar discussion with was

Peter Jackson over *The Lord of the Rings*, but I felt much less adamant about that — because I felt the films did do what they were supposed to do, which was to keep people enthralled. They were just such a fascinating scenario, and one has to be careful about not being too arbitrary about saying a film shouldn't be longer than X. Those films without end-credits were very close to three hours each, but they really did hold the audience's attention and you didn't find people straying much. And I couldn't figure out a real way to even *suggest* to Peter how to continue cutting once it had got down to that length. I mean, when the films were three hours and forty-five *minutes* there were plenty of suggestions to make, and Peter was attentive to the issues. But he did get to a point which I have to agree with. It *is* a kind of marketing/commercial negative to say you are going to see a three-hour movie.

How did Lord of the Rings *happen?*

Lord of the Rings got started at another company but they weren't allowed to invest that amount of money in the films, and we were. And even though the films went substantially over-budget, we acceded to the over-budget requirements, because we liked what we saw. A lot . . .

How much did you see?

There have been three scripts that have been transmuted to such a degree that, I must admit, I'm going to see the third film in a couple of weeks and I have no idea what it's going to be like except that the people who *have* seen it say it's the best of the three.

Was it a risk taking on a film in that genre?

Yes, a tremendous risk. But I think we've mitigated it with considerable intelligence from a financial perspective, so that the risks ultimately were not going to be any bigger than the kind of risks we've had to take on a number of lower-budget films, because of the interest the films have had from our international distribution partners and a number of other financing devices that we capably used that mitigated the risk. But there's no question it was a risk. It was just one of those things that I believed had incredible marketing momentum behind it. So from a purely business point of view I thought was a good risk, with high-reward potential.

7. Get a job

Ted Turner purchased New Line in 1993. In 1996, Turner merged with Time Warner, which then merged with AOL in 2002. What is the corporate status of the company now?

We are part of Time Warner, which includes *Time* and *Fortune* magazines.

Has that been a good merger for you?

No, because what happened was there was a big bamboozle somewhere, and AOL and Time Warner and everybody lost a lot of money including me personally. It was a good step for us to join with Ted Turner and for Ted Turner to join with Time Warner. But it should have stopped there.

As to the future . . . would you say you have achieved what you set out to do?

No. I am still on the road to fulfilment and inspiration. And the great thing about the movie business is you're only as good as your next movie. It's not like I ever get bored, because I find there are always new stories to tell, new groups of people to entertain.

What do you say when you are asked how to become a producer in Hollywood?

I think anyone who wants to be in the movie business should just get up and do *something* — whether it's working as an unpaid intern, or in a job that gets you closer to the business. You've got to start moving yourself around. Because not only do people not know what creating, producing and distributing motion pictures is outside of Hollywood — most of them haven't a clue *inside* Hollywood. It's just a lot of people milling around, some more cheeky than others. Cheek is necessary to catalyse talent most of the time, especially if you're going to be independent, and not just take a regular job. But taking any job in the business is a good idea to get yourself going . . .

The Lord of the Rings marched on, and The Return of the King had its clean sweep on Oscar night in February 2004.

Take 19

JAMES SCHAMUS

Screenwriter, academic, studio president and producer — James Schamus first got himself noticed on *Poison* by Todd Haynes (1991, as executive producer); Tom Kalin's *Swoon* (1991, as executive producer); and Alexandre Rockwell's *In the Soup* (1992, as associate producer). Schamus founded Good Machine with Ted Hope in 1991. He distinguished himself further as a collaborator with Ang Lee, producing *Pushing Hands* (1992), producing and co-writing *The Wedding Banquet* (Golden Bear, 1993 Berlin Film Festival), co-writing and associate producing *Eat Drink Man Woman* (1994 Best Foreign Film Oscar nominee), and continuing with Lee in a partnership that has since brought forth *Sense and Sensibility, The Ice Storm, Ride with the Devil, Crouching Tiger, Hidden Dragon, The Hulk,* and *Brokeback Mountain.* Good Machine executive-produced and sales-agented *The Brothers McMullen* by Edward Burns and *Clean Shaven* by Lodge Kerrigan. *Safe* (1995), *She's the One* (1996) and *Happiness* (1998) confirmed their eminence. David Linde joined the Good Machine team in 1996, and in 2002 the company was acquired by Universal, and merged with USA Films to become Focus Features. Schamus is also a professor of film at Columbia University.

1. *Possessory credit*

HELEN DE WINTER: *The combination you have achieved of the roles of screenwriter and producer is quite exceptional, isn't it?*

JAMES SCHAMUS: It's a combination that is predominant in television, so it's not such an odd thing in the audio-visual moving-image world. It's odd in film only because of the historical constructs by which both the studios and the different guilds and creative parts of the whole matrix of filmmaking inform themselves, in particular over the last thirty to forty years.

Around 1960 you had Lew Wasserman and Alfred Hitchcock doing deals at Universal which gave Hitchcock possessory credit and kind of allowed him to retain partial ownership of a great deal of his work.[21] The studios started giving more power to directors. Then all of a sudden you had *Cahiers du Cinema*'s appreciation of Hollywood genre products, and whereas once you either identified the film by its star or its genre, you now started identifying it by the signature of the directorial presence. Which is something you just don't do that much in television. There is no directorial signature. It is more 'Created by' or 'Executive Produced by', whether it's *Six Feet Under* or *Sex in the City*. In television, which moves much more quickly, you have a balance of power that turns away from directors and is much more in the interests of the industry.

As a writer/producer, are you able to be more intimately involved with screenwriters developing and fixing script problems?

It depends. It's easy to identify that as part of my activity because I happen to be a screenwriter, but quite frankly that's what good executives do — they develop material and work on it.

2. 'Hey, we're here to help'

Did you set out to write or produce?

I didn't set out for anything. But once I got to New York I was picking up internships and odd jobs, and realized that the internships — meaning free labour — were not 'paying the rent'. So I very quickly got through the development slate of the place where I was interning and offered to rewrite one of the scripts, which was basically a dog, and said I could offer them something for much less than what they were used to paying. This was for a company that was then called Program Development Company which made primarily made-for-television films of theatre pieces for American Playhouse, which at that time was beginning to really be a centre for the nurturing of what would end up being called independent cinema. In terms of the rewriting, by the time that I stepped in the original writers had long disappeared into their next jobs, so there was no other feeling but that it was about attempting to save projects that had died, in which they had already invested a lot of money in development.

21. When MCA was an agency Wasserman made deals for Hitchcock at both Paramount and CBS that gave the director ownership of his films and his hit TV series, enriching the filmmaker considerably.

Did your rewrite go into production?

It didn't. The first script I rewrote was called 'The It Girl', it was about Clara Bow. I delivered it and it got a lot of attention, and for a moment it looked as though it was going to be made for cable, which was then a young business, with Virginia Madsen, the then top 'Q-rated' star, as they say. But that fell apart. I then adapted a novel and delivered that script the week before the famous Writer's Guild strike in 1988, which was a bloodbath, basically. I got on a plane to Hollywood, and the day I flew was the start of the strike. I landed and suddenly I wasn't able to meet anybody.

What then was the genesis of starting Good Machine?

Through all of this — especially having a window on to the Hollywood scene during the strike — I realized that screenwriters, especially those who intended to do it passionately and were active, tended to be people who look like I do now — overweight middle-aged guys. They tended to be very macho, they tried to look like Joe Eszterhas, that was the style back then at least, and they were very angry, and they were rich. You could be paid a lot of money to be serially humiliated. And I thought 'Well, I've been looking at that as a future, and I love to write, blah, blah . . .' But as an identity it just didn't seem like a healthy one. I thought you would need a stronger ego than I had, and an internal support system to withstand that career path. Also I was simultaneously getting involved in the 'independent scene' . . .

And what was that?

It was just a bunch of people who had come out of college recently and had seen Spike Lee's *She's Gotta Have It* or Jim Jarmusch's *Stranger Than Paradise*, and realized that there was a transient interest from — shall we say — the last gasp of a public television-dominated European landscape. That is to say that most of the European countries had yet to see the commercial television revolution take place. So there were slots in late night arts programming where, for very modest licence fees — but still big for us — you could actually sell independent work, whether it was to ZDF in Germany or LA SEPT in France, or to Channel 4 in England. All these territories were either acquiring or buying interesting films. And at the same time it was the birth of home video, and a flood of new capital was coming in through companies like Vestron that were just insatiable in their appetite for product. And since the studios were holding on to their libraries, trying to figure out whether video was going to sell them or not, there was just an enormous sellers' market for a while. You could have some ridiculous, mind-numbing, idiotic, independent film but you could get $600,000 for the video rights — you just needed a colour picture to put on the cover, especially if you had somebody on the cover who had their top off . . .

Was this the time that you met Ted Hope?

Ted and I were both readers or 'script analysts' at New Line and I had hooked up with the Wooster Group, a wonderful theatre company here in New York. I didn't have a lot of — or I should say 'any' — real physical production experience. But Ted had gone to NYU and spent a long time on set. So we joined forces at that point.

How did you set yourself up as 'The Kings of Guerrilla Film Making'?

We set that as one of our mandates from the very beginning, because there was a need. There were a lot of auteurs, a lot of eighteen-year-old geniuses running around with NYU film degrees. Some were older . . . but they were everywhere, I mean Sundance is full of them. But there were no producers, because it wasn't really a role that was articulated within the independent sector at that time. You had the old-school 'independent' producers, but there was no organized way of thinking about what the business was. So it was a very opportune moment to say, 'Hey, we're here to help auteurs do their thing, we can provide that kind of support.'

How did you set about creating an identity for Good Machine? Who were you seeking to work with?

I think it was a fairly long list. There were filmmakers who had only made short films and had yet to make their first features and we were very interested in seeing that process take place. Others were people who already had some films under their belt but who were outside the mainstream who we felt were interesting. So the list is pretty much a list of people we ended up working with, except obviously the list was a lot bigger at the start. The identity we had hoped for would be created as a result of the work of filmmakers who had a signature style. You take the auteurist philosophy, ideology — whatever you want to call it — and you realize that you can't afford movie stars but if you have a relatively good-looking, articulate person making the movie, *that's* your star.

Things changed, obviously, especially with movies like *Pulp Fiction*, when suddenly stars who *had* been stars but weren't any more, but were about to be again, such as Travolta and Bruce Willis, cut their fees significantly to be in an independent film. Up until that point, agents were very scared of independent producers of low-budget films because they thought that if they allowed their client to work for less, the studio would say, 'Hey, you worked on *that* for the minimum, so what's with this $2 million for *our* movie?' I think what Willis did to break through that particular injunction was to introduce a two-tier system: 'There is my price for the little low budget indie and there is my price for the big studio picture.' And the studios played along because, of course, that's how they were starting to get into the business themselves, buying Miramax et cetera, so they understood the benefits of linking that system to the various parts of production.

What skills did you have to be an independent producer?

Like with most skills, you *pretend* you have them before you have them, and then you do them and you learn as you go along . . . I think it's interesting in the last fifteen years there has grown up a fairly large industry of publishing and film schools in terms of training for producers, and certainly there are bodies of knowledge that are worth having before you pull the trigger — especially if you are holding the gun directly to your own head. But the skills are quite varied. There are different styles of producing as there are different styles of directing and at the end of the day the skills are still very much to prioritize what it is you are trying to do, and maximize your ability to motivate people so they hook up.

What financial risks did you take when you started?

Well we didn't have any money so it's difficult to take risks. It's kind of that simple — if you're always broke, then you never go bankrupt, and if you don't have a nickel, what's the risk? We were hand-to-mouth for years and years and there was a constant thing of 'How are we going to pay the rent next month?' That was going on even after a decade. We continued in that way while, at the same time, remaining fairly fiscally conservative overall. Our business practices were always very, very conservative even if the aesthetic practices were, from time to time, a little outlandish.

So a budget had to match pretty much what you could sell it for?

It depends. You have different partners at different times, who have different appetites for different levels of risk. Sometimes people were appealed to on an equity basis, to take a gamble. Other times you had to pre-sell. One of the things that we understood from the very beginning was the multiplication of sources of support and income, having a multiplicity of partners, understanding that there was no such thing as an 'American film' and that it was really an international marketplace that sustained it from the very beginning — either through video or European television or Taiwan or various partners in Holland et cetera. Each one of these potential partners had their own scale of comfort and interest, so the goal, always, was not to pre-sell the film in its entirety — because then there is no upside, you're simply just making a film, which is fine, but you're not really making money and you're not sustaining a business. But David Linde joined us and after a few years we started putting a lot of thought and effort into building an international company, because *that's* a business.

Was there a turning point for you as a producer, a point where you felt you had really achieved something?

The most obvious movie is *The Wedding Banquet*, which came when the company was, as usual, on its last legs. We had no international sales to speak of, or even a domestic sale. We had a sale in Taiwan, a couple of regional output deals, but nothing really, and we couldn't even get sales companies interested to represent it. So we decided to do it ourselves, since we now had some experience with different international distributors over different movies. We went to the Berlin Film Festival, screened the film in competition, it went through the roof and we spent the next week interviewing every distributor in every territory and thinking through who were the best logical partners, for Ang as well, and who was going to support the film. We were able to return an enormous amount of money to our partners in Taiwan and earn very healthy fees for the service on this side of the movie. At that point, we understood ourselves to be as much a distributor and sales agent as we were filmmakers, and we pretty much stayed on that path right up until meeting David Linde.

And that has enabled you to executive-produce other people's films as well?

As far as we were concerned, unlike the figure of the producer as the cigar-chomping guy who is in charge of everything, the goal was to be of service, in any productive way we could across the whole gamut of producing activities, whether it was financing, being on set or line producing and making sure the electricity was being paid for. Different filmmakers and filmmaking teams needed different kinds of assistance and we could offer that without being a threat to their own producing teams. It's been a very collegiate process, that's why over time we have worked with as many producers as directors. Right now, here at Focus, it's interesting to work with producers because we know where they're coming from and they know we've done it before.

Do you think the independent sector can be seen as a victim of its own success? The marketing costs can cost more than the film and as so many independents are now owned by the studios there isn't the appetite to do that any more?

Take a very successful company like Miramax. Suddenly it had an enormous infrastructure and overhead, and in order to feed that you then have to look at what's going to be the next 'break out' or 'crossover' film. Every independent film is now judged by whether it's going to be the next independent success so you become news as Miramax or New Line has now become. At Focus we never want to become a studio but we also take risks quite prudently on budgets — they are nothing compared to studio budgets — but these are substantial numbers that require a real audience response. There is this enormous pressure on the marketing side. Miramax just changed the game completely and made this a very expensive game to play. At the same time it's a business, though I'm not saying it's a good business because the economics of specialty film don't make a *lot* of sense to me, but they make just enough sense, with the benefit of Oscars, so that we'll keep going.

3. *Unpleasant, to say the least*

Given your track record, why was it so difficult to put Crouching Tiger, Hidden Dragon *together?*

There were a number of reasons. One was that in Hollywood you're only as good as your last failure. At that point *Ride With the Devil* had that aura of defeat around it, and it was very difficult to put together what would have been the most expensive Chinese film in history, in a genre that was disreputable and had no track record at the American box office. Whatever one's reputations are, it's still real money that people have to spend, and it's a real risk.

Wasn't there a Taiwanese billionaire who wanted to invest in the film?

He was there for a while . . . I guess there were a couple of these guys, he was one, and he was there for a while. Then that interest dissipated . . .

So you travelled the globe looking for money?

Well, by that point of our careers we had got everyone's phone numbers and there was Cannes et cetera. We pre-sold distribution rights to a number of territories in Europe and they put up letters of credit, or cash guarantees or contracts that we could sell to the bank to cashflow. We then went to Sony Classics, a division of Sony's affiliate with Columbia, they bought the domestic US rights, and then Columbia bought a couple of foreign rights. So there were two separate deals to be done there. Plus we ended up selling the soundtrack rights to Sony Classical, because they had Yo Yo Ma who Dun Tan, our composer, wanted to work with. Then there was a co-producer in China, as well as the co-producers and producer in Taiwan, and the co-producer in China had to do a co-production agreement with the official Chinese state government. We had to get all these deals together in such a way that the bond company could sign off on the actual production side of things and the bank could sign off on releasing funds against the contracts. Then Mr Billionaire kind of disappeared pretty close to when we were starting pre-production, and we were talking about pulling all this together with everyone signing circular agreements in a timescale of about a month and a half . . . it was unpleasant, to say the least. Bill Kong, our producer in Hong Kong, really held the film together.

When production started in the Gobi Desert, were you on set during production?

I went back and forth. I didn't kid myself that I could physically line produce the movie, and I was in a state of exhaustion by the time we pulled the finance together. So I was commuting to China. But I wasn't that helpful on set, put it that way.

Does post-production suit your interests more than production?

I think that because of the way I do things, from the writing to the running of the companies, and also as the years go by with Ang, I don't feel the necessity to be there during production. And I *don't* need to be there looking over his shoulder. But I do enjoy post-production.

Is your writer's imagination affected by your producing discipline?

Writing screenplays is a very instrumental job, as I said before. When you write a poem, at the end of your effort you have a poem, but when you have a screenplay, what you have is simply a document that's begging people for money, and attention, and casting. It's work. Yet the goal is not the screenplay, the goal is the movie. So writing is very much part of this continuum, it's part of the same process.

4. 'They fight' . . .

How did you and Ang Lee go about conceiving the action sequences necessary for The Hulk?

Well, that was easy because it was all digital, so you could do anything. At the same time, one doesn't want one's imagination to soar, but it was soaring as we headed towards production as opposed to the writing itself. On *Crouching Tiger* I knew that Ang and [action choreographer] Yuen Hou Ping were going to do their thing. When I started the screenplay I thought it had to read as the greatest martial arts film ever with the greatest martial arts sequences, and in my genius while writing I discovered two words to describe each fight, which were 'They fight' . . .

With *Hulk* I needed, from a direction point of view, to let everyone know what was really going to be involved in those sequences so I was much more specific with the action. In the event, about half of those were transformed into very specific things that Ang was doing and about half remained as they were in the script, which I thought was a reasonable mix. But what was good about that was that at the various different stages the guys at Industrial Light & Magic and our effects producer could say, 'OK, here's the sequence, it's going to be this many shots, it's going to have about this much action, we're going to have to plan these miniature sets.' Otherwise it would be a nightmare.

In producing terms, did you feel a leap to a film like The Hulk?

They are all leaps. Obviously *Crouching Tiger* was a leap, *Ride with the Devil* was a leap and so was *The Ice Storm*. We've managed it in a pretty organic way and as you take these jobs and as the numbers get bigger and the number of people et cetera, you're still doing what you always do which is build a team of people who know what they're doing. It's not like on Ang's first movie *Pushing Hands* even I knew how to get electricity out of a telephone pole for a night scene, which is about as low-level a thing as an electrician on set can do. So from there, to the *Hulk*, with tens of thousands of hours of digital rendering time — well, I didn't know how to do that, but I do now, and we have people around us who can help us figure out who to work with and what the goal is.

Where do you go from The Hulk?

Good question . . . I am finishing *Hulk* 2 just to see what they'll do and we will take it from there. *Hulk* isn't a Focus movie, it was the last Good Machine movie actually, so it's with Universal. But time will tell whether it's going to become a franchise.

5. 'Go do your thing'

How has the independent environment changed from when you started?

It's changed substantially. I think that, as you said, victimization by success is probably just as pernicious as victimization by failure. *Now* I think a lot of younger directors who come out of film school and who maybe make a first feature that gets some good notices, they are accompanied by agents and managers and publicists and are always expecting to get $1 or 2 million for their next feature. So you have to deal with that. But Ang's first feature didn't even get distribution in the United States until after *The Wedding Banquet*. Nobody after their first feature is going to get paid a million bucks. And sometimes it takes time to become a director.

The independent sector internationally has shrunk quite a bit as it has here. There is no question that when we were starting, in each territory you had four or five or six viable small companies who had just enough money to get you the money you needed to be able to make or finish the movie and sell it at the right price. Those companies have in many places disappeared into or morphed into companies who don't have any money for an advance, but if you want your film distributed they will distribute it. So you have fewer buyers and those buyers are much more interested in the kinds of movies that essentially we produce here at Focus, as a rule, which are movies that have movie stars who have cut their fees to do something interesting. It means we can make interesting movies and risky movies, no question about it, but our buyers are interested in particular kinds of profiles.

Are you a workaholic?

I probably am, and I am trying to reform myself a bit. But I'm pretty notorious here, because I have kids, so I shoot out of the office, where-as most people are here until 7.30 p.m. and going out to drinks and then home. I guess part of my reticence is because of my writing, and then I also travel so much that when I'm home I'm just pretty remiss. But it's hilarious, you would not believe how under budget I am with my entertainment and expense account. I'm *trying* . . . I should go out more and meet people.

Have you ever done the schmoozing circuit?

Not really. I don't go to the receptions, I don't go to the clubs and it's not because I'm anti-social. The thing is I can go home, put the kids to bed, make my phone calls to LA and then write a bit.

What's your strategy now for going forward?

I don't really have one. I very much enjoy this job, but I wasn't really born for it, as David Linde was. David is truly a genius, he is an exceptional executive, I'm just having a good time and trying to be helpful.

That's very modest.

Well, it's just kind of true actually . . . it may sound like false modesty. There's a reason I come to the office, and I work hard and it's a great team of people. But, that said, you really know the difference if you spend time with David, and see his ability to have a complete grasp and command of the details of this part of the business and all the different aspects of our international partnerships.

How do you keep current?

That's very much a part of my job and why we're working with Alejandro González Iñárritu and Christine Jeffs, who we just did *Sylvia* with; it's her second film. We're very interested in new voices, but there is an ageism in this business that has always driven me mad — the idea that it's good if it's *new* doesn't make a lot of sense to me. Sometimes it's good if it's *good*, how's that? Rather than the preoccupation with the emerging new voice. The thing is to remain un-snobbish and open.

Is Focus independent within Universal?

There is no such thing as complete independence. Ted, my former partner, is completely independent except that his company is paid for by this company through a first look deal. So you tell me . . . it's a feeding chain here. I have to say, though, that Universal has really looked after us and it's an interesting mixture which would seem to be contradictory but we have had total support in really preserving the value of what we're doing. If we have a problem, I can pick up the phone to Universal and they are genuinely helpful. Have they ever said 'No' to anything we have ever proposed? No, they have always said, 'Go do your thing.' They have been great.

Is producing a fraternal environment?

I would say collegial. Yes, at least in New York. In LA there is a more competitive edge to it and I think there is some of that here with petty jealousies but for whatever reason, the generation that we have grown with have all worked with each other at different times and then separately.

Are you considering making cheaper, digital movies?

I like to make a good movie so it doesn't matter if that's digital or not. But we made the first digital feature, Frank Grow's *Love God*, which was wild.

Is it financial success that enables you to continue making films?

Sure. If I had made a lot of wonderful, wonderful films that had been abject failures and consistently lost money I wouldn't be sitting here.

When The Ice Storm *didn't perform at the box office did that have a negative impact on your plans for other movies?*

It did somewhat, I think. The good news was that when it got ditched at the box office we weren't too embarrassed . . . I mean if it had been a complete, abject failure it would have been a problem, but this can happen every year. In a mix of twelve films you are looking for one or two breakouts, you are looking for every other one to break even and make some change. Sometimes you lose money on *really* good movies and sometimes you make money on complete piles of crap.

Given your knowledge and experience, do you mentor others in the business?

I don't think so, no, it's not a role that I like and I think there's always a certain pomposity in the phrase 'mentor'. The best way that I can mentor people is just by using my knowledge. If I get my job done then I am naturally helping thousands of other filmmakers just by doing what I am doing. I've always had a couple of rules of thumb and one of them is, the most important aspect of the thing, before you go ahead and make the film, is knowing that everyone involved is making the same movie — the people who are financing it, the people distributing it, the people acting in it, and whoever is directing it. There's no use in thinking, as a lot of people can do 'Well, the studio thinks we're doing *that* but actually I'm making *this*, so we've fooled them.' That's just a recipe for unhappiness and disaster. So I would say to other producers, in my *mentor-mode*, it's not always the amount of money on the cheque you get to produce the movie, it's who's signed the cheque. Sometimes it's better to say 'No thank you' if you know that the people signing the cheque are deluded as to what it is they are signing for.

Have you been in that position?

I've never been *completely* in that position because I'm kind of ruthless about making sure I just don't go there. But for directors it's even more dramatic. It's difficult and scary for producers, but for directors it's *existential*. But you see it again and again, especially out there in the independent world where there are a lot of equity financiers who don't have the experience. Or sometimes in the studios where they say, 'This is going to be *big*, it's going to break out', and they hire artistes to do their artistey *thing* . . . those stories are legion.

In the year of the comic book hero, you have The Hulk *but you're also getting behind films like* Autofocus. *Is that diversity important to you?*

You know, *Hulk* is the weirdest and most risky movie that I have ever made frankly because of its entire take on the superhero genre. This isn't a guy wearing long underwear saving a bus full of kids. He's not fighting with the American flag on his back, he has the army fighting *him*. He's a little bit different. We don't have a brief here or think we will always do a certain kind of movie. If there is an interesting film-maker with an interesting idea, why not? At the same time, we're not apologetic or defensive about the fact that when we make movies, we want people to see them and we want them to do the numbers so that it pays for the movie, so we can have a little extra and can go on and make the next one.

The Hulk punched its weight at the summer box office of 2003 to the tune of $132 million domestically. Schamus's next project with Ang Lee, *Brokeback Mountain*, won the Golden Lion at Venice in 2005 and was nominated for 9 Oscars in 2006.

Take 20

CHRIS HANLEY

Chris Hanley's track record as a culture entrepreneur since the 1980s is quite outstanding, and *very* New York City. He has passed through rap and hip-hop and the art world into a movie-producing career, specializing in bringing acclaimed cult literature to the screen through his company Muse. If Alison Owen could be said to cover the literary waterfront in the UK, Hanley is definitely the man down at the docks on the other side of the Atlantic.

1. *'Chris Hanley is edgy'*

CHRIS HANLEY: I was an English and philosophy major, and after college I moved to New York and started working in the music business — we had a recording studio and we shot videos. The music world in New York in the early 1980s was a mix of Africa Bambaata, Soul Sonic Force, and different hip-hop and rap artists. We were electronic musicians and we kind of contributed to rap music having drum machines and synthesisers that played the human voice — so all that came out of our studio. Directors would come in and we would do scores of tiny new wave-type movies or short art-house experimental films — strange little movies with transsexuals like Terri Toye who was a famous transsexual actress. A lot of these films ended up in the Whitney Museum. At the time we were hanging out with Andy Warhol and people like Richard Hell, Debbie Harry and David Byrne . . .

I also worked as a contemporary art dealer in New York and Warhol was always part of the film and music community. We used to hang out, not that much, but we would go to the Gulf and Western Building and watch movies with some of his guys and the musicians would come over who were part of the Warhol Factory.

Then I started my own company, Rock Video International, with a Japanese partner and got into distributing music videos across Asia.

This was just as MTV was starting — we brought karaoke to the Western world, and my wife Roberta directed Steve Buscemi in a karaoke video . . .

But by the end of the 1980s the whole New York scene had got messy and difficult, the economy was collapsing, and my activities in music weren't paying off financially. At that point we wanted to get into the film business though there wasn't that much film stuff happening in New York. Roberta and I started our own company, Muse Productions, and we were given a project to look at called *Neuromancer*, a William Gibson novel. It had Chuck Russell attached to direct but it was going to cost a huge amount of money because of the special effects — CGI was not what it is today. We thought we should pursue what we had always liked, so we started buying up book rights, which went back to my days of being interested in literature at college.

HELEN DE WINTER: *What did you acquire?*

We bought the rights to Bret Easton Ellis's *American Psycho* which was published in 1991, then in 1993 we bought Jim Thompson's *The Killer Inside Me*. Thompson wrote *The Grifters, The Getaway, After Dark, My Sweet,* and Kubrick's *The Killing.* And we got Jeffrey Eugenides's *The Virgin Suicides.* A screenwriter called Matthew Bright wanted to adapt the Thompson novel so I read his own screenplays including *Freeway,* and I liked them and we got the rights to those. Within a month of acquiring *Killer,* Sean Penn and Val Kilmer wanted to be involved and at the time I remember thinking it didn't seem like everything was going to be so hard . . . but we're still developing the script today . . .

Would you say you are drawn to particular material?

Well, there is a tendency to say 'Chris Hanley is edgy', but I'm interested in anything that dramatically explores something important. Over ten years we have been pretty successful licensing books and getting them made into films, so I can call up any literary agent and they will call me back. A producer starting out probably wouldn't be able to buy the rights in the first place, because guys like me or Scott Rudin or the studios are eliminating opportunities for new producers to get going.

I don't consciously choose projects about outsiders but, to me, outsiders are the heroes of their own universe. So when you isolate an individual within their own community, like Valley Stream in *Buffalo '66,* or New York City in *American Psycho,* or Gross Point, Michigan, in *The Virgin Suicides*, these are individuals who are alienated from their particular community so the films explore them and their communities more closely. Perhaps I'm interested in them because they're all malcontents and ostracized. What interests me is to seek out the directors who would be interesting to work with, and then try to figure out what they would need — but if it's more than I think I can get, then we can't move forward.

2. The 'Guinness guy'

While you were developing the books how did Muse get going?

The same group of people that brought us *Neuromancer* had a sort of sci-fi exploitation monster movie called *Split Second* that they wanted us to finance. It was Rutger Hauer running around trying to catch a monster and you didn't know if it was real or not. The director was British, Tony Mahlin, and we had the creature effects guy who had done *Alien*, Steve Norrington. It wasn't necessarily the type of film we wanted to make. But at that point we just wanted to take the opportunity to get into the business so we decided it was economically do-able and we were shown interest from New Line and Gaga Communications in Japan with just the attachment of Rutger Hauer who at the time was the 'Guinness guy', and the Japanese really went for it. Then we hired Kim Cattrall to play the female lead. It was interesting to us, because it kind of felt like instant financing. We had a sales agent, Vic Bateman at Victor Films, and he basically showed us documents that proved there was interest from four territories in pre-buying the film with Rutger Hauer in the lead, and this added up to $4.2 million of pre-sales. So the distributors in those territories signed deal memos in one afternoon at the American Film Market and we were off.

*Was **Split Second** a good experience?*

Yeah. We made the film in London, and I went there and treated the process like any other business. I think we probably scrutinized the process more closely than any of my later films except maybe *Buffalo '66* which had its own scrutinies that needed to take place.

When did you begin to feel secure about production?

The film where I was the most structured was *Split Second*, because I sat with the accountant — who later became a line producer, then a producer, and now a financier — and we went through every aspect of the cost versus what we were doing with the funds. I looked carefully at every single expenditure for every hour of every day, to make sure that we weren't exceeding our limits too much. I find now that you sort of 'back into' a budget. I can tell by reading a script whether the budget is sufficient or not. Sometimes you have to farm out costs to computer graphics, special effects, prosthetics or unusual costume companies because you can't guess what those costs are going to be without them breaking it down and analysing how many hours it's going to take them to do the animation or Claymation. Then I will have a meeting with two or three people competing for the work to discuss the costs.

When *Split Second* opened in May of 1992, during the Rodney King riots, it started in twenty theatres in LA during the curfew but it did more than $3.74 million in its first weekend. Then it went to one thousand theatres and to number four at the box office and it ended up grossing $5 or 6 million. Then it did another $5 million from video, and I think it scored a couple of million when it was shown on HBO. From that, we recouped our initial financing costs, and a percentage on top of the investment.

What did this success mean?

It brought us opportunities to meet people, because it proved we could provide finance. The industry didn't really acknowledge Muse or Roberta and I as filmmakers, but I was able to start having meetings. Afterwards I flew from New York to Los Angeles and Roberta said, 'Well, if we're going to do this, let's do it properly.' So we packed up and left New York. In those days Miramax was just about the only company in New York that was doing anything, though it wasn't so much to begin with. New Line was in New York too, but they had already predominantly come out to LA. Jim Jarmusch was in New York. But don't forget there was no *Mask*, no *Crying Game*, no *Pulp Fiction* — *Reservoir Dogs* was only just coming out. No *Four Weddings and a Funeral*. All these films came out in the early to mid nineties and gave people like me an opportunity to pursue and develop material that was not typical studio fare. I would say that the big break for me came with two films: Steve Buscemi's *Trees Lounge* and Matthew Bright's *Freeway*. Oliver Stone was also involved with *Freeway* as an executive producer.

What was interesting to you about Freeway?

Matt Bright's screenplay was pretty good all along. Reese Witherspoon was dramatically very interesting in the film, and she was only about nineteen at the time. The film got into Sundance and we had a lot of interested buyers but the reviewer from *Variety* misunderstood the film, and some of the buyers were badly affected by the review. That was a terrible moment for us because festivals are important for sales. But Rex Reed then came out with a review that said something like 'Reese Witherspoon's performance in *Freeway* makes Alicia Silverspoon in *Clueless* look like a wind-me-up burp-me-doll from K-Mart'. We had a mixture of derision and acclaim, there was a division between the Moral Majority-type of critic versus the more ambitious critics who go to festivals looking for films that test limits.

Did the commercial success of Split Second *mean that agents were willing to introduce you to new talent?*

I was always able to locate up-and-coming talent because our movies make the public aware of the artist. If they've previously got locked into a particular kind of movie, our movies break the pattern. For example Christina Ricci impressed the film community and general public in *Buffalo '66* with what she could do dramatically, as opposed to *That Darn Cat* or *The Addams Family*. We cast Brittany Murphy in *Freeway*. And when we cast *Trees Lounge* we put Chloe Sevigny in the picture; and she had just done *Kids* which we had seen at Cannes. Later she came in and we told Steve to hire this girl, and he did.

3. *Steve knew exactly what he was doing*

How did Trees Lounge *come together?*

We knew Steve Buscemi from the music scene in New York, he had bar-tended at Vasiks or B-Bar as we called it on Thompson Square Park. Back then he was doing theatre with Mark Boone Jr., who he still works with. Steve had passed the screenplay around and my wife got it but I didn't read it. Then probably two years went by and in 1993 an agent, Cassian Elwes, got in touch with me and said he was trying to sign Steve Buscemi and that he could probably get the financing for this movie he had heard about. He knew we knew Steve from New York so we called Steve at home and tried to get the rights to produce the movie. Then Roberta said to me, 'I've been trying to get you to read this all along, Chris.' So I called up Mark Boone Jr. and he called up Steve, and then Boone was out here in LA and the next thing we knew Quentin Tarantino's attorney, Carlos Goodman, was writing some kind of sixty-day right to arrange financing. Live Entertainment put up the entire budget, which was about $1.27 million, and at the time they had done *Reservoir Dogs* and *Bad Lieutenant*. In point of fact, Live then spent nearly $3 million on advertising alone and they had ads for *Trees Lounge* going during baseball games, during the World Series.

How did you feel about working with an actor who hadn't directed before?

Steve had done a short, though I'd never seen it. But we showed it to Live. At the time some people were like 'This is going to be a lot of work . . .' But the truth of the matter is Steve knew exactly what he was doing. He said he could deliver certain actors, and Mimi Rogers, Debbie Mazar, Anthony LaPaglia and Sam Jackson all came and did the movie for him and worked for scale. Steve was limited by his budget and I think certain producers, financiers and marketing guys would have preferred a different ending — if his character had walked away from the alcohol and got in his car and maybe driven away from his life in Valley Stream and started a new life, then maybe more tickets would have been sold. But Steve wanted to tell the story in a particular way and the film was well received for it. It got into the Director's Fortnight at Cannes.

Buscemi has said he found directing Trees Lounge *overwhelming at times.*

Well, Steve was also playing the main character, so he would have to perform then look at the monitor and think about what the shot looked like. And that's very hard to do. We had a pretty good first AD but he was always on the back of Lisa Rinzler, the cinematographer. Lisa is very careful about the way that she shoots, and she shoots beautifully, but she doesn't do that many set-ups a day — at least, not back then. She had some fantastic ideas that took time to set up, a lot of time, particularly in the first third of the movie. So on some days we were only shooting the minimum number of set-ups, maybe nine or ten. We didn't have a second camera — if we had, we might have done seventeen or nineteen set-ups a day. It's all a matter of coverage, and you can do it sloppily or carefully, and Lisa was extremely careful. So almost everything she shot was usable, and what Steve had to work with in the edit were good shots, so in the end we had what we needed.

4. *Vinny*

Vincent Gallo was another first time director with Buffalo '66. *How did you meet him?*

I first knew him from the recording studio in New York back in 1983/4. He was a Sicilian from Buffalo who had acted in a movie with Steve Buscemi and Mark Boone, it was called *The Way it Is* and it was kind of like Cocteau's *Orphée* — black and white, 16mm. The director, Eric Mitchell, was a new wave-type director, Vinny was also the composer, and a hip-hop break dancer with the cardboard and spinning. Vinny and Michel Basquiat were artists working out of Lexington and 56th Street making money any way they could. Besides the music and everything else he was doing, Vinny had made these fresco paintings on metal of still-life fruit and they would come up in Sotheby auctions — and don't forget I was an art dealer at the time and I was dealing in Warhol. Then he had come out to LA before we did and he had got a couple of acting jobs, including *Arizona Dream* for Emir Kusturica. So we had always known Vinny, but now I have an agreement that we are never going to speak again in this lifetime. There was a real incident with him that took place in Cannes this year that I'm not going to discuss.

How did you put Buffalo '66 *together?*

An actress called Tara Subkoff had been in *Freeway* and she said to me, 'Chris, you gotta get me a part in Vinny Gallo's movie. He's written a screenplay and he's got some director doing it.' I said, 'What screenplay?' Vinny had sent me one years ago, about birthday cakes melting and masturbating with Vaseline jars by his bed, and crying because his mother didn't love him. And one year in Cannes he had pitched me a thing called 'The Shaver' about a mad guy who shaves people's hair off and runs away. Vinny was saying it was going to be a huge hit . . . So I had figured that he would have at least told me if he'd got some script written down. I called him up in New York and he said, 'Oh yeah, Mark Romanek was going to do it and Propaganda offered me $450,000 but I told them to fuck off so I gave it to Monte Hellman. Why not give Monte a call?' So I called Monte and they sent over the script and I read it. And it was kind of like a revamped, updated, comedic and interesting version of one of those earlier screenplays like the one with the melting birthday cake and torturing Mom . . . I said, 'Vinny, no one can direct this but you, it's your story.' He goes, 'Really? You think I can direct it?' I was like, 'Yeah, why not?'

Why did you think Gallo could direct a feature?

Well, he was an artist. Matthew Bright hadn't directed anything before *Freeway*, Steve Buscemi hadn't directed anything before. I thought

Vinny had a lot of potential energy. He's turned out to be a real director although he directs with fury all the time. Frequently a first-time director comes up with a nice film because their attention and their passion is more focused. Vinny was certainly focused on *Buffalo '66*. Also actors have a particular experience that makes it propitious to directing well — they learn what the camera is recording when they are in front of it, and they have a tendency to know their way around performances and whether the drama is being successfully captured, and how realistic it is. I think actor-directors have real intuition about these things, and Steve and Vinny are great actors.

How did the financing come together?

Roberta found out through Steve Buscemi about a company called Cinepix who did independent financing and were based out of Toronto and Montreal, and she sent them the script. By this point Vinny had acted with Meryl Streep in the magic realism picture *The House of Spirits*. Vinny said, 'Meryl Streep loves me and I'm with ICM and they're backing me and I'm sure I can get Barbra Streisand and Anjelica Huston because I'm friends with them . . .' He knew he could get a 'name' to play the mother, and Christina Ricci had shown interest. Cinepix read the script and thought it seemed like a cool comedy and it was like 'We have Meryl Streep . . .' Plus Vinny had a little bit of notoriety, having been an Armani fashion model, and a strong member of the art community in New York and likewise in the film community in Los Angeles. Cinepix thought it was a bit different and they said, 'OK, we'll finance it for this much money, but you have to get either Meryl Streep, Barbra Streisand or Angelica Huston for a full green light.' We went to Meryl Streep and she said no. Then we went to Barbra Streisand . . . Then Anjelica called back and at a certain point she agreed to do it, so then it was just a question of picking up the money.

We left for Toronto a couple of days later and we were in pre-production really quickly. We got a budget of about $1.8 million or so, discounting banking costs. Cinepix put up the money and it was one cheque. When the film was finished Cinepix became Lion's Gate and the film came out under their banner and did $2.6 million at the US box office. It was a hit in England and a massive hit in Japan where it did something like $4.5 million.

Was the process straightforward?

Well, it wasn't easy. Vinny was calling me every night and saying he was going to stab me in the face if I didn't do some deed for his assistant . . . He gets very involved in the details of filmmaking and he requires everything to be in place so that he can achieve what he wants. And if that fails there is only one person you can turn and complain to and that's your producer. So producers have to run around and organize other departments, whether it's the art department not finishing the bathroom and the height of the ceiling isn't high enough to put up the lights so you can't get the shot, or the strip club you're shooting in has changed their mind and now they won't let you shoot there, so you end up having to shoot there in the morning . . . you know, all kinds of things happen. On *Buffalo '66* we had the power to the generators cut in the middle of a shot with Anjelica Huston because we hadn't signed the union signatory agreement. So I had to go out at midnight, and I was on the phone with the head of the union agreeing to sign it in the morning. Maybe these things don't happen if your budget is at studio level. It's my feeling that these things happen at *every* level of filmmaking. Though, perhaps, there is proportionally a greater risk of catastrophic events affecting your film if it's low budget.

5. *Some mistakes*

How do you see your role when a film is shooting?

You should only be hands-on in the editing process or during principal photography if things aren't going well. I prefer the director to satisfy whatever vision they have if I can get away with it. I try to satisfy the financiers, but I usually do my best to back the director first.

On a few occasions we have exceeded our financial limits and you have to take drastic steps in order to cut some shooting time or certain other things. If you have used up your time on other shots it can compound into serious problems. There can be problems with the unions. Some films are union and some are not. If the movie is under $1 million, which is not that common these days, the union usually waives it, but it can be union up to $2 million. Many of the crew people in the US who are worth working with are in the union and if you are shooting in areas like New York or Los Angeles even the lowest budgets require you to have a union signatory. It's not against the law to shoot non-union, but the union has the right to organize, and in certain states they have the right to come on the set and do that during a lunchbreak. If the crew votes not to continue supplying their services because they want the shoot to be a signatory to the union, then they have the right to do that. If that happens, you no longer have a crew unless you sign with the union — or you have to go out and find a new crew.

There is a tendency for the non-union shoots to be on a twenty-four-day shoot which is about a month of six-day weeks of work. The union will be five-day weeks of work and the time and a half and double time pay under the union signatory agreement come in a bit differently in terms of structure — so actually it optimizes as being cheaper to shoot a five day week. You get this 'golden time' situation so if you are on the sixth day and you go past your twelve hour day or you go past fourteen hours of shooting then you get into double wages. So when you multiply that by ninety people you can be burning more than the entire cost of a day's shoot just from the overtime.

What are you doing if the shoot is going smoothly?

Well, that's very boring for a producer . . . unless something is going wrong, and then it's not boring, but sort of hard.

In post-production I like the director to enjoy the full authority of the mix and work on the sound the way they see it. Sometimes you can make a mistake because a director might not be confident in all areas, particularly with music. I have seen first cuts where the music was making it hard to hear the dialogue, and it was interfering with the drama. There are different ways to work sound and music in post, and I find that a good temp score indicates the direction they would like to go in — or sometimes putting some good tracks on, even if we don't necessarily have the money, will suggest the commercialism of the picture. This can go both ways, though. Billy Corgan scored *Spun* for us and he's a composer who likes to record the music while we are making the movie and then give it to the director, who'll start to mix it in — so a lot of his music ends up in the finished movie. When we were making *Bully* we used an Eminem/Dr Dre video in the film; their record company gave us permission to use the video so we shot it with Brad Renfro in the scene, and it was a great scene. Then later, in post, I was looking at it and I said, 'Where's the master-use licence for the recording rights and publishing rights?' We had the synchronization licence to synchronize the track to the picture but we hadn't thought about the master-use licence. And it was like 'Oh no!' So we called Eminem and Dre and they said they wanted $400,000. I mean, this was a $2-million movie. Maybe we could have squirrelled away $20,000, but there was no way we could find that kind of money when it wasn't in the budget. I guess Larry kind of knew them because he got them on the phone and Eminem looked at the movie and said, 'Fuck it, this is cool.' So I think we got the rights for $20,000. Then Studio Canal, who had financed the movie with Lion's Gate in North America, cut a deal so we could go with it without going over budget. Did Larry know it was going to be $400,000 in the first round? No. Who got blamed for not getting the synchronization licence? Well, it wasn't the director . . .

As a producer, sometimes I feel I'm not learning anything unless you have a problem that needs solving. But I have seen a lot of different things that happen that can be detrimental to the process of making a film, and I know now that there are so many possibilities and how to address them. I've made some mistakes and, in most cases, I know what to do now, after ten years of making films. On *This World, Then the Fireworks*, we had a twenty-four-day shoot and it was non-union up in Wilmington, North Carolina, and the director Mike Oblowitz likes to shoot a lot of film so we had two cameras going; Mike is a cinematographer who came out of commercials and music videos, and it was his second feature film but he got fourteen-hour days out of the crew. In England if you go above eleven shooting hours you're dead meat. We had eleven eighteen-hour days in twenty-four days. I had gone to the *Trees Lounge* premiere in Director's Fortnight in Cannes two days before the end of the shoot, and before I left the second AD pitched up at four in the morning and she was barely standing. I turned around and crew members would be lying flat out on the ground — these guys were working so hard they would just drop.

American crews are a little bit different to what we find in England or when we shot in the Isle of Man or other places in Europe; Americans really like to make their overtime money. In the Isle of Man or in London we would give bonuses to everyone for every hour we went over; I think we gave everyone an extra $10 but when you multiply that by ninety you're spending anything between $900 to $3,000 extra per day. I mean, truck drivers like nothing better than to do a twenty-seven-hour day. They are pissing mad if they are not on double time.

How do problems in the shoot affect post-production?

Production is like an iceberg that's moving, so an increase in the amount of film you shoot can cause drastic changes to the whole process — because every activity is contingent upon each other. Shooting a lot of unbudgeted footage compounds because your post-production costs increase.

Have you ever had to step in if a shoot has got out of control?

Sometimes a producer has to get on the phone and say, 'That's it, there is no more film.' If the director is supposed to shoot nine thousand feet a day and they go over, you just have to say, 'Look, you shot eleven

thousand feet today, you're not having any more film, take it or leave
it.' If one day you shoot *twenty* thousand feet then the financier can
see that you're getting into extreme financial difficulties. Filmmaking
is all about the art of the possible, but if you start to do stuff that isn't
financially within the limits that you have been set, then the bond
company is very quickly going to step in and stop you exceeding those
limits. Every director is different in how they deal with the tough conversations; they may have shot a lot and still know that they haven't
got what they need for it to be a good movie. And they may realize
that there has been a failure of some sort and it nevertheless has to
be corrected or else the movie won't be that good. At the same time
the financiers might be thinking that they made the wrong choice of
director and that the director can't be controlled and that perhaps
the movie isn't going to be as good as it should be. Bottom line, no
financier is going to spend more money. So that's the challenge for the
producer and director. And in those circumstances the director needs
to be parsimonious in order to achieve his vision. Does every director
understand that? Sometimes . . . But you have to learn really fast to
get the most out of what tools you have in production.

*Do you think you have become more adept at helping a director find
creative solutions if there is a problem?*

That might be the fact of the case. But the director doesn't necessarily
think of a producer contributing creatively in any way. Ultimately,
though, since it will affect what is being viewed on screen, there might
be some kind of involvement in the creative process for the producer
— like discussions about whether the story is going to work if we
shoot it this way, or whether the script should be rewritten because
now we've seen the shot perhaps it would be better for the story to
shoot it a different way. So the producer and director might sit down
and have a conversation like that at lunchtime. Sometimes that conversation doesn't happen, and sometimes it *has* to happen. Sometimes
it's difficult, and there are times when it's smart to talk because you
might be choosing to do something that means maybe the film won't
be quite as good as you hoped, but it's your only choice. Ultimately it's
the director's choice if they want to talk to the producer because they
know they need an opinion other than their own. Sometimes, just to
make the budget work, you might have to cut an entire scene. Or there
are times when you know what you have shot and you know what
you have to shoot to make the story work, and you are imagining a
particular scene, and the director, or the producer, or often the first

assistant director — who has done the scheduling — knows that a particular scene isn't going to make it in the edit and asks, 'Why do we have to shoot that? It isn't even going to be in the movie.' And the director goes, 'Yeah, you're right, we don't need it.' So it gets cut.

6. *Impossible situations*

How did you meet Larry Clark?

Larry and I originally met through Harmony Korine and Chloe Sevigny when Larry came to the *Trees Lounge* premiere after-party. Afterwards Roberta and I stayed in touch with Larry a little bit and specifically with respect to *Bully*. John Murphy, one of our producing partners, had the rights to the book and the screenwriter, David McKenna, had been put in touch with Larry. At the time Larry was going to direct *American History X* before Tony Kaye, but there was a connection between David and Larry so John had hired David to write the screenplay. Larry was interesting to us because he had done *Kids* and then *Another Day in Paradise* with Natasha Wagner. We always liked *Kids* and Larry was also a stills photographer, so he was quite well known in my world of art-dealing as well. Larry's stills were these vérité shots of heroin addicts shooting up and teenagers having sex and that sort of thing . . . and he got known for getting into impossible situations where real life is going on and he's snapping pictures almost like a journalist in a world of drug dealers and teenage trash and their personal sexual experiences. He would record this, which is hard to do, and it became something of a focus in the art world. When Larry made *Kids*, it put him on the map, and it did quite well, and we liked it. So we called him on the phone and said we wanted to make *Bully* with him and he said he would do it.

So I took the project to Canal Plus who were interested in financing a slate of our films, and they said yes. Then it was just a question of casting, so Bijou Philips came in and Nick Stahl, Kelly Garner, Rachel Miner and Brad Renfro. In addition to the book there had also been a documentary about the story, but while the real story was interesting to us and the book had plenty of anecdotal material, inevitably in an investigative situation like that a lot of people were in jail so if you are making a film about events and real lives you are never going to get to the bottom of what happened. Actually we weren't interested in depicting the actual events so much as taking a specific event which seemed Columbine-esque and exploring it from different angles. *Bully* is based on a true story about a bully in a high school who psychologically tortured his best friend and this led to the friends of the bully taking the bully's life. The book explored how they lost track of their own lives without realizing it. It was interesting for us to explore the skateboarding, surfing mall worlds of Fort Lauderdale, Broward County and Hollywood, Florida and look at the relationships between the parents and their kids and the teenagers of a real community — to examine, dramatically, how an event like that could have happened. We shot around the courthouse where the murder was tried, the same courthouse that became the focus for the Bush/Gore voting quagmire in 2000. There were four separate trials because each defendant was tried separately. Most of them went to jail for life, and death penalties were commuted, though one was commuted to life imprisonment. Larry changed the script quite a lot and ultimately David took his name off because he thought the movie had become too pornographic, but the script is a lot of Larry's work and because of the nature of his previous work and his stills photography background that's the way he works; he creates his own images, he does it on his own and he makes his own decisions and that's just the way it is. If you don't like it, don't hire him. Larry is really an extreme final-cut director and by that I mean he gets to do what he wants.

Bully didn't get into Cannes but it did get into Venice, which is the one and only time I've had a film there. It got a standing ovation. I don't know if they do that with every movie, but they were very nice to us.

7. *Numbers*

CH: Today I find I'm doing even lower budgets than I have ever done: some are bigger than I've ever raised previously, but with digital technology there was a time when the technology became the motivating factor in financing, because the thinking was that films could be made for $1 million or less. I have no problems doing that, but I can't make much of a living from it. I don't really need to increase Muse's reputation by getting these things off the ground. But if the financing falls into place or some of the guys in my office or outside producers can use the auspices of Muse Productions to round up casting directors and properties and produce, co-produce or executive-produce these projects, then I can oversee it to the extent that it needs to be sold in North America. Or if you need a particular cast, then I think Muse now stands for a certain type of movie that can get made.

Do you go overseas to raise funds?

I lived in Paris for a while, going over projects. We have worked a lot with Studio Canal who are now The Wild Bunch since the break-up of the company. They are a company who bring anything between eight to thirteen films per year to the Cannes Film Festival, year after year, with six or seven of those going to the Toronto and Venice Film Festivals. They have a sales and distribution pipeline that like-minded financiers/ distributors want to exploit, so festivals are very important to them, and to us. They like to work with the David Lynchs and Michel Gondrys of the world, and if a producer can provide an access-pipeline to talent, whether it's the actors or directors, then that's of significant value to them. So we go back and forth between New York, London, Paris and Berlin, taking our properties around. We keep an office in Paris which we share with Wild Bunch and I have a partner called Fernando Sulichin who I have worked with for a number of years. He's produced four or five movies with me, and together we're constantly looking for new sources of finance. We work with territorial incentives — even in the US there are certain states who offer subsidies, and in the UK there is a sub-stantially successful tax-incentive programme for filmmakers seeking between ten and forty per cent of the budget.

But truthfully it's probably more unstable and harder now that it's ever been to finance independent films. I am not completely isolated from the studios because several of them have their boutique divisions like Fox Searchlight, Paramount Classics and Sony Classics who han-dle more artistically orientated films. But I think there is a tendency for the blockbuster films to suck up all the capital that could be available to filmmakers, and the funds within the specialty divisions are more limited now than they have ever been. There are limits in independent financing as to how much you can raise in a budget. You can try to take a crack at studio-level financing but an independent producer doesn't want to get too bogged down, because a studio can afford to spend a lot of money and not make the movie, whereas I can't afford to do that — not even if they paid me back my development money. Besides, what's the point of spending years in development? For the studios it's all about numbers, patterns of population, tracking the entertainment culture, and how the marketing and public relations divisions think. Their sole conversation is about what people want or expect, so, based on that thinking, there are only a limited selection of films they can choose from. And meanwhile the spend on blockbusters gets bigger and bigger. It's the same in the music business: we used to think that a handful of artists at the top of the pyramid would fund alternative bands, and for a time there was reciprocity between both ends of the business. In the eighties Michael Jackson and Madonna were paying for the music business. In the film business, a Jim Carrey movie or a Russell Crowe movie or a Nicole Kidman movie accounts for ninety per cent of a studios's profits compared to the A or B list. I don't think in terms of $50-million budgets but, on the other hand, sometimes the mathematics of a bigger spend does justify commercial success. *Trees Lounge* had a budget of just over $1 million, but the prints and advertising spend was just under $3 million, so now you have $4 million invested in a little movie. Whereas *American Psycho* cost $6 million but we and Lions Gate invested $9 to 10 million in prints and advertising just for North America, so now you're spending $16 million on a low-budget movie. But it took $15 million at the US box office, and that made it possible for the film to have a big video release and it did about $15 million in video sales and did good TV sales. So the film was worthwhile. And in foreign sales the film was a hit in the UK, it probably did $6 million there when it was only estimated to earn back ten per cent of the whole budget. So we find that spending more money on the prints and advertising means you might as well spend more money on the film itself. And, of course, if there is something you can put on the screen that means audiences will pay more to see it, whether it's special effects or a big name actor, then your public awareness increases. We have a film with Brittany Murphy due for release in the UK called *Spun*, and Brittany is going to be very good for the movie.

Generally, a studio doesn't like to go below $10 million on a film. They can jump from ten to thirty million quite easily but once you get to between $50 and a $100 million, constructing that sort of movie can take years. But, you know, I have no interest in being part of a studio. And I'm happy if a studio says it doesn't understand my pictures.

8. 'Sofia is in love . . .'

You had the rights to The Virgin Suicides *for some time?*

There were other directors who had written drafts of scripts, and there was even a script written for Disney that we could have obtained the rights to — because Disney had the book before us. Sofia Coppola had read it and without even knowing that Muse was holding the rights she had tried her hand at writing the screenplay. I don't think she thought that script would end up being made with her directing it, but when she finished the first draft her dad read it and thought it was great. Sofia checked out the rights and saw they were held by us. We had dinner with her a few times and she kind of knew us. Then her sister-in-law Jackie Coppola called up Roberta and said, 'Come *on*, get rid of this other director, Sofia is in *love* with this and you have *got* to let her do it.' I hadn't been able to put a cast together based on earlier drafts with other directors attached, and I knew that if we joined forces with Francis Ford Coppola and Sofia, given what Muse had by then established in independent filmmaking, that between us there was no way we were not going to be able to cast the movie, and then it would attract finance. Which is exactly what happened . . .

We split the development costs we had put in up to that point, then we became partners and went looking for the money. Fred Roos, who casts a lot of Francis's movies, helped with the casting. James Woods wanted to meet me because he also wants to direct, so I met with him and he liked the screenplay then met with Sofia, and an hour after meeting me he goes to her, 'Let's do it.' So that was pretty solid. Then we got Danny DeVito, Kathleen Turner and Scott Glenn attached. We ended up having to get the budget in bits and pieces so we went to the American Film Market and Cannes and ended up with a budget of something close to $4.3 million. When we were in pre-production in Toronto, Kirsten Dunst was in town, but initially Sofia wasn't sure — remembering her from *Interview with the Vampire* when she was a little girl. So the script went to Scarlet Johanssen, but Scarlet didn't want to do it. Kirsten was available, then after Sofia met Kirsten she immediately said, 'I've changed my mind, you're right, I think she's great.' Kirsten's manager, Iris Burden, also looked after Josh Hartnett and another casting director friend had recommended him as a hot up-and-coming dude, so we said, 'OK, we'll hire Josh.'

I think initially it was tricky to finance because of the title. You couldn't pitch it like a high school movie, like *American Pie*. This wasn't a movie that was going to have a sequel. My pitch to financiers was if you want to make a movie that dramatically is Oscar-orientated material then this is your movie. It was a story that explored high school and suburbia in the seventies with a kind of sentimental attachment to that period, through the passage of time. Jeffrey Eugenides had been a religion scholar at Stanford, and before had gone to Brown University and studied philosophy and religion, before becoming a novelist. A few months ago he won the Pulitzer Prize for *Middlesex*. He's a very smart guy. The script needed a bit of work as far as we and the author were concerned, we thought maybe it could be better, but Sofia proved to us that there were certain ways of reading the screenplay where you could satisfy the story requirements visually in film as opposed to finding it within the dialogue and she proved that was the case.

We were present during pre-production and photography, then the film was edited up in San Francisco. I didn't watch any dailies, I just saw a rough cut, which I liked. Then they wanted to re-cut every scene frame by frame. The time to really study a film is when the director and editor have had at least six to eight weeks after photography to do whatever they want with it, so they can come up with something interesting. Then you look at the film. And that's what we did. I liked it a lot. We were very happy with the movie.

9. Like a zombie

What kept American Psycho *in development for so long?*

Ed Pressman shared the rights to *American Psycho* with us from the beginning to the end. He's an experienced producer and we learned a lot working with him — but we also probably learned more not making *American Psycho* during the six years it took to make than in actually buying the rights or making the film.

For a time David Cronenberg was attached, then after about nine months or a year David said he didn't have the vision to do it. Then Roberta spent a whole year rewriting the screenplay with Bret Ellis. Roberta's script was very gory but it was the real-deal *American Psycho*. We kept on renewing the option, and about five years went by, and I was at Sundance with *Freeway* and one of the movies showing at the festival was *I Shot Andy Warhol*. Roberta said, 'Why don't we recommend Mary Harron for *American Psycho*?' I said I didn't think she was that kind of director. Then I thought about it and when we were introduced to her, I was told she had made four documentaries for FilmFour and the BBC, and I thought it would be pretty interesting if a documentary technique was used to shoot *American Psycho*. That would stop the film from being over-the-top and it might feel as though these events were really happening. Ultimately I don't think that's how Mary made the film. But she was intrigued because we were casting her against type. So she read Roberta's script and suggested we meet. At the meeting Mary had a strong idea of which direction she wanted to go in so Mary and Ed Pressman met and she said she wanted to get back to the book. Marie got Gwen Turner and together they started the screenplay again from scratch. Mary did some great stuff that was unique to her writing — she merged action scenes with some of the hyper-boring obsessive dialogue about the Phil Collins and Whitney Houston discography while the murder scenes were taking place. So I think we achieved the level of irony while covering both aspects of the book that were essential to the theme. The book objectively records the surface gloss of Manhattan at the end of the eighties so Mary isolated 1987 as the year the film was set, and the art she put on the walls was incredibly accurate; we licensed some Richard Prince, and Peter Halley, some Cindy Sherman, and we worked hard to get permission from the artists to recreate the work and make copies of the paintings. So this all became part of the design, and the pseudo-documentary feel.

Originally we had Billy Crudup attached to star then he dropped out. And Mary wanted Christian Bale and he was passionate about the project but Mary wasn't consulted when Lions Gate said, 'Let's throw this out to Leonardo DiCaprio' — because his loft was on the same floor as Lion's Gate's offices in New York. The script went out to DiCaprio's management company over the weekend and Mary was upset about that because she didn't really want him, she wanted Christian Bale. DiCaprio wasn't told there was a director attached, and he was offered $10 million pay-or-play; and on the following Monday he accepted, even though our budget at that point was around $6 million. After this happened I was in Cannes, and there was a formal announcement with his management that DiCaprio had accepted the role of Patrick Bateman in *American Psycho*. I was OK with it but my first concern was that DiCaprio had not been made aware of Mary's firm attachment to direct the project. He was under the impression that he had control over the choice of director, and he hadn't been told otherwise. The controversy immediately started and some of the stuff that appeared in *Variety* was pure spin. Then DiCaprio denied he was attached to the film, but you know his management company were right there, changing the press release in their own handwriting. The press release said this was going to be DiCaprio's next film, and the word 'next' was crossed out so that he was just attached. Later he didn't want it categorically confirmed that he had agreed to do *American Psycho* as his *next* film. In point of fact, he did *The Beach*, so we would have to wait.

I decided to be technically smart, so I suggested that we should be pay-or-play with Mary because we didn't know if she was going to make the finish line if we had a big actor like DiCaprio, and she couldn't be expected to just wait around and see what happened. DiCaprio had his own list of approved directors, he was one of the biggest stars in the world. I also wanted to make sure that if anything unforeseen happened with DiCaprio that she was still committed to the movie.

It got to the point where DiCaprio approved Oliver Stone to direct and Oliver agreed, which was tricky, given that Oliver and I went back to *Freeway*. But by then things had got pretty explosive. We then had cast readings — I think Cameron Diaz and DiCaprio read together at Oliver's. By then DiCaprio was complaining that the end of the screenplay wasn't like the book — which is not the case, because Marie's screenplay closely follows the book. We had some discussions about changes to the script and DiCaprio was *still* not happy, but then he went off to make *The Beach*. So Lion's Gate asked his management if it was going to be his next movie after that or not, because they had to guarantee this. But it was like 'Well, obviously he *wants* to do the movie but we can't *guarantee* that it will be his next film.' So Lion's Gate said, 'We are a small company, not a studio that's in the business of developing for months and months. And we are holding a lot of finance on this. So, thanks, but we're not going to use Leonardo DiCaprio because there is no guarantee from you that he won't delay for another six months and then another six months.' So Lion's Gate made their decision and we called up Mary and said, 'Let's make the movie.' We got everyone back, Christian Bale came back, and frankly it was a relief to get the development process over and recoup the $200,000 that had already been spent by that point. By the time we made the film it was well structured and ran smoothly in Toronto and New York. But it had taken so many years I couldn't believe it was actually happening. I was like a zombie . . .

Do you enjoy *producing?*

The financing is always tortuous and rude, and I suppose I must like it to take it . . . There's no financial stability in it, and it's a twelve-hour day job and right through the weekends. I guess the studios have their problems too . . . I would like to get away and enjoy life more. Producing is probably not the ideal artistic situation for me, and perhaps I would rather be directing — not that I am suggesting that, but I think I could do that just as easily. But then somebody else would have to do all this . . .

Since our interview Chris has produced Asia Argento's *The Heart is Deceitful Above all Things* and a film of David Mamet's very edgy stageplay *Edmond*.

Take 21

SYDNEY POLLACK

Sydney Pollack has been the recipient of one Best Director Oscar (for *Out of Africa* in 1986) and two further nominations (*They Shoot Horses, Don't They?* in 1970 and *Tootsie* in 1982). He has competed with honour at Berlin (*Absence of Malice*, 1981) and Cannes (*Jeremiah Johnson*, 1972). And yet, over the years — just as he has made use of his formative stage training in order to work as an occasional screen actor for the likes of Kubrick, Altman and Woody Allen — so Pollack has similarly translated his deep knowledge of the filmmaking process into the task of producing for other directors, so much so that his producing credits in the past decade far exceed the number of his directorial assignments. So much, then, for the old saw 'What I really want to do is direct . . .'

1. *Something to offer*

HELEN DE WINTER: *What is it about producing that has taken you away from directing?*

SYDNEY POLLACK: Well, I would say it was mostly a mistake . . . or rather I didn't ever *intend* for it to take me away from directing. But I'm a rather lazy director — I avoid directing for as long as I can. I am not somebody who thinks directing is a great song and dance. I envy those directors who just can't wait to get on the floor and direct something.

Even after all these years?

Oh sure, sure. It's agony for me to direct. I get nervous about it and I always worry or think that I'm going to fail. It's a lot of pressure — though I think the pressure is a self-imposed one. But it's pressure nonetheless.

As a producer I think that I've been able to offer something to directors that often other producers can't, which is the experience of having been there myself. Most of my career has been directing. Other than producing my own films, which I have done for thirty-five years, I didn't start producing other people's films until 1985 when I started Mirage. Now I have a partner in the company, the wonderful Anthony Minghella.

But back around the mid-eighties my intention really was to feel more useful to myself and to the rest of the world. During the long periods of time I was taking to decide what I would direct next, I thought that, instead of coming to the office every day and feeling useless — because I was reading scripts and saying, 'No, no, no' — maybe I should produce a picture or two. So we started a very small company, Mirage. Previously, the first time I did any producing was when the singer Willie Nelson asked me to produce a movie. I gave Willie his first acting job in a movie called *The Electric Horseman* [1980] with Robert Redford and Jane Fonda, and he had a project of his own, *Honeysuckle Rose* [1980], that he wanted me to direct. I didn't want to direct it so he asked me if I would oversee it instead. So I produced the film with Gene Taft, and Jerry Schatzberg directed.

And when you say you produced it — ?

I didn't finance the movie, I was the creative supervisor, which meant having an opinion about the script, working a bit with the writer, talking to the director about the casting, looking at the dailies, commenting on them, looking at the edit, working through the cut and making suggestions.

But with each movie the job depends on what is needed. Let's take *Presumed Innocent* [1990]. I got Warner Bros. to buy the book and then I developed the screenplay, working every day with the writer. Then I hired Alan J. Pakula . . . Well, Alan Pakula didn't need me to stand around on the set. Once he had said he would do it, there wasn't any sense in me doing anything except saying 'Bon voyage, and if you need me I'm here.' Until I saw the cut . . . and then I had some strong feelings about what I felt had been a mistake in departing from the book with a different ending. Alan had felt he couldn't get away with the book's ending, which, in a sense, lets the murderer off the hook. But for me that was precisely what was so powerful about the novel. So I got involved in that issue with Alan and talked him into trusting the book's ending and going with it.

But, overall, Alan was on a level where I had no value to him. Anthony Minghella doesn't need me either, but he *wants* to have me there just as I would want *him* to be around for me. I don't need a producer with me on set, but if I have Anthony standing around so I can talk to him, it's only going to help.

As a director, have you ever felt unsupported by a producer?

It's not a question of being unsupported, but I *have* felt at odds creatively with a producer. Sometimes you know right away that you are working with the wrong producer. And I have made films with producers who I just didn't feel were going to be of any help. The terrible problem with our business is that we are accustomed to the virtues of what we think of as a democratic process, and yet it doesn't apply in this field because there simply are people who aren't as good as others, but nevertheless they still want to exert the same control and they want to define themselves as 'the producer'. In those circumstances, if I've got a producer who's not very good — in my opinion — then half of my job is going to be spent defusing the power of the producer. And, you know, you don't hire the producer if you are a director — usually it's the producer who has some legal ownership or control of the property that makes him 'the producer'.

2. *Catastrophes, mostly*

What, in your opinion, are the most difficult aspects of producing?

Often it's difficult to get a film set up that you believe in, because you can't get the right cast for the right number of dollars. The financier will say, 'If you bring me actors X, Y, and Z then I will give you $21 million. But if you don't I'll give you $12 million.' You say, 'But I need $15 million!' and it's 'No, $12 million is the most I can give you.' And you just know you can't do it for $12 million, so that's a difficult time.

But once you start making the movie it's all about trying to make it as good as you can. Most movies, in my opinion, are a train wreck — it's really a question of managing the blood flow and keeping it as minimal as possible. Once in a while there is this marvellous thing where everything goes smoothly and the weather is perfect and the actors come out of their trailers on time and we all get along and everything is wonderful. I have never had one of those experiences as a producer . . . Most of the time, it's a catastrophe that needs management, particularly when you have a hundred and fifty people on the crew and you find that having chosen a particular location because you were told it had just one rainy season, you get there, start shooting and find it has five . . . On *Cold Mountain* back in the fall of 2002, we were in the middle of Romania, and Central Europe was having the worst floods it has ever had. Berlin was flooded, the Charles River Bridge in Prague was submerged, and we were just next door shooting in Romania. I mean, this *never* happens . . . so you have to deal with these problems, and unless you're making a studio film then you don't have their deep pockets. Instead, you have a bond.

Most of my working life as a director has been spent working with the studios, and it's certainly easier in that you don't have to bond the picture — so if it goes over budget then the studio pays for it. As a director I have never had an experience with a bonded picture. It was only when I started producing these smaller movies that I had to do all that.

The people in the bond company can take over a film if it goes ten per cent over budget — so you are constantly trying to manage that. I have never had a film taken over by a bond company, but it *is* a possibility, and you find you always have to try to hide money in other parts of the budget, so that when you go two days over you know you have a little money saved that you can still use.

Do you get involved in that level of detail when you're producing? Do you attend bond meetings?

Sure. I mean, it's not the best use of my time, and frankly I would rather hire somebody who could do that for me. But because I have to give the OK to everything, then I am the person whom the financier is looking to. And when the bond company get angry, they're not going to go to the other guy. They're going to come to me and say, 'Wait a minute! I thought Mirage was taking care of this? Why aren't you over there?' I got screamed at by Intermedia almost every week during the production of *The Quiet American* [dir. Philip Noyce, 2002]. They would say, 'How come you're not in Vietnam?' But the fact is, I went to Vietnam for a while and then at some point, I didn't want to stand on the set with Philip Noyce, because he's a grown-up director, and the production was running smoothly and they didn't need me there. So I thought 'This is crazy', I went on set and patted everyone on the back and I came home. But Intermedia got upset and would say, 'How come nobody from Mirage is over there?' Well, because we had a very good line producer in Vietnam, and that guy was signing the cheques, and we trusted him. And every day we would be looking at the dailies and the shooting schedule, and it was all going fine.

3. 'We might as well be in business together'

It's interesting that you have formed a close working relationship with another director, Anthony Minghella. Why did you want to work with Anthony in particular?

I was a huge fan of *Truly Madly Deeply*, the picture Anthony wrote and directed in 1990, and later I met him at a party and it turned out we were mutual fans of each other's work. But, generally, I was just very taken with him when we met. He was very smart, and — how can I say this? — he was atypical [in terms of our business], in the sense that if he was a narcissist, then I certainly didn't see it. I felt he actually listened, which is not something you see much of the time in our business. This is a business in which the people in it are paid so much attention by the public that they become spoilt. So to meet somebody who is genuinely interested in other things, and particularly interested in people . . . I was just very taken with that.

First we became friends, and then he sent me his screenplay of *The English Patient* and asked if I had any thoughts about it. So we met in London and I had some notes and we talked about them. After he shot the film he invited me to San Francisco to see it, and then asked if I would come up for a weekend and work with him a bit in the editing room. Anthony had made a previous film called *Mr Wonderful*, an American film with William Hurt, that didn't quite work, but it was a bigger film. But then he made enormous strides forward when he did *The English Patient*. That was a beautifully directed and realized movie. By then Mirage had bought *The Talented Mr Ripley* by Patricia Highsmith, and so Anthony was officially working for me, in a way, because I was the producer on that. Then Mirage found *Cold Mountain* and sent that to him too. And then eventually I said, 'This is getting silly . . . We might as well be in business together.' So Anthony came into the company, and since then it's been a very good experience. Together we've produced *Heaven* [dir. Tom Tykwer, 2002], *Iris* [dir. Richard Eyre, 2001], and *The Quiet American* [dir. Philip Noyce, 2002]. We're going to make a film adapted from an English novel by Allison Pearson, a bestseller called *I Don't Know How She Does It*. Philip Noyce is shooting a film in South Africa that we're co-producing with *Working Title*. We're doing Kenny Lonergan's new movie, *Margaret*. Kenny made *You can Count on Me*, an independent movie, with Laura Linney and Mark Ruffalo. It was a lovely movie. Kenny is a brilliantly talented writer/director/playwright.

How did you get involved with producing Sliding Doors?

I made a producing deal with Intermedia, and that was the first film I did with them. John Hannah happened to be visiting my office on a general appointment, and he was depressed, so we asked him why. And he said he had this movie he had been going to do, at the time it was going to be with Minnie Driver, and Peter Howitt was going to direct, but the finance had fallen apart. So I asked, 'How much was the budget?' and he said, '$3 million' — it was going to be a $3-million picture. So I said, 'Gee, let me read it. I think I can help you with $3 million.' I read it and I thought it was a very clever script, and it made me laugh and it made me think, so I called John and I said, 'I have a feeling I can get you your money . . .'

I had met Guy East at Intermedia just once and I didn't really know him, but he had said, 'I know you've done all your movies with studios but we're financing movies, please bring us movies.' So I thought, 'I'll try Guy and see what happens.' I made one phone call and he was cautious. 'Are you sure this guy can direct?' he asked and I said, 'No, I'm not sure, but he wrote a wonderful script that's smart and original and I trust that.'

What had Peter Howitt directed at this stage?

Nothing. He was mainly an actor. Though he showed me something he did at film school — a little short or something.

What convinced you as a producer and director that Peter could pull it off?

The script, more than anything — talking to Peter about the script. It was a small movie, about the right size for a first film, and it was beautifully written, Peter wrote a terrific script. Peter's a really good guy. He struggled a bit with the film, because it was his first. And it's a tough film to organize, because it's telling two stories with the same person. It's difficult to know where you are all the time in the story. It wasn't easy to break down properly. I worked on the script with Peter, and I was there in casting sessions with him, and at the cast reading. I spent a certain amount of time on the set, but I'm too much of a director myself to be able to go and talk to a director when he is directing. So I stayed outside the set mainly, and looked at the monitor. More than anything I felt I was trying to get a bird to fly, saying: 'Go on, go on . . . you do what you want.' Until we got to the editing. A lot of the work I ended up doing was after the filming. I got very involved in the editing because it was a picture that required precise editing to know where you were all the time and for the audience to be able to find the movement between the A and B stories. I felt that Peter needed some help, so I worked pretty hard on that part of it and was able to make a contribution to it just because it was complicated for a director the first time around.

After *Sliding Doors* we wanted to do some other films with Intermedia, and at the time I had my offices over at Sony Pictures and they were paying the overhead on Mirage. I found I just couldn't keep doing it, because it was an expensive company to run, there were six other people at that time and we were paying their salaries. So I decided to transfer the deal to Intermedia, and that's when I brought Anthony into the company. We were about to start working on *Cold Mountain*. Ultimately the relationship with Intermedia didn't work out, because films like *Iris* and *The Quiet American* didn't make their money back — in *time* they are going to make their money back, but ultimately they were not going to make enough money soon enough to justify what they were spending on us. So Anthony and I decided we should support the company ourselves. We trimmed Mirage down to a lean, mean group and what we have now is basically just Anthony and myself and a development executive in each office — one in London and one here in LA — and then a few support staff.

It seems that the smaller films such as Iris, *have been more difficult to produce?*

Iris was a combination of Scott Rudin talking to me, Richard Eyre talking to Anthony, and all of us talking to Intermedia. It was a patchwork so it was partially Harvey Weinstein at Miramax, partially Intermedia and partially Paramount, so there were three of us and partially the BBC. It was cobbled together financially. I think the director, Richard Eyre, had done one other movie before *Iris* that was a small movie but he did a beautiful job on the film.

Unfortunately the bulk of the movies I produce, I don't make much money on, so I make my money as a director. I produce a lot of movies where everything is deferred. We were paid literally zero on *Iris*. On *Heaven* it was almost nothing. We're not going to make money on *Margaret* and neither will Scott Rudin, but it's a beautiful film. Sometimes I will put Mirage with another company, like Scott Rudin's company. When we started on *Margaret* I called Scott because I knew he was chasing this film, so now we're doing it together.

There have been times when we've produced a film not intending to make money — like *Sense and Sensibility* [dir. Ang Lee, 1995] — and suddenly it's a hit and makes money. We've made more money on *Sliding Doors* than almost anything else we've done because it was a huge hit compared to its modest cost. It wasn't that big in the US, but it's made a fortune everywhere else and the film only cost $7 to 8 million. So it turned into a very profitable movie for the company. But I don't direct or produce films to make money because I don't know what makes money. I choose movies the way I choose what I am going to wear in the morning, it's not logical. If I knew what made money, I would never make anything but hits, and I have made a lot of flops.

Have you produced a flop?

Yes.

And what is that experience like?

Not as bad as directing a flop. To direct a flop feels like a public humiliation . . . you feel like they are going to drag you through the streets and point at you or something. With producing, in some way, you're one step removed from total responsibility — 'Well, you know, I didn't direct it, so . . .'

4. *September the 10th, 2001*

Have you had projects in development that have taken a long time to get off the ground?

Sure. Mirage had *The Quiet American* for fourteen years.

What changed in order to get the film made?

I'm not sure . . . though there was the advantage of Michael Caine being somebody who could get a studio interested.

It was interesting that the film came out when it did. Did that change how the film was perceived?

Well it was an accident, of course. The film previewed in New York on September the 10th, 2001. The catastrophe happened on the following morning and it definitely changed the perception of the film . . . forever after. It was looked at completely differently.

Why had you always wanted to make the film?

It presented a side of innocence that is not what it seems to be — that was the genius of the material, but it was also its fault, and why we couldn't get a completely successful screenplay. Even Graham Greene, as good as he is, didn't write the American character as a fully three-dimensional character. What he wrote was a man who has a really sinful kind of naivety which had been innocent but ended up being destructive. We tried to be faithful to Graham Greene but as a result we could never create a character who we could cast, because the American was a Boy Scout right up until the end, and then he becomes a killer. It was the same with the love story; he meets the young girl, then he is in love with her and then he proposes to her so the story feels like it's written in headlines. There was a lack of anything three-dimensional about the character, so developing him took a long time. As it was, Brendan Fraser did a great job of filling him out, but it was tough to get off the page.

How did you find Cold Mountain?

The book came to Mirage from two other producers, Albert Berger and Ron Yerxa, who have a production company called Bona Fide. One of the guys at Bona Fide was a childhood friend of Bill Horberg who worked for me at the time and they came over and said to Bill, 'Do you guys want to partner up with us on this?' Albert and Ron had got a free option from the agent, but they needed a little more muscle because they knew that it was going to be an expensive book and they weren't real well known at the studios. We had a bigger profile at Mirage.

Do you pitch projects to studios or do you work solely with scripts?

I really don't like to pitch. I try not to do that. I'm not good at listening to pitches and I don't like doing the pitching. Once in a while I have to go and do it but most of the time I'll pick up the phone and call an executive at a studio and say, for example, 'Would you like to read Kenny Lonergan's new script?' I might briefly say it's about a seventeen-year-old girl coming to moral grips with an adult world — or something like that. I would say, 'It's probably going to cost somewhere in the region of $15 to 16 million.' If they say yes to the read then I send it to them, and usually I get a call back saying, 'Can we talk? Could you bring Kenny in?' or they'll say, 'We like it, we have great respect for Kenny and we love you but it's too long and it's not for us.' But I don't go and do pitch meetings because I just find it a waste of time on both sides.

And frankly, I believe this is an execution business, not a concept business. Although for some studio heads a lot of movie-making is concept-driven. Something like *Spider-Man* is basically a concept picture, whereas with Kenny's film *Margaret*, it's all about execution — it's all in the writing and how the film is going to be realized, how the characters are going to be played. I wouldn't understand how to pitch that.

5. Get the gun out fast

Over the course of your career, has working with the studios got better or worse?

Worse. Much worse. The complexion of the business has changed a lot. Films today carry the burden of a repeatable product, because it's usually companies which make repeatable products that own film studios. They don't want to re-invent the wheel every time they make a movie. The philosophy of marketing has taken over the picture business and the marketing department of a movie studio make as many creative decisions today as the people running the production department. That's never been true before. Many times the head of a studio cannot greenlight a picture unless the people who have to sell it, the marketing department, say yes. They want to be able to see the poster in their heads first — to imagine the trailer and know the cast — to protect their ability to sell it to a cinema chain that will give you three thousand theatres.

It isn't the way movies used to be made. Today executives are under a different kind of gun. On the one hand they have to try to make what appeals to them but they also have to try to provide a programme of pictures where the quarterly reports that go to the stockholders look as healthy as the parent company's car sales or book sales quarterly reports. Multinational conglomerates like AOL/Time Warner, Viacom or Newscorp are the studios today.

How involved do you get in marketing and distribution decisions?

As much as I can. I don't claim to be a marketing expert, but I have been around a long time so I know enough to say 'I don't think we should go wide with this' or 'I think this ought to be a platform movie' or 'I think we should hold this for the fall' or 'I don't think we should sell this as a thriller.'

Do you think audiences have changed in the time that you have been making films?

Yes. Back in the seventies, on Friday or Saturday nights, college kids would watch foreign movies. Audiences were composed of all ages.

Today most audiences are younger and they're watching special effects movies. Most films made today are geared for a demographic that provides repeat business. And that's eighteen- to twenty-five-year-olds. Many movies are sort of 'video game' movies. They go after your attention as fast and furiously and loudly as possible. There isn't much patience with a slowly developing narrative line. Things have to go quickly. The film-going experience is influenced by what happens at home with DVDs and VHSs — you eat, talk on the cellphone, comment out loud . . . It's an entirely different thing than it was in the seventies — or even the eighties.

Would Three Days of the Condor *[1975] be green-lit today?*

I don't know. The climate has changed. At the time that film was critical of the CIA in a certain way, because that was the political climate of the US in the 1970s. Back then, we were outraged as we were learning stuff that we had done. But that's not the feeling today.

In terms of my own pictures — well, a strange picture like *Jeremiah Johnson* [1972] wouldn't get made today because it doesn't fall into any clear genre. It's not a western . . . It had a lot of success in its day. But it's not a movie that would get made today. I wouldn't know how to pitch it. Or *They Shoot Horses, Don't They?* [1969], where at the end of the movie a woman ends up saying 'Please shoot me' and the guy does . . . You just wouldn't make those movies today.

Does that depress you?

Well, yeah — except I try not to get depressed about stuff I can't do anything about. It's like the weather. Here's the thing — when I was a young director and I would meet great older directors, they were all depressed about what had happened to the movie business. And secretly I felt bad for them, because I kept saying to myself, 'I guess that's what happens when you get old — you lose touch and you think it was always better in your day.' So I have always been on guard about not wanting to get that way.

On the other hand, I know that there has been a real sea-change in the quality of American movies. And that is not an opinion, it's a fact. If you look at the movies that were made in this country between, say, 1965 and 1980, that was really the golden age of Hollywood — more than the 1930s and the 1940s, though they were great in their own way too. But look at the movies made during that period and it's extraordinary. All of us were doing serious stuff, and it wasn't about special effects or a $60-million opening weekend. Back then you didn't give a damn about that. Now, in a way, we have to make movies that are designed for huge opening weekends rather than shelf life. Movies have become fast-food, in a way. Every studio has to make twenty films a year, which means they have got to open one almost every three weeks. If one movie does just one huge opening weekend, then after its theatrical life its residual income will pay for the flops. DVDs are making more money than the theatrical releases. So the afterlife of these movies that have a $60-million opening is substantial. Take *The Hulk*. It did $60 million in the week it opened, then the drop-off at the box office this weekend was seventy per cent, and that's a $135 million negative. Historically that would be a catastrophe. But today, with merchandising, syndication rights, VHS and DVD sales, the after-life will save it and the studio will maybe eke out its investment. And the thing is, there is such an appetite for this stuff . . . that's the reality. It's interesting that Intermedia have just opened *Terminator 3* or *T3* because they are going to rise or fall on the basis of it.

At the moment we're having trouble making *Margaret*, yet it's one of the best scripts I have ever read. Peter Rice, head of Fox Searchlight loves this movie, but he can't pay more than $12 million for a picture and we can't make it for that. So now Scott and I are trying together to see if we can raise a budget of $16 million. That's a big difference, because $4 million is one-quarter of the budget. But if I was looking for $44 million instead of $40 million it would be easier. But I want to see it get made, so Scott's doing it for nothing and we are doing it for nothing. It's not a high concept movie and there's no action in it. When you look at what people go to see, it's often comic books. I'm not knocking it but that's how it is. When you have people turning out for $60 million grossing weekends with comic book films, then that is what you are going to get more of. This generation of moviegoers grew up with very short attention spans, they grew up multi-tasking, doing homework with earphones on listening to rock music and the TV on with no sound coming from it. Beginnings and endings are not interesting, audiences want the high point, which means you've got to get to it and get to it *now* — get the gun out fast, the clothes off quick.

In the last few years, you've produced more than you have directed.

Because it has often taken me two or three years to find something that I really got excited about directing. But during that time I've had all these other things in the works — *The Quiet American, Heaven, Cold Mountain, Iris.* Some of them took a long time . . . But I'm getting ready now to direct a film called *The Interpreter*. It takes place at the

UN, it's a contemporary mystery thriller about a female, white, South African interpreter, who while interpreting hears something through the headphones that she's not supposed to hear about an African dictator and this puts her in danger. And there's a love story. I'm about three months into working with the writer, and at this point I'm struggling to see the plot all the way through . . .

The Interpreter was an international hit upon its release in 2005. *Margaret* was shot in 2005, as was Pollack's latest production with director Minghella, *Breaking and Entering*.

AFTERWORD

Woody Allen once said (and I paraphrase) that there are two types of film producer – those who get out there and do the job, and the *life-style producers* who talk about producing over lunch. It's clear that the interviewees in this book fall firmly into the first category, even if – as Barbara De Fina attests – producers in LA take their lunch dates *very* seriously.

One of the intentions of this book was to shed some light on the varied paths that people can take into producing for a living. It seemed to me that there was a job to do at the outset in explaining that producers are not just 'money people', but a diverse group of individuals from a range of backgrounds. True, many have been apprenticed in cinema by some means or other – whether as distributors or programmers or First ADs, graduates from talent agencies or film schools. But this anthology shows that producers may, in previous lives, have been lawyers or art dealers, City financiers or property developers. They may even have believed once that contemporary dance was their calling. And I noted with interest that more than one had grown up with parents in the grocery business, and obviously inherited a flair for making a sale, amongst other qualities.

Into the mix was the challenge of proving that raising money is a complex and lengthy process, given today's reality that most films are independently financed. Hollywood studios remain the hub of the business – British 'studios' might have sound stages and facilities but they *don't* fund movies. Still, the business changes with tastes and times. Moving around LA I was intrigued to discover that even if a studio does give its producers the money to finance their films, there are nonetheless studio producers such as Gary Lucchesi and Tom Rosenberg who have been smart enough to see that it is wise to have a separate financial entity to handle the sale and distribution of films on which the studio might pass. Similarly, studio veterans Mike Medavoy and Arnie Messer realised in setting up Phoenix Pictures that it made business sense to take on more financial risk for the sake of retaining more independence. Perhaps the most startling example of an independent micro-studio is Nigel Sinclair and Guy East's Intermedia, a bi-coastal 'multi-headed monster' that produced both low-budget and high-concept fare.

But if you really want to produce, there is no getting round the 'tortuous and rude' job of raising the cash to make the movie. In that effort, most producers in this book, almost by default, have had to acquire some fairly sophisticated skills, as they find, negotiate and patch together budgets from a variety of sources, be they banks or insurance companies, high-worth individuals or the latest European territory offering the best tax breaks or public subsidies. The film world attracts shysters, too, and both Mike Medavoy and James Schamus have had sobering encounters with phantom billionaires who wasted their time while trying to con their way into the business.

If you have read this far then you will have gathered that producing is rarely about dinner parties, private jets, fat cigars, Harry Winston diamonds and fine gowns – unless you happen to have been nominated for an Oscar. Rather, the reality of producing is a complex bundle of responsibilities, physically and mentally challenging, extraordinarily risky, occasionally rewarding. However excessively hard you graft, movies can still fall apart – witness Stephen Woolley's *Borgias* experience, Stephen Evans' struggles with *Wings of the Dove*, Alison Owen's long-gestating adaptation of *Tulip Fever*. You may collapse at the very last hurdle if your project doesn't happen to suit the limited windows of availability for Brad, Russell, Reese, Nicole or whoever else is A-List at the time you were dreaming of getting into production. You can even get the movie onto screens only for a war to start that same weekend, as befell Mike Medavoy, Arnie Messer, and *Basic*.

It should by clear by now that *real* producing is not about choosing an enviable lifestyle – for one thing, it's far too financially precarious a profession – but, rather, a process of carving out a life in film. When I met with Alison Owen, her working schedule involved overseeing the general release of one film, with another in production, a third preparing to shoot, and a raft of others in development. As Lawrence Bender says, from his own hard-won experience, 'There is no such thing as having a life.' In light of Working Title's output over recent years it's understandable when Eric Fellner remarks that he hasn't had more than two weeks off since 1985. Even if one isn't shooting, cutting, or preparing to shoot, there is potentially precious material to read, and either acquire or pass on.

It's universally accepted that film-making is a team-process. But the flair and the dynamism that producers must possess in order to initiate projects and get them off the ground is very definitely born of an entrepreneurial mind-set. Within that, they also exhibit a unique set of skills that are, nevertheless, not particularly obvious. Most people apply for jobs requiring specific skill-sets, and promote themselves on the basis of what their CV says they can do. But for film producers there is a valuable currency in the sort of skills that employers would not necessarily take at face value if you flagged them up in interview. It is one thing to say 'I like to take risks and I have to trust my intuition in order to do that.' Or 'There's no point doing it if I don't feel passionate about it.' But as these pages show, these sorts of statements are the guiding principles of producers. Their hunches and risks can consume years of time, at considerable personal cost, but they are practiced in the fine art of never giving up. When we hear directors or stars describing the years it took to bring such-and-such a film to the screen, we should know that in most cases it could only have happened through the determination of the producer. As such, the successes, if and when they come, are understandably sweet.

Of course, Paul Brooks never dreamt that a tiny $3 million dollar movie called *My Big Fat Greek Wedding* would become a global phenomenon. Tim Bevan and Eric Fellner probably never imagined their *Billy Elliot* would dance his way from Easington to Broadway. But having the foresight to appreciate the full creative and commercial possibilities in the invention of a piece of copyright is a key to good producing. Nigel Sinclair and Guy East *knew* the market value of the *Terminator* franchise when they had the idea to invite Arnold Schwarzengger back to our screens, but it was also their carefully developed and executed creative/ business plan that made *T3* happen to the tune of hundreds of millions of box office receipts. In a similar vein, in November 2006 Barbara Broccoli and Michael J Wilson will unveil their new James Bond, Daniel Craig, in *Casino Royale*, a reworked approach to the franchise. The results will be keenly scrutinized, but as this duo point out, it's down to them, as keepers of the flame, to keep audiences excited by Bond.

When I asked Bob Shaye why he committed so much of New Line's money to the *Lord Of the Rings* films, he testified to his belief in Peter Jackson and his own business instinct that the films would be a success. Similar convictions had paid off for him years before with the *Nightmare On Elm Street* films. Let's not forget that an instinct for material and talent ought to be far-reaching. Steve Golin knew about the quirky and perennially interesting Charlie Kaufman long before Spike Jonze decided that *Being John Malkovich* was the script he wanted to make as his first movie. But while Golin is candid about his initial reticence over the project, nonetheless, at a particular moment he was sufficiently convinced by Jonze and Kaufman to put his job on the line to get the movie made.

Sometimes a producer's instinct is essentially about people and their talent. Why else did Stephen Evans set aside his lucrative profession to lay a bet on the young Kenneth Branagh? We all watch movies and

form our own views of the leading man or lady but how many of us
have the ability to recognize the precocious talent of a newcomer and
decide that a star has been born, in the way that Alison Owen felt
about Cate Blanchett and Gwyneth Paltrow before they were house-
hold names? Uncovering talent and sticking with it is a process that
James Schamus and his then producing partner Ted Hope committed
to when they drew up a list of names of directors who had made interesting short films. Years later, Ang Lee has proved the most enduring
creative relationship for Schamus, but he also notes that ultimately he
worked with everyone else on that shortlist. There is, of course, something very compelling about the long-term creative partnerships of
producer and director: to the example of Schamus and Lee add Bender
and Tarantino, Woolley and Jordan, Channing-Williams and Leigh,
and so on.

When I conducted the bulk of these interviews, there was a prevailing industry gloom caused by the perception that the 'comic-book
movie' was the dominant global genre, responsible in turn for killing
off interest in riskier and more challenging movies. The key offenders
at the time were *The Hulk*, *Tomb Raider 2*, and *Terminator 3*. In fact,
there were no fewer than seventeen sequels on wide release that summer of 2003. The marketing spend on those films was gigantic, but the
risks just as huge, as illustrated when *The Hulk*'s takings dropped a
staggering 62% in its second weekend. Has the ecology changed at all
over the time of preparing this book for publication? For sure, Batman
and Superman and X-Men still devour enormous budgets in the hope
of commensurate receipts. But in March 2006 the Best Picture Oscar
went to *Crash*, surely the most independent of 'indie' movies to
emerge from Hollywood in recent times. In fact, fellow nominees
Good Night & Good Luck, *Brokeback Mountain*, *TransAmerica*,
Capote, *Syriana* and *The Constant Gardener* made the 2006 Oscars
something of a celebration of independent film.

Given the pressures and uncertainties of the business, it's fair to say
that every film that gets made is something of a triumph. In that context I found it interesting to note the exceptional – almost excessive –
modesty of my interviewees. And yet, while many were reluctant to
take too much credit for their work, the issue of *on-screen* credits
struck me as one of some complexity. No producer will deny that
movie stars and acclaimed directors are the figures with whom the
general public and cinephiles are most fascinated. But there are sim-
pler forms of recognition that are still denied the producer. It's not just
the burying of their names within the Internet Movie Database.
Barnaby Thompson and Simon Channing-Williams offer chiming rue-

ful anecdotes of how Cannes, that auteur's paradise, conspires to shunt producers from the limelight.

Consider the very Hollywood controversy of spring 2006 when financier Bob Yari attempted to sue the Producer's Guild of America and the Academy of Motion Picture Arts and Sciences for formally denying him his producer's credit on Best Picture nominee *Crash*. The upshot of that exclusion was that, on Oscar night, Yari was prevented from taking the stage when the film won top prize. What the debacle highlighted was the shifting definition of what makes a producer. The prevailing wisdom at both the PGA and AMPAS is that a producer's worth is defined by an assessment of their contribution to the process, and the process is defined in a traditional way – a producer must prove that they have made a significant contribution to at least 30% of development, 20% of pre-production, 20% to production and 30% to post production and marketing. Bob Yari's expertise is finance, and his argument was that he had spent as much of his time financing the film as his fellow producers Cathy Schulman and Tom Nunan had devoted to the more traditional aspects of the job. Yari lost his case, but the debate remains significant in terms of the changing nature of the business and the needful skills of the producers therein.

Have I convinced you yet that the producer has grounds to feel generally overlooked, and sometimes downright slighted? If not, consider a survey of *The 50 Greatest Movies Of All Time* that caught my own eye in the September 2005 edition of *Vanity Fair*, the glossiest of glossy magazines, and one that pays extravagant attention to movies both new and old. For each of the films on the honour-roll, the name of the screenwriter, the director, and leading cast members were duly cited. A short paragraph listed Academy Awards won, accompanied by some interesting behind-the-scenes anecdotes. Of the fifty titles, nine had won Best Director Oscars, and eight had won Best Picture statuettes, no doubt gratefully received at the time by the producers of said pictures. And yet not a single producer's name was mentioned.

If what you really want to do is direct, join the queue – and you could hardly be blamed for it. But no student or exponent of filmmaking can afford to ignore the role of the producer. As I hope we have seen, it's more than just teas, transport and toilets...

Helen de Winter

July 2006

ACKNOWLEDGEMENTS

I am deeply indebted to the professionalism of agents, assistants and PRs who assisted me in my approach to the interviewees, then helped coordinate diaries to set up interviews or, later in the process, became super-heroes by working as efficient go-betweens during an intense period of revisions – a time when the interviewees seemed busier than ever. My thanks as well to the generosity of individuals who made introductions to hard-to-track producers or made interesting suggestions and provided contact information for people I wanted to meet. Heartfelt thanks, then, to all of the following: Claire Broughton, Ian Smith, Aliza James, Chloe Dorigan, Devon Wilson, Chris Prapha, Ruth Jackson, Caroline Hutchings, Chris Payne, Jonna Smith, Ciara Parkes, Sarah Feinberg, Craig Sherman, Ron Puckett, Keri Wilson, Joan Smith, Jessica Cox, Ilsa Berg, Jeremy Baxter, Matthew Gerber, Suzie Halewood, Anne Batz, Karin Padgham, Anne Bennett, Faye Ward, Rachel Connors, Rikki Jarrett, Jo Laurie, Gailor Large, Dawn Oliver, Scott Herbst, Jennifer Hoffman, Patrick Brennan, Cassandra Sigsgaard, Daniele Bernfeld, Lynda Dorf.

Books, just as movies, must be finite when it comes to their length, and these considerations of space meant, alas, that after the manuscript was submitted a handful of my interviews had to remain in the cutting room. With apologies for same, and in deep appreciation of their time and insight, I would like to thank Gary Winick, Elaine Goldsmith Thomas, Jeremy Thomas, Alan Greenspan, Sidney Sheinberg, and Gareth Wigan.

Special thanks to family and friends for their kindness, generosity and helpfulness on the journey round the US (particularly for accommodation, sustenance and getting to grips with the geographical labyrinth that is LA) or for practical support back in London when faulty tapes and technical matters caused temporary headaches: Susan Matheson, Richard Morson, Jerry Teague, Fleur Fontaine, Franco Carbone, Sa & Taegan Goddard, Jeremy & Charlene Kay, Yves Salmon, Shirley & Leonard Pardon

Love and thanks to my partner Alister Campbell, without whom...

Thanks are also due to Walter Donohue, my commissioning editor at Faber, who gave me the opportunity to write this book on the basis of no track record other than a curiosity for the subject and a conviction that there was something worth saying about producers. I thank him deeply for his trust in me. And, most particularly, to my editor Richard T. Kelly. At the outset, the notion of a book's editor was as mysterious to me as, say, the role of a film's producer is to many. Several times during the long process of editing and revisions Richard reminded me that making a book is not dissimilar to the process of crafting a film. Reassuring emails, the odd telephone call, fine suggestions, patience, a superior knowledge of film, a wry sense of humour and sharp wit were just some of what Richard called upon in his arsenal of talents to keep me focused and passionate. Not one moment of that went unnoticed or unappreciated and I sincerely thank him for that.

I dedicate this book to the interviewees and thank them for their time, trust and support. Yes, it took longer than I imagined, having had to wrap this passion-project around the demands of a working life. But I believe your stories are unique and will inspire new producers to come forward and contribute to the epic journey that is the task of turning money into light.

HdW

Index